The American Presidents

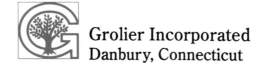
Grolier Incorporated
Danbury, Connecticut

Contents

THE PRESIDENCY

In the course of some 200 years, the presidency of the United States has become the most powerful office in the world. The duties and responsibilities of the office are immense. Unlike many of the democratic governments of Europe and elsewhere that have both a chief of state and a head of government, the U.S. system of government has only one chief executive, the president. The holder of that office serves not only as head of government but also in the primarily ceremonial post of chief of state. As chief of state, the president performs many of the public and ceremonial duties undertaken by the king or queen of the United Kingdom, other monarchs, and the governor-general of Canada and other Commonwealth nations. Although some of the duties the president performs as chief of state may seem trivial, the role helps the occupant of the office maintain contact with the overall populace. As head of government, the president is the chief executive of the nation, the director of the government. In addition, the president serves as commander in chief of the armed forces of the United States and the voice of the American people.

According to presidential scholar Clinton Rossiter, the presidency is a one-person job. The person "who holds it can never escape making the final decisions in each of many areas in which the American people and their Constitution hold him or her responsible." A sign that was always prominently displayed on the presidential desk of Harry S. Truman, the nation's 33rd chief executive from April 1945 to January 1953, expressed the idea perfectly: "The buck stops here." According to Rossiter, "that, in the end, is the essence of the presidency. It is the one office in all of the land whose occupant is forbidden to pass the buck."

THE ROLE AND DUTIES OF THE PRESIDENT

The role of the president has expanded considerably beyond that envisaged by the Founding Fathers in the Constitution. During such crises as the Civil War, world wars I and II, and the depression of the 1930s, Congress and the nation both turned to the executive for leadership and guidance. Crisis powers given to the president were to a great extent retained afterward, thereby adding new stature to the office. Likewise, as foreign affairs increased in importance during the 20th century, the president's role as the voice of the nation added new prestige and responsibilities to the office. Governmental efforts to provide for the social and economic welfare of its citizens, initiated in the depression of 1929–33 and subsequently expanded, have contributed to the president's duties and powers in the economic and social spheres. Likewise, the necessity for an expanded bureaucracy serving the president has heightened his prestige and influence at the expense of the legislative branch.

Such chief executives as Thomas Jefferson, Andrew Jackson, Abraham Lincoln, Theodore Roosevelt, Woodrow Wilson, Franklin D. Roosevelt, and Harry S. Truman have shaped the office of the presidency. Normally regarded as "strong presidents," these individuals, exercising their prerogatives as leaders of the nation, utilized their influence to initiate major changes in American society. In so doing they added to the magnitude of the office. Although the Vietnam war and the Watergate scandal of Richard Nixon's administration strained the presidency during the 1960s and early 1970s, President Gerald Ford and his successors worked hard, and successfully, to restore the office to its former status.

The President as Leader of the Nation. The president as leader of the nation is confronted with a multiplicity of problems and tasks. As the only executive official elected by the people at large (the vice president is assigned a legislative post as president of the Senate), he represents the nation to the world. His responsibilities do not stop there, for he is the chief policymaker for domestic and foreign affairs. In this capacity, although he is acknowledged as the leader of one of the political parties, he must represent all the people.

John Marshall, who was to become chief justice of the United States, recognized, as secretary of state, the inherent responsibilities of the president in the domain of foreign affairs. "The president," he noted in 1799, "is the sole organ of the nation in its external relations, and its sole representative with foreign nations." In receiving the credentials of foreign delegates, the president exercises the prerogative of recognizing or rejecting the credentials of other governments. Likewise, he has the power to withdraw such recognition. He alone may address foreign governments or be addressed by them. Diplomatic communications are generally carried out through the numerous ministers and envoys who represent the president and the United States in other countries. Ambassadors are appointed by the president.

The president, with the advice and consent of the Senate, consummates treaties in his capacity as leader of the nation. (He signs treaties as chief of state.) Should he ignore the Senate's role in treaty making, especially by disregarding the Senate in the making of a pact, the president may endanger his own position. Thus President Wilson, by ignoring the senators in the negotiations on the Treaty of Versailles and the League of Nations, created acrimonious feelings that later led to the rejection by the United States of the treaty and the league. In addition to this, the president must recognize the need for congressional appropriations for his foreign policy measures. Consequently he must cultivate congressional support for his programs.

As leader of the nation, the president must determine the course of foreign and domestic policy. The Constitution stipulates that the executive "shall from time to time give to the Congress Information of the State of the Union, and recommend to their Consideration such Measures as he shall judge necessary and expedient." In his messages to Congress, including those on the annual budget, the state of the union, and the economic condition of the nation, the president suggests the programs and measures for legislative enactment that he considers vital to the nation's welfare and betterment. The chief executive then may have to use political influence to see them enacted.

Elected by the people, the president, unlike members of Congress, represents the entire nation rather than a district or state. Hence he must be a national leader. This he accomplishes by diverse means. In addition to his messages to Congress, he utilizes television and radio, including the live televised address and press conference, to inform the people of his position concerning the issues and problems confronting the nation.

Although elected specifically as a member of one political party, the president must work with both parties in determining public policy. Nevertheless, as the nominee of a specific party, he must also work toward the realization of that party's programs and goals. To prevent a complete cleavage in society, however, the

The president of the United States shoulders broad responsibilities in both foreign and domestic policy. Opposite page: As "the sole organ of the nation in its foreign relations," President Bill Clinton hosted a White House ceremony marking a significant 1993 Middle East peace accord. Here, President Clinton watches proudly as two longtime enemies—Israel's Prime Minister Yitzhak Rabin and Palestine Liberation Organization Chairman Yasir Arafat—shake hands during the festivities. Right: A skilled promoter of domestic legislation, President Lyndon Johnson signs the historic Civil Rights Act of 1964.

Above: *Exercising his power as commander in chief of the armed forces, President Abraham Lincoln meets with military leaders during the Civil War.* Right: *President John Kennedy used the televised news conference to great effect in communicating the positions of his administration.*

president, along with the leaders of his party and the opposition, often works out programs on crucial matters like foreign affairs and national defense that are generally acceptable to both parties. If the president's party holds a majority in Congress that is in accord with his views, the president is more likely to see his program enacted. However, if his party is in a minority, or if the members of his own party disagree with his specific programs, the president's legislative measures may be ignored or defeated by Congress.

Early in 1986, President Ronald Reagan urged a major U.S. arms sale to Saudi Arabia. The Republican-controlled Senate and the Democratic-controlled House of Representatives passed a resolution blocking the sale. The president then vetoed the resolution and began a major campaign to have his veto sustained. On the morning that the Senate was to vote on the measure, all 100 senators were invited to breakfast at the White House; many senators also received presidential telephone calls on the issue. Although the merits of the sale were considered during Senate debate, some supporters of the president's position simply pointed out that the "prestige of the presidency" was "at stake" with the vote. The veto was sustained in the Senate by one vote. Eight senators, who originally voted against the sale, voted to sustain the veto. The incident is a classical example of the political clout and power of the presidency.

The President as Commander in Chief. Article II, Section 2, of the Constitution states that the president is

"Commander in Chief of the Army and Navy . . . and of the Militia of the several States, when called into the actual Service of the United States." This provision assures civilian control of the military. Although this stipulation grants the executive broad powers, the chief executive is limited somewhat by those powers left solely to Congress. These powers include the right of Congress to declare war, to appropriate funds for the armed forces, and to conscript men for military service.

Nevertheless, the executive's powers are extensive. He selects the key figures in the military establishment, including the secretary of defense, the secretaries of the Army, Navy, and Air Force, and the military chiefs of staff. He recommends the defense budget to Congress and administers laws pertaining to the defense of the nation. He directs strategy in times of war, and is held responsible for the success or failure of the entire defense program. As noted previously, the president has often been delegated extraordinary wartime powers. These include the right to make decisions pertaining to the fundamental military strategy of the nation and, on the domestic scene, to initiate measures, including the invoking of martial law if necessary, designed to win a war. In fact, in the 175 years between the late 1790s and the early 1970s, U.S. troops had been sent into military hostilities more than 200 times without a declaration of war. In the age of the Cold War and possible nuclear conflict, the case for congressional involvement in decisions involving military force seemed to be weaker than at any time in U.S. history. In the event of a nuclear attack against the United States, there very likely would not be time for a president to consult Congress.

The Vietnam war of the 1960s and early 1970s, which took some 57,000 American lives and cost the nation billions of dollars, marked a turning point. In 1964 the Congress, responding to an alleged attack on U.S. vessels in the Gulf of Tonkin off Vietnam, passed a resolution authorizing the president to take the steps needed, "including the use of armed force," to assist South Vietnam preserve its freedom. As the U.S. involvement in the conflict mounted, so did congressional discontent with the implications of the Tonkin Gulf Resolution. By the early 1970s, Congress was debating legislation to limit the president's war-making power. Finally in October 1973, the Senate and House of Representatives passed the War Powers Resolution. Although President Richard M. Nixon vetoed the measure, there was sufficient support in Congress to override the veto.

The purpose of the War Powers Resolution is stated in Section 2(a):

> *to fulfill the intent of the framers of the Constitution of the United States and insure that the collective judgment of both the Congress and the president will apply to the introduction of United States armed forces into hostilities, or into situations where imminent involvement in hostilities is clearly indicated by the circumstances, and to the continued use of such forces in hostilities or in such situations.*

The resolution requires the president to keep Congress informed both before and during any involvement by U.S. forces in hostilities. Under Section 4(a), the president is required to report to Congress within 48 hours when U.S. troops are introduced:

(1) into hostilities or into situations where imminent involvement in hostilities is clearly indicated by the circumstances;
(2) into the territory, airspace or waters of a foreign nation, while equipped for combat, except for deployments which relate solely to supply, replacement, repair, or training of such forces; or
(3) in numbers which substantially enlarge United States armed forces equipped for combat already located in a foreign nation.

A written report must be submitted to the speaker of the House of Representatives and the president pro tempore of the Senate setting forth:

a—the circumstances necessitating the introduction of the United States armed forces;
b—the constitutional and legislative authority under which such introduction took place; and
c—the estimated scope and duration of the hostilities or involvement

Only in the first circumstance (U.S. forces likely to be engaged in combat) is the length of the commitment

---

FACTS ABOUT THE PRESIDENCY

Qualifications: (1) Natural-born citizen of the United States. (2) At least 35 years old. (3) At least 14 years a resident of the United States. Candidates are usually nominated at national party conventions held in the summer of the election year. Although only men have served as president, women are eligible to hold the office.

Election: By a majority vote of the Electoral College.

Term: 4 years. A president may not serve more than 2 terms (plus 2 years of an unexpired term).

Salary: (1) $200,000 plus allowances for expenses, travel, and official entertainment totaling $150,000. (2) Provided with White House, household help, transportation, health care. (3) Lifetime pension of $97,500 annually.

Removal: May be impeached (accused of serious wrongdoing) by a majority of the House of Representatives; must then be tried by the Senate and convicted by a two-thirds vote.

Succession: If the president dies or is disabled in office, the line of succession is as follows:

(1) Vice President of the United States
(2) Speaker of the House
(3) President Pro Tempore of the Senate
(4) Secretary of State
(5) Secretary of the Treasury
(6) Secretary of Defense
(7) Attorney General
(8) Secretary of the Interior
(9) Secretary of Agriculture
(10) Secretary of Commerce
(11) Secretary of Labor
(12) Secretary of Health and Human Services
(13) Secretary of Housing and Urban Development
(14) Secretary of Transportation
(15) Secretary of Energy
(16) Secretary of Education
(17) Secretary of Veterans Affairs

---

limited by the resolution. In that event, Section 5(b) of the resolution requires the president to withdraw U.S. troops within 60 to 90 days unless the Congress authorizes their continued presence. The resolution also contains a provision, 5(c), permitting Congress, by concurrent resolution without approval by the president, to order the withdrawal of U.S. troops from hostilities abroad.

Since passage of the act, Presidents Gerald Ford, Jimmy Carter, and Ronald Reagan sought ways to avoid the trigger mechanism in Section 5(b). The three presidents reported to the Congress under the act's provisions but often without citing which precise provision in the act applied to their deployment of forces. In this way they have been able to avoid the 60- to 90-day clock. As a result, the role of Congress in the deployment of U.S. troops abroad has not been any greater after enactment of the resolution than before.

THE PRESIDENCY IN HISTORY

Origins of the Office. The presidency, and what is often termed the "presidential system of government," is of distinctly American origin. Political philosophers such as John Locke and Baron de Montesquieu had written earlier on the separation of legislative and executive functions, but the transition from theory to practice was left to the framers of the Constitution. The term "president" was not new, however, for it had been applied to the presiding officer of legislative bodies in the colonies and in the Continental Congress. Likewise the New York constitution of 1777 and the Massachusetts constitution of 1780 suggested an independent executive, whose powers were somewhat comparable to those later granted to the president of the United States.

Delegates to the Constitutional Convention in Philadelphia in 1787 faced a dilemma when they considered establishing a "national executive." The majority of the framers of the Constitution wanted an executive power capable of reaching the remotest parts of the Union, "not only for the purpose of enforcing national laws but also . . . for the purpose of bringing assistance to the states in grave emergencies of domestic disorder." The framers also wanted to avoid stirring up popular fear of the monarchy.

At the convention, Roger Sherman of Connecticut favored the notion of subordinating the chief executive to a legislature. According to James Madison's *Notes*, Sherman "considered the executive magistracy as nothing more than an institution for carrying the will of the legislature into effect," and he "wished that the number [of executives] might not be fixed, but that the legislature should be at liberty to appoint one or more as experience might dictate." Delegate James Wilson of Pennsylvania took an opposite view and argued in favor of a single executive with broad powers. Wilson, as James Madison recorded in his diary of the convention's proceedings, "preferred a single magistrate, as giving most energy, dispatch, and responsibility to the office." The executive, Wilson argued, should be independent of the legislature, and to preserve this status should be vested with an absolute veto over legislative enactments. Otherwise, he maintained, the legislature would "at any moment sink it [the executive] into nonexistence." Furthermore the president should be elected directly by the people. Wilson ended up having to compromise on a number of points, including the last one, for the convention decided that the president should be elected indirectly by the people through a college of electors. However, the core of Wilson's ideas, supported especially by Madison and Gouverneur Morris, was incorporated into the final document.

Section I of Article II of the Constitution clearly spells out and defines the basis of and qualifications for the office of president. It states:

George Washington took the presidential oath in New York City on April 30, 1789. The 20th Amendment to the Constitution later set the inauguration date as January 20.

Five living presidents gathered on November 4, 1991, in Simi Valley, California, to dedicate the new Ronald Reagan Presidential Library. Left to right: *George Bush, Ronald Reagan, Jimmy Carter, Gerald Ford, and Richard Nixon.*

The executive Power shall be vested in a President of the United States of America. He shall hold his Office during the Term of four Years. . . .

No Person except a natural born Citizen, or a Citizen of the United States, at the time of the Adoption of this Constitution, shall be eligible to the Office of President; neither shall any person be eligible to that Office who shall not have attained the Age of thirty five Years, and been fourteen Years a Resident within the United States.

In Case of the Removal of the President from Office, or of his Death, Resignation, or Inability to discharge the Powers and Duties of the said Office, the Same shall devolve on the vice president, and the Congress may by Law provide for the Case of Removal, Death, Resignation or Inability, both of the President and Vice President, declaring what Officer shall then act as President, and such Officer shall act accordingly, until the Disability be removed, or a President shall be elected.

The President shall, at stated Times, receive for his Services, a Compensation, which shall neither be encreased nor diminished during the Period for which he shall have been elected, and he shall not receive within that period any other Emolument from the United States, or any of them.

Before he enter on the Execution of his Office, he shall take the following Oath or Affirmation:—"I do solemnly swear (or affirm) that I will faithfully execute the Office of President of the United States, and will to the best of my Ability, preserve, protect and defend the Constitution of the United States.

Four constitutional amendments, relating directly to the presidency, were approved subsequently. The 12th Amendment, proclaimed on Sept. 25, 1804, clarified the election procedure and defined the office of vice president. A confused 1800 election result encouraged passage of the 12th Amendment. The 20th, or Lame Duck, Amendment was proclaimed on Feb. 6, 1933, and reduced the period between the election and inauguration of a president. The inauguration date now would be January 20, not March 4 as previously, and the session of Congress that had been held in the interim period was eliminated.

Franklin D. Roosevelt, an extremely active chief executive who took full advantage of his power, was the first and only president to be elected to four terms. As a result, sentiment in favor of limiting a president's time in office arose, and the 22nd Amendment, limiting the president to two terms, was proclaimed on March 1, 1951.

The crises caused by the illness of President Dwight D. Eisenhower and the 1963 assassination of President John F. Kennedy focused attention on the issue of presidential succession and the need to establish a procedure for filling the vice presidency when that office becomes vacant. As a result, the 25th Amendment was passed by Congress, ratified by the states and proclaimed on Feb. 24, 1967.

Section I of the 25th Amendment states that in case of the removal of the president from office or of his death or resignation, the vice president shall become president. Section II provides that "whenever there is a vacancy in the office of vice president, the president shall nominate a vice president who shall take the office upon confirmation by a majority vote of both houses of Congress."

Prior to the 25th Amendment, the vice presidency had been vacant on 16 occasions. Gerald R. Ford and Nelson A. Rockefeller were appointed vice president by Presidents Nixon and Ford, respectively, and took office in accordance with the terms of the 25th Amendment.

The amendment also provides for a means of dealing with a much more difficult aspect of presidential power: namely, that of presidential disability or inability to perform the powers and duties of the office. It provides for the resolution of the presidential inability problem in three ways. First, the president may declare his own inability, whereupon his "powers and duties shall be discharged by the vice president as acting president." In this instance, the president may reclaim the powers and duties of the office by stating his ability to perform. Second, in the event the president cannot declare his own inability, the vice president and a majority of the Cabinet may declare that such an inability exists, whereupon the "vice president shall immediately assume the powers and duties of the office as acting president." Third, in the event that the vice president and a majority of the Cabinet conclude that the president is unable to perform the powers and duties of the office and the president disagrees with this

conclusion, the matter will be decided by Congress. "If the Congress, within 21 days. . . .determines by two-thirds vote of both Houses that the president is unable to discharge the powers and duties of his office, the vice president shall . . . discharge the same as acting president; otherwise, the president shall resume the powers and duties of his office."

At various times there have been calls for reform of the presidency. A single, six-year term as well as a parliamentary government system have been suggested. During the 1950s, Sen. John W. Bricker, a Republican from Ohio, proposed an amendment to limit the power of the president under executive agreements. Generally, such efforts to change the office have not met with much success.

As presidential scholar Thomas E. Cronin has noted, "the original job of presidency has grown and yet the Founding Fathers wrote a marvelously flexible job description that is almost as appropriate today as it was when the nation was a new republic. The flexibility plus the willingness of the American people to place confidence in effective presidents give a president an enormous opportunity to serve the nation."

1st PRESIDENT OF THE UNITED STATES (1789–1797)

Born: *February 22, 1732, in Westmoreland County, Virginia*
Occupation: *Planter, soldier*
Party: *Federalist*
Vice President: *John Adams*
Wife: *Martha Dandridge Custis*
Died: *December 14, 1799, at Mount Vernon, Virginia*

"To the memory of the Man, first in war, first in peace, and first in the hearts of his countrymen." So wrote Congressman Henry Lee in 1799, upon the death of George Washington. Lee, better known as "Light Horse Harry", was a hero of the Revolutionary War and a good friend of Washington's. His famous words accurately described the feelings of Americans for their first president.

EARLY YEARS

Washington was born in Westmoreland County, Virginia, on February 22, 1732. His father was Augustine Washington, a prosperous farmer; his mother, Mary Ball, was Augustine's second wife. Both his parents were descended from families who had emigrated from England to Virginia in the 1650s.

After his father's death in 1743 George lived for a time with his half-brother Lawrence at Lawrence's estate, Mount Vernon. Washington had no formal schooling but, as was common in Virginia at the time, was taught by his family and probably by tutors. At the age of 16 he went with one of his Fairfax "cousins" (Lawrence had married

Anne Fairfax) on a surveying expedition in the Shenandoah Valley, then a distant frontier. The next year George, now grown into a tall and vigorous young man, was appointed surveyor for Culpeper County, Virginia, and he lived for many months in the wilderness. In 1751 he sailed with Lawrence to Barbados in the British West Indies, where Lawrence hoped to regain his health. It was to be Washington's only trip outside his country. Lawrence died the following year, and George became heir to Mount Vernon.

Young men matured early in that day, and at 20 Washington was already managing the family plantations and serving as adjutant of the Virginia militia. Then in 1753 he stepped onto the stage of history.

Both the British and French had long been struggling for control of the lands west of the Allegheny Mountains and for the friendship and help of the Indians in that area. Hearing that the French were pushing deep into the Ohio Valley, Virginia's Governor Robert Dinwiddie sent the 21-year-old Washington to warn the French that they were encroaching on British territory. Washington was further instructed to get on good terms with the Iroquois Indians in the area and win them over to the British.

With six companions Washington set off into what was then the far West. After a long, difficult journey he found the French at Fort Le Boeuf near Lake Erie and delivered Governor Dinwiddie's message. The French were polite but had no intention of giving up any territory. As for the Indians, Washington was not successful with them either. The trip back, through the deep winter snows, was full of danger. Washington had to walk most of the way. An Indian shot at him. He fell into the icy waters of the Allegheny River and almost drowned. Finally, a month after leaving Fort Le Boeuf, he arrived back in Virginia and reported to Governor Dinwiddie.

George Washington

1st president, 1789–97   Federalist

1732 Born on February 22 in Westmoreland County, Virginia.

1752 Inherited Mount Vernon, an estate on the Potomac River.

1755–58 Was commander in chief of Virginian troops for the balance of the French and Indian War.

1759 On January 6, married Martha Dandridge Custis, a widow with two children.

1759–74 Served in the Virginia House of Burgesses.

1774 Was a delegate to the First Continental Congress.

1775 Elected a delegate to the Second Continental Congress; named commander in chief of the Continental Army.

1776 Forced British troops to evacuate Boston; after a series of defeats in New York, crossed the Delaware River on December 25–26 to take 1,000 British prisoners.

1781 Defeated British forces at Yorktown. Lord Cornwallis surrendered to end the Revolutionary War.

1787 Served as president of the Constitutional Convention.

1789 Unanimously elected president of the United States.

1797 Retired to Mount Vernon after two terms as president.

1798 Named commander in chief of new U.S. Army.

1799 Died on December 14 at Mount Vernon.

Highlights of Presidency

1789 Judiciary Act established federal court system; first tax laws were adopted.

1791 Bank Act established a nationwide banking system. The Bill of Rights became law on December 15.

1792 Unanimously reelected to a second term. Coinage Act gave the government power to mint coins.

1793 On April 22, proclaimed U.S. neutrality in war between Britain and France.

1794 Federal troops suppressed the Whiskey Rebellion, armed resistance to excise tax.

1795 The Jay Treaty, under which Britain gave up its frontier forts and ensured continued trade with the United States, was ratified.

1796 Delivered Farewell Address, announcing his retirement and advocating a strong central government and neutrality in foreign affairs.

THE FRENCH AND INDIAN WAR

Washington had suggested the building of a fort at the forks of the Ohio River, where Pittsburgh now stands. Dinwiddie sent some men to build the fort and dispatched Washington, now promoted to lieutenant colonel, with 150 men to guard it against the French. Washington set off in the spring of 1754. When he reached the Ohio, he found the French had already established Fort Duquesne on the same spot. At Great Meadows in Pennsylvania, Washington's men defeated a small French force. The French responded by sending out a larger force, and Washington was compelled to surrender.

Returning to Virginia, he resigned his commission and tried to give his attention to farming. But Great Britain and France were now unofficially at war. (War was formally declared in 1756.) In 1755 British General Edward Braddock was chosen to head an expedition against the French. Braddock named young Washington to his staff, so along he went on that ill-fated expedition. The Indians caught Braddock by surprise and all but destroyed the British force. Washington had two horses shot from under him, and four bullets ripped through his uniform. But he emerged unhurt and with a reputation for bravery under fire. No sooner was he back in Mount Vernon than the governor named him commander in chief of the Virginia militia, with responsibility for defending the far-flung frontiers against the Indians. Then, in 1758, Washington went along with another expedition against the French. This time he had the satisfaction of seeing the French retreat and the British capture Fort Duquesne, which they renamed Fort Pitt.

RETIREMENT TO MOUNT VERNON

The fortunes of war had changed, and Washington now retired from the army. On January 6, 1759, he married Martha Dandridge Custis, and settled down to manage his extensive farms. Although he and Martha had no children of their own, he adopted her son and daughter from her first marriage to Daniel Parke Custis. A wealthy Virginia planter, his death had left her a widow at 27. Washington himself was not yet 30, but he was already Virginia's foremost soldier and a member of the House of Burgesses, the Virginia legislature. He was a great planter, rich, respectable, and connected with most of the leading families of the colony. For the next 15 years Washington divided his time between the affairs of Virginia and of his estate. He experimented with scientific farming, bought and sold western lands, hunted and fished, and enjoyed the pleasures of country life. But this was just an interlude in what was otherwise a life of constant toil and anxiety, responsibility, and service.

THE APPROACHING REVOLUTION

All through the 1760s and into the 1770s relations between the American colonies and Great Britain were growing more strained. Finally in 1774 resentment by the colonists against what they thought was unjust treatment

George and Martha Washington are portrayed late in life with Martha's grandchildren, George Washington Parke Custis (left) and Eleanor Washington Parke Custis. The "Father of His Country" had no children of his own. (Painting by Edward Savage.)

by Parliament and by King George III led to open revolt. In this crisis many of the rich planters and merchants in the colonies stayed loyal to Great Britain. But Washington took his stand without hesitation on the side of the American rebels. When Parliament passed a series of so-called Intolerable Acts punishing the city of Boston for its "Tea Party," Virginia rallied to Boston's support.

"Shall we supinely sit and see one province after another fall a prey to despotism?" wrote Washington, as he met with other Virginia Burgesses at the famous Raleigh Tavern in Williamsburg to plan measures of resistance. "The crisis is arrived when we must assert our rights or submit to every imposition till custom and use shall make us tame and abject slaves."

Washington voted for a general meeting of all the American colonies and was sent as a delegate to this First Continental Congress, which met in Philadelphia in 1774. He was sent again to the Second Continental Congress, which met the following year after the fighting at Lexington and Concord. On June 15, 1775, at Philadelphia, Washington was unanimously elected to the command of all American forces. Washington accepted the charge out of a deep sense of duty, adding that he would serve without pay. He rode off at once to take command of the American troops outside Boston.

COMMANDER IN CHIEF

For eight years Washington carried almost the whole burden of the American cause on his broad shoulders. Thirteen colonies not yet a nation, with a population of less than 3,000,000 who were sharply divided among themselves, had defied the greatest military power in the world. Great Britain had just emerged from a tremendous victory over France, and its navy ruled the seas. The British controlled Canada to the north and could count on many supporters in the American colonies. Great Britain had many times as many people and was many times as rich as America.

The new United States (actually it did not come into existence until 1776) had no regular army, no navy, no treasury, no foreign service. Indeed, it had hardly anything with which to fight a war. Washington had to hold his little army together and rebuild it almost every year. He had to train it and discipline it and find food, clothing, and arms. He had to win the support of the Continental Congress for his plans and enlist the governors of 13 states that often acted as if they were independent nations. Without Washington the army would have fallen apart; without him the nation itself would probably have fallen apart.

Washington was not a great general like Hannibal or Marlborough or Napoleon or Lee. But he had just the qualities needed for the success of the American cause. He

DID YOU KNOW?

- *Washington was the only president elected unanimously, receiving all 69 of the electoral votes cast.*

- *At his inauguration, Washington had only one tooth. At various times he wore dentures made of human or animal teeth, ivory, or lead—never wood.*

- *In addition to the nation's capital and the state, 31 counties and 17 communities are named in his honor.*

- *The mature Washington stood 6 feet, 2 inches tall, weighed 200 pounds, and wore size 13 shoes.*

- *Washington is the only president who didn't live in Washington, D.C., during his presidency.*

knew when to attack and when to retreat. He could show audacity, as when he crossed the icy Delaware River and struck at the Hessian camp in Trenton, New Jersey. He showed patience in avoiding battle, as during much of 1779 and 1780. But he could seize an opportunity, summon all his resources, and strike with marvelous speed and force, as he did at Yorktown. Washington insisted on discipline but was always just, and he shared the hardships of his soldiers, who were devoted to him. John Adams said that he made every crowned head in Europe look like a valet, and many men spoke of Washington as godlike. Yet he never presumed on his power and always respected the civil authority. He was, in short, the ideal leader for a democratic people.

THE REVOLUTIONARY WAR

Once in command, he hemmed in the British at Boston. When he had enough cannon he moved, on March 4, 1776, onto Dorchester Heights, overlooking Boston. The city was at his mercy, and General William Howe, the British commander, had no choice but to evacuate it. Howe sailed to New York City to renew the fighting. Washington hurried to meet him. But the British had both a navy and a larger army, and they pushed Washington's weak forces off Brooklyn and chased them out of Manhattan. Finally Washington was forced to retreat across the Hudson River to New Jersey.

Weakened by losses and desertions, he retreated all the way across New Jersey and into Pennsylvania, with the British after him.

Trenton. Then, when winter seemed to have ended the fighting, Washington struck back. He crossed the Delaware River on Christmas night and defeated the surprised Hessians (mercenaries hired by the British) at Trenton. That, plus a victory at Princeton, forced the British to give up New Jersey. Washington spent the winter at Morristown, training his men and gathering strength for the spring.

Saratoga. The year 1777 was one of decision. General John Burgoyne invaded New York from Canada but got caught in the forests and in the end had to surrender his whole army at Saratoga to the Americans under General Horatio Gates. A few people thought that perhaps Gates ought to become commander in chief instead of Washington, but nothing ever came of this.

General Howe, instead of going to Burgoyne's aid, attacked Philadelphia. Washington fought two brilliant battles, at Brandywine Creek and Germantown, to save Philadelphia. But the British were victorious, and Washington retired to nearby Valley Forge to suffer through the bitter winter months. However, American fortunes were looking up. In the spring of 1778 came the good news that France had entered the war on the American side.

Fighting in the South. Most of the fighting from 1778 to 1780 was along the western and northern frontiers or in the far South. Howe's successor, General Henry Clinton, decided that if the war could not be won in the North it could be won in the South. In 1780 the British captured Charleston, South Carolina, taking more than 5,000 American prisoners. Then General Charles Cornwallis marched through the Carolinas, winning one battle after another.

Now the British had the upper hand, and the American cause seemed desperate. There were mutinies in the army, which seemed on the verge of falling apart. The states were bickering among themselves, and the nation was bankrupt. And now Cornwallis was laying waste Virginia. Washington was in despair.

"Instead of having everything in readiness to take the field," he wrote, "we have nothing, and instead of having the prospect of a glorious offensive campaign before us, we have a bewildered and gloomy offensive one—unless we should receive a powerful aid of ships, land troops and money from our generous allies."

Yorktown. Fortunately for the American cause, that is just what happened. In July 1780, General the Comte de Rochambeau arrived in America with 5,000 French troops. Then, in midsummer of 1781, Washington received word that Admiral the Comte de Grasse was sailing with his French fleet for Chesapeake Bay. Washington and de Rochambeau agreed at once on their course of action. They would march swiftly to Virginia and together with the French fleet bottle up Cornwallis at Yorktown.

On September 5, 1781, the British fleet appeared off Yorktown. But it was too late—de Grasse was already there and he sent the British scuttling back to New York. Then de Grasse ferried Washington's army to Yorktown. Now for the first time in the war the Americans had more soldiers than the enemy and controlled the seas as well. Cornwallis fought gamely, but with help cut off he had no chance. On October 19, 1781, the British army marched out in surrender and stacked its arms while the bands played "The World Turned Upside Down."

Peace. Yorktown was really the end of the war, though nobody quite realized that yet, not even Washington. In fact after the victory at Yorktown things took a turn for the worse. Happily for America the British were just as tired of the war as the Americans. Soon American and British diplomats were drawing up the terms of peace, which were finally announced in April 1783.

Washington still had to deal with many difficult problems. The discontent of soldiers who had not been paid by Congress threatened to blow up into a rebellion. The states still acted as if they were independent. And Spain was growing hostile to the United States. But in December 1783, Washington was able to take farewell of the Army and the Congress. "I retire from the great Theatre of action," he said, "and take my leave of all the employments of public life."

Washington had hoped to retire to Mount Vernon to put his tangled affairs in order, restore his broken fortunes, and enjoy his old age in quiet. But his country would not let him do this. He was not only a public figure, he was the most important public figure in the United States. Nothing could really be done without him.

THE CONSTITUTION

Clearly if the new nation were to survive, it would have to have a stronger national government. All who understood this turned to Washington for leadership. The first talks that eventually led to the Federal Convention of 1787 were held at Mount Vernon. And when in 1787 Congress finally voted to call a convention to strengthen the old government, Washington headed the list of delegates from Virginia.

Early on the morning of May 9, 1787, Washington mounted his horse and started off on the long ride from Mount Vernon to Philadelphia. Everywhere he was greeted by cheering crowds, by waving flags, by enthusiasm. Whatever the American people might think about the Convention or about politics, there was one thing they all agreed on—their admiration for George Washington. As soon as the Convention met, it chose Washington as its president. This decision was one of the most important things that happened in the whole Convention. At one stroke it made the Convention respectable, and made

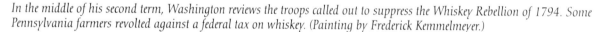

In the middle of his second term, Washington reviews the troops called out to suppress the Whiskey Rebellion of 1794. Some Pennsylvania farmers revolted against a federal tax on whiskey. (Painting by Frederick Kemmelmeyer.)

Mount Vernon, the estate Washington inherited from his half-brother, Lawrence, in 1792, was purchased by the Mount Vernon Ladies' Association of the Union in 1858. Today they continue to maintain it for the visiting public. Both George and Martha Washington are buried there.

sure that whatever came from it would receive a hearing from the people.

It was the Virginians who took the lead in making the old Articles of Confederation into a strong Constitution. Everyone knew where Washington stood, for ever since the war he had worked for a stronger government. Finally, the nationalists—or as they came to be called, the Federalists—were successful in drawing up a new Constitution, which provided for a real national government. On September 17, 1787, 39 delegates from 12 states (Rhode Island did not attend the Convention) signed the Constitution. Washington's name headed the list.

It was one thing to write a Constitution, another to get the people of the 13 states to accept it. It was a hard fight, for many of the people were suspicious of a government that was new and afraid of a government that was strong. What influenced them as much as anything else was the fact that Washington had presided over the Convention, that Washington had signed the Constitution, and that Washington was expected to head the new government. If Washington were thus committed to it, it

must be all right. One by one the states ratified the Constitution. Within a year 11 states had accepted it; the two laggard states, North Carolina and Rhode Island, came in later.

FIRST PRESIDENT

The Constitution had created a new office for the new nation. Instead of a king or an emperor, who would rule by inheritance and by Divine Right, it provided for a president who would be elected by the people themselves. The first election took place on February 4, 1789, and Washington received every vote cast. John Adams became vice president.

Actually the presidency was the last thing that Washington himself wanted. He had, so he wrote, "no wish but that of living and dying an honest man on my own farm." But as always he responded to the call of duty. Once more he rode off from Mount Vernon to take up the burdens of office.

Washington's trip to New York City, the first national capital, was a triumphant procession. Every town was decorated; songs were sung and poems recited; there were pageants and triumphal arches with girls strewing roses in front of him. At New York hundreds of ships sailed out in the harbor to greet him, their flags fluttering in the breeze. Along the shores crowded thousands of cheering spectators. Bands played, cannon boomed, and church bells rang. One observer called it "a universal chorus of welcome to the great deliverer."

On April 30, 1789, Washington took the oath of office as first president of the United States. What a task faced the new president! Everything had to be done. Washington had to hold the new nation together, get the machinery of government working, and attract first-rate people to run it. He had to set its finances in order, get its commerce going again, defend the frontiers against the Indians, and defend the nation itself against the threats from Great Britain and from Spain.

As for the presidency itself, it was up to Washington to decide what was really meant by the term "the executive power" in the Constitution, and to fix the place of the presidency in the American Government. Was the president to be a real force in government, or merely a figurehead? Washington interpreted "executive power" to mean real power. It was his idea that the president was to represent all the people. He was to be above political parties and battles. He was to be the leader at home and in foreign affairs as well. He was to be a symbol of the people and of the nation. He was never to abuse his power, but he was never to fail to use the power that the people and the Constitution had entrusted to him.

Washington's Administration

As a first step, Washington brought the ablest men into government service. Thomas Jefferson was appointed to head the Department of State. Alexander Hamilton became secretary of the Treasury. John Jay was appointed Chief Justice of the United States. With the aid of these and other members of his cabinet, and of the Congress, Washington got the government going. A financial system was set up that got the United States out of debt and enabled it to pay its way. The supremacy of national over state laws was established. The so-called Whiskey Rebellion (1794), a revolt of Pennsylvania farmers against the tax on whiskey, was put down, proving that the federal government was strong enough to enforce federal law. Peace was made with the Indians, and new lands in the West were acquired, including the sites of Detroit and Chicago. Three new states, Vermont, Kentucky, and Tennessee, were admitted to the Union.

Problems of foreign relations were equally serious, and Washington managed them with equal skill. When all Europe went to war in 1793, he decided that the United States should stay out and issued a proclamation of neutrality. He sent John Jay to England to make a treaty (Jay's Treaty, 1794) whereby the British agreed to give up the posts they had kept in the Northwest. He sent Thomas Pinckney to Spain to make a treaty (Pinckney's Treaty, 1795) that opened the Mississippi River to American commerce and set what was then the southern boundary of the United States. These were great achievements. They kept the United States at peace and established its independence from other nations.

RETIREMENT

Washington had been reelected in 1792. He could have been elected to the presidency again in 1796, but he decided that two terms were enough and refused to run again. Before he retired, he prepared his Farewell Address to the American people. The Farewell Address was a plea for Union, for a union of hearts and minds, for understanding. It was a warning against the dangers of political parties and rivalry between the different sections of the country. It urged friendship and commerce with all nations but warned against permanent alliances with any.

At the close of his second term on March 3, 1797, Washington returned once again to his beloved Mount Vernon, hoping to enjoy at last that peace which had been so long denied him. But it was not to be. On December 13, 1799, he became ill with a severe throat infection. As his illness grew worse he said, "I am not afraid to go." On December 14, 1799, two months before his 68th birthday, he died. Martha Washington died on May 22, 1802, and is buried next to her husband.

Washington's death marked the end of an era in American history. He had led the American colonies in their struggle for independence and helped create a new nation. For eight years he had guided its growth, setting it on the road to independence and freedom. Few men in history were ever given such opportunities for shaping the destiny of a nation; none ever responded more greatly to the opportunity. He is truly the "Father of His Country."

The Washington Monument, opened to the public in 1888, soars 555 feet, 5½ inches over the District of Columbia.

JOHN ADAMS

2nd PRESIDENT OF THE UNITED STATES (1797–1801)

Born: *October 30, 1735, at Braintree (now Quincy),*
Massachusetts
Occupation: *Lawyer*
Party: *Federalist*
Vice President: *Thomas Jefferson*
Wife: *Abigail Smith*
Died: *July 4, 1826, at Braintree, Massachusetts*

Of all the early presidents of the United States, John Adams has been the least understood and appreciated. His reputation, both during his lifetime and after, has suffered from this lack of understanding. Yet he was a remarkable man who contributed greatly to the creation of the United States during the American Revolution and in its formative years.

FAMILY LIFE

Adams was born on October 30, 1735, in Braintree (now Quincy), Massachusetts. His great-grandfather Henry Adams had emigrated from England. But both his grandfather Joseph Adams and his father, John Adams, had been born in Braintree. His mother, Susanna Boylston Adams, came from the nearby city of Boston.

Adams grew up on his father's farm, doing the usual country chores, including feeding the horses, milking the cows, and chopping wood. In 1751, at the age of 16, he entered Harvard, then a small college, and graduated four years later. He then taught school during the day and studied law at night. In 1758 he became a lawyer. Perhaps his most famous case, which showed Adams' characteris-

tic courage, was his successful defense of the British soldiers who were arrested after the Boston Massacre in 1770.

In 1764, Adams married Abigail Smith. She was an intelligent and sprightly woman whose letters are still a source of interesting information. The marriage was happy and successful. It lasted 54 years, until Abigail Adams' death in 1818. Their eldest son, John Quincy, later became the sixth president.

POLITICAL BEGINNINGS

Altogether, Adams spent about 25 years in public life. He became interested in politics quite early in his career as a lawyer. In 1765 a crisis arose when the British Government passed the Stamp Act. This was an unpopular tax on public documents, newspapers, licenses, insurance policies, and even playing cards. Adams wrote powerful articles against the tax in the Boston *Gazette*. These articles helped to establish his reputation as a political thinker, as an opponent of Britain's colonial policies in America, and as a champion of individual liberties.

The Continental Congress. Adams served as a delegate from Massachusetts to the First Continental Congress in Philadelphia in 1774 and to the Second Continental Congress, which met in 1775. With brilliance and persistence, he argued for American independence from Britain. When the fighting broke out in 1775 that marked the beginning of the Revolutionary War, Adams proposed George Washington as the commander of American military forces.

Adams was a member of the committee that drafted the Declaration of Independence. Although the Declaration was written chiefly by Thomas Jefferson, Adams bore the burden of defending it on the floor of the Continental Congress. It was adopted on July 4, 1776.

Abigail Adams was the wife of one president, John Adams, and the mother of a second, John Quincy Adams. She was the first First Lady to occupy the White House.

Diplomatic Service. Adams' diplomatic career began in 1778 when he was sent to France to help negotiate a treaty of alliance. In 1780 he returned to Europe as minister to arrange for loans and trade agreements in France and the Netherlands. Two years later Adams, together with Benjamin Franklin and John Jay, signed the preliminary peace treaty with Britain. The treaty, known as the Treaty of Paris, was finally concluded in 1783. It ended the Revolutionary War and crowned Adams' long struggle for American independence.

In 1785, Adams was appointed the first U.S. minister to Britain. He tried to win British friendship and economic cooperation, but without success. One reason was that he was too outspoken in defense of American interests. He was happy to return home in 1788, after having spent some ten years abroad.

Vice President. In the first presidential election in the United States, in 1788, George Washington won all the electoral votes cast for president. Adams became the first vice president. Both men were reelected in 1792 without opposition.

In spite of his general agreement with Washington's policies, Adams was impatient with his position as vice president. Adams was eager to lead and to act. Instead, he had to confine himself to the largely ceremonial job of presiding over the U.S. Senate.

PRESIDENT

Adams' frustration was ended by his victory in the presidential election of 1796. Running as the Federalist candidate, he edged out Thomas Jefferson, leader of the

---

John Adams

John Adams

2nd president, 1797–1801 Federalist

1735	Born on October 30 in Braintree (now Quincy), Massachusetts.
1755	Graduated from Harvard College.
1758	Began law practice in Braintree.
1764	Married Abigail Smith on October 25. Five children would be born to the couple.
1765	Wrote resolutions opposing the British Stamp Act.
1775	As a delegate to the Second Continental Congress, argued for independence and the formation of an army.
1776	Headed Continental Board of War and Ordnance; served on committee drafting Declaration of Independence.
1779	Drafted most of the Massachusetts state constitution.
1780	In France and the Netherlands, negotiated treaties and a $1,400,000 loan for the United States.
1782	Helped negotiate peace treaty with Britain (the Treaty of Paris, signed Sept. 3, 1783).
1785–1788	Was U.S. minister to Britain.
1789	Elected as the nation's first vice-president.
1792	Reelected vice president.
1796	As the Federalist candidate, successfully opposed Thomas Jefferson, the Democratic-Republican candidate, in presidential election. Jefferson became vice president.
1801	Retired to Braintree.
1826	Died on July 4 in Braintree.

Highlights of Presidency

1797	XYZ Affair brought the United States to the brink of war with France. (Peace was secured by the Convention of 1800.)
1798	Alien and Sedition Acts were adopted. The laws, supported by the Federalists, were highly unpopular.
1800	U.S. capital moved from Philadelphia to Washington, D.C. In the presidential election, Adams and the Federalists were defeated by the Democratic-Republican candidates, Thomas Jefferson and Aaron Burr.

Democratic-Republicans (also called the Republicans). According to the laws of the time, Jefferson thus became vice president. As a result, the new president and vice president belonged to opposing political parties.

John Adams was the first president to occupy the White House. He and Abigail moved in near the end of his term, in the fall of 1800. The President's Palace, as it was then known, was still unfinished and littered with debris.

Adams' one term as president was marked by troubles, both international and domestic. The foreign affairs crisis involved American neutrality at a time when Britain and France were at war. French attacks on American ships stirred up a warlike atmosphere in the United States, even inside Adams' own Cabinet. The situation was aggravated by the so-called XYZ Affair.

The XYZ Affair. Adams had sent a diplomatic mission to France to arrange a treaty in 1797. There the diplo-mats were visited by three agents of the French foreign minister Talleyrand. These agents, known as X, Y, and Z, asked for a bribe of $240,000. When news of this XYZ Affair reached America, it caused an uproar and led to an undeclared war between the United States and France. But despite immense pressure, including that of members of his own Federalist Party, President Adams knew that the United States was not strong enough to fight the French Empire. He persisted in his efforts for peace, which was finally achieved by the Convention of 1800. Adams considered it his great accomplishment. He said, "I desire no other inscription over my gravestone than: 'Here lies John Adams, who took upon himself the responsibility of the peace with France in the year 1800.'"

Adams' courageous but unpopular peace policy and his stubborn independence in other political matters cost him the support of his own party. The leading Federalists,

John Adams (standing, in rust-colored suit) and the four other members of the drafting committee present the Declaration of Independence to the Second Continental Congress in this painting by John Trumbull. The 56 signers of the Declaration are as follows:

Connecticut: Roger Sherman, Samuel Huntington, William Williams, Oliver Wolcott.

Delaware: Caesar Rodney, George Read, Thomas McKean.

Georgia: Button Gwinnett, Lyman Hall, George Walton.

Maryland: Samuel Chase, William Paca, Thomas Stone, Charles Carroll.

Massachusetts: John Hancock, Samuel Adams, John Adams, Robert Treat Paine, Elbridge Gerry.

New Hampshire: Matthew Thornton, Josiah Bartlett, William Whipple.

New Jersey: Richard Stockton, John Witherspoon, Francis Hopkinson, John Hart, Abraham Clark.

New York: William Floyd, Philip Livingston, Francis Lewis, Lewis Morris.

North Carolina: William Hooper, Joseph Hewes, John Penn.

Pennsylvania: Robert Morris, Benjamin Rush, Benjamin Franklin, John Morton, George Clymer, James Smith, George Taylor, James Wilson, George Ross.

Rhode Island: Stephen Hopkins, William Ellery.

South Carolina: Edward Rutledge, Thomas Heyward, Jr., Thomas Lynch, Jr., Arthur Middleton.

Virginia: George Wythe, Richard Henry Lee, Thomas Jefferson, Benjamin Harrison, Thomas Nelson, Jr., Francis Lightfoot Lee, Carter Braxton.

including the powerful Alexander Hamilton, turned bitterly against him. This led to a hopeless split in their party.

The Alien and Sedition Acts. President Adams' unpopularity was aggravated by the Alien and Sedition Acts. These acts were a direct result of the excitement over the trouble with France. The country was divided into pro-French and pro-British groups. Adams' Federalist Party was strongly anti-French. The opposition Democratic-Republican Party, led by Jefferson, was just as strongly anti-British.

The Federalists were convinced that opposition against them was aroused by the French and Irish living in America. They were sure that the country swarmed with French spies. The Federalists controlled Congress. In 1798 they decided to crush the opposition through legislation that came to be known as the Alien and Sedition Acts.

The Alien Act contained three provisions. One required that the period of naturalization for foreigners be changed from 5 to 14 years. The second authorized the president to deport all aliens considered dangerous to the peace and security of the country. The third gave the president the power to imprison or banish citizens of an enemy country in time of war.

More serious was the Sedition Act, which was aimed at American opponents of the government. This act made it a crime to oppose the administration directly or indirectly. Even those who voiced criticism in print were made subject to harsh penalties.

The Sedition Act resulted in the prosecution of 25 persons and the conviction of 10 of them. All were prominent Democratic-Republicans.

These acts were violently unpopular. They were considered an attack on the basic liberties of the American

Final plans for the White House were drawn up by the Irish architect James Hoban and construction began in 1792. President John Adams and his family became its first occupants in 1800.

people. President Adams was not personally responsible for them, but they were passed by his party and he signed them. Therefore the blame fell upon him. In the election of 1800, Adams and his party suffered disastrous defeat. The Federalist Party never recovered.

On March 4, 1801, after the inauguration of President Jefferson, Adams retired from public life. He returned to Braintree and devoted the remaining 25 years of his life to intellectual pursuits, mainly reading (philosophy, religion, political thought, science) and letter writing.

He resumed his friendship and correspondence with Thomas Jefferson in 1812. The two men had been separated for 12 years because of political differences. On July 4, 1826—the 50th anniversary of the Declaration of Independence—John Adams died at Quincy. That same day Jefferson died at Monticello, Virginia.

POLITICAL PHILOSOPHY

Adams expressed his ideas in a number of essays and books, as well as in his letters. There are three main elements in his philosophy. One is Adams' view of human nature. Another is his conception of inequality. The third is his idea of government.

Adams did not agree with democrats like Jefferson that human beings were naturally good and decent. On the contrary, he believed that people were basically selfish and only good because of necessity.

Adams also denied the democratic idea of equality. He pointed out that among all nations the people were "naturally divided into two sorts, the gentlemen and the simple men." The gentlemen, being superior in abilities, education, and other advantages, were therefore qualified to rule.

These views underlay Adams' philosophy of government. Since human beings were greedy and selfish, it was necessary for society to keep them in check. The average person, he felt, could not be entrusted with power.

Adams believed in liberty and was opposed to tyranny. Though he was sometimes accused of being a monarchist, he actually preferred a republic. But instead of a Jefferson-type democracy, Adams favored a republican government run by an aristocracy of talented men.

Such views, expressed with his typical bluntness, gained Adams unpopularity and even hostility among the American people. But he was not one to seek popular favor. He died as he had lived, an independent, toughminded, somewhat opinionated and irritable Yankee—but always a courageous patriot and scholar.

DID YOU KNOW?

SEAL OF THE PRESIDENT OF THE UNITED STATES

- *Adams was the great-great-grandson of John and Priscilla Alden, Pilgrims who landed at Plymouth Rock in 1620.*

- *As president, Adams refused to attend any Washington's birthday celebrations because he considered them a form of deification.*

- *Adams and Jefferson were the only presidents to sign the Declaration of Independence, and they both died on its 50th anniversary, July 4, 1826.*

- *Adams lived 90 years, 247 days, longer than any other president, in spite of a life of poor health.*

3rd PRESIDENT OF THE UNITED STATES (1801–1809)

Born: *April 13, 1743, at Shadwell Plantation, Virginia*
Occupation: *Lawyer, planter*
Party: *Democratic-Republican*
Vice Presidents: *Aaron Burr (1801–05); George Clinton (1805–09)*
Wife: *Martha Wayles Skelton*
Died: *July 4, 1826, at Monticello, near Charlottesville, Virginia*

Thomas Jefferson is best known as the author of the Declaration of Independence and as 3rd president of the United States. He was also a diplomat, an architect, a musician, a scientist and inventor, a pioneer advocate of public schools, the founder of the University of Virginia, and the most eminent patron of learning and the arts in his generation. Though he lived 83 years, he never ceased to be young in spirit. He was always learning something new, always trying to contribute to human progress. His fame as a champion of freedom and democracy was great in his own time. It grew even greater in the 20th century, when dictators arose in so many parts of the world.

As a person, Jefferson will always be fascinating because he did so many different things so well. In his range of interests perhaps no other great American except Benjamin Franklin ever matched him.

EARLY LIFE

Though he became renowned as a friend of all the people, Jefferson was a member of a favored class by birth and training. He was born on April 13, 1743, at Shadwell

Plantation in what is now Albemarle County, Virginia, then on the edge of western settlement. His father, Colonel Peter Jefferson, was a large landholder as well as a noted explorer. He provided his son with excellent opportunities for education and left him a considerable estate. His mother, Jane Randolph, belonged to one of the leading Virginia families.

Jefferson was educated privately in his early years. He studied Latin and Greek before going to the College of William and Mary in Williamsburg at the age of 17. He learned French early and afterwards acquired a knowledge of Italian and Spanish. At college Jefferson's interest was aroused in science and mathematics. And in the colonial capital of Williamsburg he saw government in operation. This in itself was a political education. Jefferson was not good-looking. He was tall and rather awkward, sandy-haired, and inclined to freckle. But he was strong in body and a fine horseman, and he made and kept many friends.

For five years Jefferson studied law under George Wythe, the most noted law teacher in Virginia, preparing himself with unusual care for his profession. At the age of 24 he was admitted to the bar, and he rode the circuit as a lawyer until the American Revolution closed the courts. Like other lawyers he had trouble collecting his fees, and he was chiefly supported by the income from his farms. His lands were doubled by the inheritance of his wife, Martha Wayles Skelton, whom he married in 1772. But his wife's estate was burdened with a heavy debt from which he never escaped.

Jefferson owned about 10,000 acres of land in Virginia, much of it forested, and from 100 to 200 slaves. He was always opposed to slavery, but his proposals for its abolition in his own state failed. He himself was a notably kind master.

On a little mountain he built a house, later extensively remodeled, which he named Monticello—meaning "Little Mountain" in Italian. (Jefferson pronounced the "c" as in the word "cello.") He was his own architect and builder.

Because of his position as a leading planter, Jefferson was expected to share in the government of his county and province. At the age of 25 he was elected to the Virginia House of Burgesses, and he served there until the Revolution. He disliked speaking in public, partly because his voice was not strong. But he excelled on committees and soon showed his skill as a writer. From the beginning he was a member of the group that most strongly upheld colonial rights against the British Government. He was no orator like Patrick Henry. But it was afterward said that he was the pen of the American Revolution, as George Washington was the sword.

REVOLUTIONARY PATRIOT

Jefferson said many times that he never liked public life. And this unusually domestic man might have remained at home (except for brief trips to Williamsburg) if the conflict between the colonies and the British Government had not become critical. After the Boston Tea Party in 1773 and the severe British measures against Massachusetts, the issue, as he saw it, was between freedom and tyranny. There was no doubt where Jefferson stood. His entire career was dedicated to protecting and extending the liberties of the American colonists. When he became a member of the Continental Congress in 1775, he was known to be an ardent patriot. Because of his "masterly pen" and because he was a representative of the largest colony, he was chosen to write the Declaration of Independence. He was only 33 years of age at the time. If he had done nothing more than that, he would have gained lasting fame.

The Declaration is one of the two most famous documents of the United States. The other one is the Constitution, but the Declaration came first. After it was adopted on July 4, 1776, by representatives of the 13 original colonies, it was written on parchment and signed by 56 delegates. Today it can be viewed in its glass case at the National Archives in Washington, D.C.

But in Jefferson's eyes, his services in Virginia during the next few years were of comparable importance. He believed that the American Revolution was not only a struggle against foreign rule but also a fight for the rights of individual human beings. Therefore, as a member of the legislature, he set out to reform the laws of Virginia. He hoped to replace the artificial aristocracy of birth and wealth, to which he himself belonged, with a natural aristocracy of talent and virtue. He did this by opposing laws

Jefferson was a self-taught architect and designed his own home, Monticello, which is situated on a hilltop near Charlottesville, Virginia. He first drew up the plans in the 1760s. The house was completed after he left the presidency in 1809 and is now a national historic landmark.

restricting liberty, and he came to be known as the "Man of the People."

Jefferson set highest value on his Bill for Establishing Religious Freedom, which was passed in 1786, seven years after he introduced it. It called for the complete separation of church and state and for the freedom of people to think as they liked. Unfortunately, his Bill for the More General Diffusion of Knowledge, which would have started a system of public schools in Virginia, did not pass. Jefferson was ahead of his time in this.

In 1779, at the age of 36, Jefferson was elected governor of Virginia, succeeding Patrick Henry. His two terms as governor were troubled. He had little power under the existing state constitution. And in 1781, just as his term was ending, the British invaded the state. Since the main American armies were elsewhere, nobody could have done much to stop the British, but Jefferson was blamed. The legislators fled, and for a time the state had no governor. Later an inquiry was made into Jefferson's conduct. He was cleared of all charges and regained his popularity in Virginia. However, the old charges came up years later, when he was a candidate for the presidency. Meanwhile, he was so distressed by the criticism, which he thought unjust, that he determined never to return to public life. During his retirement he prepared his *Notes on Virginia*. Much of his reputation as a scientist rests on this important book.

Jefferson probably would not have left Monticello if his wife had not died in 1782, leaving him lonely and desolate. He sent his two very young children to live with an aunt (where one of them afterward died), but he kept his eldest daughter, Martha, with him. Yielding to the wishes of friends, he accepted election to the Continental Congress in 1783.

During his brief service in the Congress, Jefferson was its most useful and industrious member. He recommended the adoption of the dollar and the decimal system of money. This saved Americans from the confusion of English pounds, shillings, and pence. His report on the government of the western territory was especially important. It anticipated the Northwest Ordinance of 1787, which formed the basis for the creation of new states from western lands. On this system the nation as it exists today was gradually developed. Throughout his career Jefferson recognized the rights of the settlers in the West and tried to promote their interests. For that reason he was always popular there.

MISSION TO FRANCE

But Jefferson soon had to turn his eyes eastward. For in 1784 he was appointed to join Benjamin Franklin and John Adams in Paris, to negotiate treaties of commerce with European countries. They had little success, but after a year Jefferson was appointed Franklin's successor as minister to France.

Jefferson's five years in Paris were among the most interesting of his entire life. He took his daughter Patsy

Benjamin Franklin (left) and John Adams (center) made some suggestions, but the Declaration of Independence was largely the work of Thomas Jefferson, who headed the five-man drafting committee.

(Martha) with him, and after a time he sent for his other daughter, Polly (Maria). He lived in style in the most polite court in Europe, enjoying to the full the architecture, art, and music of the Old World. He bought books by the dozen and made friends of scholars and scientists. He learned many of the secrets of French cooking and became an authority on French wines. He visited England, the south of France, northern Italy, and the German Rhineland. He kept careful records of the things he saw, wrote American friends about them, and sent home samples of European animals and plants. He sent to Virginia drawings of a classic temple at Nimes in France, to serve as a model for the state capitol in Richmond. Though the building there did not come up to the original or to his plans, it started the classic revival in American architecture. From this time on, white columns appeared on the façades of public buildings and private houses. Others had a part in this movement, but Jefferson more than anyone else began it in the United States.

Jefferson's eldest daughter, Martha (Patsy), was born in 1772. She went with her father to Paris in 1784.

Jefferson became the first secretary of state in 1790. This portrait is attributed to Charles Wilson Peale (1741–1827).

A polite and friendly man, Jefferson was a skillful diplomat as well as a close observer. He formed a low opinion of the kings of Europe and especially disliked the monarchy of France. However, the French Government had shown friendship to the United States during the American Revolution. And Jefferson was determined to strengthen this tie at a time when the young republic had hardly any other friends. The Marquis de Lafayette, who had fought on the American side in the war and was his close personal friend, helped him greatly.

Jefferson saw the start of the French Revolution in 1789, his last year in Paris. He feared that it would get out of hand, as it did later. But he approved of this revolt against the tyranny of a king, and he was disturbed when other European kings tried to put it down.

FIRST SECRETARY OF STATE

Jefferson returned home with his two daughters in 1789. Rather reluctantly he accepted the invitation of President George Washington to become the first secretary of state under the new Constitution. He took office in the spring of 1790 and served as secretary of state to the end of 1793. During this time occurred his historic conflict with Alexander Hamilton, the young and brilliant secretary of the treasury. In foreign affairs Jefferson, who believed that the British were still enemies of the United States, tried to keep the United States friendly to France and the cause of liberty it now represented. Hamilton favored the British and

preferred the rule of kings in Europe to that of the French revolutionaries. But when war broke out between France and Great Britain, both men believed that the United States should keep out of it. Jefferson was embarrassed by the demands and reckless actions of the fiery French minister, "Citizen" Genêt, who hoped to win American support for the Revolutionary government. But he upheld the policy of neutrality to Washington's satisfaction.

What Jefferson sought was full independence for the United States. Later, as president, he followed the same policy as Washington. That policy came to be called isolation and lasted more than a century, until world political conditions changed.

Jefferson objected to certain of Hamilton's policies as favoring merchants and financiers rather than farmers. Most of the people in the country were farmers, and Jefferson always thought of himself as one. He believed in human liberty more than Hamilton did and trusted the people more. He thought that Hamilton relied too much on force and was trying to increase the power of the national government beyond what was permitted by the Constitution. He favored the strict interpretation of the Constitution, in order to prevent tyranny. The country owes much to both of these men. Hamilton did more than any other man of his day to make the national government strong. Jefferson did more than anybody else to make it democratic and to leave men as free as possible.

Thomas Jefferson

3rd president, 1801–09 Democratic-Republican

1743 Born on April 13 at Shadwell, Virginia.

1762 Graduated from the College of William and Mary.

1767 Admitted to the bar; began practicing law.

1769 Elected to the Virginia House of Burgesses.

1772 Married Martha Wayles Skelton on January l. Only two daughters of six children would live to maturity.

1775 Elected a delegate to the First Continental Congress.

1776 As a delegate to the Second Continental Congress, chosen to write the Declaration of Independence.

1776–79 A member of the Virginia House of Delegates, supported proposals on land reform and religious freedom.

1779–81 Served as governor of Virginia.

1783–84 As delegate to Congress from Virginia, helped establish the nation's coinage system.

1785–89 Served as minister to France.

1790–93 Was secretary of state under George Washington.

1796 Accepted Democratic-Republican nomination for president but was narrowly defeated by John Adams and thus became vice president.

1800 In the presidential election, defeated Adams but tied with his running mate, Aaron Burr. The election went to the House of Representatives, which chose Jefferson on Feb. 17, 1801.

1809 Retired to his Virginia estate, Monticello.

1819 Founded the University of Virginia.

1826 Died on July 4 at Monticello.

Highlights of Presidency

1803 Supreme Court ruling in *Marbury v. Madison* established the principle that the court could declare unconstitutional a law passed by Congress. The Louisiana Territory was purchased from France.

1804 Elected to a second term as president. Meriwether Lewis and William Clark began to explore the Northwest.

1808 The importation of African slaves into the United States became illegal.

1809 The 1807 Embargo Act was replaced by a law banning trade with Britain and France.

VICE PRESIDENT

In the presidential election of 1796, a successor to George Washington had to be chosen. John Adams was supported by the Federalist Party and Jefferson by the Democratic–Republicans. At the time, Jefferson was in retirement at Monticello, directing his farms and rebuilding his house.

Adams was elected by a majority of three electoral votes. According to the laws then in effect, Jefferson became vice president. There has never been another situation like this, for Jefferson was also the recognized leader of the party opposed to the government. This was the time of what Adams called the "half-war" with France. Diplomatic relations were broken, and there was fighting at sea. Jefferson was charged with favoring the French, though in fact he did not do so. It was also the time of the Alien and Sedition Acts, when foreigners were threatened and newspapermen who criticized the policy of the government were sent to jail.

THE ELECTION OF 1800

Adams finally broke with the extremists in his own party and made peace with France. But he was defeated in the election of 1800. Under the confused electoral system (afterward corrected by the 12th Amendment to the Constitution), Jefferson was tied with Aaron Burr, who was the Democratic–Republican candidate for vice president. It was long uncertain who would be president. At length Jefferson was elected by the House of Representatives, as the majority of the people wanted him to be. That is the most important thing about this famous election. It showed that the wishes of the majority of the people must prevail.

PRESIDENT

Jefferson was nearly 58 when he became president. He served two terms, winning reelection by a huge majority. He was the first president to be inaugurated in Washington, D.C., which had become the seat of government during the last year of the Adams administration. Though it was called a city, Washington was then merely a village in the wilderness. Only one wing of the original Capitol had been built, and the President's house looked like a big, bare box. The columns were not put on during Jefferson's presidency. Still, he had the big house furnished handsomely and gave delicious dinners there. Jefferson did not like formality and ceremonies, however. He acted just as he did at Monticello. The British minister did not like such informality, and he was one of those who thought Jefferson careless about his clothes. Others said that Jefferson did not believe in God and was an immoral person, though neither charge was true.

No American president ever had worse things said about him falsely. Yet Jefferson was enormously popular with the American people for most of his two terms. This was chiefly because he believed in the people and respected their wishes. He reduced taxes, abolished offices

A highlight of the Jefferson presidency was the transfer of the Louisiana Territory to the U.S. in 1803. At more than 800,000 square miles, the purchase doubled the size of the country at a cost of about $15 million.

that he thought unnecessary, and tried to leave everybody as free as possible. He was a friendly man, who did not often order people to do things. Nevertheless, he nearly always got Congress to do what he wanted. He was the first president who was also the leader of a political party. And he led his party so well that the Federalists never had a chance to elect another president.

The Louisiana Purchase

One of the most important achievements of Jefferson's presidency was the purchase of the Louisiana Territory from France in 1803, doubling the size of the United States. This action aroused alarm in the minds of many Easterners, especially New Englanders, who feared that their small states would become unimportant. But it delighted most Americans. Jefferson himself wondered if in purchasing Louisiana he had not done more than he had the right to do under the Constitution.

The Federalist Judges

Jefferson's struggle with the judges also aroused fears. They were all Federalists, and some of them brought their politics into the courtroom. Congress abolished the positions of some and tried to get rid of one Supreme Court Justice by impeachment, but without success. The main lesson the new government learned from this struggle was that judges should be independent and stay out of politics. Most of them did remain apart from politics afterward, though Chief Justice John Marshall and Jefferson continued to be political enemies.

Aaron Burr

Jefferson gave the American people what they wanted and needed most: freedom and a chance to develop the country by their own efforts. He was troubled by a movement to separate New England and New York from the Union, but this died away. He was also troubled by the strange actions of Aaron Burr. After killing Alexander Hamilton in a duel, Burr made a mysterious expedition down the Mississippi River. Burr was suspected of conspiring to set up an independent empire in the Southwest. He was tried for treason but acquitted by a court over which John Marshall presided. This was a blow to Jefferson, who had said that Burr was guilty.

The Embargo

Jefferson's greatest difficulties as president grew out of the war between the British and the French, which had been resumed. The chief trouble was with the British, who controlled the seas. They interfered with American commerce by stopping American vessels, searching them for British seamen, and impressing (forcing into service) Americans. But Jefferson did not want to get into this war on either side. Therefore he tried an embargo. He hoped that if American foreign commerce was stopped altogether, the British and French, who needed American products, would cease their objectionable actions. Measures of this sort had been used by the colonists against the British before the Revolution. However, the embargo was bitterly opposed by shippers, especially in New England. They claimed that it did more harm than good, and that the government was tyrannical in enforcing it. The failure of this law was painful to Jefferson. It was repealed at the very end of his presidency.

Jefferson's friend and secretary of state, James Madison, was elected to succeed him as president in 1808. After the wars in Europe ended, Jefferson largely regained his popularity, though some old foes continued to attack him. In spite of some failures he was a great president. But Jefferson himself took more pride in what he did during the American Revolution and his final retirement.

INGENIOUS INVENTOR

Not only was Jefferson a self-taught architect, he was also an inventor. All his life, but especially while at Monticello, he came up with ideas and gadgets to make his life as a farmer and scholar easier. He made his own nails on his property and invented an improved plow. Jefferson also perfected a hemp-making machine and a folding ladder. He had voluminous correspondence to take care of, and the adjustable table and swivel chair he invented helped to lighten this task. He also invented the polygraph, to make copies of his letters as he wrote them. And the automatic doors on today's buses are based on a Jeffersonian concept. He had so many interests—literature, botany, art, music, French wines (from his trips abroad)—and he was so competent in all of them, that he was known as the "Sage of Monticello."

FINAL RETIREMENT

Jefferson lived 17 years after he left office. At Monticello, his mountaintop home, he was surrounded by grandchildren, whom he adored. But he had so many visitors that

DID YOU KNOW?

- *Jefferson was the first president to shake hands with guests. Previously, people bowed to Presidents Washington and Adams.*

- *Jefferson's library of some 6,000 books formed the basis of the Library of Congress. They were purchased from him for $23,950.*

- *He took his oath of office in Washington, D.C., the first president to do so.*

- *Jefferson designed his own tombstone and wrote his own epitaph, omitting the fact that he was president of the United States.*

- *The U. S. Military Academy was founded during Jefferson's presidency.*

At the Jefferson Memorial in Washington, D.C., on the edge of the Tidal Basin, cherry blossoms and other plantings form a fitting background for statesman and gentleman planter Thomas Jefferson.

he fled for a time every year to another place of his, Poplar Forest, near Lynchburg, Virginia.

Jefferson rode horseback almost every day until the end of his life. But he spent most of his time writing letters. Many of them were to John Adams, with whom he discussed books, government, religion, and almost everything else. He was in financial difficulty in his last years. This was partly because of the old debt he never could get rid of, partly because he had spent more than he made as president, partly because of small returns from his crops, and finally because he endorsed a large bank note for a friend who could not meet it. He was practically bankrupt at his death.

Jefferson's last great public service was the founding of the University of Virginia in 1819. It was the only accomplishment he valued as much as his authorship of the Declaration of Independence and the Virginia act for religious freedom. He designed buildings for the University that have been much admired. He selected the first professors and laid down the course of study.

Jefferson and John Adams died on the same day, July 4, 1826—the 50th anniversary of the Declaration of Independence. Two centuries after his birth a memorial to Jefferson was dedicated in Washington, D.C. He has taken his place, with Washington and Lincoln, among the greatest of Americans.

JAMES MADISON

Born: *March 16, 1751, at Port Conway, Virginia*
Occupation: *Lawyer*
Party: *Democratic-Republican*
Vice Presidents: *George Clinton (1809–12); Elbridge Gerry (1813–14)*
Wife: *Dolley Dandridge Payne Todd*
Died: *June 28, 1839, at Montpellier, Virginia*

James Madison is perhaps best known to Americans as the father of the Constitution. This title was given him because of the leading part he played in framing the charter of government under which the American people have lived since 1789. Madison was only 36 years old when that work was completed, but he had been in public life for 11 years and was unsurpassed as a student of government.

BACKGROUND AND EARLY YEARS

Madison was born on March 16, 1751, at Port Conway, Virginia. His great-great-grandfather, a ship carpenter, had emigrated from England in 1653 and become a tobacco farmer in the Virginia tidelands. Later generations of Madisons pushed westward as the country opened. James Madison's grandfather and father built up a farm of about 6,000 acres in what is now Orange County, Virginia. This great farm, Montpellier (now spelled Montpelier), remained James Madison's home throughout his 85 years.

James was taught to read and write by his mother and grandmother. Soon after his 11th birthday he was sent to Donald Robertson's famous boarding school in King and Queen County, Virginia. After a year devoted to English, mathematics, French, and Spanish, James took up Latin at the age of 12. Within two years he was reading Virgil, Horace, Justinian's *Institutes*, Ovid, Phaedrus, Terence, and Sallust. The intellectual fare fed to the teenage boy also included Montesquieu's *Spirit of Laws*, John Locke's *Essay Concerning Human Understanding*, and Descartes' astronomy. Long afterward Madison said of schoolmaster Donald Robertson: "All I have been in life I owe largely to that man."

Two years of tutoring at home by the local Episcopal rector made the boy ready for college. James was sent to the College of New Jersey (now Princeton University). He completed the four-year course in two years, sleeping only five hours a night and considerably damaging his health. Madison acquired his basic knowledge of government and international relations at college. Then, for five years after his graduation in 1771, he continued his extensive studies at home. These included a good part of a lawyer's training, though Madison had no intention of becoming a lawyer. At the same time he was teaching the younger children of the family.

During these years young Madison witnessed scenes that made him think religious persecution the worst of all evils. In a neighboring county half a dozen dissenting clergymen were in jail for preaching according to their own beliefs. All Madison's efforts to win their release were in vain.

The approaching Revolutionary War, however, turned Madison's thoughts in another direction. Three Madison brothers enlisted for military service in the Revolution. But James was forced to drop out, because of the physical strain, before his company was called to active duty. He turned at once to political service.

EARLY POLITICAL CAREER

In 1776 the 25-year-old Madison was elected a delegate to the Virginia Revolutionary Convention. There he wrote a strong guarantee of religious freedom in the Virginia Declaration of Rights. He helped pass a resolution asking the Continental Congress to issue the Declaration of Independence. Madison then served a year in the Virginia legislature but was defeated for reelection because he refused to furnish whiskey to the voters. He was immediately appointed a member of the governor's council, which managed the state's war efforts. After two years of this work he was sent as a delegate to the Continental Congress. Though he was one of its youngest members, and was boyish in appearance, Madison quickly rose to leadership, especially in the conduct of American relations with France and Spain. Through his efforts, too, the vast vacant lands of the West came under national ownership.

With the coming of peace in 1783, Madison devoted his efforts to strengthening the weak national government set up under the Articles of Confederation. Elected again to the Virginia legislature, he persuaded his state to issue a call for a convention of the states. He went as a delegate to the Annapolis Convention of 1786 and then to the Constitutional Convention at Philadelphia in 1787. Madison's understanding of government made him a leader in the work of framing the Constitution. His devotion to democratic self-government helped make it the keystone of the American political system. He became known as the "Father of the Constitution."

Madison's Ideas on Government

The essential problem facing the framers of the Constitution was to find some way to establish power and yet maintain liberty. This called for the republican form of government, in which the people are sovereign (supreme) but rule through elected representatives. Up to Madison's time most students of government had assumed that small republics were more virtuous than large ones. Madison observed that the opposite was true in America. Tyrannical majorities ruled the smallest states. In the larger ones, however, the greater diversity of interests prevented one faction, or interest group, from acquiring undue power.

So, Madison reasoned, let the United States have the republican form of government at all levels, with each state controlling its local affairs. Let a supreme federal government manage national affairs and interstate matters—those between the states. The larger such a federal republic became, the more liberty it could enjoy with safety, for the different interests of the various sections of the country would split the factions that might produce tyranny in a small republic.

Madison presented this idea to the delegates at Philadelphia. It overcame the fear many of them had of democracy, and the government of the United States was built on the basis of Madison's ideas. He then joined with Alexander Hamilton and John Jay in writing

---

James Madison

4th president, 1809–17 Democratic-Republican

1751 Born on March 16 at Port Conway, Virginia.

1771 Graduated from the College of New Jersey (now Princeton University).

1776 Served on the committee that drafted Virginia's constitution and declaration of rights.

1777 Elected to Virginia governor's council, where he served under Patrick Henry and Thomas Jefferson.

1780 Elected to Congress as a delegate from Virginia.

1784 Returned to Virginia, where he served in the legislature.

1787 As a delegate to the Constitutional Convention, argued for a strong central government and a system of checks and balances. Also contributed to *The Federalist* papers.

1788 Debated for and won Virginian ratification of the U.S. Constitution.

1789–97 Served in the House of Representatives.

1794 Married Dolley Payne Todd on September 15.

1798 Wrote the Virginia Resolutions, defending states' rights and opposing the Alien and Sedition Acts.

1801–09 Was secretary of state under Thomas Jefferson.

1808 Elected president over Federalist candidate C. C. Pinckney.

1817 Retired to his Virginia estate, Montpellier.

1826 Succeeded Jefferson as rector of the University of Virginia.

1836 Died on June 28 at Montpellier.

Highlights of Presidency

1810 Congress ended a ban on trade with Britain and France, who continued to be at war.

1811 Trade with Britain was ended again, after Britain continued to enforce its blockade of France by attacking U.S. ships. Indian forces allied under Chief Tecumseh were defeated in the Battle of Tippecanoe on November 7.

1812 Citing continued attacks on its ships, the United States declared war on Britain in June. Reelected to a second term.

1814 Treaty of Ghent, ending the War of 1812, was signed on December 24. British troops earlier had burned the White House.

1815 Began a wide-ranging domestic program that included reorganization of the National Bank and development of roads and canals.

DID YOU KNOW?

- *He was the first president to wear trousers rather than knee breeches.*

- *"The Star-Spangled Banner" was written during his presidency by Francis Scott Key.*

- *Madison was the first president to face enemy fire, during the War of 1812.*

- *At 5 feet, 4 inches, he was our shortest president.*

- *His widow, Dolley, in 1844 sent the first personal message by Morse telegraph.*

The Federalist papers, explaining the Constitution to the people in order to secure its ratification. Madison led the supporters of the Constitution at the Virginia ratifying convention. The people of Virginia then elected to the House of Representatives in the First Congress of the United States.

DRAFTING THE BILL OF RIGHTS

James Madison is also considered the "Father of the Bill of Rights." In his campaign for a seat in the House of Representatives under the new Constitution, he promised his voters that he would energetically push for the adoption of a bill of rights. True to his word, he took the lead in the First Congress in pressing for the desired amendments.

On June 8, 1789, drawing from proposals made by the various state ratifying conventions, Madison proposed to the Congress nine amendments to the Constitution, containing nineteen specific provisions (many of which are now contained in the Bill of Rights). The House and the Senate modified some of Madison's proposals, eliminated others entirely, and added some new ones as well.

As it finally emerged from Congress, the proposed Bill of Rights consisted of twelve amendments and was offered to the states for ratification. The first two proposed amendments were never ratified by the states. On December 15, 1791, Virginia ratified the remaining ten amendments, and the Bill of Rights officially became part of the Constitution.

GOVERNMENT SERVICE

Madison served in Congress from 1789 to 1797, rising to leadership of the entire House of Representatives. Then, as political parties began to form, he became leader of those men (later called Democratic-Republicans) who wished the government to give special thought to the welfare of the common people. Opposed to this was the Federalist Party, led by Alexander Hamilton, who wanted to strengthen the new government by linking it with the interests of persons of wealth and power. Hamilton's party won in Congress.

Early in this contest Thomas Jefferson arrived home from France, where he had been American minister, and took over leadership of the Democratic-Republicans. Madison became his foremost supporter. When Jefferson was elected president in 1801, Madison was appointed secretary of state. In this capacity Madison helped promote the purchase of the Louisiana Territory from France.

Meanwhile, in Europe the Napoleonic Wars were raging. Great Britain was impressing (forcing into service) seamen from American ships to man its navy against France. Both Great Britain and France were seizing American ships and cargoes. Secretary Madison strongly upheld the right of a neutral country to trade with warring nations through unblockaded seaports. But all his

Dolley Dandridge Payne Todd married Madison in 1794. She was a distant relative of Martha Washington.

The American warship Constitution, *affectionately known as "Old Ironsides," defeated the British* Guerrière *on August 19, 1812 in a key battle of the War of 1812. Opponents of the conflict called it "Mr. Madison's War."*

protests were ignored. President Jefferson attempted to preserve peace by the Embargo Act, forbidding American ships to leave port. But this only resulted in violations of the act.

DOLLEY MADISON

About this time, at the age of 43, Madison married Dolley Dandridge Payne Todd on September 15, 1794. She was 17 years younger than Madison, and became one of the most famous first ladies in U.S. history. She acted as White House hostess first while her husband was secretary of state under Jefferson, who was a widower, and later during her husband's own two terms. She was noted for her graciousness and charm and for her ability to entertain guests and preside at dinners. During the British invasion of Washington in 1814 when they set fire to the White House, she escaped to Virginia carrying important state papers and the famous Gilbert Stuart portrait of George Washington, among other valuables. She would outlive Madison by 13 years.

PRESIDENT

Thomas Jefferson's support helped Madison win election to the presidency in 1809. Madison's first action on becoming president was to inform Great Britain that if it would stop interfering with American commerce and France continued to seize American ships, he would ask Congress to declare war on France. At the same time a similar offer was made to France—to go to war against Great Britain if France would stop its seizures and Great Britain continued them. But both countries continued to seize American ships. In 1810 Congress authorized the President to cut off trade with either country if the other agreed to stop its oppressions. An agreement to do so by the French, though false, led to a commercial break with Great Britain in 1811 and to war in 1812.

The War of 1812

Congress, however, was more willing to declare war than to provide the means of fighting it. The War Department consisted of a secretary of war and eight clerks. The United States had virtually no army and only a small navy. While the little American navy was winning brilliant triumphs at sea, the inexperienced soldiers met with defeat after defeat. Washington, D.C., itself was captured by the British. Part of the city, including the White House, was burned, and Madison was forced to flee with other members of the government. Young army officers, however, were gaining experience, and so was the president. Newly disciplined American troops drove the Duke of Wellington's veterans from the field in successive battles. This change of fortune led to a satisfactory peace in the Treaty of Ghent in 1814.

All through the War of 1812 the Federalist Party of New England had opposed what they called "Mr. Madison's war." Nevertheless, Madison had refused to

Montpellier as it looks today. The land was originally purchased by Madison's grandfather in what is now Orange County, Virginia. Madison lived there all his life and is buried there with his wife.

place any restraints on speech or the press. Amid the rejoicings over peace the Federalist Party broke down and soon vanished from existence.

When Madison left the presidency in 1817, the citizens of Washington held a mass meeting at which he was congratulated on "the untarnished glory" of his administration. During the war, they declared, Madison had held

Madison is known as the Father of the Constitution, but he was also the principal author of the Bill of Rights, which became the first ten Amendments in 1791. Today they are on display at the National Archives in Washington, D.C.

military authority within its proper limits, directed it with energy, and "won power and glory . . . without infringing a political, civil, or religious right."

LATER YEARS

During the remaining 19 years of his life Madison engaged in scientific farming at Montpellier. He originated methods of agriculture that did not become common until a century later. With his wife, Dolley, he welcomed visitors from all over the United States and Europe. Equally welcome were the children of relatives, for Madison had no children of his own.

Although a slave-owner by inheritance, Madison hated slavery and did all he could to put an end to it. As an adult he never belonged to any church, but in his mature years he expressed a preference for the Unitarian faith. After Jefferson's death in 1826, Madison succeeded his old friend as rector (in effect, president) of the new University of Virginia.

Madison's last great service to the United States began in 1828. In that year South Carolina claimed the right to nullify (declare null and void) acts of Congress. For the next six years the aged statesman fought this doctrine of nullification. He wrote articles against it when he was so crippled with rheumatism that he could barely move his fingers.

Madison died at Montpellier on June 28, 1836. His earliest political thought had been for the liberty of America. His last thought and his final message to his countrymen concerned the way in which that liberty could be preserved: "The advice nearest to my heart and deepest in my convictions is that the Union of the States be cherished and perpetuated." He is buried in the family plot at Montpellier, as is Dolley, who died in 1849.

JAMES MONROE

5th PRESIDENT OF THE UNITED STATES (1817–1825)

Born: April 28, 1758, in Westmoreland County, Virginia
Occupation: Lawyer
Party: Democratic-Republican
Vice President: Daniel D. Tompkins
Wife: Elizabeth Kortright
Died: July 4, 1831, in New York, New York

In Virginia the young officer "formed a connection," as he put it, with a man who was to shape his career and affect his whole life. The man was Thomas Jefferson, then governor of Virginia. Jefferson made the young man his protégé and, among other things, taught him law.

The intimacy between the two men lasted for 46 years, until Jefferson's death in 1826. Jefferson, Monroe's senior by 15 years, unfailingly helped the younger man to advance his political career, all the way up to the presidency. His confidence in Monroe never wavered. Jefferson said of him: "He is a man whose soul might be turned wrong side outwards, without discovering a blemish. . . ."

POLITICAL CAREER

Monroe embarked upon his political career with single-minded concentration. No rebuff halted him, and no defeat slowed him for long. From 1782, when he was elected to the Virginia House of Delegates at the age of 24, until 1825, when he left the White House at the age of 66, he was in public office almost without interruption.

Monroe was a member of the Congress of the Confederation, by which the United States was governed before the adoption of the Federal Constitution. He was a delegate to the Virginia Ratification Convention, where he opposed adoption of the Constitution because he felt it centered too much power in the federal government. He was a United States senator, acting in opposition to the Federalist Party. He was four times governor of Virginia. He was minister to France, Spain, and Great Britain. He was secretary of state as well as secretary of war. Finally, he was a two-term president of the United States.

DIPLOMATIC MISSIONS

In 1794 President Washington sent Monroe to Paris. Washington hoped to win a favorable reception among

James Monroe was the last of the Virginia Dynasty presidents. (These included Thomas Jefferson and James Madison.) He was a professional politician who spent virtually his whole adult life in public service, steadily rising to ever higher office. A modest man, Monroe was overshadowed by the brilliance of his great contemporaries. Yet his modesty and integrity won him wide esteem and the unwavering loyalty of his friends.

EARLY YEARS

Monroe was born on April 28, 1758, in Westmoreland County, Virginia, the son of Spence and Elizabeth Jones Monroe. At the age of 16 he entered the College of William and Mary, but he left within two years, in 1776, to join the Third Virginia Regiment as a lieutenant. He took part in some of the famous battles of the American Revolution. At Valley Forge in the winter of 1777 Monroe served as aide-de-camp to one of George Washington's generals. In the following year, on General Washington's recommendation, the 20-year-old Monroe was commissioned lieutenant colonel of a regiment to be raised in Virginia.

This illustration of James Monroe's Westmoreland County, Virginia, birthplace, a small plantation which grew mostly tobacco, originally appeared in The Family Magazine *in 1839. The future president was born there in 1758.*

the French revolutionary leaders there and to conciliate their sympathizers in the United States. The French Government gave Monroe an enthusiastic reception. Monroe returned the enthusiasm. But his open pro-French sympathies so antagonized President Washington's anti-French Cabinet that it urged Monroe's recall. The President agreed, even though Monroe's removal deepened the anti-American feelings of the French Government.

The major achievement of Monroe's second mission to Europe involved the Louisiana Purchase. After 1800 there was growing fear in the United States that the Spanish cession of Louisiana to France would bottle up the Mississippi River, a vital artery for western American trade. "The day France takes . . . New Orleans," President Jefferson said, ". . . we must marry ourselves to the British fleet and nation." Jefferson decided, however, upon diplomatic measures first.

For so delicate and grave a mission the president needed a man in whom he and his followers had complete trust. Such a man was James Monroe. Jefferson wrote him in 1803:

"You possessed the unlimited confidence of the administration . . . and generally of the republicans everywhere; and were you to refuse to go, no other man can be found who does this—All eyes, all hopes are now fixed on you."

Monroe carried with him to Paris President Jefferson's unlimited confidence and his special instruc-

tions. These were, primarily, to buy New Orleans and to acquire the right of free navigation on the Mississippi. He arrived in Paris in April 1803. There he joined the regular American minister, Robert R. Livingston. The French surprised them with the sudden offer, by Napoleon, to sell the United States the whole Louisiana Territory. After some haggling with the French minister of finance, Monroe and Livingston signed the treaty, which was dated April 30, 1803. By its terms the United States acquired all of the Louisiana Territory for a total cost of 80,000,000 francs (about $15,000,000). The Louisiana Purchase was beyond a doubt the greatest real estate bargain in history. In one stroke it doubled the territory of the United States. The transaction also enhanced Monroe's reputation.

After Paris, Monroe went to London, and then for about a year to Madrid, as American minister. In these wartime capitals (the Napoleonic Wars were then raging) his diplomatic activities were not fruitful, partly because of British hostility. In 1807 he returned home. There his Virginia friends were trying to promote him as successor to Jefferson in the presidency. Monroe was willing, but the nomination and election went to James Madison. Monroe refused the governorship of Louisiana and resumed political life in Virginia, first as a member of the state legislature and then as governor.

In 1811 Monroe accepted President Madison's offer of the post of secretary of state. He held this position throughout the War of 1812 and until the end of Madison's

James Monroe

5th president, 1817–25 Democratic-Republican

1758 Born on April 28 in Westmoreland County, Virginia.

1774 Entered the College of William and Mary.

1776 Joined the Virginia Militia, enrolling as a lieutenant. Fought at White Plains and Trenton.

1782 Elected to the Virginia House of Delegates.

1783 Elected to Congress of the Confederation.

1786 Married Elizabeth Kortright of New York City on Febraury 16, and returned to Virginia to practice law. The couple would have two daughters, and a son who died in infancy.

1790 Elected to the U.S. Senate, where he opposcd greater centralization of government.

1794 Named minister to France by President Washington. His pro-France sympathies led to his recall in 1796.

1799 Elected governor of Virginia.

1803 Sent by President Jefferson to France, to negotiate the Louisiana Purchase. Subsequently named minister to Britain.

1808 Defeated by James Madison in bid for the Democratic-Republican presidential nomination.

1811 Appointed secretary of state by President Madison. His attempts to avert war with Britain were unsuccessful.

1814 Replaced John Armstrong as secretary of war following the British burning of Washington.

1816 Elected president by a wide margin.

1825 Retired to Oak Hill, near Leesburg, Virginia.

1829 Presided over the Virginia Constitutional Convention.

1830 Moved to New York to live with his daughter.

1831 Died on July 4 in New York, New York.

Highlights of Presidency

1818 The Convention of 1818 fixed the boundary between the U.S. and British North America.

1819 Spain agreed to give Florida to the United States in exchange for the cancellation of $5 million in debts.

1820 Congress adopted the Missouri Compromise, temporarily quieting sectional disputes over the expansion of slavery. Won election to a second term in a nearly unanimous vote.

1822 Vetoed a plan for the federal government to improve internal roads.

1823 On December 2, proclaimed the Monroe Doctrine, warning European powers not to interfere in U.S. affairs.

second term. In 1814 Monroe also became secretary of war. His energetic policies as war secretary were given some of the credit for the American victories at Plattsburg in 1814 and at New Orleans in 1815. They also helped him toward his nomination for the presidency in 1816.

PRESIDENT

Monroe was elected president in 1816. He received about 84 percent of the electoral votes cast (183 out of 217 votes) and carried 16 of the 19 states of the Union. In 1820, when he ran for a second term, his triumph was even greater. This time he received all but one of the electoral votes (231 out of 232). He would have received all the electoral votes had not one elector felt that nobody should share that historic honor with George Washington.

Monroe's administration came to be known as the Era of Good Feeling. It was a period of national optimism, expansion, and growth. There were no major domestic problems to trouble the president. In regard to internal improvements, Monroe in 1822 vetoed the Cumberland Road bill as unconstitutional. However, he recommended a Constitutional amendment to give the federal government power in the field of "great national works."

The Missouri Compromise of 1820–21. In 1818, and again in 1819, the Missouri Territory applied for statehood as a slave state. The U.S. at that time was divided between free and slave states. A bitter controversy ensued, and then Maine applied for admission as a free state. The looming slavery issue was settled, at least temporarily, by admitting Missouri and Maine as slave and free states, respectively.

Foreign Affairs

The Monroe Administration was especially notable in the field of foreign affairs. The able diplomacy of Monroe's secretary of state, John Quincy Adams, resulted in a number of achievements of lasting benefit to the United States. The Convention of 1818, held in London, settled the boundary between the United States and British North America (Canada) and fixed the northern line of the Louisiana Purchase. In the following year the western limit of the Louisiana Territory (from the Sabine River, on the Gulf of Mexico, along the Red and Arkansas rivers to the Pacific Ocean) was defined by the Adams–Onís Treaty with Spain. In the same treaty the United States also acquired East Florida and a claim, which Spain renounced, to West Florida.

The Monroe Doctrine. The most memorable event connected with Monroe's presidency was the proclamation of the Monroe Doctrine. In 1822 the Austrian, French, Russian, and Prussian monarchies considered the possibility of restoring Spanish power in South America. But the British foreign minister, George Canning, was unwilling to see the European nations, especially the French, intrude into the Western Hemisphere. He approached the American minister in London about a joint action on

Latin America. This proposal was reported to Monroe. After consulting with his Cabinet and seeking the advice of Jefferson and Madison, Monroe decided to take a step independently of Great Britain. This was a public declaration of American policy, expressed in a message to Congress on December 2, 1823.

The Monroe Doctrine, as embodied in the President's message, comprised four main points: (1) The political system of the Americas was different and separate from that of Europe; (2) the Americas were no longer to be regarded as subjects of European colonization; (3) the United States had no intention of interfering with the European "colonies or dependencies" already existing in the Americas; (4) the United States would be hostile to any extension of European power in the Americas.

For more than a century this doctrine remained the foundation of American foreign policy. It guided United States relations with Europe, particularly in regard to Latin America.

President Monroe declared the cornerstone of his foreign policy, the "Monroe Doctrine," in a message to Congress on December 2, 1823. He signed the message at this desk, now on view at the James Monroe Museum and Memorial Library in Fredericksburg, Virginia.

DID YOU KNOW?

- *As a U.S. senator, Monroe obtained the rule change which opened Senate sessions to the public.*
- *His first inaugural was the first to be held outdoors.*
- *Monroe's daughter was the first to be married in the White House.*
- *The U.S. Marine Band played at his second inaugural and at every inauguration since.*
- *Monroe was the first president to ride on a steamboat.*
- *He was the first U.S. senator to become president.*

LATER YEARS

Upon his retirement from the presidency, in March 1825, Monroe returned to Oak Hill, his home in Loudoun County, Virginia. In 1826 he became a regent of the University of Virginia. And in 1829 he presided over the Virginia State Constitutional Convention. After the death of his wife, Eliza, in 1830, Monroe, lonely and ill, went to live with his daughter, Mrs. Samuel L. Gouverneur, in New York City. There he died on July 4, 1831, at the age of 73. In 1858, on the 100th anniversary of his birth, his remains were moved to Richmond, Virginia.

Monroe was about six feet tall, with grayish blue eyes and a lined face that conveyed an expression of kindliness. Somewhat colorless, he yet inspired universal respect for his modesty, solid judgment, and quiet administrative ability. The crusty John Quincy Adams, who followed Monroe in the presidency, paid his predecessor this tribute:

"Monroe . . . was . . . of purposes always honest and sincere, of intentions always pure, of labors outlasting the daily circuit of the sun . . . ; of a mind anxious and unwearied in the pursuit of truth and right; patient of inquiry; patient of contradiction; . . . sound in its ultimate judgments; and firm in its final conclusions."

Unavoidably, Monroe has suffered by comparison with his brilliant contemporaries, particularly Jefferson and Madison. But his many years of devoted service to the United States in the country's most formative period entitle him to esteemed remembrance.

6th PRESIDENT OF THE UNITED STATES (1825–1829)

Born: July 11, 1767, at Braintree (now Quincy),
   Massachusetts
Occupation: Lawyer
Party: Democratic-Republican
Vice President: John C. Calhoun
Wife: Lousia Catherine Johnson
Died: February 23, 1848, in Washington, D.C.

Many Americans have sought the office of president of the United States and have deliberately shaped their lives to that end. John Quincy Adams' parents prepared him for the presidency from boyhood. But although Adams achieved his goal of becoming president, his term in the White House was overshadowed by his two other political careers—as America's greatest diplomat and as its greatest defender of human freedom in the U.S. House of Representatives.

AN UNUSUAL CHILDHOOD

John Quincy Adams was born on July 11, 1767, in Braintree (now Quincy), Massachusetts. His father was John Adams, who would later become the second president of the United States. His mother, Abigail Smith Adams, was the most accomplished American woman of her time. Young Adams grew up as a child of the American Revolution, which began when he was seven years old.

John Quincy's education began in the village school and continued under his mother's guidance. His education was inspired by letters from his father, who had been serving in the Continental Congress in Philadelphia since 1774.

During the Revolutionary War, John Quincy accompanied his father on two diplomatic missions to Europe. In 1781, at the age of 14, he acted as French interpreter to his father on a mission to Russia. In 1783, John Quincy served as his father's secretary when the elder Adams was minister to France. Young Adams was present at the signing of the Treaty of Paris in 1783, which ended the Revolutionary War.

In Paris, John Quincy Adams began his famous diary. He was to continue it for over 60 years. On the title page of the first volume was the proverb that ruled his life: "Sweet is indolence and cruel its consequences." Adams never had a lazy day.

Young Adams returned to Massachusetts in 1785 to complete his education at Harvard College. He graduated in 1787 and then studied law.

EARLY DIPLOMATIC CAREER

He had barely developed a law practice when the French Revolution broke out. Articles Adams wrote for a Boston newspaper attracted the attention of President George Washington. In 1794 Washington appointed the 28-year-old John Quincy Adams minister to the Netherlands. Adams' official dispatches and his letters from the Dutch capital at The Hague convinced the president that this young man would one day stand at the head of the American diplomatic corps.

In 1797, while on a mission from the Netherlands to England, Adams married Louisa Catherine Johnson, daughter of the American consul in London.

From The Hague, Adams (whose father was now president) was assigned to the Court of Prussia. There he negotiated a treaty of friendship and commerce. He continued his letters and dispatches about the war of the French Revolution. Because of political reasons, John Adams recalled him after Thomas Jefferson was elected president in 1800.

Adams' experiences had convinced him that the United States must never be caught in the "vortex" of European rivalries and wars. This lesson guided him through his later diplomatic career and influenced United States policy for a century afterwards.

A SHORT TERM IN THE SENATE

When he returned to Boston, Adams found the practice of law frustrating. He had a strong desire to enter politics. In 1803 the Massachusetts legislature elected him to the United States Senate. Though elected as a Federalist, Adams felt that party politics stopped at the ocean's edge. To the disgust of Massachusetts Federalists, he voted for President Jefferson's Embargo of 1807. The embargo was aimed at protecting United States neutrality in the wars between England and France. It stopped all American trade with the two countries. Adams' vote in favor of the embargo cost him his Senate seat. The legislature held a special election ahead of time to replace him with a more faithful Federalist.

DID YOU KNOW?

- *As president, Adams swam nude in the Potomac River every day, weather permitting.*

- *He was the first to be elected president without receiving either the most popular votes or the most votes of the electoral college.*

- *He was the first president married abroad.*

- *Adams was the first of three presidents who were Phi Beta Kappa.*

- *He is the only president to be elected to the House after his presidential term.*

This portrait of Louisa Catherine Johnson Adams dates from the 1820s. The harp and book symbolize her love of music and literature.

DIPLOMAT AGAIN

In 1809 President James Madison appointed Adams the first American minister to Russia. Adams was in Russia when the War of 1812 broke out between the United States and Great Britain. He served on the delegation that brought about the Peace of Ghent in 1814. The following year he became minister to Great Britain, where he served until 1817.

By now Adams was in his 50th year. He was without question the most experienced man in the United States diplomatic service. Because of his European experience, Adams had become a confirmed isolationist. He felt that the future of the United States lay in expansion across the North American continent rather than in European alliances.

SECRETARY OF STATE

In 1817 President James Monroe called Adams home from Great Britain to become secretary of state. The most important achievements of Secretary Adams were the treaties he negotiated, which brought much of the Far West under American control. The famous Transcontinental Treaty of 1819 (ratified 1821) with Spain gave the United States access to the Pacific Ocean. This was regarded by some historians as one of the greatest diplomatic triumphs ever achieved by one man in the history of the United States. Adams was also responsible for treaties with the newly independent countries of Latin America.

Adams sat for this portrait in 1847, at age 79. At the time he was serving in the U.S. House of Representatives.

The Monroe Doctrine

John Quincy Adams had a major role in forming the Monroe Doctrine. That famous document made it clear that the United States would not tolerate any new European colonization in the Americas. The doctrine properly bears President Monroe's name, for it was Monroe who in 1823 first declared its principles to the world as American foreign policy.

The Election of 1824

Adams was never a dynamic politician. But his accomplishments brought him before the people in the national election of 1824. There was no real party contest. The old political parties had disappeared during the so-called Era of Good Feeling of Monroe's administration. It was a contest of leaders.

General Andrew Jackson, the hero of the battle of New Orleans during the War of 1812, received a majority of the popular vote. But no candidate received the necessary majority in the electoral college. Jackson had 99 electoral votes; Adams, 84; William H. Crawford of

John Quincy Adams

6th president, 1825–29 Democratic-Republican

1767 Born on July 11 at Braintree (now Quincy), Massachusetts, the second child and eldest son of John and Abigail Adams.

1787 Graduated from Harvard College.

1790 Began law practice in Boston.

1791 Wrote the first of three series of articles supporting President Washington's policy of neutrality.

1797 On July 26, married Louisa Catherine Johnson. The couple would have four children.

1797-1801 Served as U.S. minister to Prussia.

1803 Elected to the U.S. Senate as a Federalist; however, his independent policies led the party to replace him before the end of his term.

1809-14. Was minister to Russia.

1814 Served on commission negotiating the Treaty of Ghent, ending the War of 1812.

1815-17 Was minister to Britain.

1817 Appointed secretary of state under James Monroe.

1824 Ran for president, opposed by Henry Clay, William Crawford, and Andrew Jackson (all Democratic-Republicans). Jackson received the most votes, but as none of the four had a majority, the election went to the House of Representatives. In the House, Clay, who had won the fewest electoral votes and was thus out of the running, threw his support to Adams and ensured his election in Febraury 1825.

1829 Returned to Quincy after four years as president.

1830 Elected to the House of Representatives, where he would serve for 17 years. As a Congressman, argued for government's right to free slaves and against the annexation of Texas.

1848 Died on February 23 in the Capitol.

Highlights of Presidency

1825 Divisions in the Democratic-Republican Party increased when Adams appointed Henry Clay secretary of state, leading to charges that the two men had made a bargain in the election of 1824.

1824 Opposition in Congress prevented Adams from enacting most of his domestic program. Erie Canal, linking New York City and the Great Lakes, was completed.

1828 Congress imposed stiff duties on imported manufactured goods. Soundly defeated by Andrew Jackson in bid for reelection.

Georgia, 41; and Henry Clay of Kentucky, 37. Under the Constitution the election had to be decided by the House of Representatives. The voting there was by states and was limited to the first three candidates. On February 9, 1825, Adams was elected president by a bare majority of states.

John Adams, then 90 years old, was delighted at his son's victory. But Abigail Adams did not live to see the presidency come to rest on her son's shoulders. She had died in 1818.

PRESIDENT

President John Quincy Adams appointed Henry Clay secretary of state. Clay had thrown the votes of his supporters in the House of Representatives to Adams rather than Jackson. At once Jackson and his followers raised the cry of "corrupt bargain." That there was a political deal seems fairly certain, but there is nothing to show that it was dishonest.

The charge of corrupt bargain was the beginning of a quarrel with Jackson that marred Adams' administration. Jackson had strong support among the voters of the newly admitted states. Adams, after all, had not received a majority of the popular vote. The Jacksonians were out to get rid of Adams and seize office themselves.

The four years of Adams' presidency were prosperous and generally happy years for the United States. Adams' ambition was to govern "as a man of the whole nation," not as the leader of a political party. He believed in liberty with power. He favored more power for the federal government in the disposal of public lands and in building new roads and canals to keep up with the westward movement. He supported federal control and protection of the Indian groups against invasion of their lands by the states.

This program hit at the narrow interpretation of the Constitution under the old Jeffersonian concept of states' rights. It thus aroused Adams' opponents. In the election of 1828, Andrew Jackson was elected president by an overwhelming majority.

With his term as president over, Adams' career seemed finished. He returned sadly to Quincy, Massachusetts. However, he was still willing to serve his country in any office, large or small. In 1830 he was elected to the House of Representatives. Nothing could have been more pleasing to Adams, for the ghost of the presidency still haunted him. He hoped for the nomination again. But these hopes soon faded.

Adams spent the last 18 years of his life, from 1830 to 1848, in Congress. He died two days after collapsing there while giving a speech against the war with Mexico.

"OLD MAN ELOQUENT"

During Adams' years in the House of Representatives, the stormy issue of slavery faced the United States. At heart Adams was an abolitionist: he wished to do away completely with slavery. But he was politically prudent, and did not say so publicly. He became a leader of the antislavery forces in Congress but limited his efforts to constitutional means. He sought to abolish slavery in the District of Columbia. He opposed its expansion into the territories of the United States. And he championed the right of petition to Congress for abolition of slavery.

As secretary of state and as president, Adams had tried to obtain Texas from Mexico. But in Congress he resisted to the last the movement for annexation of Texas. By that time the entry of Texas into the Union would have meant the creation of one or more new slave states. On the other hand, he championed the annexation of Oregon, where slavery did not exist. "I want the country for our Western pioneers," he said.

Adams was a patron and supporter in Congress of scientific activities, especially in the fields of weights and measures, and astronomy. He led the movement for establishment of the Smithsonian Institution, in Washington, D.C., one of the nation's foremost centers of learning.

"Old Man Eloquent," as Adams was called, opposed the war with Mexico that followed the annexation of Texas in 1845. He considered it an unjust war. On February 21, 1848, while giving a speech protesting the award of swords of honor to the American generals who had won the war, Adams collapsed on the floor of the House of Representatives. He died two days later in the Capitol. He was 80 years old.

During most of his early career as a diplomat, John Quincy Adams was little known throughout the country. His term as president was unpopular. Always a reserved man, he seemed cold and aloof to the people. His career in the House of Representatives made him a violently controversial figure. It was not until the final years of his life that Adams won esteem and almost affection, especially in the hearts and minds of the millions of Americans who hated slavery. Representatives of both political parties journeyed to Quincy, Massachusetts, for his funeral. In death, John Quincy Adams seemed at last to belong to the whole nation.

ANDREW JACKSON

7th PRESIDENT OF THE UNITED STATES (1829–1837)

Born: *March 15, 1767, in the Waxhaw settlement, South Carolina*

Occupation: *Lawyer, soldier*

Party: *Democrat*

Vice Presidents: *John C. Calhoun (1829–32); Martin Van Buren (1832–37)*

Wife: *Rachel Donelson Robards*

Died: *June 8, 1845, at Nashville, Tennessee*

A visitor to the White House in 1832 wrote of Jackson: "In person he was tall, slim and straight. . . . His head was long, but narrow, and covered with thick grey hair that stood erect, as though impregnated with his defiant spirit; his brow was deeply furrowed, and his eye . . . was one to 'threaten and command'. . . . His whole being conveyed an impression of energy and daring." Someone whispered a message in the President's ear, and he jumped up, exclaiming, "By the Eternal! I'll smash them." Jackson was engaged in one of his political battles, and he did indeed smash his opponents.

EARLY YEARS

Jackson's parents, Andrew and Elizabeth (Hutchinson) Jackson, came from northern Ireland to the Waxhaw settlement on the South Carolina frontier in 1765. There Jackson was born on March 15, 1767, a few days after his father's death. He was raised, with his two older brothers, by his widowed mother, who lived with relatives. He acquired some schooling and grew up a tall, lanky boy with reddish-sandy hair and a quick temper. At the age of nine, as he later proudly remembered, he publicly read the newly arrived Declaration of Independence to 30 or 40 people who gathered at his house.

During the Revolutionary War, Jackson, at the age of 14, fought with the patriots against the British in the battle of Hanging Rock. He was captured, and a British officer demanded that he clean his boots. When Jackson refused, the officer slashed him with his sword. Jackson bore the scar on his head for the rest of his life. He was soon released from prison but was orphaned by the death of his mother. "I felt utterly alone," Jackson later wrote, "and tried to recall her last words to me."

Andrew Jackson made such a lasting impression upon his times that the years when he was president are usually referred to as the Era of Jacksonian Democracy or the Age of Jackson. As the victor in the battle of New Orleans, during the War of 1812, he was one of the nation's most famous military heroes. As president he stood for equality of opportunity for the common man—for the right of every American to better himself. The average American responded by taking a far more active interest in politics than ever before. When Jackson was first inaugurated, in 1829, one admirer wrote: "It was a proud day for the people—General Jackson is their own president!"

Jackson's hardiness when marching with Tennessee militiamen and his unwavering devotion to their welfare led them to nickname him Old Hickory. The name stuck and well fitted Jackson as president. With vigor and determination he smashed the second Bank of the United States because he regarded it as a monopoly exploiting the people. And he threatened military action against South Carolina when it defied the Federal Union.

At 16 Jackson occupied himself in Charlestown, South Carolina, spending a substantial legacy from his grandfather. He returned to the frontier with a horse and no money. He tried schoolteaching and then studied law at Salisbury, North Carolina. He was remembered there as "the most roaring, rollicking, game-cocking, horse-racing, card-playing, mischievous fellow, that ever lived in Salisbury. . . more in the stable than in the office." He also acquired the manners, as well as the vices, of a gentleman.

EARLY CAREER

Before he was old enough to vote, Jackson had passed his bar examinations. In 1788 he went westward with the first group of pioneers to travel a new trail to Nashville, Tennessee. This city was then a cluster of log cabins within a stockade on the Cumberland River. There Jackson's fortunes flourished along with those of the town and the territory, which in 1796 became the state of Tennessee.

In 1791 he married Rachel Donelson Robards, thinking that she was divorced. But the divorce decree was not granted until two years later. They were remarried in 1794. Jackson was devoted to his wife and furiously resented any gossip about the marriage.

Jackson improved his fortunes by speculating (buying and selling) extensively in land. In 1795 he obtained a tract of land where he raised cotton and in 1819 built his graceful home, The Hermitage. Nearby he owned a store. While his personal fortunes were improving, he was advancing with equal rapidity as a lawyer-politician. Whatever Jackson's deficiencies in legal knowledge may have been, he made up for them with a forthright common sense that made him one of the most popular men in Tennessee. He became prosecuting attorney. Then in 1796, when Tennessee became a state, he became its first representative in Congress. He resigned in 1797 and was elected to the United States Senate. But business reverses led him to resign from the Senate in 1798 and return to Nashville. His ambition was to become major general of the Tennessee militia, and in 1802 the field officers elected him by the margin of a single vote.

It was this post that brought Jackson fame when the War of 1812 broke out. The governor of Tennessee gave him the command of troops sent to punish Creek Indians who had massacred settlers in the Mississippi Territory. At Horseshoe Bend in March 1814, he routed the Indians and first won a military reputation. He was commissioned a major general in the United States Army and became responsible for the defense of New Orleans.

When financial problems forced Jackson to resign from the Senate in 1798, he returned to the plantation he had purchased near Nashville, Tennessee in 1795. He built The Hermatage, which became his much-loved home, in 1819. He is buried there, beside his wife.

Jackson, who was called "Old Hickory" by his admirers, capped his military career with an impressive victory in the Battle of New Orleans in 1815. His success as a soldier and his devotion to the average American led, almost inevitably, to the presidency.

The Battle of New Orleans

On January 8, 1815, a force of approximately 5,000 British soldiers attacked the city. Jackson's militiamen, reinforced by Creoles, African Americans, and pirates (about 4,500 men in all), were concealed behind log breastworks. They concentrated a deadly fire upon the advancing columns of British redcoats. Three times the British advanced, and three times they were repulsed. They suffered over 2,000 casualties, including the death of their commander, before breaking off the battle.

The American victory saved New Orleans and the vast Louisiana Territory, and Jackson became one of the most celebrated of American heroes. Actually, the Treaty of Ghent with Great Britain had already been signed, ending the war, although the news had not yet reached New Orleans. But had the British won, they might have made new demands rather than ratifying the treaty. In any event, Jackson came to stand for American victory, the triumph of simple frontiersmen.

THE ROAD TO THE PRESIDENCY

Jackson's fame was to lead almost inevitably to the White House. But meanwhile, his friend James Monroe was president. The headstrong Jackson became involved in controversy when, in 1818, he led his troops against the Seminole Indians and pursued them into Spanish Florida. Secretary of State John Quincy Adams averted

trouble with Spain, and the United States purchased Florida. Jackson served briefly as governor of the new territory. Then he retired to The Hermitage. There old friends with political ambitions began to promote him for the presidency. A first step was to return him to the United States Senate in 1823. The next was to launch him nationally as a candidate in the presidential election of 1824.

The Election of 1824

Running against John Quincy Adams, Henry Clay, and William H. Crawford, Jackson won the largest number of popular votes. But none of the candidates received a majority of the electoral votes. The election, as provided by the 12th Amendment, was decided by the House of Representatives. There Clay threw his support to Adams (who had received only 84 votes to Jackson's 99). Adams, after his election, made Clay secretary of state. Jackson's followers raised the cry of "bargain and corruption" and aroused Old Hickory himself to anger. Four years later, however, he was to even the score.

The Election of 1828

The campaign of 1828 revolved around personalities rather than issues. Enthusiastic voters, though lacking any clearcut idea of Jackson's views, voted overwhelmingly for him. Three times as many men went to the polls in

Andrew Jackson

7th president, 1829–37   Democrat

1767 Born on March 15 in the Waxhaw settlement, South Carolina.

1780 Joined state militia; captured by the British in 1781.

1787 Admitted to the bar, after reading law in North Carolina.

1791 In August, married Rachel Donelson Robards. The couple remarried on Jan. 17, 1794, on learning that Mrs. Jackson's divorce from her first husband was not final until 1793. They had no children.

1796 After being a member of the Tennessee constitutional convention, was elected to the House of Representatives.

1797 Won a U.S. Senate seat; resigned a year later.

1798–1804 Served on the superior court of Tennessee.

1806 Killed Charles Dickinson, a Nashville lawyer, in a duel sparked by remarks he made about Mrs. Jackson.

1812 Mobilized a force of 2,500 for the War of 1812.

1815 Defeated the British in the Battle of New Orleans.

1817 Successfully led an expedition into Florida, to stop Seminole raids on U.S. territory.

1821 Named provisional governor of Florida.

1823–25 Served in the U.S. Senate.

1824 Defeated by Adams in presidential election.

1828 Won a sweeping victory in the presidential race.

1837 Retired to The Hermitage, his estate near Nashville.

1845 Died on June 8 at The Hermitage.

Highlights of Presidency

1829 Placed some 2,000 of his supporters in government jobs and established a "kitchen cabinet" of informal advisers.

1832 Won a second term. On December 10, federal troops were sent to South Carolina over the state's attempt to nullify federal tariff laws.

1833 Removed government funds from the Bank of the United States after vetoing a new charter for the bank in 1832.

1835 Final installment of national debt was paid, making Jackson the only president to clear the debt.

1836 On July 11, issued the Specie Circular, ordering that federal lands be purchased only in gold and silver.

1828 as in 1824. Jackson received about 56 percent of the popular vote (over 647,000 votes) and 178 electoral votes, compared with 83 for Adams.

PRESIDENT

Great crowds hailed Jackson's inauguration and jammed into the White House to shake his hand. A Supreme Court justice, mourning for older ways, lamented, "The reign of King 'Mob' seemed triumphant." The small but powerful group of men who held federal offices also shuddered. For the ambitious politicians who had promoted Jackson's candidacy hoped to obtain positions for themselves and their lieutenants. Senator William L. Marcy of New York asserted, "To the victors belong the spoils." Jackson made some concessions to his followers. In so doing he made officeholding somewhat more democratic. Some political offices had been in the hands of the incompetent and the corrupt. Jackson informed Congress that official duties could be made "so plain and simple that men of intelligence may readily qualify themselves for their performance." He adopted the principle of rotating offices among deserving candidates. His opponents charged him with introducing a "spoils system." Yet it is noteworthy that Jackson removed only one fifth of the federal officeholders, and some of these had misused government funds. Nor were the men he appointed any less well trained than the men they replaced.

During Jackson's administration another device of democratic politics came into existence. This was the national nominating convention. Originated by the Anti-Masonic Party, a short-lived third party, it was also used by the Democrats (as the Jacksonians called themselves) in 1832.

As president, Jackson soon developed clearcut positions on most of the great issues facing the nation. He was ready to utilize fully his presidential powers, on behalf of both the common man and the national government.

Indian Policy

Jackson's interest in settlers and his feelings as a former Indian fighter led him to develop a policy to remove all eastern Indian tribes to the Great Plains. The Supreme Court tried to stop Georgia from moving the Cherokees in 1832. But Jackson would not enforce the Court's decision. The Indian resettlement policy was tragic for thousands of Indians, though it was popular with the settlers in the South and the West.

Internal Improvements

Another of Jackson's policies was less popular. This was his refusal to allow federal money to be spent on internal improvements unless they were interstate in nature. In 1830 he vetoed as unconstitutional the Maysville Road Bill. This would have provided a federal subsidy to help build a turnpike in Kentucky, River past the plantation of Jackson's political opponent, Clay. However, Jackson did

This anti-Jackson political cartoon depicts him as a leader of the "spoils system." He was the first president to reward many of those who worked for his election with political appointments.

sign bills providing far more government funds than his predecessors for the building of interstate roads and for improvement of rivers and harbors.

The Clash with Calhoun

On the question of states' rights versus supremacy of the federal government, Jackson clashed sharply with his vice president, John C. Calhoun of South Carolina. In 1830 the Senate discussed a theory that Calhoun had devised. According to Calhoun's theory a state could nullify (declare null and void within its borders) acts of Congress it considered unconstitutional. Congress then would either have to drop the disputed act or obtain its validation through a constitutional amendment. Calhoun hoped to win Jackson to this states' rights view. But at a banquet honoring Thomas Jefferson, the president, looking firmly at Calhoun, offered a significant toast: "Our Federal Union—It must be preserved."

At the same time, Jackson was engaged in a troublesome personal dispute with Calhoun and his followers. This concerned their refusal to treat with respect the wife of Secretary of War John H. Eaton. Scandalous rumors were circulating concerning Mrs. Eaton. Jackson furiously defended her, for he had suffered much from ru-

mors concerning his own wife, and he was sure that they had caused Rachel Jackson's death in 1828. The combination of political and personal complications led in 1831 to the breakup of Jackson's cabinet. As a result, Calhoun's followers were eliminated from the cabinet. Martin Van Buren, who had loyally backed Jackson, replaced Calhoun as "heir" to the presidency.

The Nullification Crisis

The issue of nullification came to a head the next year, when a South Carolina convention adopted an ordinance of nullification. It declared that the high protective tariffs (taxes on imports) of 1828 and 1832 were invalid within the borders of South Carolina. It forbade collection of duties and provided for military defense.

Privately Jackson threatened to hang Calhoun. Publicly he prepared to use military force. In a proclamation he denounced nullification as treason: "I consider the power to annul a law of the United States, assumed by one State, incompatible with the existence of the Union, contradicted expressly by the letter of the Constitution, unauthorized by its spirit, inconsistent with every principle on which it is founded, and destructive of the great object for which it was formed." In the Senate, Henry Clay arranged a compromise—a gradual lowering of the tariff. The crisis ended, and the doctrine of nullification was dead.

DID YOU KNOW?

- *Jackson was the only president who served in both the Revolutionary War and the War of 1812.*
- *He was the only president to have been a prisoner of war.*
- *Wounded in a duel at the age of 39, Jackson carried the bullet, lodged near his heart, to his grave.*
- *He was the first president born in a log cabin.*
- *Jackson was the first president to ride on a railroad train.*
- *Jackson was the only president to have adopted a child.*
- *He paid off the national debt and thus became the only president of a debt-free United States.*

The Bank of the United States

With equal force Jackson moved during these same years against the second Bank of the United States. The Bank was three-fourths privately owned and was privately managed. But it was the depository of government funds. After the close of the War of 1812, it had received a 20-year charter. Because of its size and through its branches in several states, the Bank operated as a large and profitable monopoly. It was able to dominate banking throughout the United States. Strong state banks in the Northeast and weak ones in the West did not like the Bank of the United States. Most westerners did not like it. Jackson, who had lost money in a panic in 1797, did not like any banks. The president of the Bank, Nicholas Biddle, fearing Jackson, allied himself with Senators Henry Clay and Daniel Webster. Clay convinced Biddle that if Jackson vetoed a bill to recharter the bank, the veto would be so unpopular that Clay would be elected president in 1832. As expected, Jackson in 1832 vetoed the recharter bill. He denounced the Bank as un-American, unconstitutional, and dangerous. But Clay had guessed wrong. The veto was so popular that Jackson was decisively reelected in 1832. Martin Van Buren became vice-president.

Second Term

During his second term, Jackson continued his war on the Bank of the United States. (Its charter ran until 1836.) He removed deposits from it and placed them in so-called pet banks. These were boom years. But Jackson's war with Biddle, and his insistence at the close of his administration that public lands be sold only for specie (gold or silver coin), helped bring about a depression at the beginning of the administration of his successor, Van Buren.

This photo portrait was taken by Mathew Brady, the famous Civil War photographer, seven days before Jackson's death in June 1845.

The Alamo was founded as a Spanish mission in 1718 in San Antonio, Texas. In 1836, during Jackson's presidency, it became the site of a famous battle in the Texas struggle for independence from Mexico.

Texas. One of the historical highlights of Jackson's second term was the battle of the Alamo. When the Mexican dictator Gen. Antonio López de Santa Anna invaded Texas early in 1836, some 200 Texans retreated to a crumbling mission-fortress in San Antonio, called the Alamo. While Stephen Austin was in Washington vainly seeking help from Jackson, Gen. Santa Anna laid siege to the mission. On March 6, after holding out for 13 days against heavy fire, the heroic Texans were overrun. In April, however, Sam Houston led his troops to victory over Santa Anna at San Jacinto. Texas had earned its independence. For political reasons relating to the slavery issue, President Jackson resisted attempts to annex Texas. Later, in 1845, Texas was finally admitted as the 28th state.

RETIREMENT

Jackson left the White House in 1837, his popularity undiminished. He lived on for some years at The Hermitage, still standing for nationalist policies and the interests of the average American. He saw his protégé, James K. Polk ("Young Hickory"), elected president in 1844. And in 1845 he saw Texas agree to become part of the United States, as a slave state. When Jackson died on June 8, 1845, one of his admirers declared, "He was the imbodiment of the true spirit of the nation."

MARTIN VAN BUREN

8th PRESIDENT OF THE UNITED STATES (1837–1841)

Born: *December 5, 1782, at Kinderhook, New York*
Occupation: *Lawyer*
Party: *Democrat*
Vice President: *Richard M. Johnson*
Wife: *Hannah Hoes*
Died: *June 24, 1862, at Kinderhook, New York*

On March 4, 1837, Martin Van Buren succeeded his close friend Andrew Jackson as president of the United States. At the time, the country was prosperous, the Democratic Party was supreme, and the incoming president seemed superbly trained for his office. Van Buren had been vice president and secretary of state under Jackson, minister to Great Britain, United States senator, and governor and attorney general of New York. He had been nominated unanimously by his party's convention. In the election of 1836 he had been swept into power, defeating William Henry Harrison by 170 to 73 electoral votes.

But within a matter of weeks President Van Buren had a major depression on his hands. The Panic of 1837 began with the collapse of business and the wholesale failure of banks. Thousands of city people were out of work in a country that had never been through such an experience. The United States had no government machinery to underwrite loans, create jobs, feed the hungry, or bolster the farm market. In the rural sections people continued to lead normal lives. But in the cities mobs stormed the warehouses for food, flocked to the poor-houses, and committed crimes so they could go to jail, where they could at least survive. "Where will it all end?" wrote Philip Hone, a former mayor of New York City, in his diary. "In ruin, revolution, perhaps civil war!"

Fortunately the United States had a beckoning frontier, which absorbed some of the unrest, and Van Buren acted with courage and dignity to restore confidence. He believed that the panic had been caused by too much land speculation (buying and selling land for a quick profit) and that it would run its course. He was right. Within two years prosperity was returning, but too late to save him politically. Van Buren was badly defeated by Harrison in the election of 1840. He suffered what to him was the disgrace of being a one-term president.

Van Buren was the first president to be born under the American flag; the first New Yorker to hold the office of president; and the first man to be nominated for the presidency by the Democratic Party under that name. He was a short, plump, jolly man with side-whiskers. His personal charm earned him many friends, even among his political opponents. He probably had more comic nicknames than any other occupant of the White House—the Red Fox, the Little Magician, the Careful Dutchman, and variations on these themes. He was not a statesman, but he was a thoroughly honest, generous, and incredibly clever politician.

EARLY YEARS

Fittingly, this master politician was literally born at the polls. The event took place at his father's tavern in Kinderhook, New York, on December 5, 1782, just 14 months after the battle of Yorktown had secured American independence from Great Britain. Martin's birthplace was where the villagers came to cast their ballots and where they gathered to talk politics.

Van Buren bought the former Van Ness mansion, built in 1797, on the Hudson River in upstate New York and named it Lindenwald. He died there in 1862.

Martin's father was Abraham Van Buren, whose ancestor had come to the Hudson River valley from Holland in 1631. Abraham married Maria Hoes Van Alen, a widow with three children. Two daughters and three sons were born of the new marriage. As the eldest son, Martin worked in the tavern. There he heard many tales of the intense political rivalry in which he would soon take part.

Martin's parents were poorly educated and not well-to-do. But there was a farm in the family so he suffered no real hardship. He studied at the Kinderhook Academy, leaving at the age of 13 to take a job in a local law firm. There the handsome blond youth advanced from sweeping the floors and cleaning the quill pens to doing copy work and being of general assistance in court.

One day, when Martin was 16, a junior member of the firm turned to him at the end of a petty case and said: "Here, Matt, you sum up."

Matt won his first case and many others while still in his teens. He also made his start as a politician.

A neighbor, John Van Ness, was engaged to marry an heiress. But she would not have him unless he proved himself by winning a seat in Congress. It was the time of the exciting election of 1800, when Thomas Jefferson was running against John Adams for the presidency. Young Van Buren proposed himself as campaign manager for Van Ness. At the district convention he stood on a table and nominated his candidate, who won on the first ballot. For the next several weeks Van Buren toured the district in the general election and brought off a resounding victory for Van Ness. Shortly afterward, as a reward for his services, the 18-year-old Van Buren went off to New York City to a job in the law office of Van Ness' brother.

At the age of 21 Van Buren returned to practice law

and politics at home. At 24 he eloped to Catskill, New York, and married his childhood sweetheart and schoolmate, Hannah Hoes, a distant cousin.

POLITICAL CAREER BEGINS

In 1808 Van Buren managed the campaign of Daniel Tompkins, who was running for governor of New York. When Tompkins won the governorship, he appointed Van Buren surrogate (judge). Four years later, when he was not quite 30, Van Buren won a seat in the New York State Senate. Within a few years he was leader of the powerful political group called the Albany Regency. At one legislative session he wrested control of the council of appointment from Governor DeWitt Clinton. Van Buren now had control of 8,000 state jobs. He made his law partner a district attorney, his half-brother a surrogate, his brother the clerk of the court, and his brother-in-law the state printer. Hundreds of his friends and followers received minor posts. Van Buren had established the spoils system in New York state politics. Soon he would transfer that system to Washington, D.C.

AMBITION

In his autobiography, published after his death, Van Buren good-humoredly recounts his youthful adventures and climb to power. He makes no secret of his life's ambition. He wanted to become president. He called that office "the glittering prize" and "my most earnest desire."

Van Buren's career can be understood only by taking him at his word. Every office he held was a stepping-stone to the White House. In 1821 he went to Washington as a United States Senator. He left his unfinished second Senate term to run for governor of New York in 1828. He remained governor only ten weeks, returning to Washing-

Martin Van Buren

8th president, 1837–41 Democrat

1782 Born on December 5 in Kinderhook, New York.

1800 Named a delegate to the New York congressional caucus.

1803 Began law practice in Kinderhook.

1807 Married Hannah Hoes on February 21. The couple would have four sons.

1813–20 Was a member of the New York state Senate; also served as state attorney general (1816–19).

1821–28 As a U.S. senator, opposed international alliances and the extension of the slave trade.

1828 Elected governor of New York but resigned after two months to become secretary of state under Andrew Jackson.

1829–31 As secretary of state, settled a dispute with Britain over West Indies trade and obtained an agreement whereby France would pay claims for U.S. ships damaged in the Napoleonic wars.

1831 Resigned as secretary of state, bringing about the resignation of the rest of the cabinet and allowing Jackson to reorganize it.

1832 Elected vice president as Jackson's running mate.

1836 Elected president with a wide electoral majority.

1841 Returned to his farm near Kinderhook, which he named Lindenwald.

1848 Nominated for president by the antislavery Free Soil Party, which had split from the Democrats. The party split opened the way for the election of the Whig candidate, Zachary Taylor.

1862 Died on July 24 at Kinderhook.

Highlights of Presidency

1837 On May 10, banks closed in Philadelphia and New York City, marking the start of the Panic of 1837. The panic, touched off by inflation and land speculation, was followed by an economic depression that lasted the rest of Van Buren's term.

1839 A boundary dispute between Maine and New Brunswick brought the United States to the brink of war with Britain.

1840 At Van Buren's urging, Congress established an independent treasury to hold federal funds. An attempt to safeguard funds from private bank failures, the treasury was abolished in 1841 but reinstated in 1846. Defeated by William Henry Harrison in the November presidential election.

ton to be near President Jackson as his secretary of state and political manager.

Van Buren resigned as head of the State Department in 1831 to allow Jackson to get rid of his cabinet members who were followers of Vice President John C. Calhoun, Jackson's political enemy. Jackson then appointed Van Buren minister to Great Britain, but he served less than five months. The Senate rejected his confirmation by the deciding vote of John C. Calhoun. When Jackson won reelection in 1832, however, Van Buren became the new vice president. He was then, as Jackson's favorite, almost certain to win the presidency in 1836.

CHARACTER AND PERSONALITY

But any bare account of the Red Fox's wily progress fails to do him justice. Van Buren made a fortune in law and a name in politics because people trusted and admired him. His sparkling wit, his affection for people, and his occasional flashes of genius for serious statesmanship were his extraordinary traits.

Jackson once remarked of Van Buren: "It is said that he is a great magician—I believe it, but his only wand is good common sense which he uses for the benefit of his country."

The author Washington Irving, meeting Van Buren for the first time after hearing harsh criticism of him, found him "one of the gentlest and most amiable men I ever met with." Most of the criticism, in fact, stemmed from amusement at Van Buren's cleverness. Congressman John Randolph picturesquely described Van Buren as one who always "rowed to his objects with muffled oars." When Van Buren arrived to take his Senate seat in 1821, Rufus King a fellow senator from New York, wrote that within two weeks "he will know every man's opinion, but none will know his."

Yet nearly everybody acquainted with Van Buren conceded that he had talent and was capable of political courage: During the War of 1812 he wrote and submitted in the New York legislature a bill to draft able-bodied men into the Army. The measure was widely denounced as an invasion of personal liberty. But Van Buren toured his district in support of the measure and pushed the bill through to passage. A historian of the day called it "the most energetic war measure ever adopted in this country."

Van Buren's admirers often wished he would put his mind to serious affairs and give up the game of intrigue and self-promotion. Benjamin F. Butler, Jackson's attorney general, once wrote to an acquaintance: If I were Van Buren I would let politics alone. . . . This morning I heard him open a case before the [New York] Supreme Court in the most able, eloquent and exact fashion I almost ever heard."

PRESIDENT

Once Van Buren reached the White House, he did leave "politics" alone. The Panic of 1837 was no fault of his, coming when he had barely reached office. President Jackson's financial policies had sowed the whirlwind that his successor had to reap. As the first president from the West, Jackson had reason to feel that the Eastern money interests held the frontier areas in a financial vise. Old Hickory withdrew federal deposits from the Bank of America in Philadelphia and distributed them in banks around the country. The result was a splurge of investment, followed by a sudden loss of confidence in the banks.

Van Buren's handling of the crisis was superb. It was altogether devoid of crafty politics or retreat from principle. He calmly allowed the excitement of the spring and summer to subside, and he set a special session of Congress for September. He then delivered a message in the spirit of Thomas Jefferson. Van Buren said in part: "All communities are apt to look to Government for too much . . . especially at periods of sudden embarrassment or distress. But this ought not to be. The framers of our excellent Constitution . . . wisely judged that the less Government interferes with private pursuits the better for general prosperity. . . . Its real duty . . . is . . . to leave every citizen and every interest to reap, under its benign protection, the reward of virtue, industry and prudence."

Van Buren was not heartless, although his enemies painted him as such. His administration enacted legislation that established the independent treasury system and made sound-money loans available through local banks. Foreign relations were troubled during his term by a boundary dispute with Canada and by difficulty with Mexico over the secession of Texas. Van Buren skillfully negotiated the dispute with Canada. He refused to accept Texas into the Union because that would mean an additional slave state as well as war with Mexico. He was a good president who dared to be unpopular.

The expression "OK" often is attributed to the presidential campaign of 1840. "Old Kinderhook," or "OK" was one of Van Buren's nicknames.

Van Buren's defeat in 1840 can be seen as delayed punishment for his 25 years of playing politics. The Whig Party was organized and led much as the Albany Regency had been. The Whig candidate, General William Henry Harrison, was presented to the country as an "old hero." He avoided every serious issue. Along with his running mate, John Tyler, Harrison won by an electoral vote of 234 to 60 with the campaign slogan "Tippecanoe and Tyler too."

FREE-SOIL CANDIDATE

Still, Van Buren remained a powerful figure in New York State politics. In 1848 he was nominated as the presidential candidate of the Free-Soil Party, composed mainly of Northerners—both Whigs and Democrats—opposed to the expansion of slavery into the western territories. Van Buren's candidacy, however, split the Democrats and helped General Zachary Taylor, the Whig candidate, defeat Lewis Cass.

LATER YEARS

Van Buren's last years were his happiest. His marriage had ended tragically with Hannah's death in 1819. But she left him four fine sons, who brought him pride and pleasure. John Van Buren became attorney general of New York. Abraham Van Buren married a niece of Dolley Madison, and Smith Thompson Van Buren married a niece of Washington Irving. Martin Junior accompanied his father on a two-year trip through Europe. There the former president, the first to take such a journey, was admired by the crowned heads and the society figures of many countries. These family successes and personal honors helped him to bear the disappointment of being turned out of the White House.

Van Buren had purchased the old Van Ness mansion on the Hudson near Kinderhook and renamed it Lindenwald (Linden Woods) after the trees. There he spent his declining years, pampered by his daughters-in-law, honored by his neighbors and by famous visitors. He died on July 24, 1862, at the age of 79.

DID YOU KNOW?

- *Van Buren was the first president born in the United States.*
- *The only president of Dutch ancestry, Van Buren and his wife spoke Dutch at home.*
- *He took his four-years' salary as president, $100,000, in a lump sum at the end of his term.*
- *After serving his one term as president, he made three unsuccessful bids for reelection.*

9th PRESIDENT OF THE UNITED STATES (1841)

Born: February 9, 1773, at Berkeley plantation in Charles City County, Virginia
Occupation: Soldier
Party: Whig
Vice President: John Tyler
Wife: Anna Tuthill Symmes
Died: April 4, 1841, in Washington, D.C.

William Henry Harrison had the shortest term in office of any U.S. president. He died one month after his inauguration in 1841 and was the first president to die while in office.

Before becoming president, Harrison had served as a soldier, territorial governor, congressman, senator, and diplomat. But it was his military career that won him the greatest fame and popularity with American voters. During the election campaign of 1840, Harrison's supporters pictured him as the "log cabin" candidate. Actually, he had been born into one of the most distinguished families in Virginia and raised on a large plantation.

EARLY YEARS AND CAREER

Harrison was born on February 9, 1773, at his father's plantation, Berkeley, in Charles City County, Virginia. His father, Benjamin Harrison, was one of the signers of the Declaration of Independence and governor of Virginia. William Henry was the youngest of the seven Harrison children. He received his early education at home and attended Virginia's Hampden-Sidney College without gaining a degree. His father wanted him to become a doctor, so William was sent to study medicine in Richmond and Philadelphia. When his father died in 1791, Harrison gave up medicine to join the Army.

Soldier. In 1791, the 18-year-old Harrison, newly commissioned as an ensign in the First Regiment of Infantry, arrived in Fort Washington (now Cincinnati, Ohio) in the Northwest Territory. Indian wars were then raging in this frontier region, and young Harrison learned his trade as a soldier fighting Indians.

In 1792, General Anthony Wayne arrived to take command. Wayne, impressed by Harrison's abilities, promoted him to second lieutenant and made him his aide-de-camp, or assistant. In 1794 the Indians were defeated at the Battle of Fallen Timbers, in which Harrison was cited for bravery. The Treaty of Greenville, signed in 1795, divided the territory between the Indians and settlers and ended the Indian wars for a time.

Marriage and Family. Harrison was promoted to captain and placed in command of Fort Washington. There in 1795 he married Anna Symmes, the daughter of Judge John C. Symmes, a wealthy landowner and an important figure in the Northwest Territory.

The Harrisons had ten children in all, of whom four lived to see Harrison become president. One son, John Scott Harrison, was the father of Benjamin Harrison, who became the 23rd president of the United States.

Territorial Governor. Dissatisfied with the low pay and lack of advancement, Harrison resigned from the Army in 1798 and was appointed secretary of the Northwest Territory by President John Adams. The following year, Harrison was elected as the territory's first delegate to Congress.

In Congress, Harrison played a leading role in the creation of the territories of Ohio and Indiana from the old Northwest Territory. In 1800 he was appointed governor

Anna Symmes Harrison was too ill to attend her husband's inauguration on March 4, 1841. He died a month later.

of the Indiana Territory (which included all or parts of the present-day states of Indiana, Illinois, Wisconsin, Michigan, and Minnesota).

Harrison served as governor of Indiana for 12 years and was responsible for many improvements in the territory. He also tried to be fair in his dealings with the Indian tribes. But he was handicapped by the white settlers and the federal government.

Indian Disputes. Over the years the Indians were slowly deprived of their lands in the Northwest by a series of treaties. The Treaty of Fort Wayne in 1809 caused strong opposition among the tribes. Led by the Shawnee chief Tecumseh and his brother Elskwatawa, they formed a confederation to stop the settlers' advance.

In 1810, Tecumseh met with Harrison and warned him that the Indian tribes would oppose the occupation of their land under the terms of the Treaty of Fort Wayne. Harrison insisted that the treaty would be carried out. In 1811 he led a force of about 800 regular soldiers, militia, and volunteers against the Shawnees near Tippecanoe Creek. The Indians, under Elskwatawa, were defeated and their settlement was burned. The battle did little to curb the tribes, but it won fame and the nickname "Old Tippecanoe" for Harrison.

War of 1812. Meanwhile, the growing difficulties between the United States and Britain were erupting into the War of 1812. Harrison returned to military service as a brigadier general and was given command of the Army of the Northwest. Promoted to major general, he was ordered to retake Detroit, which had been captured by the British, and to invade Canada. Detroit was recaptured on September 29, 1813. On October 5, 1813, Harrison defeated the British at the Battle of the Thames in southern Ontario. In the battle Tecumseh was killed while fighting on the side of the British. Harrison's victory made him famous. But he

William Henry Harrison

9th president, 1841 Whig

1773 Born on February 8 at Charles City County, Virginia.

1790 Left college to study medicine.

1791 Abandoned his studies to enlist in the army, serving in the Northwest Territory.

1795 Married Anna Symmes in November. The couple subsequently had ten children, only four of whom survived their father.

1798 After resigning from the army, appointed secretary of the Northwest Territory in June. Was elected the first delegate to Congress from the Northwest Territory in 1799.

1800 Following the division of the Northwest Territories into Ohio and Indiana, appointed governor of Indiana.

1809 As governor, negotiated the Treaty of Fort Wayne, which secured approximately 3 million acres of land from four Indian tribes.

1811 In the Battle of Tippecanoe on November 7, defeated a federation of Indian tribes under the Shawnee chief Tecumseh, that was protesting the Treaty of Fort Wayne.

1812 Placed in command of the Army of the Northwest during the War of 1812.

1813 In October, won a major victory over combined British and Indian forces in the Battle of the Thames, in southern Ontario.

1814 Resigned from the army.

1816 Elected to the U.S. House of Representatives.

1819 Elected to the Ohio state Senate.

1825 Elected to the U.S. Senate.

1828 Resigned his Senate seat to become minister to Colombia. However, his outspoken views on democracy offended President Simón Bolívar, and he was recalled a month after his arrival there.

1836 Defeated for the presidency by Martin Van Buren.

1840 With John Tyler as his running mate, campaigned successfully for the presidency on the slogan " Tippecanoe and Tyler too."

Highlights of Presidency

1841 Inaugurated on March 4 as 9th president, delivering the longest inaugural address on record, in which he promised not to run for a second term. Having contracted pneumonia in late March, died at the White House on April 4.

William Henry Harrison became a military hero and earned the nickname of "Old Tippecanoe" for his victory over the Shawnee Indians at the Battle of Tippecanoe (in what is now Indiana) in 1841.

took part in little military activity during the rest of the war. In 1814 he again resigned from the Army.

Return to Politics

Harrison returned to his home and family at North Bend, Ohio, and in 1816 he was elected to the U.S. House of Representatives, serving until 1819. After failing to gain appointment as minister to Russia, he won election to the Ohio State Senate. In 1825 he was elected to the U.S. Senate, where he served as chairman of the committee on military affairs.

DID YOU KNOW?

- *Harrison was the only president born in the same county as his vice president.*

- *He was the only president to have studied medicine.*

- *Harrison gave the longest inaugural address—one hour and 45 minutes.*

- *His immediate job before becoming president was clerk of Hamilton County (Ohio) court.*

- *Since he was the first president to die in office, his widow was the first First Lady to receive a pension—$25,000.*

Harrison resigned from the Senate in 1828, when President John Quincy Adams appointed him minister to Colombia. Harrison's venture into diplomacy was not a success. He took the attitude that the U.S. should act as a big brother to the newly independent republics of South America. He offended Colombian President Simón Bolívar when he bluntly suggested that Bolivar take care not to become a dictator. Harrison was recalled as minister in 1829 by the new president, Andrew Jackson.

ROAD TO THE PRESIDENCY

Elections of 1836 and 1840. Harrison was nominated for the presidency in 1836 by the Whig Party, which had been formed in opposition to the policies of President Andrew Jackson and the Democrats. Although Harrison was defeated in the election by Martin Van Buren, Jackson's vice president, he made such a good showing that the Whigs again nominated him to oppose Van Buren in the 1840 election.

During the 1840 campaign, the Whigs made the most of Harrison as a military hero and a man of the people. The Democrats responded with ridicule, saying that all Harrison wanted was a barrel of hard cider, a pension, and a log cabin.

The Whigs turned this to their advantage, referring to Harrison as the "log cabin and hard cider" candidate and using a log cabin and a barrel of cider as their campaign symbols. John Tyler of Virginia was Harrison's running mate and the Whig slogan was "Tippecanoe and Tyler, too!" Harrison's popularity as well as an economic depression, which had begun in 1837, contributed to Van Buren's defeat. Harrison won an overwhelming victory, receiving 234 electoral votes to Van Buren's 60.

A Short Tenure. But the excitement of the inauguration and the demands of political job seekers proved too much for the 68-year-old Harrison. Soon after taking office on March 4, 1841, he caught a cold that developed into pneumonia. He died on April 4, 1841.

JOHN TYLER

10th PRESIDENT OF THE UNITED STATES (1841–1845)

Born: *March 29, 1790, in Charles City County, Virginia*
Occupation: *Lawyer*
Party: *Democrat, Whig*
Vice President: *None*
Wives: *Letitia Christian; Julia Gardiner*
Died: *January 18, 1862, at Richmond, Virginia*

through Congress. As a result, Tyler was expelled from the Whig Party. He was the only U.S. president to have been ousted by the party that had nominated and elected him.

After that, Tyler worked more closely with the Southern Democrats. With their aid, he was able to accomplish much in the field of foreign policy. In 1842 he and Secretary of State Daniel Webster negotiated the Webster-Ashburton Treaty with Britain, which settled the boundary between Maine and Canada. More important, in 1845, Tyler brought about the annexation of Texas to the United States. He considered this his most important contribution. It made up for all the defeats and disappointments he suffered in the presidency.

EARLY YEARS

John Tyler was born at Greenway plantation in Charles City County, Virginia, on March 29, 1790. Tyler's mother died when he was seven, and the boy was raised by his father, Judge John Tyler, who later served as governor of Virginia. As a youth, Tyler was frail and never in very good health. He was, however, an excellent student. He graduated from the College of William and Mary in nearby Williamsburg in 1807. He then studied law and in 1811 began to practice in Richmond. That same year, at the age of 21, he was elected to the Virginia state legislature.

Letitia Christian Tyler

In 1813, Tyler married Letitia Christian, the daughter of a Virginia planter. They had eight children—five daughters and three sons—all of whom lived except one daughter. The same age as her husband, she was an invalid when Tyler became president. She made only one public appearance as First Lady, at her daughter Elizabeth's wedding in 1842. She died soon thereafter.

When President William Henry Harrison died in office on April 4, 1841, John Tyler became the first vice president in American history to be elevated to the presidency. He came to power at a time when the new Whig Party was badly divided. The Northern Whigs, led by Senator Henry Clay of Kentucky, favored government aid to industry, a national bank, and government funds to build roads and canals. The Southern Whigs, headed by John Tyler, believed that government was best when it governed least. Many of them, like Tyler himself, were ex-Southern Democrats who had joined the Whigs in the 1830s because of their dislike of Democratic President Andrew Jackson. The Southern Whigs favored states' rights. They had more in common with the Southern Democrats, led by South Carolina Senator John C. Calhoun, than with the Northern Whigs.

No sooner had Tyler taken office than he became involved in a personal and political feud with Senator Henry Clay. This dispute split the Whigs further and made Tyler's years in the White House bitter and difficult ones. Indeed, he spent much of his time vetoing, or disapproving, bills that the Clay Whigs had pushed

POLITICAL CAREER

Except for the years 1834 to 1844, when he called himself a Whig, John Tyler was a lifelong Democrat. He was elected to almost every office open to a professional politician. From 1811 to 1816 and again from 1823 to 1825 he sat in the Virginia House of Delegates. From 1816 to 1821 he served in the United States House of Representatives. He was elected governor of Virginia in 1825, but he resigned in 1827 to enter the United States Senate. There he remained until 1836. In that year he resigned his Senate seat and left the Democratic Party rather than support policies of President Andrew Jackson that he believed unconstitutional. In 1836 he ran for vice president. Defeated, he returned to the Virginia House of Delegates in 1838. He was serving as speaker of that body when the Whigs nominated him to run as vice president with William Henry Harrison of Ohio in the exciting "Tippecanoe and Tyler too" campaign of 1840. "Tippecanoe" was a nickname for Harrison, who had won the Battle of Tippecanoe against the Shawnee Indians in 1811.

Tyler's nomination was designed to balance the ticket even though he was from the same state as Harrison. The Whigs thought it a shrewd idea to put a man who was a former Southern Democrat on their ballot to draw votes in the South. They did this knowing that Tyler's political principles were not supported by Harrison, Clay, or the Northern Whigs. Thus, when Harrison suddenly died in office, the surprised Whigs were faced with a man in the White House who opposed much of their program. Clay quickly set out to drive Tyler from the party and from the presidency. He wanted the presidency for himself in 1844. He was successful in disrupting Tyler's tenure, but Clay never became president.

POLITICAL PRINCIPLES

Throughout his long political career John Tyler held rigidly to certain beliefs. He could be a very stubborn man when he believed he was right. He thought that only educated men who owned property should have the vote. He was very upset when General Andrew Jackson appeared on the political scene in the years between 1824 and 1828 as the popular leader of the common people. Tyler never trusted Jackson. He worried that a military man in the White House might bypass the Constitution and establish a military dictatorship.

Tyler felt that each state should run its own affairs and that the federal government should stay within the powers assigned to it in the Constitution. Like most Southern politicians of that day, he also believed in low tariffs, or taxes on imports.

Regarding slavery, John Tyler accepted the institution as he found it. He did not think that slavery was good; he simply felt that to abolish it overnight would create more problems for the Southern whites than it would solve for the African American slaves. He favored gradual abolition of slavery.

John Tyler

10th president, 1841–45 Whig

1790	Born on March 29 in Charles City County, Virginia.
1807	Graduated from William and Mary College.
1809	Admitted to the bar.
1811	Elected to the Virginia House of Delegates.
1813	Married Letitia Christian on March 29. The couple would have eight children.
1816–21	Served in the U.S. House of Representatives.
1823	Elected again to the Virginia House of Delegates.
1825	Elected governor of Virginia.
1827	Elected to the U.S. Senate. His stand in favor of states rights eventually led him to break with the Democrats and ally himself with the Whigs.
1836	Resigned his Senate seat rather than follow the instructions of the Virginia legislature to expunge a vote of censure against Andrew Jackson. As a Whig, lost bid for the vice presidency to Richard M. Johnson.
1840	Elected vice president.
1841	Succeeded to the presidency following the death of William Henry Harrison.
1844	Two years after the death of his first wife, married Julia Gardiner on June 22. The couple subsequently had seven children.
1845	Retired to Sherwood Forest, his estate near Charles City, after one term as president.
1861	In February, chaired a peace convention attempting to avert the Civil War. At a Virginia convention, voted in favor of secession.
1862	Died on January 18 in Richmond, Virginia, before taking his seat in the Confederate House.

Highlights of Presidency

1841	Vetoed banking bills supported by the Whigs, prompting the resignation of his cabinet. Tyler quickly named a new cabinet, but the Whig Party disowned him.
1842	Seminole War in Florida ended; boundary settled between Maine and New Brunswick.
1843	In January, the Whigs introduced impeachment resolutions in the House, but the measures were defeated.
1844	A treaty with China opened the Far East to U.S. traders.
1845	Signed bills permitting Texas and Florida to be admitted to the Union.

Letitia Christian Tyler (above), John Tyler's first wife, died in the White House in 1842. In 1844, Tyler married the 24-year-old Julia Gardiner (right), becoming the first president to marry while in office.

He strongly opposed the powerful Bank of the United States. This national bank was a partnership between private business and the federal government. Tyler argued that it was an unequal partnership. He also felt that the very existence of the bank was unconstitutional. He pointed out that while the government deposited its money in this bank, it was actually run by the small group of wealthy businessmen who controlled most of the stock. Tyler charged that these men ran the bank more in their own selfish interest than in the public interest. He demanded that the government withdraw its money from the Bank of the United States and put it in various state banks. This would (and eventually did) ruin the Bank of the United States. He was happy, therefore, to see President Jackson remove the government's funds in 1833, although he did not like the way Jackson went about it.

PRESIDENT

Tyler had scarcely settled into the White House when Henry Clay decided to drive him out of it. The Kentucky senator produced two bills to reestablish the Bank of the United States. He knew Tyler would veto these bills, and he was right. During the political warfare that followed the bank bill vetoes, Clay persuaded all of Tyler's cabinet, except Webster, to resign in a body. He hoped this would cause the president to quit his office in panic and disgust. But Tyler calmly appointed a new cabinet and stood firm. Then Clay had Tyler thrown out of the Whig Party. By October 1841, the Tyler administration was a shambles. In January 1843, the Whigs tried to impeach

Tyler by introducing impeachment resolutions in Congress. Nothing came of them. Tyler had no vice president to succeed him, since at that time no provision was made for vice presidents who succeeded to the presidency to name a successor.

Annexation of Texas

Tyler wanted Americans to remember him for some great accomplishment. Because of his break with Clay, he knew that the divided Whig Party could get little done in domestic matters. For this reason he turned to the annexation of Texas, which was then an independent republic and previously had been part of Mexico. Many Southern Whigs and Democrats around the President wanted annexation because it would bring another slave state into the Union. Tyler did not want it for this reason. Instead, he saw annexation as an opportunity to expand American trade into the Southwest and as a chance to bring most of the world's cotton production under the American flag. But above all, he wanted the annexation of Texas to rescue the historical prestige of his sagging administration.

Between 1843 and 1844, Tyler and his new secretary of state, Abel P. Upshur, secretly worked out an annexation treaty with the Republic of Texas. Unfortunately Upshur was killed in an accident in February 1844. John C. Calhoun then became secretary of state. Calhoun unwisely linked Texas annexation to the expansion of slavery. This was a political blunder in an election year. The treaty quickly became involved in sectional politics, and the Senate turned it down. Many senators wanted to wait and see how the people felt on the annexation issue in the coming elections of 1844.

Meanwhile, Tyler had formed a small third party with the slogan "Tyler and Texas." He knew he himself Had no chance of reelection in 1844. He created his party only to force the wavering Democrats to support annexation. He agreed to withdraw from the race if James K. Polk and the Democrats would pledge annexation in their platform and stick to their promise. When Polk agreed to this bargain, Tyler quit the campaign. He threw his support to Polk, who defeated Clay by a narrow margin. The president-elect then urged the Democrats in Congress to support Tyler's Texas treaty. Congress finally approved the treaty in February 1845, and an overjoyed Tyler signed it just before he left office. Throughout the whole annexation debate Tyler showed great political skill and patience. Florida joined the Union as well, becoming the 27th state in 1845.

Julia Gardner Tyler

Letitia Christian Tyler, the President's first wife, died in the White House in September 1842. A few months later, Tyler began courting 23-year-old Julia Gardiner, a beautiful and wealthy New Yorker. When they were married in New York City on June 26, 1844, Tyler became the first president to be wed while in office. He was 30 years older than his bride. As First Lady, the new Mrs. Tyler captivated Washington with the size and brilliance of her White House receptions.

- *Because he was the first vice president to assume office after the death of a president, Tyler was called "His Accidency."*
- *After the Whig party disavowed him, Tyler served without being a member of any political party.*
- *Tyler was the only president to hold office in the Confederacy.*
- *His second wife initiated the practice of playing "Hail to the Chief" whenever a president appears in public.*
- *He was a granduncle of President Harry S. Truman.*

RETIREMENT

From 1845 to 1861, Tyler and his second wife spent peaceful years at Sherwood Forest, his plantation on the James River below Richmond, Virginia. Seven children were born to them there, bringing his total number of children to 15, the most of any president. Lively dinners and dances and fox hunts were held. About 70 slaves worked the corn and wheat fields of the sprawling estate. Tyler was an excellent farmer. He experimented with new fertilizers, and the harvests were good. But Julia always managed to spend more money then the plantation brought in. The Tylers were in constant financial trouble as a result of their large expenditures for entertainment, clothes, and travel.

Sherwood Forest seemed a model Southern plantation. No whips or lashes were ever used on the slaves there. The slaves appeared happy and contented, and there were no runaways. But all this was deceiving. When the Union Army overran the proud estate in 1864, the slaves quickly and gladly departed. Before they left, they sacked and plundered the main house. It was later restored.

SECESSION AND CIVIL WAR

As the Civil War approached, John Tyler was on the side of moderation. He thought that the problems of slavery and the expansion of slavery into the Western territories could be solved by compromise rather than by a bloody civil war. When South Carolina seceded from the Union in December 1860, and the Confederate States of America was formed on February 8, 1861, Tyler was deeply saddened.

Although he was now 70, tired, and sick, he agreed to leave retirement to serve as president of the Peace Conference, which met in Washington, D.C., on February 4, 1861. He soon saw, however, that this last attempt to preserve the Union was doomed to failure. At this point he returned to Richmond and became an outspoken secessionist. His vain hope was that if Virginia joined the Confederacy, the border states would follow its lead. This would make the enlarged Confederacy so strong that the federal government would not dare risk a war. Thus peace would be preserved, and the state of Virginia would not become a battleground. Tyler wanted Virginia's secession to preserve the peace; not peace to preserve the Confederacy. He was willing to sacrifice the Union to prevent bloodshed.

Following Virginia's secession on April 17, 1861, Tyler was elected to the House of Representatives of the Confederate Provisional Congress. This was the last of the many political offices he held during his more than 50 years in public service. Tyler was serving in this post when he suffered a stroke and died in a Richmond, Virginia hotel on January 18, 1862. He was 71 years old. He died in debt and in doubt, branded a traitor by the very government he had once headed. He is buried in Hollywood cemetery in Richmond.

JAMES K. POLK

11th PRESIDENT OF THE UNITED STATES (1845–1849)

Born: *November 2, 1795, in Mecklenburg County, North Carolina*
Occupation: *Lawyer*
Party: *Democrat*
Vice President: *George M. Dallas*
Wife: *Sarah Childress*
Died: *June 15, 1849, at Nashville, Tennessee*

James Knox Polk became the first "dark horse," or little-known candidate, to win the presidency when he unexpectedly defeated Henry Clay in the election of 1844. At 49 years of age, he was also the youngest president the United States had yet had. During his term of office Polk added to the United States a vast region stretching from the Rocky Mountains to the Pacific Ocean which includes present-day California. Antislavery men of his own day condemned him, for they believed that he desired only to extend the area of slavery. But modern scholars deny this and generally rank Polk as one of the 10 greatest American presidents.

EARLY YEARS

James K. Polk was born in Mecklenburg County, North Carolina, on November 2, 1795. The future president was the eldest of ten children born to Samuel and Jane Knox Polk. In 1806 the Polk family moved from North Carolina to Duck River, Tennessee. There Samuel Polk became a successful frontier farmer. James never developed the physical strength needed for farming. His parents therefore trained his mind. They provided tutors for him and

sent him to several preparatory schools. In 1815 he entered the University of North Carolina. He applied himself diligently to his studies, graduating in 1818 with honors in mathematics and the classics.

Polk then studied law and in 1820 was admitted to the bar. He began his practice in Columbia, Tennessee, and soon became a well-known lawyer. In 1823 he was elected to the state legislature. As a young politician he became friendly with Tennessee's new United States Senator, Andrew Jackson.

On January 1, 1824, Polk married Sarah Childress, the daughter of a prosperous family from Murfreesboro, Tennessee. She was a tall, handsome woman with a queenly bearing and remarkable cultural refinement.

CONGRESSMAN

In 1825 Polk was elected to the United States House of Representatives. There he championed Andrew Jackson, who had just lost the contest for the presidency to John Quincy Adams. Polk proved a courageous and able debater and blunted the effect of the worst attacks against the Jacksonian Democrats. When Jackson was elected president in 1828, Polk became one of his most trusted lieutenants, serving without expecting political reward. In 1833 Polk became chairman of the Committee on Ways and Means. Two years later he was elected Speaker of the House of Representatives. He was reelected Speaker in 1837.

During these years Polk had to preside over some of the stormiest sessions ever known in the House of Representatives. He was heckled unmercifully from the floor of the House and hounded by enemies, some of whom tried to goad him into a duel. Nevertheless, Polk served efficiently if unhappily.

GOVERNOR

In 1839 the Tennessee Democrats, hoping to capture control of the state from the Whig Party, nominated Polk for the governorship. Although he would have preferred to remain in Congress, Polk consented to run for the good of the party. He was elected and served a two-year term, from 1839 to 1841. His success proved more a personal than a party victory, for in the presidential election of 1840 Tennessee cast its vote for the Whig candidate, William Henry Harrison. Polk ran for reelection as governor in both 1841 and 1843 but suffered defeat each time.

THE ROAD TO THE WHITE HOUSE

President Harrison's death in 1841 put Vice President John Tyler in the White House. Tyler, however, was soon ousted from the Whig Party for vetoing their favorite measures. This immediately raised the question of who would become president in 1844. Senator Henry Clay of Kentucky proposed to take charge of the Whig Party and become its candidate. Former president Martin Van Buren was expected to be the Democratic candidate.

Meanwhile, President Tyler concentrated his efforts upon achieving the annexation of Texas. On April 22, 1844, he submitted a Texas annexation treaty to the Senate. The proposed treaty immediately started a national controversy. The entry of Texas into the Union was popular in the South and Southwest. But many people, in the North and elsewhere, objected because it would add a new slave state to the United States. In addition, they felt that annexation would almost certainly lead to war with Mexico.

On April 27 both Clay and Van Buren published letters opposing statehood for Texas. The Whigs nominated Clay for the presidency shortly thereafter, but all politicians agree that his letter had weakened his hold on the voters of the Southwest. Van Buren's letter, appearing just a month before the Democratic nominating convention, ruined his chances. The aged but still influential Andrew Jackson informed his friends that the Democratic party and its candidate would have to support annexation. Furthermore, Jackson believed, the Democratic candidate ought to come from the Southwest, to capture Whigs who would refuse to vote for Clay. Jackson suggested James K. Polk—who had been mentioned as a possible vice presidential candidate—as a man who could lead the Democrats to victory.

"Who Is James K. Polk?"

The Democratic National Convention met in Baltimore, Maryland, in May 1844. The delegates took Andrew Jackson's advice and nominated Polk on the ninth ballot. George M. Dallas of Pennsylvania became the vice presidential candidate. Polk's success against men much better known prompted the Whigs to ask mockingly: "Who is James K. Polk?"

DID YOU KNOW?

- *Born a Presbyterian, Polk was baptized a Methodist a week before he died.*
- *He was a great-grandnephew of John Knox, the founder of Scottish Presbyterianism.*
- *Before the advent of anesthetics and antiseptic practices, Polk survived a gallstone operation at age 17.*
- *Sarah Polk hosted the first annual White House Thanksgiving dinner.*
- *The telegraph was used to relay political news for the first time to announce Polk's nomination.*

The Democrats adopted a platform calling for the annexation of Texas and the "reoccupation" of the whole of Oregon. The vast Oregon Territory included present-day Washington, Oregon, and Idaho; parts of Montana and Wyoming; and a large area of western Canada. Since 1818 it had been occupied by both Great Britain and the United States. The Democratic platform emphasized Polk's own devotion to Manifest Destiny—the concept that the United States must continue to expand across the North American continent.

President Tyler, who had accepted renomination, withdrew from the campaign and threw his support to Polk. In return, Polk promised to support the immediate annexation of Texas. On December 3, 1844, Tyler recommended annexation by a joint resolution of Congress. The next day, December 4, Polk won the presidency over Clay by an electoral vote of 170 to 105. Polk received 1,337,243 popular votes to Clay's 1,299,062. James G. Birney of the Liberty Party, an antislavery party, received 62,300 votes. The vote for Birney's party in New York cost Clay the electors of that state and gave the victory to Polk. Tennessee, Polk's home state, gave its electoral votes to Clay by a margin of only 113 popular votes. The election was one of the closest in American history.

On March 1, 1845, just before Polk's inauguration, President Tyler signed the joint resolution authorizing the annexation of Texas. Polk had thus redeemed half of his party's platform pledge three days before entering the White House.

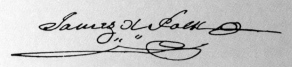

James Knox Polk

11th president, 1845–49   Democrat

1795 Born on November 2 in Mecklenburg County, North Carolina, the eldest of ten children.

1806 Moved with his family to the Duck River valley in central Tennessee.

1818 Graduated from the University of North Carolina.

1820 Admitted to the bar and began practicing law in Columbia, Tennessee.

1821 Became chief clerk of the Tennessee Senate.

1823 Elected to the Tennessee House of Representatives.

1824 Married Sarah Childress on January l. There were no children from the marriage.

1825 Elected to the first of seven consecutive terms in the U.S. House of Representatives, where he quickly became known as a strong supporter of Andrew Jackson.

1832 As chairman of the House Ways and Means Committee, supported President Jackson's efforts to abolish the national bank.

1835 Became Speaker of the House.

1839 Resigned his House seat to run for governor of Tennessee, winning by a slim margin.

1840 Sought the Democratic vice-presidential nomination but was turned down at the party's national convention.

1841 Defeated for a second term as governor.

1843 Again defeated in a bid for the governorship.

1844 At the Democratic presidential convention, the party split between opponents and supporters of Martin Van Buren. Polk took the nomination on the ninth ballot, the first "dark horse" candidate. He won the election by a slim margin, campaigning on a platform of territorial expansion.

1849 Died in Nashville, Tennessee, on June 15, a few months after leaving the presidency.

Highlights of Presidency

1846 Two key pieces of Polk's domestic program, bills setting new tariffs and reestablishing a federal treasury, were adopted. A treaty with Britain settled a dispute over Oregon, giving both nations part of the territory.

1848 A treaty with Mexico ended two-year war and gave the United States control of most of present-day Arizona, California, Colorado, Nevada, New Mexico, Utah, and Wyoming. Gold was discovered in California in December.

PRESIDENT

Polk was keenly aware that many leading Democrats doubted his qualifications for the presidency and expected to control his administration. He therefore felt a special compulsion to act firmly and with independence. His determination to exercise all his powers as president made him excessively suspicious of advice. Although he early decided to serve only one term, Polk asked all his cabinet members to pledge not to seek the presidential nomination in 1848. He hoped by this means to prevent conflicts of private ambition from interfering with public business. But his efforts weakened party leadership.

At the beginning of his administration, Polk told his Secretary of the Navy, George Bancroft, "There are four great measures which are to be the measures of my administration: one, a reduction of the tariff; another, the independent treasury; a third, the settlement of the Oregon boundary question; and lastly, the acquisition of California." Polk quickly accomplished the first two measures. In 1846 he signed into law the Walker-McKay Tariff, which greatly reduced import taxes. That same year he signed the act restoring the independent treasury system. Under this system the federal government kept its own funds instead of depositing them in state and private banks. The Independent Treasury Act remained in effect until 1913, when the Federal Reserve System was established.

Oregon

Foreign policy, however, dominated Polk's administration. A major problem was the Oregon boundary, which had long involved the United States and Great Britain in controversy. During the presidential campaign of 1844 the Democrats had demanded American occupation of all of Oregon up to 54° 40' north latitude. This included a large part of what is now British Columbia. A favorite Democratic slogan was "Fifty-four forty or fight." Polk offered to compromise by setting the disputed boundary at the 49th parallel (its present boundary). But when the British minister curtly refused, the president withdrew the offer and declared his intention to press American claims to the entire region up to 54° 40'. Influenced by Andrew Jackson's dislike of Great Britain, Polk wrote: "The only way to treat John Bull is to look him straight in the eye." War over Oregon was avoided, however, and on June 15, 1846, the United States and Great Britain signed a treaty setting the boundary at the 49th parallel.

The Mexican War

Polk had determined to acquire California, which was then a part of Mexico. On March 6, 1845, Mexico broke relations with the United States in protest against the annexation of Texas. At this time two Mexican governments were struggling for control, and the distracted nation had failed to pay an installment on some $3,000,000 in claims owed to American citizens. Polk tried to use these circumstances to persuade the government of President José

Herrera to accept the Rio Grande as the southern boundary of Texas and to sell California.

Polk sent Senator John Slidell to offer Mexico $25,000,000 plus the $3,000,000 in claims for the territory. The effort failed. Polk then decided to recommend war. In May 1846, he learned that Mexican troops had attacked General Zachary Taylor's forces along the Rio Grande, in territory claimed by both Mexico and Texas. Polk told Congress that Mexico had shed American blood on American soil, and he called for war. Congress declared war on May 13, 1846. The conflict caused great resentment in the northeastern states. Many Northerners felt that the war was unjustified and motivated by a Southern desire to expand the area of slavery.

The fighting lasted about a year and a half. General Taylor seized northern Mexico, and American forces occupied California. In September 1847, General Winfield Scott captured Mexico City. The Treaty of Guadalupe Hidalgo, ending the war, was ratified by the Senate on March 10, 1848. By its terms the United States acquired California and New Mexico (including parts of present-day Nevada, Arizona, Utah, and Colorado). The United States paid Mexico $15,000,000 and assumed the $3,000,000 owed to American citizens.

The Polk Doctrine

In his first annual message to Congress in 1845, Polk set forth the Polk Doctrine, an extension of the Monroe Doctrine. Polk declared that the United States opposed "any European interference" in any country in the Americas. In addition, the United States would resist even the voluntary transfer of such a country or territory to a European power. In 1848 Polk applied this doctrine to prevent Yucatan, a rebellious province of Mexico, from uniting itself to Spain or Great Britain. Latin-American nations, now fearful of the United States, challenged the Polk Doctrine as an invasion of their sovereignty. Polk defended it on the ground that only a firm stand by the United States would prevent European control of weak American nations.

Polk's administration represents the point when the United States began to regard itself as the equal of Europe. In his last annual message to Congress, Polk proudly announced that with the addition of the new territories "the United States are now estimated to be nearly as large as the whole of Europe."

Other Events

Many other events occurred during Polk's administration. The Department of the Interior was established. Wisconsin and Iowa as well as Texas became states, while Minnesota and Oregon became federal territories. Congressman David Wilmot introduced the Wilmot Proviso to prohibit slavery in any territory acquired from Mexico. Though Wilmot's measure did not pass the Senate, it became the basis of the antislavery Free-Soil Party and later of the Republican Party.

Dark shading shows the area ceded to the U.S. by Mexico in the Treaty of Guadalupe Hidalgo of 1848. Polk was determined to acquire California. The present-day states are shown by dashed lines.

PERSONAL LIFE

Polk showed little imagination or humor. He organized his life methodically, seeking workable answers to practical problems. He labored harder and longer than perhaps any other president of the United States. During his four years as president Polk spent only 37 days away from his desk. He arose at daybreak and applied himself to state business, usually until midnight. Before going to bed, he carefully recorded in a diary the details of the day's activities.

Sarah Polk greatly aided her husband. She maintained social life at the White House on a dignified and formal level, permitting no card-playing, liquor, or dancing. She had political intelligence and social grace, and she was able to give her husband some protection from the constant pressure of office-seekers, and she served as his personal secretary for many years. The Polks had no children.

Polk was succeeded as president by General Zachary Taylor, a hero of the Mexican War. Worn out by his unceasing labor, James K. Polk died on June 15, 1849, scarcely three months after leaving the White House. He was buried at his home, Polk Place, in Nashville, Tennessee. Despite Polk's wishes to the contrary, his home was demolished after his wife's death in 1891. In 1893 his body was moved to the state capitol grounds at Nashville.

ZACHARY TAYLOR

12th PRESIDENT OF THE UNITED STATES (1849–1850)

Born: *November 24, 1784, near Barboursville, Virginia*
Occupation: *Soldier*
Party: *Whig*
Vice President: *Millard Fillmore*
Wife: *Margaret Mackall Smith*
Died: *July 9, 1850, at Washington, D.C.*

Before he became president of the United States in 1849, Zachary Taylor served his country for nearly 40 years as an army officer. He fought with courage and honor in the War of 1812, the Black Hawk War, the Second Seminole War, and the Mexican War. At the close of the Mexican War he was the second highest officer in the United States Army. Taylor was the first of only two Whig presidents. His term as president was cut short by death before much had been accomplished, but not before Taylor had made clear his devotion to the preservation of the Union, his absolute integrity, his unyielding firmness, and his modesty. His soldiers affectionately nicknamed him "Old Rough and Ready" because he paid little attention to his appearance.

EARLY YEARS

Taylor was born near Barboursville in Orange County, Virginia, on November 24, 1784. His father was Lieutenant Colonel Richard Taylor, a veteran of the Revolutionary War and a member of a long-established Virginia family. Through his father, Zachary Taylor was related to the fourth president James Madison and the brilliant future

Confederate general Robert E. Lee.

In the spring of 1785, when Zachary was only a few months old, Richard Taylor took his family west to Kentucky (then a part of Virginia) to settle on lands he had received for his service in the Revolution. His new plantation was along the banks of the Muddy Fork of Beargrass Creek, a few miles east of the village of Louisville. Here Zachary Taylor spent his boyhood. At first the population of this wilderness region was small. But gradually the frontier was pushed back, and life for the Taylors became more comfortable. The family grew to include six sons and three daughters. Zachary probably had little, if any, formal education beyond that received at a small school in Louisville. Additional instruction was likely given him by his parents.

Zachary Taylor remained at home, assisting in the operation of the plantation, until 1808. In that year he was appointed first lieutenant in the Seventh Infantry Regiment. The appointment marked the beginning of a military career that, except for one brief period, continued until Taylor's election as president 40 years later.

MILITARY CAREER

Between 1808 and 1837, Taylor was stationed at various army posts, mostly on the Northwest frontier but occasionally in the Southwest. During the War of 1812 (1812–14) he took part in a number of military campaigns against the British and their Indian allies, most notably in the defense of Fort Hamilton. He slowly advanced in rank, receiving his commission as major in 1815. Later that year, when the Army was reduced to peacetime strength, he resigned rather than return to the rank of captain. But after less than a year in civilian life, which he spent growing corn and tobacco near Louisville, Taylor was appointed major in the Third Regiment. In 1819 he was promoted to lieutenant colonel.

By 1832, Taylor, now 47 years old, was a colonel, commanding the First Regiment. The Black Hawk War broke out the same year, and Taylor took part in the hard-fought campaign against Chief Black Hawk and the Sauk Indians in Illinois.

FAMILY AND HOME LIFE

This same period of nearly 30 years was important in Taylor's family and domestic life. In 1810 he married Margaret Mackall Smith, daughter of a Maryland planter. Five daughters and one son were born to them. Two of the daughters died in early childhood. A third, Sarah Knox, died only a few months after her marriage to Jefferson Davis, then a lieutenant in Taylor's regiment and later to become the president of the Confederacy. The other two daughters also married army officers. Taylor's youngest child and only son, Richard, became a lieutenant general in the Confederate Army.

In addition to his military career, Taylor took an active interest in planting. In 1823 he purchased a 380-acre cotton plantation in northern Louisiana. In later years he bought Cypress Grove, a much larger plantation in Mississippi.

Mary Elizabeth Taylor Bliss was the Taylors' youngest daughter. Because Mrs. Taylor was a partial invalid, Mary Elizabeth served as the White House hostess.

DID YOU KNOW?

- *Taylor was a second cousin of James Madison, fourth cousin once removed of Robert E. Lee, and fourth cousin three times removed of Franklin D. Roosevelt.*
- *A nondrinker and nonsmoker, Taylor chewed tobacco.*
- *He served in the regular Army for 40 years.*
- *He never voted, never belonged to a political party, nor took any interest in politics until he ran for president at age 62.*
- *Taylor was elected in the first national election held on the same day (November 7, 1848) in all states.*
- *He pastured his old Army horse, Whitey, on the White House lawn. Visitors would take horse hairs as souvenirs.*

THE SECOND SEMINOLE WAR

In the summer of 1837 Taylor was ordered to take his regiment to Florida. Since late 1835 the Army had been fighting the Seminole Indians, and reinforcements were needed. This was the start of events that were to make Taylor a national hero and carry him to the White House.

In December 1837, with a force of nearly 1,100 men, including regular soldiers, volunteers, and some Shawnee and Delaware Indians, Taylor set out in search of the Seminole. On December 25, after hard marching through very rough and difficult country, he found the Seminole at Lake Okeechobee and defeated them in a desperate battle. This victory won for Taylor the thanks of President Van Buren and a brevet (honorary) commission as brigadier general. But the war continued, and in 1838 Taylor was placed in command. For two years he directed the fighting against the Seminole. His efforts were commended by the secretary of war, but he had no greater success in subduing the Seminole than had his predecessors. In 1840, at his own request, he was relieved of command and assigned to duty in the Southwest. Here his main concern once again was with the Indians.

THE MEXICAN WAR

In 1836, after winning its independence from Mexico, Texas had established itself as an independent republic. Early negotiations for Texas to join the United States had failed, but in 1844 these negotiations were renewed. Mexico, however, strongly opposed American annexation of Texas, and the Texans, fearing attack, requested protection from the United States.

Taylor was ordered to Fort Jesup, close to the Texas-Louisiana border. He remained there until July 1845, when he was ordered to move his forces to the coast of Texas.

Z. Taylor

Zachary Taylor

12th president, 1849–50   Whig

1784 Born on November 24 near Barboursville, Virginia.

1785 Moved with his family to a plantation near Louisville, Kentucky, where he grew up and was educated by tutors.

1808 Entered the U.S. Army as a first lieutenant.

1810 Married Margaret Mackall Smith on June 21. The couple subsequently had six children, two of whom died in infancy.

1812 As commander of a company under William Henry Harrison, successfully defended Fort Harrison from Indian attack; subsequently brevetted a major.

1814 Led U.S. troops against British and Indian forces at Credit Island in Illinois Territory; outnumbered, he was forced to withdraw after some initial successes.

1829–32 Was Indian superintendent in the Northwest, at Fort Snelling, Montana.

1832 Promoted to colonel; fought in the Black Hawk War.

1837–40 Earned the nickname "Old Rough and Ready" while fighting the Seminole Indians in Florida.

1841 Named commander of the second department of the army's western division, with headquarters at Fort Smith, Arkansas.

1846 Advanced with a small army to the Rio Grande, in anticipation of conflict with Mexico. After war began, defeated Mexican forces at two battles, forcing their retreat across the Rio Grande. Later launched an attack against Monterrey, capturing the city after a prolonged fight.

1847 Leading a force mostly of volunteers, defeated a much larger Mexican force under Santa Anna on February 22–23; the battle secured U.S. victory in the war and made Taylor a national hero.

1848 Elected president as the Whig Party candidate, defeating Lewis Cass of the Democratic Party and Martin Van Buren, who ran on the Free-Soil ticket.

1850 Died in the White House on July 9.

Highlights of Presidency

1849 Sectional debates over the extension of slavery occupied Congress, with Taylor supporting the admission of California without conditions.

1850 The United States and Britain signed the Clayton-Bulwer Treaty guaranteeing the neutrality of a future canal across Central America.

Early in 1846 he was ordered to advance to the Rio Grande, the river that Texas claimed as its border with Mexico. On April 25, 1846, Mexican troops crossed the Rio Grande and attacked a U.S. detachment. In May a larger Mexican force crossed the river. Although badly outnumbered, Taylor gave battle, defeating the Mexicans at Palo Alto and Resaca de la Palma.

The American people hailed Taylor as a hero. Promoted to major general, he became the second ranking officer in the U.S. Army. He was outranked only by Major General Winfield Scott, the commanding general of the Army.

After Congress declared war on May 13, 1846, Taylor crossed the Rio Grande. On September 25, he captured the Mexican city of Monterrey. By November 1846, he had advanced some 200 miles (320 kilometers) into Mexico.

Meanwhile, President James K. Polk had given General Winfield Scott command of a new Mexican expedition, and most of Taylor's best troops were transferred to Scott's forces. The angry Taylor claimed that Polk had acted so for political reasons. (Both Polk and Scott were Democrats.) Despite orders to remain on the defensive, Taylor advanced with his weakened forces. On February 22–23, 1847, at the battle of Buena Vista, he defeated a Mexican army under General Antonio López de Santa Anna that was four times larger than his own. This was Taylor's last battle of the war.

THE PRESIDENCY

Although Taylor had no political experience, belonged to no political party, and never voted, leaders of the Whig Party urged his nomination for the presidency in 1848. Taylor at first refused but later accepted the nomination. In the election Taylor carried eight southern and seven northern states, exactly half of the total. But he won 163 electoral votes, 36 more than Lewis Cass, the Democratic candidate. Martin Van Buren, a former president, ran unsuccessfully as the Free Soil Party candidate.

The Slavery Crisis. When Taylor was inaugurated in 1849, the nation faced a crisis. Controversy between North and South over the question of slavery in the Western territories had grown increasingly bitter. Opponents of slavery insisted that Congress had the constitutional authority to keep slavery out of the territories. Southerners were equally certain that Congress had no such authority, and Southern extremists threatened secession (to leave the Union) if Congress took such action. Compromise proposals to settle this and other slavery problems were introduced into Congress by Henry Clay. Taylor opposed them. This was partly because he had already suggested a plan of his own, partly because of a growing feud with Clay, and partly because he believed that the Union could not be preserved by compromise reached in the face of threats of secession.

Though a Southerner and slaveholder, Taylor had no sympathy with the southern position in this crisis. He

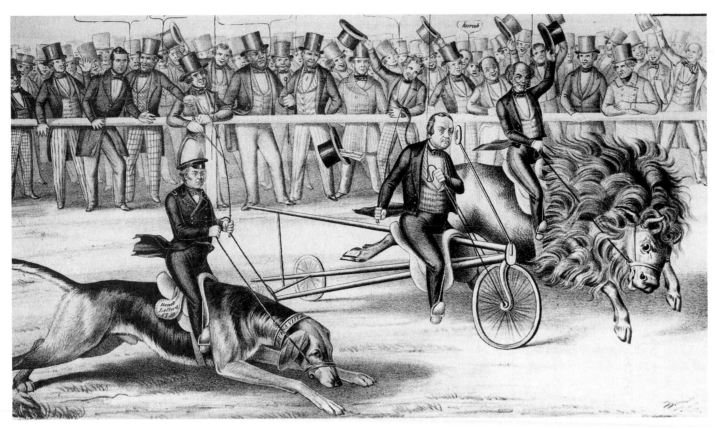

A political cartoon of the time depicts the "race" for the presidency in the election of 1848: from left, Whig Zachary Taylor, Lewis Cass, the Democratic candidate, and Martin Van Buren, who ran as the Free-Soil party candidate.

was ready to take the field and lead the Army himself if rebellion occurred. The measures known as the Compromise of 1850 were not enacted until after Taylor's death, and his death was one of the factors that made their passage possible.

Gold Rush. The great California Gold Rush brought tens of thousands of gold prospectors, called forty-niners, into California in 1849 to seek their fortunes. The gold had first been discovered in 1848 on the site of John Sutter's mill near Sacramento. Taylor encouraged both New Mexico and California to apply for admission to the union as free states, which angered his Southern followers. The rush for gold helped to populate California and other future western states.

Foreign Affairs. In the field of foreign affairs the chief accomplishment of the Taylor administration was the negotiation of the Clayton-Bulwer Treaty with Great Britain in 1850. The treaty provided that neither country would have exclusive control over any ship canal through Central America or could fortify such a canal. Trouble with Spain over Cuba threatened but was avoided, and honest friendship with all nations was maintained.

TAYLOR'S DEATH

Taylor was of medium height, short-legged, and heavy-set. He dressed plainly, at times carelessly, and made an undistinguished appearance. He was a man of absolute honesty, straightforward and simple in manner, strong-minded and firm almost to the point of obstinacy. He was not a military genius, but he was a hard-working, successful officer. He was not a great statesman, but he was a faithful servant of the people.

Although Taylor had earned the nickname "Old Rough and Ready" as a younger man, he was no longer in robust health by the time he reached the White House in 1849, at age 64. On July 4, 1850, he took part in the ceremonies at the laying of the Washington Monument cornerstone. After long exposure to the hot sun he returned to the White House. He developed a stomach ailment after dining and died on the evening of July 9, 1850. He is buried in Zachary Taylor National Cemetery, near Louisville, Kentucky. His wife died in 1852. Vice President Millard Fillmore succeeded him as the 13th president.

In 1991, historians pointed out that Taylor's symptoms were consistent with arsenic poisoning. It was thought that since he opposed slavery, supporters of that issue could have plotted against his life. However, when his remains were exhumed and tested, no trace of arsenic was found. It was concluded that he did, in fact, die of natural causes stemming from food poisoning or cholera.

MILLARD FILLMORE

13th PRESIDENT OF THE UNITED STATES (1850–1853)

Born: *January 7, 1800, at Summerhill, New York*
Occupation: *Lawyer*
Party: *Whig*
Vice President: *None*
Wives: *Abigail Powers; Caroline Carmichael McIntosh*
Died: *March 8, 1874, at Buffalo, New York*

On July 9, 1850, President Zachary Taylor died in office. The next day Vice President Millard Fillmore was sworn in as the 13th president of the United States. He was the second vice president to assume the presidency after the death of a president in office.

Fillmore has been considered one of the lesser U.S. presidents. Yet he was a statesman whose support for the Compromise of 1850 helped to prevent civil war and preserve the Union for ten years. He was also a diplomat whose dispatch of a U.S. expedition to Japan helped open that nation to world trade.

EARLY YEARS

Fillmore was born on January 7, 1800, in Summerhill, or what was then the frontier village of Locke, in Cayuga County, New York. He was the second child of Nathaniel Fillmore and Phoebe Millard Fillmore, who had come from New England. The Fillmores were poor tenant farmers, and young Millard spent his early years working alongside his father.

As he grew older, Millard realized that his formal schooling was meager. He used his spare moments to ed-

ucate himself. Even while tending a machine as an apprentice to a cloth maker, he found time to memorize the definitions of words from a dictionary. He did manage to attend New Hope Academy for six months.

At the age of 19, Fillmore became clerk to a county judge, under whom he studied law. In 1823 he was admitted to the bar and opened a law office in East Aurora, New York.

Gaining confidence in himself, Fillmore courted Abigail Powers, the dark-haired daughter of the Reverend Lemuel Powers. They were married in 1826. Two children were born to them, Mary Abigail and Millard Powers. In 1830 the family moved to Buffalo, New York, where Fillmore soon was one of the leading lawyers in the city.

EARLY POLITICAL LIFE

As a young lawyer Fillmore became active in local politics, when the anti-masonic movement swept western New York. In 1828 he won election to the New York legislature. In 1832 he was elected to the U.S. House of Representatives.

Fillmore began his career in Congress at a time when the question of slavery was being hotly debated. Those who hated slavery hoped that it might at least be banished from the nation's capital. But Southern representatives were able to "gag" (prevent) discussion of this issue. Fillmore attracted attention when he presented a petition to abolish slavery in the District of Columbia (Washington, D.C.). Fillmore also became chair of the House Ways and Means Committee, and worked for the passage of the Whig Tariff Act of 1842. He supported former president John Quincy Adams in the battle for free speech and the right of petition. Adams later recalled that Fillmore was "one of the ablest, most faithful men" with whom he served in public life.

Abigail Powers (left) was Fillmore's first wife who died in 1853. She was in poor health during his presidency, but she did take part in White House functions. Fillmore married widow Caroline Carmichael McIntosh (right) in 1858. Her wealth enabled him to purchase their mansion in Buffalo, New York. She died in 1881.

In Congress, Fillmore generally followed the lead of the Whigs and of Henry Clay of Kentucky. The Whig Party had been formed in the 1830s and represented a combination of various groups opposed to President Andrew Jackson.

After serving four terms in Congress, Fillmore decided not to run again in 1842. In 1844 he tried but failed to win the Whig nomination for vice president. He also ran for governor of New York but was defeated.

VICE PRESIDENT

At the 1848 Whig National Convention, General Zachary Taylor, a popular Mexican War hero, was nominated for the presidency. Taylor lived in Louisiana and owned slaves. Abbott Lawrence, a wealthy cotton manufacturer from Boston, was proposed for the vice presidency. But the antislavery Whigs refused to "have cotton at both ends of the ticket." In order to satisfy this group, Fillmore was nominated for vice president. In the election of 1848, Taylor and Fillmore defeated the Democratic candidates, Lewis Cass and William O. Butler.

The election came at a crucial time. The United States had just defeated Mexico in the Mexican War and acquired an enormous amount of territory, including present-day California. The question was whether slavery should be allowed to expand into this new territory. With 15 free and 15 slave states in the Union, the admission of California would upset the balance in the U.S. Senate.

Millard Fillmore

13th president, 1850–53 Whig

1800	Born on January 7 in Cayuga County, New York.
1814	Apprenticed to a firm of clothmakers.
1823	Began to practice law in East Aurora, New York.
1826	Married Abigail Powers, a teacher, on February 5. The couple would have two children.
1828	Elected to the New York state House of Representatives on an Anti-Masonic platform. Was reelected twice.
1830	Moved to Buffalo, and began a law practice.
1832	Elected to the House of Representatives, again on the Anti-Masonic ticket.
1836	Reelected to the House as a Whig. Kept House seat until 1843.
1840	Became chairman of the Ways and Means Committee. He used that position to guide new protectionist tariff laws through Congress.
1844	Lost bid for the governorship of New York.
1846	Became the first chancellor of the University of Buffalo.
1847	Elected New York state comptroller.
1848	Elected vice president, on the Whig ticket with Zachary Taylor.
1850	Zachary Taylor died in office on July 9. Took presidential oath the following day.
1853	Resumed his law practice in Buffalo.
1856	Nominated for president by the Whig Party and the American (Know-Nothing) Party. Ran third in the election, which James Buchanan won.
1858	Five years after the death of his first wife, married Caroline Carmichael McIntosh on February 10.
1874	Died on March 8 in Buffalo.

Highlights of Presidency

1850	In September, Congress passed the Compromise of 1850, which delayed conflict over slavery by admitting California as a free state, organizing the territories of Utah and New Mexico without reference to slavery, abolishing slavery in the District of Columbia, and establishing a stronger fugitive slave law.
1852	Authorized a mission to Japan by Commodore Matthew C. Perry. Rejected in his bid for nomination for a full term by Northern antislavery Whigs, who favored Gen. Winfield Scott.

There were other serious disputes. Southerners demanded the return of fugitive (runaway) slaves. Northerners demanded the ending of the slave trade in Washington, D.C. Some people predicted the breakup of the Union because of the controversy. Alarmed at the increasing hostility, Henry Clay, with the support of Daniel Webster, introduced a number of resolutions in the Senate as a compromise between North and South.

PRESIDENT

Compromise of 1850. While the debate on the compromise raged, President Taylor died suddenly. There was no question where the new president stood on the issue. In his first annual message to Congress in December 1850, Fillmore urged acceptance of the compromise as the best means of restoring peace to the nation and maintaining the Union. He named Daniel Webster as his secretary of state.

The Compromise of 1850 was the outstanding domestic achievement of Fillmore's administration. Under its terms, California joined the Union as a free state. The other territories won from Mexico were organized without restriction on slavery. The slave trade was ended in the District of Columbia. But a stronger law for the return of fugitive slaves was to be enforced.

Japan. With California in the Union, the United States took greater interest in the Far East, especially Japan. For more than two centuries, Japan had been virtually closed to the Western world. Only one port, Nagasaki, was open to foreigners.

In late 1852, Fillmore authorized a special naval expedition to Japan to deliver a letter to its emperor suggesting closer relations with the United States. A U.S. squadron under Commodore Matthew C. Perry arrived in what is now Tokyo Bay in 1853. Perry delivered Fillmore's letter to the emperor's representatives in a golden casket. The Treaty of Kanagawa, signed in 1854, a year after Fillmore had left the presidency, opened two Japanese ports to U.S. commerce. Additional treaties were later signed with the U.S. and with other Western nations.

Election of 1852. Fillmore failed to win nomination by his party for the presidency in 1852. By accepting the Compromise of 1850 and strictly enforcing the Fugitive Slave Law, he lost the support of the Northern antislavery Whigs. Only the Southern Whigs supported him. General Winfield Scott won the nomination but lost the 1852 election to Democrat Franklin Pierce. Fillmore thus became the last Whig president.

RETIREMENT AND REMARRIAGE

After leaving the White House in 1853, Fillmore returned to his law practice in Buffalo. Abigail Fillmore died that same year. In 1858, Fillmore married Mrs. Caroline Carmichael McIntosh, a widow. They had no children.

In Buffalo, Fillmore was active in civic affairs. He was a founder of the General Hospital, the first president of the historical society (where his letters are now kept), and chancellor of the University of Buffalo.

Know–Nothing Candidate

During the 1840s and 1850s a tremendous wave of immigrants arrived in the United States. Among them were many Irish who had come to America to escape the famine caused by failure of the potato crops in Ireland.

Some Americans saw these immigrants as a threat. They feared that the thousands of new arrivals would take jobs away from native-born Americans. Anti-immigrant feeling led to the formation of secret societies. However, when suspected members of these societies were questioned about their activities, they said they "knew nothing" about them. For this reason they came to be known as Know-Nothings.

The Know-Nothings wanted only American-born Protestants elected to public office. They also demanded a 21-year residency before allowing immigrants to become U.S. citizens. In the election of 1856, Fillmore ran for president as a candidate of the American, or Know-Nothing, Party. But he carried only Maryland, and Democrat James Buchanan won the election. The Know-Nothing party split up and disappeared by the 1860s. When the Civil War broke out in 1861, Fillmore was a loyal supporter of the Union, although he was critical of President Abraham Lincoln's policies.

He died in Buffalo on March 8, 1874, and is buried in Forest Lawn Cemetery.

DID YOU KNOW?

SEAL OF THE PRESIDENT OF THE UNITED STATES

- *Fillmore didn't meet his running mate Zachary Taylor until after they were elected.*
- *When he moved into the White House it didn't even have a Bible. He and his wife installed the first library.*
- *Fillmore installed the first bathtub and kitchen stove in the White House.*
- *Illiterate in Latin, he refused an honorary degree from Oxford University, saying a person shouldn't accept a degree he cannot read.*
- *The first cartoon depicting Uncle Sam as the symbol of the United States was published in 1852.*

FRANKLIN PIERCE

14th PRESIDENT OF THE UNITED STATES (1853–1857)

Born: *November 23, 1804, at Hillsborough (now Hillsboro), New Hampshire*
Occupation: *Lawyer, Public Official*
Party: *Democrat*
Vice President: *William R. King*
Wife: *Jane Means Appleton*
Died: *October 8, 1869, at Concord, New Hampshire*

When Franklin Pierce was inaugurated president of the United States in 1853, he was 48 years old. Young Hickory of the Granite Hills, as he was called (Andrew Jackson was called Old Hickory), had been a general in the Mexican War, a successful lawyer, a congressman, and a senator. As president he was faced with a crisis over slavery that brought on a war in Kansas and gave the territory the name "bleeding Kansas."

BOYHOOD

Pierce was born in a log cabin in Hillsborough (now Hillsboro), New Hampshire, on November 23, 1804, one of eight children born to Benjamin and Anna Kendrick Pierce. Benjamin Pierce was a rough frontier farmer. He had served during the Revolutionary War, became a general of the state militia, and was twice elected governor of New Hampshire. As a boy Franklin Pierce heard so much about the military exploits of his father in the Revolutionary War and of his older brother in the War of 1812 that at first he wanted to become a soldier.

Pierce attended school at Hillsborough Center and later went to Hancock Academy. Disliking the stern disci-

pline there, he ran away from school and came home. His father surprised him by saying nothing about his truancy. But after lunch he hitched up the carriage and told young Frank to get in. Halfway back to Hancock his father told him to jump out and walk to school. He had to hike the rest of the way in a rainstorm. Later, Pierce wrote that this lesson in discipline marked a turning point in his life.

In 1820 Pierce entered Bowdoin College in Brunswick, Maine. There he began a lifelong friendship with one of his classmates, Nathaniel Hawthorne, who was later to become a famous author. Pierce's carefree and irresponsible attitude toward his studies soon carried him to the bottom of his class, though he became a favorite among the students. However, after applying himself to his studies, he graduated fifth in his class in 1824. He then studied law and in 1827 was admitted to the bar.

EARLY CAREER

That same year his father became governor of New Hampshire. Pierce now began to take an active part in state politics as a member of the Jacksonian (later the Democratic) Party. He entered the state legislature in 1829. In 1833 he was elected to Congress. He remained in Congress for four years, loyally supporting President Andrew Jackson's political program. In 1837 New Hampshire sent Pierce to the U. S. Senate. At the age of 33 he was the youngest member of the Senate.

Jane Means Appleton

On November 19, 1834, Pierce married Jane Means Appleton, daughter of a former president of Bowdoin College. The Appletons, an aristocratic New England family, did not approve of Jane's match with the young Democrat from the backcountry. Mrs. Pierce found life in

Franklin Pierce

14th president, 1853–57   Democrat

1804   Born on November 23 in Hillsborough, New Hampshire.

1824   Graduated from Bowdoin College.

1827   Admitted to the New Hampshire bar.

1829   Elected to the New Hampshire state legislature.

1833   Elected to the U.S. House of Representatives, where he became known as a supporter of Andrew Jackson.

1834   Married Jane Means Appleton in November. The couple later had three sons, all of whom died young.

1837   Elected to the U.S. Senate.

1842   Resigned his Senate seat under pressure from his wife, a temperance advocate. Returned to Concord to practice law and conduct a temperance drive.

1845   Appointed federal district attorney for New Hampshire.

1847   After enlisting to serve in the Mexican War, promoted to colonel and then brigadier general. Led an army to join Winfield Scott in attacking Mexico City and was wounded at Churubusco.

1852   After being nominated by the Democrats on the 49th ballot, defeated Whig candidate Winfield Scott for the presidency.

1853   En route to Washington, the Pierces' only surviving child, Benjamin, was killed in a train accident.

1857   After leaving office, traveled widely.

1860   Settled permanently in Concord.

1869   Died on October 8 in Concord.

Highlights of Presidency

1853   The Gadsden Purchase settled boundary disputes with Mexico and gave the United States a southern railway route to the Pacific.

1854   The Kansas Nebraska Act, endorsed by Pierce despite misgivings, was adopted. The law touched off rivalry between pro- and anti-slavery settlers that eventually led to fighting. The Ostend Manifesto, a document detailing a plan to buy Cuba from Spain, caused a furor when it was leaked to the press.

1856   Ordered federal troops into Kansas in an effort to end the fighting there. The Democrats, concerned about Pierce's connection with the Kansas issue, nominated James Buchanan for the presidency.

Washington, D.C., so distasteful that her husband agreed to abandon his political career. He resigned his Senate seat in 1842 and returned to Concord to practice law.

The early years of the Pierces' marriage were saddened by the loss of two of their three sons. Franklin, Jr., the first child, lived only a few days after his birth. The second son, Frank R., died at the age of four. Only Benjamin, the youngest, born in 1841, was left to them.

The Mexican War

When the Mexican War broke out in 1846, Pierce enlisted as a private in the Concord Light Infantry. He was soon appointed a colonel and then a brigadier general of volunteers. In June 1847, he arrived in Mexico and led his 2,500 men inland. At the battle of Churubusco, Pierce suffered a painful leg injury when his horse reared and fell. The next day, while advancing into battle, he wrenched the injured leg so sharply that he fainted from the pain and was unable to take part in the fighting. In later years his political enemies twisted this incident into a charge that he had been cowardly under fire. Pierce remained in the field until the capture of Mexico City in September 1847. Then he returned to his law practice at Concord.

Presidential Candidate

In the years that followed, Pierce's friendliness, kindness, and concern for people gained him increasing political popularity. His growing law practice brought him wealth. And his military career had made him a local hero.

Thus, in 1851 many New England Democrats turned to Pierce as a presidential prospect. Few expected that he could be nominated. But some thought that he might have a chance if the Democratic convention came to a deadlock between the more prominent leaders—Lewis Cass, William L. Marcy, Stephen A. Douglas, and James Buchanan. A deadlock did arise, Pierce's friends introduced his name, and the tired delegates nominated him on the 49th ballot. William R. D. King of Alabama became Pierce's running mate. Mrs. Pierce, horrified that she might have to return to Washington, fainted upon hearing the news. Pierce's son, Benjamin, now 11 years old, said: "I hope he won't be elected."

In the campaign of 1852 Pierce ran against his former army commander, General Winfield Scott, the Whig candidate. Pierce promised, if elected, to respect the rights of the states and to concentrate on foreign policy. His simplicity and ease in meeting people gained him many votes. He had the knack of remembering the name and face of nearly everyone he met. But his desire to please led him to make promises he could not always fulfill.

PRESIDENT

Pierce won the election, carrying all but four states. He received 1,601,117 popular votes to 1,385,453 for Scott and 254 electoral votes to Scott's 42.

But a personal tragedy soon dimmed Pierce's joy over his victory. On January 6, 1853, during a family trip, the Pierces were in a train wreck. President-elect and Mrs. Pierce were uninjured, but Benjamin was killed. It was a terrible blow to the parents. Mrs. Pierce, completely overcome, lived in seclusion at the White House. She came to believe that her son's life had been the price of her husband's victory. Pierce had to bear his wife's bitter accusations, as well as his own grief.

Pierce invited into his cabinet well-meaning men without much experience. The only prominent Democrats to serve were William L. Marcy, as secretary of state, and Jefferson Davis, as secretary of war. These men held different political views, and people predicted that the cabinet would soon break up. But Pierce's cabinet proved to be the first in U.S. history to remain unchanged throughout an entire four-year term.

Pierce rose to the position of brigadier general in the Mexican War.

First Lady Jane Appleton Pierce never wanted to live in Washington.

The Kansas–Nebraska Bill

Pierce's term was marked by bitter debate over the expansion of slavery. His hopes to quiet this debate received a setback when the Kansas–Nebraska bill was introduced in January 1854. The bill proposed to create two new territories, Kansas and Nebraska, and to allow settlers there to decide whether or not to allow slavery. Pierce was not enthusiastic. But he promised to support the bill in return for Senate support of his appointments and foreign policy. The bill brought on a violent debate about slavery. The prospect of slavery in Kansas split the Democrats into Northern and Southern wings and gave birth to the Republican Party. The bill became law later in 1854, and supporters and opponents of slavery rushed to Kansas. They fought for control of the territory throughout Pierce's administration.

Foreign Affairs

In 1853, Pierce acquired from Mexico the region known as the Gadsden Purchase. This included parts of present-day Arizona and New Mexico. In 1854 he signed a treaty with Britain by which the U.S. gave trade privileges to Canada in exchange for certain fishing rights.

Pierce hoped that the United States would acquire Cuba from Spain. He told the U.S. ministers in Europe to draft a plan for obtaining the island. Their proposal was called the Ostend Manifesto, after the city in Belgium where they met. The ministers recommended purchasing Cuba but hinted that if Spain refused to sell, the United States might be justified in seizing the island.

The premature publication of the manifesto caused an uproar. Northerners objected strongly to adding any new slave territory. And Spain was insulted and refused to sell the island.

The most far-reaching diplomatic event of Pierce's term was the opening of Japan to Western trade. In 1853 a U.S. naval squadron under Commodore Matthew C. Perry arrived in Japan. The Treaty of Kanagawa, signed in 1854, opened two Japanese ports to U.S. ships. Treaties between Japan and other Western nations soon followed.

Pierce hoped for renomination in 1856. But largely because of the difficulties in Kansas, the Democrats instead chose James Buchanan. After leaving the White House, the Pierces toured Europe. Franklin Pierce died in Concord on October 8, 1869. He is buried there.

DID YOU KNOW?

- *One of the Democratic party's slogans during Pierce's campaign for president was: "We Polked you in 1844; we shall Pierce you in 1852."*

- *Because of religious considerations Pierce affirmed rather than swore the Presidential oath of office.*

- *He gave his inaugural address from memory, without the aid of notes.*

- *Pierce installed the first central-heating system in the White House.*

- *He was the first president who failed to receive his party's nomination for a second term.*

JAMES BUCHANAN

15th PRESIDENT OF THE UNITED STATES (1857–1861)

Born: *April 23, 1791, at Cove Gap, Pennsylvania*
Occupation: *Lawyer*
Party: *Democrat*
Vice President: *John C. Breckinridge*
Wife: *None*
Died: *June 1, 1868, near Lancaster, Pennsylvania*

James Buchanan, the 15th president of the United States, also served his country as a congressman, senator, ambassador, and secretary of state. But many people remember mainly two things about him: that he was the only president who never married; and that the Civil War followed his administration.

EARLY LIFE

Buchanan was born on April 23, 1791, in a log cabin near the frontier settlement of Cove Gap, Pennsylvania. His father, a Scotch-Irish immigrant, had come to America in 1783. When James was six, the family moved to Mercersburg, Pennsylvania, where his father opened a general store. James's mother had little schooling, but she loved to read and she inspired her son with a love of learning.

James was able to go to school in Mercersburg. When he was not studying, he helped his father in the store. James's father was fond of his son, but he made him work hard and pay close attention to business. Mr. Buchanan taught James that he must be ready to care for his nine younger brothers and sisters if their parents

should die. In later years, after his father died, James Buchanan became responsible for the care of his mother and four of his brothers and sisters.

When James was 16, his father sent him to Dickinson College in Carlisle, Pennsylvania. Young Buchanan was a serious student, but he also wanted to have a good time. He began to drink and smoke with some of the other students. Even though his marks were excellent, he was expelled for bad conduct at the end of his first term. James pleaded to be taken back and promised to turn over a new leaf. He was allowed to return and went on to graduate with honors.

Buchanan then went to Lancaster, Pennsylvania, to study law. Hard work and intelligence made him a very good lawyer. Before long he was earning more than $11,000 a year, a huge sum in those days.

In 1814, Buchanan became a candidate for the Pennsylvania legislature. But the War of 1812 was raging, and the British had just burned Washington. Buchanan felt that the United States should not have gone to war against Great Britain. However, he knew it was his duty to serve his country, and he joined a volunteer cavalry company.

Buchanan returned in time for the election and won his seat in the legislature. He served a second term and then returned to Lancaster to continue his law practice.

A TRAGIC LOVE STORY

As his practice grew, Buchanan became an important figure in town. He was invited to parties at some of the best homes in Lancaster. At one party he met and fell in love with beautiful Ann Coleman. In 1819 Ann and James were engaged to be married, but their happiness was destined to end quickly.

During the fall of 1819 Buchanan often had to be out of town on business. While he was away rumors

Buchanan's family moved to this house in Mercersburg, Pennsylvania in 1797, when he was six years old. His father ran a general store.

Ann Coleman broke her engagement to Buchanan in 1819.

spread that he wanted to marry Ann only for her money. There was gossip about another woman. All of this was untrue, but Ann was heartbroken. Because of a misunderstanding, she broke her engagement to James.

A short time later Ann died. Buchanan was so grief-stricken that he vowed he would never marry. Years later, after his death, a package of Ann's letters, yellow with age, was found among his papers. They were burned, according to his last wishes, without being opened.

RETURN TO POLITICS

Buchanan turned to politics to forget his sorrow. The Federalist Party was looking for a candidate for Congress. Buchanan agreed to run, and in 1820 he was elected to the House of Representatives, where he served for ten years. During his years in Congress, Buchanan changed his political party. He joined the Jacksonian Democrats (named for Andrew Jackson), and became a leader of the Jacksonians in Pennsylvania.

In 1831 President Jackson asked Buchanan to become minister to Russia. Buchanan went to Russia the following year. While there he negotiated the first trade agreement between Russia and the United States.

On his return to the United States, Buchanan was elected to the Senate. He served until 1845, and became chairman of the important committee on foreign affairs.

Buchanan applied all his training as a lawyer to his work in the Senate. The Constitution, he said, was the basis of all political power. But the Constitution also strictly limited the powers of the federal government. Buchanan believed that a constitutional republic could adjust serious differences between its people only by compromise and legal procedure.

SECRETARY OF STATE

By 1844 Buchanan had become an important political figure. Though he hoped for the presidential nomination, he gave his support to James K. Polk, who won the nomination and the election. President Polk appointed Buchanan secretary of state.

During Polk's term as president, war broke out between the United States and Mexico. Buchanan, as secretary of state, helped to arrange the treaty of peace in 1848. By this Treaty of Guadalupe Hidalgo, the United States purchased from Mexico the region extending west from Texas to the Pacific Ocean.

Another problem concerned the vast Oregon territory, which both Great Britain and the United States claimed. The dispute became so bad that war threatened. But Buchanan arranged a compromise, and the Oregon Treaty of 1846 settled the Northwestern boundary between Canada and the United States.

When Polk left office, Buchanan also retired. For four years he lived the life of a country gentleman. He bought the famous mansion, Wheatland, near Lancaster, Pennsylvania, partly to have a suitable place to entertain political guests, but mainly to care for a growing family. Although Buchanan remained a bachelor, he had over the years become a kind of foster father to a score of nephews and nieces, seven of them orphans. They often visited him at Wheatland, and two made their home with him there.

But Buchanan could not stay out of politics for long. In 1852 he was again a candidate for the presidential nomination. He was beaten by a little-known candidate, Franklin Pierce.

MINISTER TO GREAT BRITAIN

President Pierce made Buchanan minister to Great Britain in 1853. Shortly thereafter Pierce instructed the American ministers in Europe to draw up proposals to "detach" Cuba from Spain. This led to the Ostend Manifesto, named after the Belgian city where the ministers met. The Manifesto defined a plan to purchase Cuba. But it also

James Buchanan

15th president, 1857–61   Democrat

1791 Born on April 23 near Mercersburg, Pennsylvania.

1809 Graduated from Dickinson College in Carlisle, Pennsylvania.

1813 Admitted to the Pennsylvania bar and founded a law practice.

1814 After brief service in the War of 1812, elected as a Federalist to the Pennsylvania assembly.

1819 Became engaged to Ann Caroline Coleman, but the engagement was broken. She died a week later, and Buchanan never married.

1820 Elected to Congress, where he served five terms.

1831 Appointed minister to Russia.

1834 Elected to the Senate from Pennsylvania. Served there until 1845, chairing the Foreign Relations Committee.

1845 Named secretary of state by President Polk.

1852 Supporters of Buchanan and Stephen A. Douglas split the Democratic Party, giving the presidential nomination and the election to Franklin Pierce.

1853 Appointed by Pierce to be minister to Britain.

1856 Running on a "Save the Union" platform as the Democratic presidential candidate, defeated Republican John C. Fremont and Whig Millard Fillmore.

1861 Returned to Wheatland, his estate near Lancaster, Pennsylvania, where he remained a supporter of the Union.

1866 Published an account of his administration.

1868 Died on June 1 at Wheatland.

Highlights of Presidency

1857 Endorsing the concept of popular sovereignty, recommended that Congress approve a pro-slavery Kansas constitution. (Kansas antislavery forces had boycotted a vote on the measure.) The constitution was rejected, and the debate on it cost Buchanan Northern support.

1858 Northern candidates opposing Buchanan won a majority in both houses of Congress.

1859 John Brown was seized at Harpers Ferry and hanged for his attempt to start a slave revolt.

1860 Did not run for reelection but supported his vice president, John C. Breckinridge, who was defeated in the November election by Abraham Lincoln.

1861 Seven Southern states formed the Confederacy on February 4.

included a proposal many people condemned: that the United States would be justified in seizing Cuba if Spain refused to sell the island. Buchanan's political opponents severely denounced the Ostend Manifesto, and nothing ever came of the plan. Buchanan wrote of it: "Never did I obey any instructions so reluctantly."

While Buchanan was in England, Congress passed the Kansas–Nebraska Act, permitting slavery in regions of the Northwest from which the Missouri Compromise of 1820 had formerly excluded it. This new law marked the beginning of the Republican Party, which vowed to prevent any further expansion of slavery, and it split the Democratic Party into northern and southern groups. As Buchanan had been in England during the Congressional fight over the Kansas–Nebraska bill, he remained friendly with both sections of his party. When the Democrats met in 1856 to pick a new candidate for president, they needed someone who would be accepted by both the North and the South. Buchanan proved to be the man. This time he won the nomination and the election.

PRESIDENT BUCHANAN

On March 4, 1857, Buchanan was inaugurated as president. Since Buchanan had no wife, his 27-year-old orphan niece, Harriet Lane, acted as his hostess. She was very popular, and Buchanan's administration was a great social success. White House guests included the first Japanese rep-

This photograph of the president was taken about 1859, in the middle of his term as 15th president.

resentatives to the United States and the Prince of Wales (who later became King Edward VII of England). The Prince arrived with such a large party that the President had to give up his own bed and sleep on a couch.

The Dred Scott Decision

But the political situation was getting worse. Two days after Buchanan's inauguration, the Supreme Court gave its historic decision in the case of the slave Dred Scott, who sued for his freedom because he had been taken to a nonslave territory. However, the court decided that Congress could not outlaw slavery in United States territories. Buchanan thought slavery was wrong, but unfortunately the Constitution then recognized it. He hoped the Dred Scott decision would calm the country. Instead, people in the North refused to accept the court's decision. Thus the North and South became more divided than ever.

South Carolina Secedes from the Union

The crisis came in December 1860. Abraham Lincoln had just been elected president, but he did not take office until March 1861. Until that time Buchanan was still president.

When the news of Lincoln's victory reached the South, the state of South Carolina seceded from the Union, declaring that it was no longer a part of the United States. By February 1861, six more southern states had broken away from the Union. The split in the nation that Buchanan feared had taken place.

In this crisis Buchanan wanted to keep the remaining slave states loyal to the Union. He said he would do nothing to provoke a war but he would try to protect federal property and enforce the laws in the South. He asked Congress to call a Constitutional Convention and to vote him the men and money needed to enforce the laws. But Congress refused.

President Buchanan received the first delegation from Japan to the United States in 1860.

DID YOU KNOW?

- *One of Buchanan's eyes was near-sighted, the other farsighted, resulting in his head being cocked to the left.*
- *The Pony Express was inaugurated during the Buchanan administration.*
- *He was related, through his sister, to the composer Stephen Foster.*
- *Buchanan tired of being president and refused to seek renomination.*

THE COMING OF WAR

On March 5, 1861, Buchanan left Washington and returned to Wheatland. He was happy to leave the presidency and hopeful that the president who followed him could maintain peace and restore the Union. But five weeks after Lincoln's inauguration, the South fired on Fort Sumter and the Civil War began.

Buchanan spent his last years writing a book about his term as president. He died at Wheatland on June 1, 1868, and is buried at Woodward Hill Cemetery in Lancaster.

Could Buchanan have prevented the Civil War? Historians do not agree. Some say that a stronger president, one with more imagination, could have prevented the outbreak of the conflict. Others argue that the Civil War was inevitable: it would have happened no matter who was president, and if Buchanan had used force against the southern states, the war would only have started earlier.

Buchanan tried to solve the problems of the United States by acting within its laws. He failed. Whether any man could have succeeded will never be known.

ABRAHAM LINCOLN

16th PRESIDENT OF THE UNITED STATES (1861–1865)

Born: *February 12, 1809, near Hodgenville, Kentucky*
Occupation: *Lawyer*
Party: *Republican*
Vice Presidents: *Hannibal Hamlin (1861–65);*
Andrew Johnson (1865)
Wife: *Mary Todd*
Died: *April 15, 1865, at Washington, D.C.*

The election of a Republican president in 1860 provoked the Southern states to secede from the Union and led to four tragic years of civil war. In this time of grave crisis it at first seemed unfortunate that the American people had not chosen a more experienced leader. Yet the tall, awkward man from Illinois who took the presidential oath proved equal to his enormous responsibilities. Gradually, as the war progressed, Abraham Lincoln placed the mark of his greatness upon American history. He guided the nation through the perils of war to peace and reunion. He struck the fatal blow at slavery. He reaffirmed the dignity of free people in language of simple beauty. Death came to him with dramatic violence before his work was done. But death only hastened his elevation to a place beside George Washington in the memory and gratitude of his countrymen.

BOYHOOD

Abraham Lincoln was born on February 12, 1809, in a crude log cabin near present-day Hodgenville, Kentucky. His parents, who already had a little daughter named Sarah, were hardworking, uneducated pioneers. They probably saw nothing unusual about their son, except that he grew unusually fast. Thomas Lincoln, Abraham's father, was a man of ordinary abilities whose ambition apparently did not extend beyond owning a good farm. Like many Western settlers, he tended to believe that there were better opportunities somewhere over the horizon. Of Abraham's mother, Nancy Hanks Lincoln, little is known. She and her two small children experienced the usual hardships and few pleasures of pioneer life. She must have left a mother's mark upon Abraham's character, but the exact nature of her influence is lost to history.

In December 1816, the Lincolns packed their belongings and migrated about 100 miles to southwestern Indiana. They spent that winter in a rough shelter with an open side. A forest full of wild game surrounded their lonely new home. Abraham later remembered shooting a turkey, watching for bears, and listening at night to the "panther's scream." In the spring, Abraham, now eight years old, began to help his father in the hard daily labor of pioneering. They had to clear the land of trees, plant crops, build a permanent cabin, and split rails for fences. Abraham became skillful in the use of the ax but apparently never cared much for hunting and fishing. He acquired no love for the life of a farmer. It seemed to be all heavy toil with small reward.

The saddest days of Lincoln's childhood came in 1818, when his mother died and was buried in the nearby forest. A year later Thomas Lincoln married Sarah Bush Johnston, a widow with three children of her own. Between the boy and his stepmother there grew a bond of deep affection, and she lived to see him become president.

Much of Lincoln's learning was the practical kind that boys picked up from their work and play in a backwoods community. Lincoln attended school, in his own words, "by littles"—that is, only occasionally and for just a few weeks at a time. But he soon knew more than either of his parents about reading, writing, and arithmetic. In each case, school was probably a "blab school." Pupils studied their lessons aloud, and the noise could be heard some distance away. Lincoln later said that his total schooling did not amount to more than one year. Yet he read whatever he could lay his hands on. At home there was the Bible, and he walked long distances to borrow books like *Robinson Crusoe, Aesop's Fables,* and Weems's *Life of Washington.* Lincoln not only educated himself but became a master of the English language.

YOUNG MAN IN ILLINOIS

In 1830 the Lincolns moved again, this time to Illinois. They traveled in ox-drawn wagons, with Abraham as one of the drivers, and built a cabin on the prairie near Decatur. Dissatisfied there, Thomas Lincoln moved a year later to Coles County. But this time his son did not go along. Now 22 years old—6 feet, 4 inches tall, thin yet physically strong—Abraham Lincoln still had no definite ambition. But he was ready to start life on his own.

When he was 19, Lincoln had made a trip to New Orleans as a hired hand on a Mississippi River flatboat. In the spring of 1831, he undertook a similar journey down the Mississippi. On his return he became a store-keeper in New Salem, Illinois, about 20 miles northwest of Springfield. His friendliness, honesty, and talent for story-telling soon made him a popular local figure. So he decided to enter politics and in March 1832, young Abe Lincoln announced his candidacy for the state legislature.

At this point the Black Hawk War, an Indian war, began in northern Illinois. Lincoln volunteered and served for three months, first as the elected captain of his own company, then as a private under other commanders. He engaged in no actual fighting with the Indians. Back home by July, he had only a few weeks for his political campaign. Election day brought defeat, but Lincoln was encouraged by the fact that he had run eighth in a field of 13 candidates. Next, he and a partner opened a store in New Salem. Lincoln also became the village postmaster. The store was a failure, however, and he took up surveying to earn a living and pay his debts. In 1834 the 24-year-old Lincoln ran again for the legislature. This time he won, and the voters later reelected him for three more terms.

SPRINGFIELD LAWYER

It was in 1834 that Lincoln began to study law. Here again he educated himself, reading borrowed lawbooks in his spare time. He passed the bar examination two years later. Early in 1837, with Lincoln playing an important part, the legislature voted to make Springfield the state capital. There he moved on April 15 and entered a law partnership with John T. Stuart, an established attorney and fellow legislator.

For the next 24 years, with one brief interruption, Lincoln practiced law in Springfield. He did not grow

Abraham Lincoln

16th president, 1861–65   Republican

1809 Born on February 12 in a log cabin in Hardin County, Kentucky.

1832 Living in New Salem, Illionis, worked odd jobs. Served 80 days in Illinois militia during Black Hawk War. Lost election to Illinois House of Representatives.

1834 Elected to first of four consecutive two-year terms to Illinois House; aligned with Whigs.

1837 Became partner in Springfield, Illinois, law practice.

1842 Married Mary Todd Lincoln on November 4. The couple would have four sons.

1847–49 Served one two-year term in the U.S. House of Representatives, then resumed law practice in Springfield.

1858 Running as a Republican, lost election to U.S. Senate. Debates with opponent Stephen A. Douglas gained national attention.

1860 Elected president on the Republican ticket.

1865 Shot by actor John Wilkes Booth at Ford's Theater in Washington, D.C., on April 14. Died early the next morning.

Highlights of Presidency

1861 On April 12, Confederate forces attacked Fort Sumter in Charleston, South Carolina, setting off the Civil War. Lincoln moved quickly to mobilize the Union by executive order.

1862 Five days after the Battle of Antietam, Lincoln announced on September 22 that all slaves in states still in rebellion would be freed in 100 days.

1863 On January 1, formally issued Emancipation Proclamation. In the Battle of Gettysburg in southern Pennsylvania in July, Union forces led by Gen. George C. Meade turned back Gen. Robert E. Lee and the Confederate army. Lee retreated to Virginia, marking a major turning point in the war. At the dedication of the Soldiers' National Cemetery, Lincoln delivered the Gettysburg Address on November 19.

1864 The advancing Union army of Gen. William T. Sherman captured Atlanta on September 2. Sherman continued his "March to the Sea," taking Savannah in December. In November, Lincoln was elected to a second term, defeating Gen. George B. McClellan.

1865 On April 9, General Lee and Gen. Ulysses S. Grant signed terms of Confederate surrender at Appomattox, Virginia.

After a broken engagement in 1840, Mary Todd married Abraham Lincoln in 1842. They had four sons.

President Lincoln was photographed in 1864 with his youngest son, Thomas, nicknamed Tad, who is 11 years old here.

wealthy but always earned a comfortable living. Fair and conscientious, he gave clients a feeling of confidence. Never very learned in the law, he nevertheless knew the fundamentals. His greatest asset in court was the ability to go directly to the heart of a matter. Long before the presidential election of 1860 he had become one of the most distinguished lawyers in Illinois.

In 1844 Lincoln began his lasting partnership with William H. Herndon. A rather strange and excitable man ten years younger than Lincoln, Herndon nevertheless proved to be an excellent choice. The two of them worked well together in both law and politics. Herndon's biography of his partner, written many years later, is one of the classics of Lincoln literature.

Lincoln's law practice took him regularly to other towns where courts were held. This travel on the legal circuit was arduous, but it enlarged his circle of friends and helped make him better known in politics.

HUSBAND AND FATHER

Lincoln's famous romance with Ann Rutledge is apparently just a legend. He knew Ann in New Salem and was undoubtedly saddened by her death in 1835. But there is no reliable evidence that they were ever in love with each other. He did court a young woman named Mary Owens. There was a lack of enthusiasm on both sides,

however, and she refused to marry him. At Springfield, Lincoln met Mary Todd, daughter of a prominent Kentucky family. She was a popular girl in local society—attractive, vivacious, and intelligent, but somewhat temperamental. Her short and rather plump figure contrasted sharply with Lincoln's lank frame when he acted as her escort. They became engaged in 1840, then broke apart when Lincoln went through a long period of doubt and melancholy. Reconciled after a time, they were married at last on November 4, 1842.

Mary Lincoln, although not always easy to live with, was a good and loyal wife who probably spurred her husband's ambition. Their marriage had its troubled moments, but on the whole they were happy together. In 1844 Lincoln bought a house, which still stands at Eighth and Jackson streets in Springfield. There the Lincolns lived until their departure for Washington in 1861. Four children, all boys, were born to them. Robert became a corporation executive and secretary of war under two presidents. Edward died in his fourth year. William died in the White House when he was 11. Thomas, nicknamed "Tad," survived his father but died in 1871 at the age of 18. Lincoln was a loving and indulgent parent, but his frequent absences from home for his law practice placed the upbringing of the boys largely in Mary's hands.

POLITICAL CAREER

In the legislature Lincoln became a loyal member of the Whig Party, whose most prominent national leaders were Henry Clay and Daniel Webster. Lincoln's major interest at this time was the promotion of better transportation facilities. He soon advanced to the front rank of Illinois Whigs and by 1842 had emerged as a candidate for Congress. Two other men claimed the party's nomination, however, and Lincoln had to wait his turn. Finally, in 1846, he was elected.

Lincoln's congressional term began in December 1847, when the Mexican War was nearing its conclusion. Soon after taking his seat, he joined the Whig attack upon the war policy of President James K. Polk. Lincoln also introduced a moderate bill for the gradual emancipation, or freeing, of slaves in the District of Columbia, but it got nowhere. On the whole, his two years as a congressman were undistinguished.

His criticism of the Mexican War was unpopular in Illinois, and Lincoln was not renominated for Congress. He then campaigned for Zachary Taylor, helping him win the presidential election of 1848. Offered the governorship of the Oregon Territory as a reward, Lincoln declined the appointment and resumed the practice of law in Springfield. His political career had apparently reached a dead end in 1849.

THE REPUBLICAN PARTY

Five years went by, and then in 1854 came a decisive turn of events. Senator Stephen A. Douglas of Illinois, a Democratic leader in Congress, secured passage of the Kansas–Nebraska Act. The measure created the two new federal territories of Kansas and Nebraska and permitted the people there to have slavery if they wanted it. This policy, which set aside the Missouri Compromise, was called "popular sovereignty." Throughout the North there were angry protests against the Kansas–Nebraska Act from many Democrats and from most Whigs, including Lincoln. He had long considered slavery morally wrong, yet he respected the constitutional rights of slaveholders. If slavery could just be prevented from expanding, Lincoln reasoned, it might eventually die away in the Southern states. To such hopes the Kansas–Nebraska Act was a serious blow.

Soon the opponents of slavery expansion began to form a political alliance. Lincoln became a leader of this "anti-Nebraska" movement in Illinois, and his supporters almost elected him to the United States Senate in 1855. A year later, with the Whig Party breaking up, he helped organize the various anti-Nebraska groups into the Republican Party of Illinois. At the Republican national convention in June 1856, Lincoln received strong support for the vice presidency, though he did not win the nomination. He campaigned vigorously for the new party's presidential candidate, John C. Frémont, but Frémont was defeated by James Buchanan, the Democratic candidate.

DID YOU KNOW?

- At 6 foot, 4 inches, Lincoln was the tallest president.
- Mrs. Lincoln's brother, half-brothers, and brothers-in-law fought in the Confederate Army.
- He was the only president to receive a patent, for a device for lifting boats over shoals.
- He was the first president to wear a beard.
- His son, Robert, who was in Washington when his father was killed, was also on the scene when Garfield was shot in 1881 and McKinley assassinated in 1901.
- A poll of historians named Lincoln the nation's greatest president; Washington was second.

In 1858 Illinois Republicans nominated Lincoln for the Senate seat held by Douglas. Lincoln responded with his famous "House Divided" speech, in which he said: "I believe this government cannot endure permanently half *slave* and half *free*." The high points of the exciting contest that followed were seven debates between the two candidates. Douglas clung to his doctrine of popular sovereignty. Lincoln insisted that slavery must be prohibited in Western territories. The election itself was very close, but Douglas emerged the winner.

ELECTED PRESIDENT

Defeat did not hurt Lincoln's growing prestige. The debates with Douglas had brought him national attention, and before long he was being mentioned as a presidential prospect. During the next year he gained further recognition by making speeches in many states. The climax of his efforts was an address delivered on February 27, 1860, at Cooper Institute in New York City. When the Republican national convention met at Chicago in May, Lincoln had more support than any other candidate except the favorite, William H. Seward of New York. Seward took the lead in the first round of balloting, but then Lincoln pulled almost even, and on the third ballot he was nominated for the presidency.

Meanwhile, the Democrats were split over the slavery issue. The Northern Democrats nominated Douglas. The Southerners chose John C. Breckinridge . Still another candidate, John Bell, was put forward by a remnant of the Whigs called the Constitutional Union Party. Thus Lincoln had three opponents in the race. Following the custom of the time, he did no active campaigning himself but directed strategy quietly from Springfield. Out of the South came ominous warnings that his election would mean the end of the Union. At the polls on November 6 only about 40 percent of the ballots were cast for Lincoln. But since most of them were concentrated in the heavily populated free states, he won a clear majority of the electoral votes. The Republican Party had elected its first president.

SECESSION AND CIVIL WAR

South Carolina promptly seceded from the Union, in December 1860. When efforts at compromise failed, six other Southern states followed its example. Together they formed the Confederate States of America. All this happened before Lincoln became president on March 4, 1861. In his inaugural address he pleaded for harmony and insisted that the Union could not be dissolved. He hoped for a peaceful solution but was prepared to risk war rather than see the nation permanently divided.

The critical spot was Fort Sumter in Charleston Harbor in South Carolina. This was one of the few places within the Confederacy still held by Federal troops. Lincoln, proceeding cautiously, planned to send supplies but not reinforcements to the garrison there. Early in the morning of April 12, however, Southerners opened fire on the fort and soon forced its surrender. Lincoln immediately proclaimed a blockade of the Confederacy and issued a call for volunteers to suppress the rebellion. This provoked the secession of four more Southern states. As spring gave way to summer both sides were preparing hastily for war.

THE WAR PRESIDENT

From the beginning, Lincoln understood the essential nature of the Civil War better than most of his generals. The Confederacy could gain independence merely by defending itself successfully. The Union forces, however, had to conquer the enemy in order to win. Most of the material advantages were with the North. It had greater manpower, wealth, and industrial strength. Lincoln's task was to mobilize Northern superiority and make it effective on the battlefield. He favored pressing forward on several fronts to prevent the Confederates from concentrating their defenses. He also believed that the primary aim of Union strategy should be the destruction of Southern armies rather than the capture of Southern cities like Richmond, Virginia. In the early part of the war, however, Lincoln was unable to find a general capable of maintaining an offensive against the great Confederate commander Robert E. Lee.

In this Mathew Brady photo, Lincoln and General George B. McClellan meet at the latter's field headquarters after the bloody Battle of Antietam on September 17, 1862.

The battle of Bull Run in July 1861, was only the first of many Union defeats and disappointments on the Virginia front. More successful in the west, Union forces captured New Orleans and were gaining control of the lower Mississippi. At the end of 1862, however, the war was obviously still far from over.

Although military affairs occupied much of his attention, Lincoln had many other presidential duties to perform. On the whole he was content to allow his cabinet members a free hand in the administration of their departments. He rarely sought to influence Congress and seldom used his veto power. Among the important pieces of legislation that he signed were the Homestead Act, which provided free land in the West to settlers; the Pacific Railway Act; and the National Banking Act.

EMANCIPATION

Despite his own strong antislavery feelings, Lincoln insisted at first that the purpose of the war was to save the Union, not to destroy slavery. But pressure from abolitionists, who demanded an immediate end to slavery, steadily increased, and the president decided that emancipation could be justified as a military measure to weaken the enemy. It would also make the Northern cause more noble in the eyes of the world. After announcing his intention in August 1862, Lincoln issued the famous Emancipation Proclamation on January 1, 1863.

Since it applied only to the areas still under Confederate control, the proclamation did not actually free very many slaves from bondage. Yet it was a symbol and a commitment that changed the nature of the war. After that date everyone knew that a Northern victory would mean the end of slavery. Emancipation became complete and final with the 13th Amendment to the Constitution. Approved by Congress at Lincoln's urging, it was not ratified by a sufficient number of states until after his death.

ENDLESS WAR

The responsibilities of his office and the mounting toll of battle casualties weighed heavily on Lincoln's spirit. For relaxation he swapped jokes, read books of humor, and visited the theater. In his more serious moments, however, he turned to Shakespeare and the Bible. Pondering the causes of the war, Lincoln came to believe that it was a divine punishment of all Americans for the sin of slavery. The bloodshed would not end, he decided, until peace suited God's purpose.

The turning point of the war came during the first days of July 1863. Lee's army, attempting a second invasion of the North, was defeated at the battle of Gettysburg in Pennsylvania. At the same time, General Ulysses S. Grant captured Vicksburg, the last important Confederate stronghold on the Mississippi River. Later that same year Lincoln helped dedicate the military cemetery at Gettysburg. His memorable address of only a few hundred words summoned the nation to complete the great

EXCERPTS FROM LINCOLN'S SPEECHES, LETTERS, AND OTHER WRITINGS

. . . [as] soon as I discover my opinions to be erroneous, I shall be ready to renounce them.

Lincoln's first political address, as candidate for the Illinois legislature, March 9, 1832

The legitimate object of government, is to do for a community of people, whatever they need to have done, but can not do, *at all*, or can not, *so well do*, for themselves . . . .

In all that the people can individually do as well for themselves, government ought not to interfere.

Fragment, probably 1850s

As a nation we began by declaring that "all men are created equal." We now practically read it "all men are created equal, except negroes." When the Know-Nothings get control, it will read "all men are created equal, except negroes, *and foreigners, and catholics*." When it comes to this I should prefer emigrating to some country where they make no pretence of loving liberty . . . .

Letter to Joshua Speed, August 24, 1855

I will say here . . . that I have no purpose directly or indirectly to interfere with the institution of slavery in the States where it exists. I believe I have no lawful right to do so . . . .

Lincoln-Douglas Debates, Ottawa, Illinois, August 21, 1858

. . . he who would *be* no slave, must consent to *have* no slave. Those who deny freedom to others, deserve it not for themselves, ...

Letter to Henry L. Pierce and others, April 6, 1859

In your hands, my dissatisfied fellow countrymen, and not in mine, is the momentous issue of civil war. . . . We are not enemies, but friends. We must not be enemies.

First Inaugural Address, March 4, 1861

With malice toward none; with charity for all; with firmness in the right, let us strive on to finish the work we are in; to bind up the nation's wounds; to care for him who shall have borne the battle, and for his widow, and his orphan—to do all which may achieve and cherish a just, and a lasting peace, among ourselves, and with all nations.

Second Inaugural Address, March 4, 1865

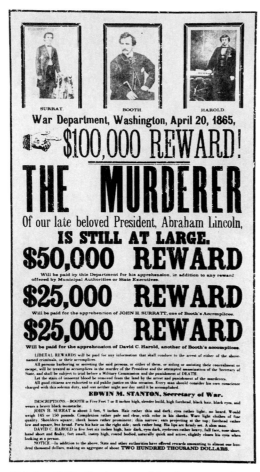

This handbill offered a reward for the capture of Lincoln's assassin, John Wilkes Booth.

Dedicated in 1922, the Lincoln Memorial in Washington, D.C., is visited by approximately 2.5 million people a year.

task in which so many men had given "the last full measure of devotion. . . ."

Early in 1864 Lincoln promoted Grant to the command of all Union armies. Grant then began the hard, bloody work of driving Lee back toward Richmond. Meanwhile, General William Tecumseh Sherman launched his famous "March on Georgia." When his troops occupied Atlanta in September 1864, the war entered its final phase.

Now the time for another presidential election had arrived. Lincoln, although opposed by some dissatisfied Republicans, won renomination without much trouble. The Democrats chose General George B. McClellan as their candidate, with a platform demanding immediate peace. For a time Lincoln despaired of victory, but Sherman's progress in Georgia helped his cause. Union soldiers voted overwhelmingly for Lincoln, and he was reelected.

THE LAST FULL MEASURE

As the Union armies pressed forward Lincoln gave increasing attention to the problem of restoring peace when victory was achieved. It must be done, he said in his second inaugural address, "With malice toward none; with charity for all. . . ." Desiring the speedy reconstruction of a united republic, he set forth a simple plan. Ten percent of the voters in a Confederate state, if they took an oath of allegiance to the United States, could organize a government and resume their old place in the federal union. By 1865 several states were putting the plan into operation. But strong opposition had developed in Congress. Many Republicans believed that such generosity was unrealistic. They felt that there should be more punishment for Southern traitors and more protection for freed slaves. The whole question of Reconstruction remained unsettled at the time of Lincoln's death.

On April 9, 1865, Lee surrendered to Grant at Appomattox Court House in Virginia. Throughout the North there were joyful celebrations. Five nights later, Lincoln attended a play at Ford's Theater in Washington. There he was shot by John Wilkes Booth, an actor devoted to the Confederate cause. The President never regained consciousness and died the next morning, April 15. Booth escaped to Virginia but was trapped and killed. While the news of the assassination sped across the country, Vice President Andrew Johnson hastily took the oath of office as president. The war had ended, but the war leader had fallen

A crowd of mourners gathered at each railway station as the funeral train rolled westward toward the Illinois prairies. In Springfield, his home, Abraham Lincoln was buried in Oak Ridge Cemetery. It was a tragic ending but also a triumphant one; for he left behind a nation reunited and a people set free. "Honest Abe," as he had come to be known, has become one of the most beloved presidents. His wife, who outlived her husband and three of her four sons, died in 1882.

ANDREW JOHNSON

17th PRESIDENT OF THE UNITED STATES (1865–1869)

Born: December 29, 1808, at Raleigh, North Carolina
Occupation: Tailor; Public Official
Party: Republican
Vice President: None
Wife: Eliza McCardle
Died: July 31, 1875, at Carter's Station, Tennessee

When President Abraham Lincoln was assassinated on April 14, 1865, just as the Civil War was ending, the man who had to fill his place and take up his unfinished work was Vice President Andrew Johnson of Tennessee. Without preparation or warning the new president was suddenly called upon to handle the most complicated problem the federal government had ever faced. This was the problem of how to deal with the defeated South and how to reunite a country that had been torn apart by four years of war.

Johnson made great efforts to carry out this task. But he was unable to reduce the bitterness between North and South and bring the country's affairs back to normal. He was a man of courage and good intentions. But he did not know how to take advice or how to work with other men, and his presidency was not a success.

EARLY YEARS

No American president ever began his life in greater poverty than Andrew Johnson. He was born on December 29, 1808, at Raleigh, North Carolina. His father, Jacob Johnson, was employed as a porter and handyman at the village inn. One winter day in 1811 Jacob rescued two local gentlemen from drowning in an icy river. But he himself died soon afterward from exhaustion and cold. His son Andrew was thus left fatherless at the age of three. The penniless widow, Polly, tried to support herself and her two boys, Andrew and William, by weaving cloth for the people of the neighborhood. But often there was no work for her, and more than one night Andrew went to bed hungry.

At 14 Andrew was sent to live with the village tailor, who taught him the trade of making coats and suits. The boy learned well and became a good workman, but before long he ran away from his master and went off to work for himself. In 1826, when he was 18, the entire family packed their belongings into a cart and started westward over the mountains. They settled in Greeneville, Tennessee. Andrew, who was full of ambition, started his own tailor shop there.

Andrew Johnson never went to school, but he had learned a little reading at the tailor's house in Raleigh. In Greeneville he married a village girl, Eliza McCardle, who taught him to write. His shop did a good business, and he bought property in the town. He became a leader of the young men of the neighborhood, who would often meet at the A. Johnson Tailor Shop to discuss politics and hold debates on public affairs.

POLITICAL CAREER

Johnson became a town alderman at 21, and a few years later he was elected mayor of Greeneville. At 27 he was elected to the state legislature. In 1842 the people elected him to Congress, where he served five terms. In 1852 he was elected governor of Tennessee. He became a U.S. Senator in 1856 and was still serving in the Senate at the outbreak of the Civil War.

Andrew Johnson

Andrew Johnson

17th president, 1865–69 Republican

1808 Born on December 29 in Raleigh, North Carolina

1827 Married Eliza McCardle on May 17. The Johnsons would have five children.

1835 Elected to the Tennessee state legislature for the first of three terms. Defeated in 1837 but elected in 1839 and 1841.

1843–53 Represented Tennessee's first district in the U.S. House of Representatives.

1853 Narrowly defeated the Whig candidate to become governor of Tennessee. Served two two-year terms.

1857–62 As a U.S. senator, he supported the Union.

1862–65 Was military governor of occupied Tennessee.

1864 Running with Abraham Lincoln on the National Union (Republican) ticket, the former Democrat was elected vice-president.

1865 Sworn in as president on April 15 following the assassination of President Lincoln.

1874 Five years after leaving the White House, and after several bids for office, elected again to U.S. Senate.

1875 Died on July 31 near Carter Station, Tennessee.

Highlights of Presidency

1865 On March 29, issued Amnesty Proclamation, pardoning all Confederates except those with property in excess of $20,000 and certain Confederate leaders. The 13th amendment, abolishing slavery, was proclaimed.

1866 Was engaged in an ongoing dispute with Congress over Reconstruction and the power of the president in Southern states.

1867 Over Johnson's continual vetoes, Congress passed its own series of Reconstruction laws, enforcing African-American suffrage and making ratification of the 14th amendment (granting citizenship to all persons born or naturalized in the United States) a condition for readmission to the Union. On March 30, the United States signed a treaty with Russia for the purchase of Alaska for $7,200,000.

1868 Ignoring the 1867 Tenure of Office Act, Johnson ordered the removal of Edwin M. Stanton as secretary of war in March. He later became the only president ever to be impeached by the House, but was acquitted in the Senate on May 26 by a one-vote margin. The 14th amendment was proclaimed on July 28.

Johnson thought of himself as a man of the common people, and he was a popular speaker among the simple mountain folk of east Tennessee. In a voice that could be heard for great distances, he would address them on the benefits of democracy and honest labor and on the evils of high taxes and government spending. Johnson often spoke of his own humble beginnings. He pointed to himself as an example of how a poor boy might rise to wealth and prominence through steady ambition and hard work. He thought that the government interfered in the daily lives of the people more than was necessary. His main idea on government was that there was too much of it.

SECESSION AND CIVIL WAR

The secession crisis of 1860–61 opened an entirely new chapter in Johnson's life. When Lincoln was elected president in 1860, the Southern states—including Johnson's own state of Tennessee—prepared to secede from the Union. Johnson, like nearly all Southerners, was loyal to slavery. But unlike most Southerners he was even more loyal to the Union. He was ready to sacrifice everything, even slavery, to prevent the Union from being broken up.

In the late winter and early spring of 1861, Johnson traveled all over his home state. He made speeches trying to persuade the people of Tennessee not to take their state out of the Union. Time after time he risked his life as he faced crowds of people who had once been his friends but were now his enemies, telling them that secession was treason. In self-defense he had to carry a loaded pistol everywhere, and more than once he was actually forced to use it. Johnson did not give up until the last hope of saving his state was gone. Tennessee finally seceded in June 1861, and joined the Confederacy. Though Johnson was now a man without a state, he stayed on in Washington, D.C., as the loyal senator from a disloyal state.

Early in 1862 the Union Army recaptured parts of Tennessee. President Lincoln, who had been deeply impressed with Andrew Johnson's courage, asked him to go back to Tennessee and act as military governor. Johnson instantly agreed, though he knew the risks were great. He stuck to his post at Nashville until nearly the end of the war, though there was hardly a week during that entire period when his life was not in danger. But his bravery had its reward. When Abraham Lincoln ran for reelection in 1864, the man he picked as his candidate for vice president was Andrew Johnson.

PRESIDENT

Lincoln and Johnson were inaugurated—Lincoln for a second time—on March 4, 1865. An incident took place that day that gave the public a very disagreeable first impression of the new vice president. Johnson had been suffering from typhoid fever, and his friends suggested that a little whiskey might do him some good. He took too

Tickets were sold for Johnson's 1868 impeachment trial, which lasted several months.

This drawing shows the vote being taken in the Senate impeachment trial of Andrew Johnson. He was declared not guilty by a one-vote margin.

much, and his inaugural speech was a drunken babble. Only six weeks later Abraham Lincoln was dead, and Andrew Johnson became the 17th President of the United States.

Reconstruction

With the war finally ended, a majority of the Northern people wanted to make sure that Southern loyalty to the Union would never again be in danger. The dispute over slavery had helped to bring on the war. The main results of the war had been the destruction of slavery and the preservation of the Union. The North now felt that the Southern states should give the newly freed Negroes the same protection and the same rights that were given to other citizens. This would be the clearest possible sign of Southern loyalty to the Union. Most Republican congressmen, however, felt that the Southern states would not take such steps without a certain amount of outside pressure. They believed that federal laws would have to be passed by Congress to "reconstruct" the South.

Johnson's failure to understand Northern feelings on this question of reconstruction led to the failure of his entire presidency. A strong believer in states' rights, Johnson felt that the South should be allowed to deal with its former slaves in its own way, without interference from the federal government. Johnson believed that he, and not Congress, should decide when the Southern states were ready for readmission to the Union. In his opinion they should be readmitted immediately. He insisted that Congress had no right to pass laws for the South when Southern representatives were not present to vote on them. Congress, on the other hand, was unwilling to readmit the Southern representatives until a full study could be made of conditions in the South.

These differences of opinion led to the bitterest quarrel that has ever occurred between a president and Congress. Matters were made worse when several Southern legislatures late in 1865 and early in 1866 passed state laws—known as Black Codes—that discriminated severely against Negroes.

Early in 1866 Congress passed the Freedmen's Bureau bill and the Civil Rights bill. These gave some federal protection to the Southern Negro. Johnson vetoed them both, though the Civil Rights bill was repassed over the president's veto. Later in the year another Freedmen's Bureau bill was successfully enacted. In the spring Congress approved the 14th Amendment to the Constitution. This amendment defined citizenship to include Negroes and entitled them to equal protection of the laws. It also stated that certain leaders of the former Confederate government could not hold public office until further notice. Johnson advised the Southern states not to ratify it (the amendment was not ratified until 1868). By the fall of 1866 the Union military commanders in the South were having great difficulty maintaining law and order.

All of these causes led finally to the Reconstruction Acts, passed by Congress in March 1867. They were vetoed by President Johnson but were repassed over his veto. These acts put the South under full military occupation, set up new state governments, and gave Negroes the right to vote and hold public office. Large numbers of Confederate leaders were forbidden either to vote or to hold office. Offices in the new state governments were filled by Northerners ("carpetbaggers"), former Southern Unionists ("scalawags"), and Negroes.

Impeachment

As a result of his stubborn opposition to Congress, Johnson came very close to being actually expelled from office. In 1867 Congress had enacted a law—the Tenure of Office Act—that forbade the president to remove certain officeholders without the approval of the Senate. Johnson had wanted to get rid of Secretary of War Edwin M. Stanton, because he thought Stanton was too friendly with leaders in Congress. Early in 1868 he dismissed Stanton. The House of Representatives thereupon impeached the president; that is, it accused him of breaking the law. In cases of impeachment, the Constitution provides that the Senate must hold a trial to decide the question of guilt. If found guilty, the accused must be removed from office. Johnson was judged not guilty by the bare margin of one vote. It was found that the Tenure of Office Act did not apply to cabinet members who were held over from a previous term. Stanton had been appointed by President Lincoln.

Alaska

The impeachment trial overshadowed almost all else in Johnson's term as president. But there were some foreign affairs activities worth noting. The Russian government, who had authorized colonization of Alaska in the 1700s and 1800s, was interested in selling its assets to the United States. The Russians feared losing Alaska to the British in the event of another war and were thus well disposed to the United States.

After the Civil War, the Secretary of state, William H. Seward, an expansionist who saw the region as having strategic importance, negotiated the purchase of Alaska in 1867. A treaty of cession was signed by Russia and the United States on March 30, 1867, and, after the treaty was ratified by the Senate, Alaska was formally transferred to

At the time this cartoon appeared, it read, "King Andy (Andrew Johnson) and his man Billy (William Seward) lay in a great stock of Russian ice in order to cool down the Congressional majority." Many were unhappy about acquiring Alaska from Russia.

the United States on October 18, 1867. The United States paid over $7,200,000 for Russia's rights in Alaska after a long and bitter debate in Congress.

During the early years of U.S. control, Alaska was called "Seward's Folly" because it was believed to be a vast expensive, and useless piece of land. The fur business had fallen off because of over-trapping, and the fishing industry was not seen as justification for this far-off acquisition. Later, in 1897-98, when gold was discovered in Klondike, Canada, another gold rush was touched off. Gold was discovered in 1899 in Nome, Alaska, and a variety of other Alaskan locations. Later, other valuable minerals and natural resources were found in the territory, and the population greatly increased. Alaska became the 49th state in 1959.

FINAL YEARS

President Johnson served out the rest of his term without further disturbance. With the inauguration of Ulysses S. Grant as president on March 4, 1869, Johnson returned to his home in Tennessee. For several years he tried without success to return to public office. Finally, in 1874, Johnson was once more elected a U.S. senator from Tennessee. He was able to attend only one session of the Senate. In July of that year, he suffered a stroke, and on July 31, 1875, he died at the age of 66. He is buried at Greeneville, Tennessee, with a copy of the Constitution beneath his head. His wife lived for one more year, and three of his five children were alive at the time of his death.

DID YOU KNOW?

- *Johnson was 18 and his wife was 16 when they married.*
- *He is the only president to serve in the Senate after his presidency.*
- *He was host to the first queen—Queen Emma of Hawaii—to visit the White House.*
- *A White House children's ball, attended by 400 children, was held to celebrate Johnson's 60th birthday.*
- *He was buried beneath a willow he had planted himself with a shoot taken from a tree at Napoleon's tomb.*

ULYSSES S. GRANT

18th PRESIDENT OF THE UNITED STATES (1869–1877)

Born: April 27, 1822, at Point Pleasant, Ohio
Occupation: Soldier
Party: Republican
Vice Presidents: Schuyler Colfax (1869-73); Henry Wilson (1873-75)
Wife: Julia Boggs Dent
Died: July 23, 1885, at Mount McGregor, New York

On February 16, 1862, during the Civil War, a Union soldier carried a message from his general to the battle-weary Confederate forces defending Fort Donelson in Tennessee. The Confederate commander had asked for terms upon which he could surrender the fort. The 39-year-old Union general, Ulysses S. Grant, replied that only "an unconditional and immediate surrender" would be accepted. This phrase, and the man who said it, at once captured the attention of the country. U. S. Grant became Unconditional Surrender Grant.

The surrender of Fort Donelson was an important victory for the North. For Grant it was also a great personal victory after years of failure. Within two years he would become commander of all the Union armies, and a few years later president of the United States.

EARLY YEARS

Grant was born on April 27, 1822, at Point Pleasant, Ohio, the eldest son of Jesse Root Grant and Hannah Simpson Grant. He was named Hiram Ulysses, but he was always called Ulysses. Ulysses loved horses. Almost as soon as

he could walk, he learned how to ride. By the time he was seven or eight years old he could handle a team of horses. Because he did not like working in his father's tannery, he did most of the work on the family farm, especially taking care of the animals. As a boy, he was thrifty, thoughtful, and hard-working, but not always too clever in business matters.

West Point. In 1839 Grant's father obtained an appointment for him to the U.S. Military Academy at West Point. The congressman who made the arrangements mistakenly referred to him as Ulysses Simpson Grant, and the name remained with him ever afterward.

At West Point his record as a student was only average, although he was good in mathematics and drawing. But he impressed everyone with his expert horsemanship. In 1843, Grant received his commission as a brevet second lieutenant. He did not like military life, however, and he expected to leave the Army after a few years of service to become a teacher of mathematics.

Early Military Career. Grant requested duty in the cavalry, but there were no openings. Instead, he was assigned to the 4th Infantry Regiment. He was in Texas when war with Mexico broke out in 1846.

Grant was not in sympathy with the aims of the Mexican War. He felt that the U.S. was not completely in the right and was bullying a smaller nation. However, as a soldier, he fought bravely in nearly all the major battles of the war and was promoted to first lieutenant.

Julia Dent Grant. As soon as the war ended in 1848, Grant asked for leave. In August 1848, he married Julia Dent, the sister of one of his classmates at West Point. Julia was to be a source of strength to Grant for the rest of his life. Grant had since given up the idea of teaching and had decided to stay in the Army for a time.

Julia Boggs Dent married U. S. Grant in 1848, when he was a young army lieutenant.

In 1852, Grant was ordered to the Pacific Coast. Because his pay as a lieutenant was so low, he could not afford to take his wife and young son with him. In 1853 he was promoted to captain. But even a captain's pay was too low to support his family in the West. Grant was lonely and homesick. According to army gossip, he began to drink, although there is no official record to support this. After quarreling with his commanding officer, Grant resigned from the Army in 1854.

Years of Failure. Grant settled with his family in Missouri, intending to become a farmer. He started a farm on land owned by his wife and labored for three years, but bad economic conditions and illness forced him to seek another form of livelihood. He then became a partner in a real estate agency, but his lack of business experience forced him to give that up too. He ran for the office of county engineer but was defeated.

In desperation, Grant took a job as a partner and clerk in a leather goods store operated by his two brothers in Galena, Illinois. But his civilian life soon was to be interrupted by war.

CIVIL WAR GENERAL

The growing troubles between the North and the South came to a head with the election of Abraham Lincoln to the presidency in 1860. In December 1860, South Carolina seceded from the Union and was soon followed by other Southern states who formed the Confederate States of America. On April 13, 1861, Fort Sumter fell. Two days later President Lincoln called for 75,000 volunteers for the Army. The Civil War had begun.

Grant offered his services to the Union and was commissioned colonel of the 21st Illinois Volunteer Regiment. In August 1861, Grant read in a newspaper that President Lincoln had made him a brigadier general.

Ulysses Simpson Grant

18th president, 1869–77   Republican

1822   Born on April 27 at Point Pleasant, Ohio.

1843   Graduated from West Point.

1846–48   Fought in Mexican War under Generals Zachary Taylor and Winfield Scott. Distinguished himself for bravery and was promoted to 1st lieutenant.

1848   Married Julia Dent on August 22. The couple would become the parents of four children.

1854   Resigned army commission and took up farming in Missouri.

1861   After outbreak of Civil War, named colonel of 21st Illinois Volunteers, then brigadier general.

1862   Took Forts Henry and Donelson, the first major Union victories in the war. Defeated at Shiloh.

1863   Forced Confederate surrender at Vicksburg, another major Union victory. Also won Battle of Chattanooga.

1864   Appointed lieutenant general and given command of all U.S. armies.

1865   Accepted surrender of Gen. Robert E. Lee at Appomattox.

1868   Elected president on the Republican ticket.

1885   Shortly after completing his two-volume *Personal Memoirs*, died of cancer at Mount McGregor, New York, on July 23.

Highlights of Presidency

1869   The first transcontinental railroad was completed.

1870   Ratification of 15th amendment, granting citizens the right to vote regardless of race, was proclaimed on March 30.

1872   Amnesty Act, restoring civil rights to citizens of the South, was enacted. Despite charges of widespread corruption in his administration, Grant won reelection, defeating Horace Greeley.

1873   Widespread bank failures set off panic. Depression lasted five years.

1875   Signed Specie Resumption Act, a "hard money" measure designed to contract the amount of paper currency in circulation. Civil Rights Act, giving equal rights to African Americans in public accommodations and jury duty, was passed.

1876   Hayes nominated for president by Republican Party, making Grant a "lame duck." Col. George Custer and his 7th Cavalry massacred at Little Big Horn, Montana.

Communications were so slow that he had received no notice of the promotion before.

Trial and Acclaim. Grant's first real battle in the Civil War took place at Belmont, Missouri. His troops drove the Confederate forces from their camp and de-

stroyed it. But the Southerners counterattacked with additional forces, and Grant had to retreat. It was a bitter lesson, but he learned from it. His next campaign led to the capture of Fort Donelson. The surrender of this important fort made Grant a hero in the North, and President Lincoln promoted him to major general of volunteers.

During the years of war that followed, Grant was both criticized and praised. After the costly battle of Shiloh, in which Union and Confederate losses totaled more than 20,000 men, Lincoln was asked to remove him from command. But the president refused, saying, "I can't spare this man—he fights." Actually, the Confederate forces were so beaten at Shiloh that they evacuated the vital fortified railroad center of Corinth, Mississippi, about a month later.

Union Army Commander. Grant repaid Lincoln's confidence by capturing the Confederate stronghold of Vicksburg, Mississippi, in 1863, giving the Union forces control of the Mississippi River. In 1864, Grant was promoted to the rank of lieutenant general and was given command of all the Union armies. He proceeded to hammer the Confederate forces in Virginia under General Robert E. Lee. It was a long, bloody campaign, for Lee was a great general. But the Southerners were greatly outnumbered, and on April 9, 1865, Lee surrendered to Grant at Appomattox Court House, Virginia.

A grateful U.S. Congress appointed Grant a full general. He was the first man to hold this rank since George Washington.

In 1864 Grant (above) was made a lieutenant general and appointed by President Lincoln to command all Union armies. Grant and his family (right) in an 1868 photograph, at the time of his nomination for president. From left to right are Mrs. Grant, U. S. Grant, Ellen (Nellie), youngest son Jesse Root, Ulysses Simpson, and eldest son Frederick Dent.

PRESIDENT

Because of Grant's great popularity, the Republicans nominated him for the presidency in 1868. Grant disliked politics and did not actively campaign, but he easily defeated the Democratic candidate, former New York governor Horatio Seymour. Grant won reelection in 1876, defeating Horace Greeley, a New York newspaper editor and publisher.

Political Scandals. Modest and unassuming, Grant tried to run the government the only way he knew—as a military operation. But his presidency was marked by scandal and corruption because he did not always choose the best men for political jobs. He was so honest himself that he found it hard to believe that anyone he trusted could betray him. Yet in one case Grant's own brother-in-law involved him in a financial scandal. His personal secretary also was implicated in one of the most notorious scandals, that of the Whiskey Ring, which sought to evade U.S. taxes in the manufacture of whiskey.

Achievements. At home, Grant supported the rights of the freed African Americans in the South. He opposed the recently-organized Ku Klux Klan (KKK), which sought through acts of terrorism to prevent blacks from voting. The most notable achievement of his administration, however, was the settlement of the *Alabama* claims dispute with Britain in 1872. The *Alabama* had been one of several Confederate warships built by Britain during the Civil War. The United States demanded compensation for damages done to the Union merchant marine by these ships and was awarded $15.5 million.

LATER YEARS

Upon leaving the White House in 1877, Grant and his wife and family, went on a two-year tour around the world. After returning to the United States, Grant was supported by some Republicans to run for the presidency again, in 1880, but he lost the nomination to James A. Garfield.

DID YOU KNOW?

- *Witness to some of the bloodiest battles in history, Grant could not stomach the sight of animal blood—rare steak nauseated him.*

- *While president, he was once arrested for driving his horses too fast and was fined $20.*

- *He signed the act that created Yellowstone National Park.*

- *Grant said he only knew two tunes: "One was 'Yankee Doodle' and the other wasn't."*

- *He smoked 20 cigars a day, which probably caused the throat cancer that resulted in his death.*

Grant's last years were difficult ones. He lost the little money he had through bad investments. Penniless, he began to write his memoirs to provide for his family. Congress restored him to the retired list, with his old rank of general, to help relieve his financial burdens. But by this time Grant had little time left, for he was dying of cancer. Although in great pain, he continued to work on his memoirs, which earned him $450,000. He finished them about one week before he died on July 23, 1885, at Mount McGregor, New York. His body and that of his wife, Julia, lie in a magnificent tomb, built especially for him, in New York City.

Grant's presidency in the years following the Civil War came at a time of political turmoil for the United States. Although he was not successful as president, he remains one of the great military leaders of American history. His personal qualities were more than admirable, and it is for these he should be remembered.

The remains of Ulysses and Julia Grant lie in an imposing tomb in New York City. Dedicated in 1897, Grant's Tomb was built with money donated by thousands of ordinary citizens. Over the entrance to the building are carved the words spoken by Grant at the end of the Civil War: "Let us have peace."

RUTHERFORD B. HAYES

19th PRESIDENT OF THE UNITED STATES (1877–1881)

Born: October 4, 1822, at Delaware, Ohio
Occupation: Lawyer
Party: Republican
Vice President: William A. Wheeler
Wife: Lucy Ware Webb
Died: January 17, 1893, at Fremont, Ohio

Rutherford Birchard Hayes had to wait four months after election day in 1876 to learn that he had been elected president of the United States. In the election of 1876, 20 electoral votes were in dispute. Both Republicans and Democrats claimed these votes, which would decide the election. In the end a compromise was reached, and the disputed votes and the presidency went to Hayes.

EARLY YEARS

Hayes was born on October 4, 1822, in Delaware, Ohio. His parents, Rutherford and Sophia (Birchard) Hayes, had come to Ohio from Vermont in 1817. Both were descended from old New England families of Scotch and English origin. Rutherford was their fifth child, but only he and his sister Fanny lived to adulthood.

His father, a storekeeper and farmer, died before Rutherford was born, and the young boy grew up as the only man in the household. His mother and sister idolized him. Fanny had great ambitions for her brother. She dreamed of him as another Henry Clay or Daniel Webster. A steadying influence was Rutherford's uncle, Sardis

Birchard, who acted as a sort of second father and helped pay for his education.

Young Hayes was educated at home and in private schools, and in 1838 entered Kenyon College in Gambier, Ohio. He was an earnest student and a very serious young man. At the age of 18 he wrote: "I am determined from henceforth to use what ever means I have to acquire a character distinguished for energy, firmness and perseverance." He graduated in 1842 and, largely because of his sister's influence, decided to become a lawyer. He studied in a law office in Columbus, Ohio, and then went to Harvard Law School. After graduating from Harvard in 1845, he was admitted to the bar in Ohio.

YOUNG LAWYER

Hayes started his law practice in Lower Sandusky (later Fremont), Ohio, where his uncle lived. Opportunities in the community were few, and he did not do well. In 1850 he moved to Cincinnati, Ohio, and opened a law office there. At first Hayes had few clients. He was so poor that he slept in his office to save money. But his practice grew steadily until he became quite successful. In 1852 he married his childhood sweetheart, Lucy Webb. Their marriage was a long and happy one. They had seven sons and one daughter, but three sons died in childhood.

Hayes took an active part in the community affairs of Cincinnati, including its political life. Originally a Whig, he became a Republican after the Whig Party broke up in the 1850s. His political career began in 1858 when he was elected city solicitor.

CIVIL WAR

Like most men in the 1850s, Hayes hoped that civil war could be avoided. However, when war broke out in 1861, he felt that it was his duty to fight. "I would prefer to go

RBHayes

Rutherford Birchard Hayes

19th president, 1877–81 Republican

1822 Born on October 4 at Delaware, Ohio.

1842 Earned B.A. degree from Kenyon College in Gambier, Ohio.

1845 Graduated from Harvard Law School, admitted to the Ohio bar and began practice of law.

1852 Married Lucy Ware Webb on December 30. The couple would have seven sons and one daughter.

1856 Helped found Ohio Republican Party.

1858 Elected city solicitor of Cincinnati; served four years.

1861 At the outbreak of the Civil War, appointed major in 23rd Ohio Volunteer Infantry. Wounded several times in combat and eventually rose to major general.

1864 Still in service, nominated and elected to U.S. House of Representatives, representing Ohio's second district. Won reelection in 1866. Supported Radical Reconstruction and impeachment of President Andrew Johnson.

1867 Nominated for governor of Ohio, resigned from Congress, and won election. Reelected in 1869. As governor, worked for social reforms.

1872 Ran for Congress and lost. Returned to private life.

1875 At urging of Ohio Republicans, ran for governor on a "sound money" platform. Election victory made him a national figure.

1876 Won Republican presidential nomination on the seventh ballot. In the most controversial presidential election in U.S. history, appeared to lose to Samuel J. Tilden. The outcome was disputed, and a special electoral commission was appointed. On March 2, 1877, it declared Hayes the winner.

1893 Died at Spiegel Grove, the family estate in Fremont, Ohio, on January 17.

Highlights of Presidency

1877 Within two months of taking office, withdrew federal troops from the South—ending the era of Reconstruction—and appointed a former Confederate, David M. Key, to be postmaster general. Called out federal troops to quell violent, widespread railroad strikes.

1878 Favoring a "hard-money" policy (specie backing of paper currency), vetoed Bland-Allison Silver Purchase Bill; Congress overrode veto.

1880 Kept pledge to serve only one term.

This 1877 photo shows Mrs. Lucy Hayes and two of the Hayes children, Fanny (right) and Scott (in dark suit), with a friend.

into [the war]," he wrote, "if I knew that I was to die or be killed in the course of it than to live through and after it without taking any part in it." He fought in the Union Army throughout the Civil War and was wounded several times.

CONGRESSMAN

In 1864, while still in the Army, Hayes was nominated for Congress. He was elected even though he was away and could not campaign. But he refused to leave the Army to take his seat until the fighting was over in 1865. In Congress he voted with his party on all important issues. He won reelection in 1866, but his career in Congress was cut short in 1867 when he was elected governor of Ohio.

GOVERNOR

As governor, Hayes earned a reputation as an able and courageous administrator. His two terms of office were characterized by thrift and honesty. He chose officials on the basis of ability, appointing Democrats as well as Republicans. This was unusual at a time when, under the spoils system, political jobs were awarded for party loyalty rather than ability.

In 1872 a split occurred in the Republican Party. Reform Republicans were dissatisfied with the record of President Ulysses S. Grant's administration. They left the party and supported Horace Greeley, a New York newspaper publisher, for the presidency. Though Hayes had much in common with these men, he remained loyal to the regular party. He ran for Congress again but was defeated because of the party split.

Hayes retired to private life—for good, he thought. He lived at Spiegel Grove, the estate in Fremont he had inherited from his uncle, devoting himself to law, real estate, and the development of public libraries. However, after Democratic victories in Ohio in 1873 and 1874, Republican leaders persuaded him to run for governor again in 1876. His victory, and a distinguished third term as governor, added to his political reputation and put him in the running for the Republican presidential nomination.

THE DISPUTED ELECTION OF 1876

The leading contender for the Republican nomination in 1876 was Senator James G. Blaine of Maine. However, the opposition of reform Republicans to Blaine was strong enough to block his nomination, and on the seventh ballot the nomination went to Hayes.

Hayes' Democratic opponent was Samuel J. Tilden, governor of New York. All signs indicated a Democratic victory. The scandals of President Grant's administration had hurt the Republican Party. Many people were dissatisfied with the Republican policy of Reconstruction, under which the South had been governed since the end of the Civil War. Finally, a depression that had begun in 1873 gave no sign of letting up. Hayes himself did not believe that he would win. "I feel that defeat will be a great relief," he wrote. "The great responsibility overwhelms me."

When the election results were in, Tilden had a majority of the popular votes. But more important were 20 disputed electoral votes: 19 from South Carolina, Louisiana, and Florida, and one from Oregon. Without these 20 votes Tilden had 184 electoral votes—one short of the necessary majority. Hayes had 165 votes. To break the deadlock, which had begun to alarm the country, Congress established an Electoral Commission in January, 1877. It was composed of five members of the House of Representatives, five senators, and five justices of the Supreme Court. On March 2, 1877, the commission awarded the disputed votes to Hayes, giving him 185 electoral votes. He was inaugurated in a public ceremony on March 5, 1877. William A. Wheeler of New York became the vice president.

Behind the decision to give the election to Hayes was a compromise between Republicans and southern Democrats. In return for the southerners' support the Republicans promised to withdraw the remaining federal troops from the South. Also, they promised to grant federal funds for improvements in the South, including aid for the Texas and Pacific Railroad, and to give southerners positions in the new administration.

PRESIDENT

Hayes was not involved in the "stolen election." Nevertheless, he abided by the terms of the compromise. As a result, federal military occupation and Republican political control of the South came to an end. Reconstruction was over, and the southern states were self-governing again. On the race issue and the South, Hayes attempted to carry out his policy "to wipe out the color line, to abol-

This 1877 cartoon by Thomas Nast (above) dramatized the controversy over the disputed Tilden-Hayes election. President Hayes (below) assumes a typical pose of the time.

DID YOU KNOW?

- *Hayes was the first president to graduate from law school.*

- *He participated in 50 Civil War engagements and was wounded four times.*

- *Mrs. Hayes was known as "Lemonade Lucy" because she refused to serve alcohol in the White House.*

- *He signed the act that permitted women to plead before the Supreme Court.*

- *The first White House telephone was installed, by Alexander Graham Bell himself, during the Hayes administration.*

- *Hayes and his wife conducted the first Easter egg roll on the White House lawn.*

ish sectionalism, to end the war and bring peace." He named a southerner—David M. Key from Tennessee—as postmaster general. His own party assailed him for this and the South repudiated his initiative. By 1878 a solidly Democratic South emerged.

The depression of 1873 continued through the first years of Hayes' administration. It caused considerable hardship, particularly among farmers and workers, who in 1878 united to form the Greenback Labor Party. The Greenbacks believed that an expansion of the currency would end the hard times. They wanted an increase in the amount of paper money (known as greenbacks) and silver coins in circulation. Thus they opposed the Resumption Act of 1875, which permitted the reduction of greenbacks in circulation, and supported the Bland Bill of 1877, which provided for unlimited coinage of silver.

Most businessmen did not share these views. Neither did Hayes. He believed that an expansion of the currency would do more harm than good, and he successfully opposed efforts to repeal the Resumption Act. The Bland Bill was modified so that it provided for limited, instead of unlimited, coinage of silver. Even so, Hayes vetoed the resulting Bland–Allison Bill, though Congress passed it over his veto in 1878.

Labor Trouble

Labor unrest erupted into violence in 1877 when railroad workers went out on a nationwide strike. Riots took place throughout the East and Middle West. Strikers fought battles with state militia and destroyed railroad property. Several state governors appealed to Hayes for federal troops. Hayes hesitated, but he believed that it was his duty to send soldiers in, and did so. Only once before, during Andrew Jackson's administration, had a president taken such action in a dispute between a private industry and its workers.

Another labor problem had to do with Chinese immigration. Workers on the West Coast resented competition from Chinese immigrants. In 1879 Congress tried to restrict Chinese immigration. However, a treaty between the United States and China had given the Chinese unlimited immigration rights. Accordingly, Hayes vetoed the measure even though it was popular in the West. In 1880 a new treaty was drawn up that gave the United States the right to regulate, limit, or even suspend Chinese immigration.

The latter part of Hayes's administration saw an improvement in economic conditions. As prosperity began to return, much of the earlier social unrest died down.

Reform

Hayes had come into office with the pledge of "thorough, radical, complete" reform in government. But his hopes for a civil service based on a merit system rather than the spoils system posed a tremendous task. For the spoils system had become a part of American political life. Hayes's efforts at reform angered leaders in his own party. His clash with Senator Roscoe Conkling, New York Republican leader, was long and bitter. (A Conkling follower whom Hayes removed from office was Chester A. Arthur, later 21st president but then collector of customs for New York.) And by the end of his term of office, Hayes was a president without a party.

RETIREMENT

Hayes had said earlier that he would not seek a second term as president. After James A. Garfield was inaugurated in 1881, Hayes retired from politics for good and devoted his remaining years to philanthropic activities, especially prison reform and international peace. He died on January 17, 1893, at Spiegel Grove, where both he and his wife are buried.

As president, Hayes's most important accomplishment was ending Reconstruction in the South. But he could also point to other important achievements. He reasserted the power and the independence of the presidency, which had been weakened by the impeachment of President Andrew Johnson and by the dependence of President Grant on Congressional leaders. Political opposition prevented actual civil service reform legislation. Yet Hayes succeeded in keeping the issue before the people and thereby helped pave the way for future reform.

JAMES A. GARFIELD

20th PRESIDENT OF THE UNITED STATES (1881)

Born: November 19, 1831, at Orange Township,
  Cuyahoga County, Ohio
Occupation: Teacher, Public Official
Party: Republican
Vice President: Chester A. Arthur
Wife: Lucretia Rudolph
Died: September 19, 1881, at Elberon, New Jersey

James Abram Garfield served as president of the United States for only a little more than six months. On July 2, 1881, less than four months after taking office, Garfield was shot as he waited for a train at a Washington, D.C., railroad station. He died on September 19, 1881, becoming the fourth U.S. president to die while in office. It was a tragic end to the career of a man who had risen from a boyhood of poverty to be come a college president, state senator, Civil War general, U.S. congressman, and finally president of the United States.

EARLY YEARS AND CAREER

Garfield was born in a log cabin in what was then the pioneer town of Orange, Ohio, on November 19, 1831. He was the youngest of five children of Abram and Eliza Ballou Garfield. When James was two years old, his father died, and James's mother was left with the difficult task of raising the young children in the rough frontier country. Life was hard for them, and all the children had to work. They were able to go to school for only three months each year, but James showed an early interest in learning and read a great deal.

When James was 16, he left home and went to Cleveland, where he hoped to get work as a sailor on the ships that sailed the Great Lakes. He could not get a job on the big sailing ships, but he was hired to work on a canalboat carrying cargo between Cleveland and Pittsburgh. One of his jobs was leading the horses that pulled the boat along the canal. Garfield later recalled that he fell into the canal 14 times before he learned how to handle the team of horses. His career as a sailor ended when he became ill with malaria and had to return home.

When he recovered, young Garfield decided that he wanted to be a teacher. He attended Geauga Seminary, in Chester, Ohio, and then studied at Western Reserve Eclectic Institute (now Hiram College), in Hiram, Ohio. To support himself, he taught school and did odd jobs. When he was 23, he left Ohio to complete his education at Williams College, in Williamstown, Massachusetts. He graduated from Williams with honors in 1856.

College President and Ohio Senator. After graduation, Garfield returned to teach at the Eclectic Institute. A year later, when he was only 26, he became president of the school. While he was teaching, Garfield studied law. He became interested in politics and spoke out about the problems facing the country at the time. The 1850s were years of bitter dispute between the North and South over the question of slavery and states' rights. Garfield joined the Republican Party, which had been founded in 1854 in opposition to the expansion of slavery into the western territories of the United States. In 1859 he was elected to the Ohio Senate. There he denounced slavery and called for the preservation of the Union.

Lucretia Rudolph Garfield. These were busy years for Garfield. Besides his other duties, he was a preacher in the Disciples of Christ Church. In 1858 he married Lucretia Rudolph. "Crete," as he called her, had been his childhood friend, a fellow student, and pupil. The Garfields had seven children in all, of whom two died as infants.

Civil War Service. When the Civil War broke out in 1861, Garfield volunteered for the Union Army. He received a commission as lieutenant colonel and helped raise a regiment of Ohio volunteers. Many of the men were his old students. Garfield had no military experience, but he was willing to learn. He studied military textbooks, and he drilled his men with a textbook in one hand.

In December 1861, Garfield was given command of a brigade in Kentucky. He was ordered to attack the Confederate forces under General Humphrey Marshall,

Garfield (below, left) volunteered for the Union Army when the Civil War broke out in 1861. Lucretia Rudolph (below, right) married Garfield in 1858. She was his childhood friend and student. Garfield (bottom)is pictured in 1870 with his youngest daughter Mary.

James Abram Garfield

20th president, 1881 Republican

1831 Born on November 19 near Cleveland, Ohio.

1848 Struck out on own and worked on a canal boat. Six weeks later, returned home seriously ill. Decided to get an education.

1851 Entered Western Reserve Eclectic Institute (later Hiram College). Studied and taught for three years.

1856 Graduated from Williams College. Returned to Hiram College, where he taught ancient languages and literature for five years, served as principal, and became a lay preacher for the Disciples of Christ.

1858 Married Lucretia Rudolph on November 11. Seven children would be born to the Garfields.

1859 Admitted to the Ohio bar. Elected to the state Senate.

1861 Volunteered for Union army after outbreak of Civil War. Made colonel of 42nd Ohio Volunteer Infantry. Appointed major general for gallantry at Battle of Chickamauga.

1862 While still in the service, elected to U.S. House of Representatives as a radical Republican.

1863 Resigned military commission to take seat in Congress. A member of the House until 1880, he supported Lincoln policies and Radical Reconstruction. Favored specie payment as opposed to paper money. Served as Republican minority leader from 1876.

1876 Was a member of electoral commission for disputed Hayes-Tilden presidential election, voted consistently for Hayes on a strict party line.

1880 Elected to U.S. Senate in January. At the Republican National Convention in May, nominated for president as compromise choice on 36th ballot. Chester A. Arthur chosen as running mate to placate disgruntled "Stalwart" faction. Despite party split, won narrow victory over Democrat Winfield S. Hancock in November election.

1881 Died on September 19 at Elberon, New Jersey, eleven weeks after taking an assassin's bullet.

Highlights of Presidency

1881 Inaugurated on March 4 as 20th president of the United States, age 49. Shot on July 12 while entering a Washington railroad station by Charles J. Guiteau, a disappointed office-seeker in the new administration. Guiteau shouted: "I am a 'Stalwart' and Arthur is president now."

an experienced soldier. At the battle of Middle Creek he defeated Marshall and forced him to retreat from Kentucky. It was not a great victory, but it was welcome news in the North, for up to this time the Union Army had won few victories. Garfield was promoted to brigadier general and fought at the bloody battle of Shiloh in Tennessee.

While his military reputation was growing Garfield became ill and had to leave the field. But he was soon active again as chief of staff to General William S. Rosecrans. He fought at Chickamauga in Georgia and for his courage and leadership was promoted to major general.

CONGRESSMAN

In 1862, while still in the Army, Garfield was elected to the U.S. House of Representatives. He remained in the Army until December 1863, when he resigned his commission and took his seat in Congress.

Garfield served in the House of Representatives for 17 years, including a period as House minority leader. He was particularly interested in matters affecting the freed blacks in the South and in education.

The Crédit Mobilier Scandal. In 1872, during the administration of President Ulysses S. Grant, Garfield became involved in the scandal of the Crédit Mobilier, a railroad construction company. Garfield and other politicians, including former Vice President Schuyler Colfax, were accused of having taken bribes from the company in exchange for political favors. Garfield denied the charge, which was never proved. But some Republicans demanded that he resign from Congress. Garfield, however, made a tour through the villages of his Ohio district, defending his conduct to the satisfaction of voters.

A political cartoon of Garfield, referring to the Crédit Mobilier scandal, appeared during the 1880 presidential campaign.

Garfield was inaugurated as president on March 4, 1881, but died a little more than six months later from an assassin's bullets.

Compromise Candidate. In 1880, Garfield was elected to the U.S. Senate. Before he could take his seat, however, he unexpectedly won the Republican presidential nomination.

In 1880 the Republicans met in Chicago to pick a candidate for president to succeed Rutherford B. Hayes. The two great rivals for the nomination were former President Grant and Senator James G. Blaine of Maine. Grant was backed by a group of Republicans known as the Stalwarts, led by Senator Roscoe Conkling of New York. Blaine was supported by a group called the Half-Breeds.

At the Chicago convention the Grant and Blaine forces were deadlocked. Finally Blaine decided to give his support to Garfield, who had impressed the delegates with his speeches. On the 36th ballot, Garfield was nominated as the candidate for president. Chester A. Arthur, a Conkling supporter, received the nomination for vice president.

During the election campaign, the old Crédit Mobilier scandal came back to haunt Garfield. The number 329 (he was charged with having received $329 from the company) was carried on posters, painted on walls and windows, and printed in newspaper headlines by his opponents. The election was very close. Garfield beat his Democratic opponent, General Winfield Scott Hancock, by fewer than 10,000 popular votes. But he received 369 electoral votes to Hancock's 155. The Republican compromise candidate had won.

This illustration shows the events of July 2, 1881, when President Garfield was shot while waiting for a train to take him from Washington, D.C., to a speaking engagement. Secretary of State James G. Blaine, accompanying the president, pointed out the assassin, Charles J. Guiteau, who was tried and hanged in 1882. Garfield died on September 19, 1881, at a summer resort in New Jersey.

PRESIDENT

A Divided Party. Garfield began his administration as the head of a divided party. He had offended the powerful Senator Conkling by appointing Blaine, a Half-Breed, to the post of secretary of state. Other Half-Breeds were given important government jobs, while the Stalwarts generally received only minor posts. Their dispute became worse when Garfield appointed William H. Robertson, Conkling's worst political enemy, collector of customs for New York.

At the time, a more serious situation faced the president. Certain post office officials were accused of cheating the government on western mail routes. These were the so-called Star Route frauds. The men were brought to trial. But before the case could continue, the nation was shocked by the news that President Garfield had been shot.

The Assassination. On the morning of July 2, 1881, Garfield, accompanied by Secretary of State Blaine, was preparing to leave Washington to visit Williams College. As they waited at the Washington railroad station, a man approached Garfield from behind and shot him twice. The man, Charles J. Guiteau, was a Stalwart who had been refused a government post.

Garfield was nursed at the White House and then at a summer resort cottage at Elberon, New Jersey, where his family was staying. He died at Elberon and was buried in Cleveland, Ohio. Vice President Chester A. Arthur succeeded to the presidency. Guiteau was arrested and tried for murder. He was convicted and hanged in 1882, even though many people thought he was insane.

AN AROUSED NATION

Garfield's friends collected a large sum of money to help the president's widow and her five children. One of their sons, James R. Garfield, later became secretary of the interior under President Theodore Roosevelt. A second son, Harry A. Garfield, became president of Williams College.

Garfield became president at a time when there was a great need for reform in politics. Although his tragic death cut short a promising political career, it aroused the nation to the necessity for such reform.

DID YOU KNOW?

- *The last of seven presidents born in a log cabin, Garfield weighed 10 pounds at birth.*

- *On election day, November 2, 1880, he was at the same time a member of the House, Senator-elect, and President-elect.*

- *His mother was the first president's mother to attend her son's inauguration.*

- *After Garfield's shooting, repeated probing for the bullet with non-sterile instruments resulted in blood poisoning which eventually killed him.*

CHESTER ALAN ARTHUR

21st PRESIDENT OF THE UNITED STATES (1881–1885)

Born: *October 5, 1829, at North Fairfield, Vermont*
Occupation: *Lawyer*
Party: *Republican*
Vice President: *None*
Wife: *Ellen Lewis Herndon*
Died: *November 18, 1886, in New York, New York*

EARLY YEARS

Chester Alan Arthur was born October 5, 1829, in North Fairfield, Vermont. He was the oldest son in a family of seven children. His father, William Arthur, was a Baptist minister.

The Arthur family moved about a great deal. The Reverend William Arthur was a man of strong beliefs and did not hesitate to speak his mind to his congregations. As a result, he did not stay in one place very long. At the age of 15, Chester entered Union College, in Schenectady, New York. He helped pay for his college expenses by teaching school during vacations. He studied hard and, in 1848, graduated with honors. Arthur then studied law. But he continued to teach to support himself until 1853, when he went to New York City to begin his career as a lawyer.

The future president first gained prominence when he became involved in the slavery question that was soon to lead to civil war. William Arthur had been opposed to slavery, and Chester shared his father's feelings. He sympathized with the plight of black slaves and took part in two important cases in their defense. In one his law firm gained freedom for eight blacks accused of being runaway slaves.

The other case dealt with the problem of segregation. It arose when a women named Lizzie Jennings was not allowed to ride on a streetcar in New York City because she was black. Arthur won $500 for her in damages. And the court decision stated that blacks had the same right to ride on New York streetcars as anyone else.

POLITICAL CAREER

Like most lawyers of the time, Arthur also took part in politics. In 1860 he helped organize the New York State Republican Party, and he supported its candidate for gov-

O n July 2, 1881, President James A. Garfield was shot in the back by an insane man. For two months the president lay between life and death. On September 19, Garfield died, and early the next morning Vice President Chester Alan Arthur became the new president of the United States.

Arthur was a handsome man. Tall and broad-shouldered, he impressed people with his dignified bearing and elegant manners. He was courteous and friendly.

But many people considered the handsome vice president unfit to be president. Arthur had long been associated with the spoils system. Under this system government jobs were awarded for service to a political party, whether the candidates were honest and able or not. In fact, the man who killed President Garfield explained that he did so because he had been refused a government job. People were alarmed that Arthur, a product of the spoils system, had become president.

Arthur's administration, however, proved to be quite different than his country expected. It was marked by honesty and by the replacement of the spoils system with the present Civil Service system based on merit.

Chester A. Arthur (signature)

Chester Alan Arthur

21st president, 1881–85 Republican

1829 Born on October 5 in Fairfield, Vermont.

1848 Graduated from Union College in Schenectady, New York. Took up private law studies and teaching.

1854 Admitted to the bar after receiving training in a New York city law office.

1856 Formed law firm in New York City. Gradually became known as a leading New York attorney.

1859 Married Ellen Lewis Herndon on October 25. The Arthurs would become the parents of three children.

1861 After outbreak of Civil War, became inspector general and quartermaster of New York, responsible for furnishing supplies to large numbers of troops.

1863 Returned to private law practice.

1871 Appointed by President Ulysses Grant as collector for the Port of New York.

1878 After a year-long federal investigation of the New York Customs House for political patronage and mismanagement, Arthur was removed from the position of collector by President Rutherford B. Hayes. The action created a rift in the Republican Party.

1880 As a member of the party's "Stalwart" faction, supported Grant at Republican National Convention in May. When the convention settled on James Garfield as a compromise candidate, Arthur was nominated as vice president to placate "Stalwarts." Garfield-Arthur ticket narrowly won November election.

1881 On September 20, took oath as 21st president, one day after the death of President Garfield.

1886 Died in New York City on November 18.

Highlights of Presidency

1882 Vetoed the Chinese Exclusion Bill as well as a "pork barrel" appropriation for river and harbor improvement. Was overridden by Congress on both measures.

1883 The Pendleton Civil Service Act, a major reform of federal civil service, was signed into law on January 16. Tariff reform legislation and the Edmunds Anti-Polygamy Bill, aimed at the Mormons in Utah, also passed.

1884 With major railroads reaching the Pacific Coast, westward settlement came into full swing. Defeated for Republican presidential nomination by James G. Blaine.

ernor. As a reward the governor made Arthur engineer in chief and then quartermaster general of New York State. During the Civil War, Arthur's position was very important, for all Union Army volunteers were equipped by the state before they were sent on to the Army. Arthur proved skillful and honest in providing thousands of New York soldiers with food, shelter, guns, tents, and other equipment.

COLLECTOR OF NEW YORK

Arthur's work for the Republican Party brought him to the attention of Senator Roscoe Conkling, the political boss of New York State. Arthur became Conkling's lieutenant and worked with him to win the election of Ulysses S. Grant in 1868. For his help President Grant in 1871 appointed Arthur collector of customs for the port of New York.

The collector was in charge of the New York Custom House, which received most of the customs duties of the United States. He also had the power to distribute more than 1,000 jobs. Under the spoils system these jobs went to faithful Republicans. They were expected to work for the party as well as for the Custom House. In the years that Arthur held the position, he simply followed the old system, although he himself remained an honest and able administrator.

But many people were becoming angry about the inefficiency of the spoils system. They wanted a merit system, under which officeholders would be chosen on the basis of ability. In 1877 Rutherford B. Hayes, a believer in the merit system, became president. Hayes ordered an in-

This newspaper cartoon of the 1880s shows President Arthur turning his back on his old crony, New York state boss Roscoe Conkling. The woman represents the Republican Party.

- *Nicknamed "Elegant Arthur," he at one time owned 80 pairs of trousers and changed clothes several times a day.*

- *He enjoyed walking at night and seldom went to bed before 2 A.M.*

- *Arthur had 24 wagonloads of old furniture and junk removed from the White House before moving in.*

- *A man-about-town, he entertained lavishly and often, and enjoyed going to nightclubs.*

- *"I may be President of the United States but my private life is my own damned business," Arthur told a temperance group that called on him at the White House.*

- *He destroyed all of his personal papers before his death.*

and independent voters if he acted simply as a tool of Boss Conkling.

Arthur therefore determined not to let his administration be disgraced by the spoils system. He also tried earnestly to deal with some of the serious political problems the nation faced. But he was not so successful as he wished because he never had the full support of Congress.

For many years the Senate and the House of Representatives had gained power at the expense of weak presidents. Even such a strong personality as Abraham Lincoln had trouble with Congress. And his successors—Johnson, Grant, and Hayes—had let themselves be dominated by powerful Congressional leaders. Arthur was especially defenseless. He had become president by accident, and he did not command the support of any strong group in Congress.

Furthermore, Congress was itself divided. Both the Democratic and Republican parties were split into warring groups like the Stalwarts and the Half-Breeds. Some questions, such as the tariff (the tax on goods imported into the country), also divided the legislators. Other issues, such as the currency, set farmers, laborers, and manufacturers fighting one another.

Most important of all, the country was expanding and growing rich. Many people thought only of what they could get for themselves. Their representatives did

After President Garfield was assassinated in 1881, Chester Arthur was inaugurated as the 21st president at his home in New York City.

vestigation of the New York Custom House, and in 1878 Arthur was dismissed from his post. The conflict caused a deep split in the Republican Party. The supporters of the old system became known as Stalwarts. The reformers were called Half-Breeds.

VICE PRESIDENT

In 1880 the Republicans who met to pick a new candidate for president were still bitterly divided. The delegates voted 36 times before they agreed on a candidate whom no one had expected—James A. Garfield, a Half-Breed. However, Senator Conkling was Garfield's political enemy. And to gain the support of the Stalwarts, the Garfield men nominated Arthur for the vice presidency. The Republicans won in a close election. Ten months later Garfield was dead, and Arthur became the 21st president of the United States.

PRESIDENT

As president, Arthur surprised both his friends and enemies. Arthur wished to make a good record for himself and was eager to be renominated and reelected. He knew that he would never gain the support of reform not vote according to what was best for the nation as a whole. Instead they voted for laws that would gain the most for their supporters. Under such conditions it was difficult even for an able president to work out a good national policy. Arthur tried his best. But his achievements were limited.

The Pendleton Act and the Merit System

Before Arthur took office, it became known that some postal officials had collected money illegally in arranging mail routes. They were brought to trial in the famous Star Route cases. They were never convicted, but the trial made many more Americans aware of the evils of the spoils system.

With President Arthur's support, Congress now tried to introduce the merit system. In 1883, Arthur signed a law that helped take thousands of government jobs out of politics. This was the Pendleton Civil Service Act. It required candidates for many government jobs to pass tests before they could be accepted. Men who qualified were protected against being dismissed for political reasons. The Pendleton Act was the beginning of the present United States Civil Service.

Too Much Money

During the 1880s the United States had an unusual problem: there was too much money in the treasury. In one year the government collected $80,000,000 more than it spent. This kept money out of circulation, hurt business, and caused prices to fall. Arthur wanted to solve the problem by lowering the tariff. Congress, however, refused to go along. It preferred to spend the money on a "pork-barrel" bill. This was a law that authorized federal funds to be spent on river and harbor improvements. Such a law won votes for the congressmen and senators of the favored states. Arthur rejected the bill even though he knew that this would make him unpopular. But Congress passed it over his veto, and the tariff problem was not solved during Arthur's term in office.

Chinese Exclusion

Congress also passed the Chinese Exclusion Act of 1882 against the president's wishes. Its aim was to prevent Chinese from immigrating to the United States. Arthur opposed the bill because it violated a treaty between China and the United States. His opposition forced Congress to rewrite the law so that it had fewer harsh restrictions against the Chinese.

The Geneva Convention

The first Geneva Convention, which provided for the humane treatment of the wounded, prisoners of war, and civilians in time of war, was signed in 1864. Representatives of 16 countries pledged to respect the neutrality of civilians and of medical personnel and hospital ships bearing the emblem of the Red Cross. The American Red Cross was founded in 1881 by Clara Barton. In 1882, the U.S. Senate ratified the Geneva Convention.

PERSONAL LIFE

In 1859 Arthur had married Ellen Lewis Herndon, the daughter of a Virginia naval officer. Mrs. Arthur died in 1880, before her husband became president. Each day President Arthur honored her by placing fresh flowers in front of her picture.

The president's favorite sport was fishing. He was considered one of the best salmon fishermen in the country. Arthur was also fond of good food and companionship. He enjoyed the dinners to which he was invited and hated to leave. Since none of the guests could politely leave before the president, the dinners sometimes lasted until midnight.

Arthur liked elegant surroundings, and he had the White House completely redecorated. He installed new plumbing, a new bathroom, and the first elevator in the White House. His sister, who acted as hostess, helped him make it Washington's social center.

REPUBLICAN REJECTION

In 1884 the Republicans did not renominate Arthur for president. The Half-Breed reformers were still not satisfied with him, and his old Stalwart friends, of course, were now against him. James G. Blaine was nominated and later lost the election to Democrat Grover Cleveland.

Arthur returned to his old law practice. But his health was failing. On November 18, 1886, at the age of 56, he died at his home in New York City. He suffered from Bright's disease and was buried in Albany, New York.

Chester Arthur was an honest and courageous president. But the political situation of his times did not permit him to deal successfully with the country's great problems. The greatest achievement of his administration was the Pendleton Civil Service Act. However, he will be best remembered as the spoils system politician who became president by accident, and who proved himself a better man than anyone expected.

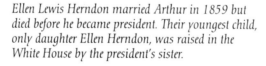

Ellen Lewis Herndon married Arthur in 1859 but died before he became president. Their youngest child, only daughter Ellen Herndon, was raised in the White House by the president's sister.

GROVER CLEVELAND

22nd and 24th PRESIDENT OF THE UNITED STATES (1885–1889, 1893–1897)

Born: *March 18, 1839, at Caldwell, New Jersey*
Occupation: *Lawyer*
Party: *Democrat*
Vice Presidents: *Thomas A. Hendricks (1885-89);
  Adlai E. Stevenson (1893-97)*
Wife: *Frances Folsom*
Died: *June 24, 1908, at Princeton, New Jersey*

Grover Cleveland was one man, but he is counted as two presidents. In 1884, Cleveland was elected the 22nd president. He ran again in 1888 but lost to Benjamin Harrison, who became the 23rd president. However, in the election of 1892, Cleveland came back to defeat Harrison. A question then arose: Was Cleveland the 24th president—or was he still the 22nd? The usually accepted answer is that he was both.

BOYHOOD

Stephen Grover Cleveland was born on March 18, 1837, in Caldwell, New Jersey. He was the fifth of nine children. His father, the Reverend Richard Falley Cleveland, was minister of the Presbyterian church in Caldwell. When Grover was four, the family moved to Fayetteville, New York. Here Cleveland lived until he was 13.

Though he was named Stephen Grover, he was always called Grover. He was chubby and round-faced, with blue eyes and sandy hair. By the time he was 13, "Grove" could outswim and out-wrestle most of the other boys of his age. He learned to fish, and that remained his favorite sport all his life.

In his early years, Grover attended school in a one-room, one-teacher schoolhouse. However, in 1850 the family moved to Clinton, New York, where Grover attended the Liberal Institute. He was a good student, but more because he worked hard than because he was unusually bright. Generally, his childhood was not much different from that of most American boys of his time, although as a minister's son he probably had to attend church more often than most. Like most boys, he sometimes got into mischief. There are stories about Grover's rigging up a device to ring the school bell at midnight, and helping to carry off garden gates on Halloween.

The Clevelands had a large family but not very much money. So when he was 14, Grover went to work as a clerk in a store at Fayetteville at a salary of $50 a year. Here he learned something about bookkeeping, and here, too, his true character began to show. The clerks in the Fayetteville stores often entertained each other at ham-and-eggs suppers by filching the refreshments from the stores. Cleveland refused to attend any party unless everything was paid for. This made enemies of some of the clerks. But it was the only honest thing to do, and he was brave enough to do it.

EARLY CAREER

In 1853, when Grover was 16, his father died suddenly. Grover had hoped to go to college to study law, but now, with four young children for Mrs. Cleveland to take care of, there was no money for college. One of his older brothers was a teacher at a school for the blind in New York City, and Grover got a job there as an assistant instructor. But after a year in the school, he made up his mind to go someplace where a young man's chances were better. He decided on the city of Cleveland, Ohio.

Grover Cleveland

22nd and 24th president, 1885–89, 1893–97 Democrat

1837 Born on March 18 in Caldwell, New Jersey.

1841 Family moved to Fayetteville, New York. Spent his boyhood there and in nearby Clinton.

1853 After father's death, moved to Buffalo, New York. Worked for an uncle and later as a law clerk.

1859 Admitted to the bar and entered law practice.

1863–65 Was assistant district attorney of Erie County, New York.

1871–73 Served as sheriff of Erie County.

1881 Elected mayor of Buffalo.

1882 Backed by reform Democrats, elected governor of New York.

1884 Nominated for president at Democratic National Convention. Narrowly defeated James G. Blaine in November.

1886 Married Frances Folsom in a White House ceremony on June 2. The couple would have five children.

1888 Lost election for second term to Benjamin Harrison, despite garnering a larger popular vote. After leaving office, practiced law in New York City.

1892 Elected a second time to the presidency, defeating Harrison.

1908 Died on July 24 in Princeton, New Jersey.

Highlights of Presidency

1886 Dedicated the Statue of Liberty in New York Harbor on October 28.

1887 Interstate Commerce Act, the first major federal program to regulate railroads and private business, was adopted. Tenure of Office Act was repealed.

1893 Financial panic began, leading to a four-year depression. Sherman Silver Purchase Act of 1890 was repealed.

1894 Jacob S. Coxey led march on Washington of 500 unemployed Midwesterners. "Coxey's Army" demanded unemployment relief. In July, President Cleveland called out federal troops to quell Pullman strike rioting in Chicago. To keep U.S. mails moving, trains ran under military guard.

1895 In support of Monroe Doctrine, Cleveland received Congressional authorization to appoint commission to resolve border dispute between Venezuela and British Guiana.

1896 Lost Democratic presidential nomination to William Jennings Bryan.

On the way he stopped to visit an uncle who had a fine herd of dairy cattle near Buffalo, New York. His uncle made Grover an offer. If he would stay and help him, he would pay Grover $50 and would also try to find him a permanent job as clerk in a lawyer's office. Cleveland accepted the offer, and his real career began in Buffalo.

LAW AND POLITICS

At that time there were few regular law schools. Most young men gained their training for the bar by working as clerks for lawyers and studying law in their offices. Cleveland worked and studied hard. Less than ten years after he came to Buffalo, he had not only been admitted to the bar but had also been made assistant district attorney for Erie County.

Cleveland's record of honesty and fairness in the district attorney's office led to his election as sheriff of Erie County. And in 1881, when the city government had become so corrupt that it disgusted many voters, the Democrats nominated Cleveland for mayor. As mayor he threw out the dishonest politicians and their friends and broke up their deals ruthlessly. This made Cleveland many enemies, but honest men liked him.

Then in 1882 the reform Democrats nominated the young mayor of Buffalo for governor of New York, and he was elected. As governor, Cleveland followed the same course of strict honesty and was hated equally by dishonest Democrats and dishonest Republicans.

Cleveland was the perfect presidential candidate for the Democrats in 1884. In that year the country was rocked by scandals in Washington, and the Republican candidate, James G. Blaine, had been involved in some of them. The Democrats had not elected a president since James Buchanan in 1856. It was plainly good politics for them to name a man famous for his honesty. The speaker who seconded Cleveland's nomination explained, "We love him most for the enemies he has made."

The campaign was dirty. The Democrats tried to prove that Blaine was a thief, which he was not. And the Republicans, since they could not attack Cleveland's honesty, tried to prove that he was immoral and a Confederate sympathizer. But many reform Republicans, called Mugwumps, disliked Blaine. They deserted their party and supported Cleveland. Near the end of the campaign, one of Blaine's friends called the Democrats the party of "Rum, Romanism and Rebellion." This so offended the Irish Catholics in New York that many of them voted for Cleveland. By carrying New York he won a majority of the electoral votes, though he beat Blaine by only a small number of popular votes.

FIRST TERM

In winning the presidency Cleveland also won a great deal of trouble. The Democrats had elected a majority in the House of Representatives. But the Senate remained Republican, and was not inclined to do anything that would help a Democratic president. More than that, after

Frances Folsom (above) married Cleveland in 1886 at the White House. Photograph shows Cleveland (below) some time during his second presidency.

24 years out of office the Democrats naturally wanted to put their own men in every federal job. Some of the party leaders recommended men who were useful to them but not fit for the job. Cleveland refused to appoint such men, which made the leaders furious.

One of the most difficult issues that faced Cleveland was the long-unsolved problem of the tariff (the tax on goods imported into the United States). The high tariff was causing an unhealthy surplus of money in the treasury as well as high prices on some products. Though Cleveland asked Congress to reduce the tariff, the tariff bill that resulted was a failure.

Another problem was the flood of pension bills for Union veterans of the Civil War that Congress sent to the president for his signature. Many of the pension claims were false. Although it angered the veterans, Cleveland vetoed many of the bills.

The one bit of really good fortune that came to Cleveland during this term was his marriage, on June 2, 1886, to Frances Folsom, daughter of one of his former law partners. The wedding ceremony was performed in the White House, the only time a president has been married there.

DEFEAT

In the election of 1888 the Republicans nominated Benjamin Harrison, a grandson of President William Henry Harrison. Cleveland seemed likely to win. But just before the election, the British minister in Washington, D.C., made the mistake of writing a letter stating that the British government hoped to see Cleveland reelected. This was regarded as foreign interference in American affairs. It so infuriated many anti-British people that Cleveland lost New York and with it the electoral vote, even though he got 95,000 more popular votes than Harrison.

Cleveland retired to New York, where he spent four years contentedly practicing law and going fishing with friends. He would have been satisfied to stay there the rest of his life, but the party needed him. Harrison got into trouble with Republican leaders. And by 1892 it was fairly plain that Cleveland, but probably no other Democrat, could beat him. So Cleveland was nominated for the presidency again. This time he received over 350,000 more votes than Harrison and won easily.

SECOND TERM

Cleveland had hardly taken office when the great business panic of 1893 broke and was followed by a long depression. Cleveland called a special session of Congress and asked for repeal of the Sherman Silver Purchase Act of 1890. Under this act the government was required to buy a set amount of silver each month and coin it into money. This caused a drain on the gold supply in the treasury. Cleveland favored a "hard," or gold, currency and felt that silver money would cause wild inflation. The repeal of the Silver Purchase Act antagonized many western Democrats—silver mine owners and farmers who favored silver. It caused a split in the Democratic Party that was to lead to its defeat in the election of 1896.

There were other problems, too. During the campaign Cleveland had promised to lower the tariff. However, conservative Democrats combined with the Republicans to pass the Wilson–Gorman Tariff in 1894, which was so bad that Cleveland called it "party perfidy and party dishonor." During the Pullman Strike that same year, Cleveland sent in federal soldiers to break up railroad strikers in Chicago, although the governor of Illinois, J. P. Altgeld, protested they were not needed. So the President was out of favor with his own party because of the silver question, the tariff, and his use of federal troops over states' rights.

Foreign Affairs

During President Harrison's administration American sugar planters in Hawaii had staged a revolution against the native king. A treaty to annex the islands had been sent to the Senate. But Cleveland felt that the United States had taken advantage of a weak country and withdrew the treaty.

A revolution also broke out in Cuba, which was then a Spanish colony, and some Americans tried to help the Cubans. Since this was against international law, Cleveland stopped them.

A more serious dispute arose in 1895 between Venezuela and Great Britain over the boundary of British

- *While sheriff of Oneida County, New York, Cleveland was also the public executioner and personally hanged two murderers.*

- *Drafted for service during the Civil War, he paid a substitute to take his place since he was the sole support for his family.*

- *In his first term Cleveland vetoed 414 bills, more than double the 204 vetoes cast by all previous presidents.*

- *He is acknowledged to be the hardest-working president.*

- *His daughter, Esther, was the only president's child born in the White House.*

A cartoon shows President Cleveland as a missionary, trying to convert congressmen ("Indians") to his policies.

IN DARKEST CONGRESS.

Guiana. When Great Britain extended its claims into Venezuelan territory, Cleveland told the British that their action was a violation of the Monroe Doctrine. He did so in such blunt terms that there was almost a declaration of war.

In each case Cleveland did what he believed was the honest thing, but in each case he angered some powerful group in his own party. So in 1896 the Democrats turned away from Cleveland and chose as their candidate William Jennings Bryan, who was defeated by Republican William McKinley.

Cleveland retired to Princeton, New Jersey, where he lived until his death on June 24, 1908. His wife lived until 1947 and four of his five children lived long lives.

For a time Cleveland was ignored by politicians and almost forgotten by the public. But as the years passed, men began to realize how often his decisions, though unpopular, were wise and right. Slowly it became clear that even when he was mistaken it was an honest mistake. He asked no favors. At the height of the panic of 1893, doctors told Cleveland that he had cancer of the mouth. He went secretly on board a ship, where an operation was performed. He had recovered and was back at work before the country learned that he had been ill.

Grover Cleveland is not considered one of the great presidents in American history, but for courage, honesty, and patriotism he has never been surpassed.

23rd PRESIDENT OF THE UNITED STATES (1889–1893)

Born: *August 20, 1833, at North Bend, Ohio*
Occupation: *Lawyer*
Party: *Republican*
Vice President: *Levi P. Morton*
Wives: *Caroline Lavinia Scott; Mary Scott Lord Dimmick*
Died: *March 13, 1901, at Indianapolis, Indiana*

Law, Marriage, and Politics. After graduation, Harrison studied law and opened a law practice in Indianapolis, Indiana. In 1853 he had married his Farmer's College sweetheart, Caroline Lavinia Scott. They had two children, Russell and Mary. A third child died at birth. A devout Presbyterian, Harrison taught Sunday school and became an elder of the church.

Considering his family background, it is not surprising that Harrison went into politics. His family were Whigs, traditional opponents of the Democrats. But the Whig Party was breaking up, partly because of the issue of slavery, which divided the country. Harrison joined the Republican Party, a newly formed anti-slavery party, and was elected or appointed to several political posts.

Civil War Service. The outbreak of the Civil War in 1861 interrupted Harrison's promising political career. He helped raise the 70th Indiana Infantry and commanded the regiment as a colonel. Although he had no military training, Harrison became an excellent officer. He served in Kentucky and took part in General William T. Sherman's march to Atlanta. He was a fearless soldier and took good care of his men, who called him "Little Ben," although his insistence on strict discipline made him unpopular. When the war ended in 1865, he held the brevet (honorary) rank of brigadier general.

"Grandfather's hat fits Ben," sang the Republicans in the presidential election campaign of 1888. "Ben" was Benjamin Harrison, whose grandfather William Henry Harrison had been ninth president of the United States. In response, Democratic cartoonists drew pictures of a little man in a huge hat—for Harrison was only 5 feet 6 inches tall. Whether the hat fit him or not, Harrison soon got a chance to wear it. He was elected 23rd president and became the second Harrison to live in the White House.

EARLY YEARS

Harrison was born on his family's large farm at North Bend, near Cincinnati, Ohio, on August 20, 1833. He was the second son of John Scott Harrison and Elizabeth Ramsey Irwin Harrison. The Harrisons had 14 children in all, two of whom were adopted.

Young Ben attended the log-cabin school that his father built for his children. At the age of 14 he entered Farmer's College near Cincinnati. After three years he transferred to Miami University at Oxford, Ohio. There he won a reputation for public speaking and in 1852 graduated fourth in his class.

RETURN TO POLITICS

Senator. Harrison returned to his law practice, his church work, and politics. He soon became one of Indiana's leading lawyers. With success came wealth and social and political prominence. In 1876 he ran for governor of Indiana. The Democrats called him "Kid Gloves Harrison" and said he was "cold as an iceberg." Harrison's chilly, reserved personality was always a political handicap. His opponent, a farmer, won the election.

Benjamin Harrison

23rd president, 1889–93 Republican

1833 Born on August 20 in North Bend, Ohio, the grandson of William Henry Harrison, 9th president of the United States.

1852 Graduated from Miami University in Oxford, Ohio.

1853 Married Caroline Lavinia Scott on October 20. The couple would have a son and a daughter.

1854 Admitted to the bar and established law practice in Indianapolis.

1857 Ran successfully for city attorney of Indianapolis.

1860 Elected reporter of Indiana supreme court; re-elected twice.

1862 After the outbreak of the Civil War, raised the 70th Indiana Volunteer Regiment. By 1865, had risen to rank of brigadier general.

1876 Lost election for governorship of Indiana.

1877 Became Republican Party leader in Indiana.

1880 Elected to U.S. Senate.

1888 Defeated Grover Cleveland in November presidential race despite having fewer popular votes.

1896 Married Mary Lord Dimmick on April 6. A daughter, Elizabeth, was born in 1897. (The first Mrs. Harrison had died in 1892.)

1897 Published *This Country of Ours*, a series of essays on how the federal government works.

1899 Acted as senior counsel for Venezuela in dispute with Great Britain over boundary with British Guiana.

1901 Died on March 13 in Indianapolis.

Highlights of Presidency

1889 The first Pan American Conference, encouraging cooperation between the United States and Latin America, was held in Washington.

1890 Four major bills were signed into law: Sherman Antitrust Act, outlawing trusts and monopolies that hinder trade; Sherman Silver Purchase Act, increasing amount of silver that could be coined; McKinley Tariff Act, setting duties at record high levels; and Dependent Pension Act, benefiting Civil War veterans. Battle of Wounded Knee, last major conflict between Indians and U.S. troops, was fought on December 29.

1892 Defeated for reelection by Grover Cleveland. Did not campaign because of wife's illness.

Nevertheless, Harrison remained the "favorite son" of Indiana Republicans. President James A. Garfield offered him a post in his cabinet, but soon after, in 1881, Harrison was elected to the U.S. Senate.

In the Senate, Harrison supported civil service reform, a high tariff (a tariff is a tax on imported goods), a strong Navy, and federal regulation of the railroads. In 1887 he ran for reelection but was narrowly defeated

The Election of 1888. When James G. Blaine of Maine, the leading figure in the Republican Party, declined to seek the presidential nomination in 1888, Harrison was chosen as the Republican candidate. Levi Morton, a New York banker, was nominated for vice president. The Democratic candidate was President Grover Cleveland, running for reelection.

The chief issue of the campaign was the tariff. The Democrats wanted a low tariff or free trade (no tariff at all). The Republicans said that this would ruin business.

During the 1888 presidential election campaign, Democrats pictured Republican Benjamin Harrison as too small to wear his grandfather's hat. Harrison's grandfather, William Henry Harrison, had been elected president in 1840.

Benjamin Harrison was born on his family's 600-acre farm at North Bend, Ohio, in 1833. He lived there until he left home at age 14 to attend college.

They wanted a high tariff, to protect American industries against foreign competition.

In the election, Cleveland received nearly 100,000 more popular votes than Harrison. But Harrison won the presidency by 233 electoral votes to Cleveland's 168.

PRESIDENT

Legislation. The Republicans controlled Congress as well as the presidency, and in 1890, they passed four important pieces of legislation.

For Civil War veterans of the Union Army, most of whom had voted for the Republican Party, Congress passed the Dependent Pension Act. It provided a pension for any disabled veteran, even if his disability had not been caused by the war.

For businessmen, who had contributed heavily to Republican campaign funds, Congress passed the McKinley Tariff. (It was named for Congressman, later president, William McKinley.) The McKinley Tariff raised tariffs to record highs. It also raised prices and the cost of living.

Between 1889 and 1890 six new states entered the Union—North Dakota, South Dakota, Montana, Washington, Idaho, and Wyoming. It is interesting to note that Wyoming was the first state to grant women the right to vote, in 1890. Four of these were mining states. For farmers, who wanted "cheaper" money, and silver-mine owners, Congress passed the Sherman Silver Purchase Act. Under this act the government bought almost all the silver mined in the country and increased the amount of silver coined for money.

To help small businessmen and consumers, Congress passed the Sherman Antitrust Act, which was designed to regulate monopolies and prices. The act was not vigorously enforced, however, until Theodore Roosevelt's administration, more than ten years later.

Harrison had promised civil service reform. However, politicians were hungry for jobs, so the spoils system of awarding government jobs for party loyalty continued to flourish.

Foreign Affairs. During Harrison's term of office the United States began to show greater interest in international affairs, especially in Latin America and the Pacific. The first Pan American Conference took place in Washington, D.C., from 1889 to 1890. All Latin American countries except Santo Domingo (now the Dominican Republic) were present. The Conference organized the Pan American Union to promote goodwill and cooperation among the American nations.

The United States, along with Germany and Britain, established a protectorate over the Samoan Islands in the Pacific. A dispute with Britain and Canada over seal hunting in the Bering Sea was successfully settled. So, too, were disputes with Italy and Chile.

Early in 1893, Americans in Hawaii led a revolt against the native ruler, Queen Liliuokalani. They set up a temporary government and asked the United States to

- *An excellent extemporaneous speaker, Harrison once made 140 completely different speeches in 30 days.*

- *Mrs. Caroline Harrison set up the first White House Christmas tree.*

- *The wearing of kid gloves to protect his hands from skin infection is said to have cost him the working-class vote. It did earn him the nickname of "Kid Gloves" Harrison.*

- *When the Harrisons moved into the White House, it was in such a dilapidated state that plans were made to build a new mansion elsewhere in Washington.*

- *His last daughter, Elizabeth, was younger than his four grandchildren.*

Harrison met his first wife, Caroline Lavinia Scott (left), while in college. She died in 1892, near the end of his term in the presidency. He remarried in 1896, three years after leaving office. His second wife was Mary Scott Lord Dimmick (right), a widow.

annex the islands. Harrison sent a treaty of annexation to Congress. But his term of office ended before the Senate acted on the treaty, and it was later withdrawn.

Defeat. Harrison ran against Cleveland again in the election of 1892. Harrison's chances were not good. The McKinley Tariff and the heavy federal spending were very unpopular. Government handling of strikes had angered workers. Western farmers were discontented enough to form their own party—the Populist Party—and run their own candidate, James B. Weaver. The illness of Mrs.

Harrison (she died two weeks before the election) also limited Harrison's campaigning.

Cleveland won the election, receiving 277 electoral votes to Harrison's 145. Weaver, the Populist candidate, received 22 electoral votes and more than one million popular votes.

END OF AN ERA

The 1890s marked the end of the Gilded Age and the beginning of the Progressive Era. The 20 years preceding Harrison's term was a time of vigorous, exploitative individualism. Despite widespread suffering by industrial workers, southern sharecroppers, displaced American Indians, and other groups, a mood of optimism possessed the U.S. Ambitious and imaginative capitalists ranged the continent looking for new opportunities. The country's industrial base grew rapidly. Factories and mines labored to provide the raw materials and finished products needed for expansion. Settlers moved west and immigrants poured in on both coasts. Ranching and then farming pushed out the native Americans whose protests subsided when the buffalo were slaughtered by the mid 1880s. Labor protests against appalling working conditions brought on reform and unions. The population of the U.S. in 1890 was 63 million, double the 1860 number. It was time to look outward and become more a part of the global community.

LATER YEARS

Harrison was not sorry to leave the presidency. Its duties had been a burden to him. He returned to Indianapolis and his law practice. He also spent some time lecturing, as well as campaigning for Republican candidates. He wrote a book on the federal government and the presidency called *This Country of Ours*. It sold widely and was used in colleges as a textbook. In 1899 he served as senior legal counsel for Venezuela in its boundary dispute with British Guiana.

Harrison remarried in 1896. His second wife was Mary Scott Lord Dimmick, the niece of his first wife. They had one child, Elizabeth. Harrison died on March 13, 1901. He was buried in Indianapolis.

As president, Benjamin Harrison was hardworking, honest, and dignified, although never really popular. Since he lacked power in his party, he left legislation to Congress. He tried to steer a middle course on the political, economic, and social issues raised by the industrialization of American life. In this he was much like the presidents who immediately preceded him in office. Political leaders had not yet begun to turn their faces toward the rapidly approaching twentieth century.

Benjamin Harrison McKee (left), was President Harrison's grandson by his daughter Mary and her husband, James McKee. The boy spent much time with his grandfather in the White House.

WILLIAM McKINLEY

25th PRESIDENT OF THE UNITED STATES (1897–1901)

Born: January 29, 1843, at Niles, Ohio
Occupation: Lawyer
Party: Republican
Vice Presidents: Garret A. Hobart (1897-99); Theodore Roosevelt (1901)
Wife: Ida Saxton
Died: September 14, 1901, at Buffalo, New York

fice in Canton, Ohio. There he remained, except when public duty interfered, for the rest of his life. Within two years he was elected prosecuting attorney, and a career in politics began to open up for him.

In 1871, McKinley married Ida Saxton, daughter of Canton's most prominent banker. They were devoted to each other. However, after the death of their two young children, both girls, Ida became ill and remained an invalid for the rest of her life.

CONGRESSMAN AND GOVERNOR

In 1876, McKinley was elected, as a Republican, to the U.S. House of Representatives. He was reelected almost continuously until 1890. In that year the Republicans lost the election because of a tariff—the McKinley Tariff.

In 1890 the business interests of the country were determined to pass a high tariff, or tax on foreign goods, in order to protect American industry from competition. McKinley firmly believed in such a policy, and overcoming all opposition, he got his tariff bill passed. However, resentment over the tariff, especially in the West and South, cost the Republicans heavily in the election, and McKinley lost his seat in Congress.

Undiscouraged by his defeat, McKinley won the governorship of Ohio in 1891. Earlier he had impressed a wealthy Cleveland businessman, who offered to help McKinley further his political career. This businessman was Marcus Alonzo Hanna, one of the most influential men in the Republican Party. A close relationship developed between the two men and grew into a lifelong friendship. Under Mark Hanna's steady direction McKinley would attain the presidency.

In 1892 McKinley was appointed chairman of the Republican National Convention. Some members of his party were so enthusiastic about McKinley that they

William McKinley was one of the kindliest and most peace-loving of U.S. presidents. Yet he led the United States at a time when most Americans were determined to go to war. And the life of this gentle and sympathetic man was brought tragically to an end by bullets from an assassin's gun.

EARLY YEARS

McKinley was born in Niles, Ohio, on January 29, 1843, the seventh child of William and Nancy Allison McKinley. Young McKinley grew up a serious boy, possessed of a quiet determination to succeed. He attended school in Poland, Ohio, and then went to Allegheny College in Meadville, Pennsylvania. He left college before graduating and became a teacher in a rural school. When the Civil War broke out in 1861, the 17-year-old McKinley enlisted as a private in the 23rd Ohio Volunteer Infantry Regiment. Though short and slight, he impressed his superiors with his initiative, and he rose to become a brevet major.

At the war's end, McKinley left the Army and returned to Ohio to study law. In 1867 he opened a law of-

William McKinley

25th president, 1897–1901 Republican

1843 Born on January 29 in Niles, Ohio.

1860 Studies at Allegheny College in Meadville, Pennsylvania, cut short by illness. Taught school briefly.

1861 At outset of Civil War, enlisted as private in 23rd Ohio Regiment, under Rutherford B. Hayes. Saw considerable action and left the Army a brevet major.

1865–67 Studied law in an Ohio law office and at Albany (NY) Law School. Admitted to bar and opened practice in Canton, Ohio.

1869 Elected prosecuting attorney of Stark County, Ohio.

1871 Married Ida Saxton on January 25. Two daughters would be born to the couple; both died very young.

1877 Entered U.S. Congress as representative of Ohio's seventeenth district. Served until 1891, except for 1884–85.

1891 Elected governor of Ohio. Served two terms.

1896 Defeated William Jennings Bryan in November presidential election.

1901 Died on September 14 in Buffalo, New York, eight days after being shot at Pan-American Exposition.

Highlights of Presidency

1897 Dingley Tariff passed, raising average duty to a record 57%.

1898 On February 15, the U.S. battleship *Maine* was blown up in Havana harbor. On April 25, the United States declared war on Spain. In Battle of Manila Bay on May 1, Adm. George Dewey led major U.S. victory over Spain.

1899 Treaty of Paris, ending the war, was approved by the U.S. Senate on February 6. Spain ceded Philippines, Puerto Rico, and Guam and agreed to independence for Cuba. In May, U.S. troops captured Emilio Aguinaldo, ending revolt in the Philippines. In September, U.S. Secretary of State John Hay sent notes to major European nations calling for Open Door trade policy toward China.

1900 U.S. troops joined international force in putting down Boxer Rebellion in China. Gold Standard Act passed, making the gold dollar the sole standard of currency.

1901 With Theodore Roosevelt as running-mate, re-elected for a second term.

Although Ida Saxton McKinley was an invalid when William McKinley became president, she entertained frequently at the White House. She died in 1907 and is buried beside her husband in Canton, Ohio.

wanted him to become the Republican presidential candidate. But McKinley felt that he was not yet ready for so important an office. Instead he gave his support to the renomination of President Benjamin Harrison. McKinley's decision not to seek the nomination was a fortunate one. While Harrison was defeated by Grover Cleveland in the election of 1892, McKinley went on to be elected governor of Ohio for a second term.

By 1896, McKinley felt ready to accept his party's nomination for the presidency. At the Republican National Convention in St. Louis, Missouri, he was nominated on the first ballot. The Republicans were confident of victory, for the Democratic administration of President Grover Cleveland had been plagued by an economic depression.

THE CAMPAIGN OF 1896

The Democrats, with William Jennings Bryan as their candidate, campaigned on the issue of "free silver." Many people, especially farmers in the West, felt their economic hardships would end if the government restored unlimited coinage of silver money. Bryan toured the country urging such a policy. He was a forceful orator, and McKinley was hard pressed to compete with him.

Taking his friend Mark Hanna's advice, McKinley did not try to out-talk Bryan. Instead, he stayed at his home in Canton and conducted a "front-porch" campaign, speaking to groups of people who flocked to his home to listen to him. Businessmen and workers in the

During the campaign of 1896, Republicans praised the McKinley tariff bill, as shown in this cartoon.

East gave him their support, and a good farm crop in the West helped restore prosperity. McKinley received 7,102,246 popular votes to Bryan's 6,492,559 and 271 electoral votes to Bryan's 176.

PRESIDENT

McKinley's first term of office was an eventful one for the United States. The nation was seething with new growth, and many different interests sought dominance. McKinley seemed ideally suited to the task of harmonizing such clashing interests.

Cuba and the Spanish–American War

The most important event in McKinley's administration resulted from a crisis in Cuba. Revolts by Cubans against Spanish rule had broken out, and the Cubans appealed to the United States for help. Stories of Spanish cruelty toward the Cubans began to arouse American public opinion against Spain. Soon an avalanche of sympathy for Cuba Libre ("Free Cuba") began to descend on McKinley. The President, above all a man of peace, had already pledged his opposition to any armed interference in another country's affairs. In his annual message to Congress he urged that Spain "be given a reasonable chance" to right the situation. Yet his concern over the plight of the Cuban people was real. He issued a Christmas Eve appeal for public contributions to a Cuban relief fund. And at his initiative over $250,000 of aid was sent to Cuba by the Red Cross.

Early in 1898 two events occurred that left McKinley helpless to avoid war with Spain. The first was a private letter written by the Spanish minister in Washington, D.C. Intercepted by a Cuban, who turned it over to a reporter, the letter was published in American newspapers. In it the minister, De Lôme, called McKinley "a would-be politician . . . weak and a bidder for the admiration of the crowd. . . ." Though the minister promptly resigned and the Spanish Government apologized, the De Lôme letter turned popular opinion even more strongly against Spain.

Then, a few days later, the United States battleship *Maine* was blown up in Havana harbor, with a loss of 260 American lives. Newspapers across the country blazed the headline that Spain was responsible and that war was now certain. Actually, no one knows to this day what caused the disaster. But without waiting further, Congress rushed through a bill appropriating $50,000,000 for national defense.

Though McKinley continued to press for peace, Congress and the vast majority of the American public were convinced that war was the only honorable road left open to the United States. A popular newspaper cartoon of the day showed an angry Uncle Sam straining to fight Spain while the president held him back by the coattails. The caption read, "Let go of him, McKinley!"

Soon the President feared that unless he gave way, Congress would declare war over his head. Finally he decided to yield to popular demand, and in April 1898 war with Spain was declared. Yet McKinley always felt that, left to himself, "I could have concluded an arrangement with the Spanish government under which the Spanish troops would have been withdrawn from Cuba without a war."

The Spanish–American War lasted less than four months and resulted in a victory for the United States. The United States won control over the former Spanish

The battleship U.S.S. Maine *was blown up on February 15, 1898, in the harbor at Havana, Cuba. This was the final straw that led the United States to declare war on Spain.*

possessions of Puerto Rico, Guam, and the Philippines, while Cuba gained its independence.

The Issue of Imperialism

After the war some Americans were undecided as to whether the United States should keep the territory won from Spain. They argued that the United States should not hold on to such possessions as the Philippine Islands, which were far from the country's shores. As the islands of Hawaii had also been acquired during this time, there was a growing fear that the United States was becoming an imperialist power.

McKinley was tormented by his conscience as to what course he should take. Though he felt that the United States had had to interfere in Cuba for "humanity's sake," he found it hard to justify holding the Philippines. However, others in his party urged him to keep them as legitimate possessions. Finally, after walking "the floor of the White House night after night until midnight," McKinley decided to acquire the islands.

China and the Open-Door Policy

With major possessions in the Far East, American interest in China and in world politics in general increased. At the time, Great Britain, France, Germany, and Japan were acquiring large "spheres of influence" in China. In 1899, McKinley's secretary of state, John Hay, called on the other powers to allow equality of trade in China. After the unsuccessful Boxer Rebellion in 1900, in which the Chinese revolted against foreign domination, Hay declared that it was American policy to respect the independence of China. He called on the other countries to do the same. This policy of equality of trade with China and respect for its territorial integrity was the basis of the famous Open-Door policy.

McKinley was shot on September 6, 1901, in Buffalo, New York, by Leon F. Czolgosz, an anarchist. McKinley died eight days later.

DID YOU KNOW?

- *McKinley was the first president to use the telephone while campaigning.*
- *He is thought to hold the record for presidential handshaking—2,500 per hour.*
- *Known for his devotion to his ailing wife, one politician said McKinley made it hard for other husbands in Washington.*
- *McKinley exercised very little; had he been in better shape, his doctors said, he might have survived his assassin's bullet.*

The Election of 1900

The election of 1900 found McKinley more popular than ever. Bryan, who was again the Democratic candidate, tried to raise the issue of imperialism. But its effect was limited by the fact that the United States was prospering more than ever. The "full dinner pail" became a McKinley slogan. The result was an easy victory for McKinley and his vice president, Theodore Roosevelt.

ASSASSINATION

On the afternoon of September 6, 1901, at a public reception in Buffalo, New York, President McKinley was happily shaking hands with his many admirers. Suddenly a man walked up to the president with a handkerchief-covered revolver in his outstretched hand. Two shots rang out, striking McKinley at point-blank range. While being carried to an ambulance, he pleaded with police not to beat the assassin. Eight days later McKinley died, and Vice President Theodore Roosevelt was sworn in as 26th president. The assassin, Leon F. Czolgosz, was an anarchist. He was speedily brought to trial and sentenced to death on September 26. Czolgosz was executed in the prison at Auburn, New York, on October 29.

Amid great mourning, McKinley was buried in Canton, Ohio. Ida McKinley died in 1907 and was buried beside her husband in a great memorial tomb. Another memorial to McKinley was erected at Niles.

With the passing of McKinley the United States, too, passed from one era to another from an era of internal growth and expansion to one of growing participation in world affairs.

THEODORE ROOSEVELT

26th PRESIDENT OF THE UNITED STATES (1901–1909)

Born: October 27, 1858, in New York, New York
Occupation: Author, Public Official
Party: Republican
Vice President: Charles Warren Fairbanks
Wives: Alice Hathaway Lee; Edith Kermit Carow
Died: January 6, 1919, at Oyster Bay, New York

Theodore Roosevelt was one of the most popular American presidents as well as one of the most important. With his zest for life and his love of controversy, he captured the public's imagination as no president since Andrew Jackson had done. His willingness to shoulder the burdens of world power and to struggle with the problems caused by the growth of industry made his administration one of the most significant.

Roosevelt was a strong nationalist and a dynamic leader. He greatly expanded the power of the presidency at the expense of Congress, the states, and big business. He made the United States the guardian of the Western Hemisphere, especially in the Caribbean. He increased regulation of business and encouraged the labor movement. He led a long, hard fight for the conservation of natural resources. And he broadly advanced the welfare of the people as a whole. At the same time he was a compelling preacher of good government and responsible citizenship.

Roosevelt was sworn in as president on September 14, 1901, following the assassination of President William McKinley. At 42 years of age he became the youngest

president in American history. Fortunately, 15 years of public service in local, state, and federal posts made him one of the best prepared. His most valuable experience had been as governor of New York. There he had shown the striking capacity to lead that made his presidency so notable. He had also become painfully aware of the need for social and economic reform. In fact, it was largely because of his efforts to regulate business and run the government honestly that New York Republican bosses decided in 1900 that Roosevelt should be eased out of the state by being made vice president.

EARLY YEARS

No president led a more varied, interesting, or adventurous life than Theodore Roosevelt. He was a hunter, rancher, and explorer as well as a soldier, naturalist, and author. As a youth, however, he had to struggle against poor health. From his birth in New York City on October 27, 1858, until his late teens, he suffered from asthma and was generally weak and frail. Otherwise he had many advantages. His father, after whom he was named, came from an old New York Dutch family of moderate wealth and high social position. His mother, Martha Bulloch, belonged to a prominent family from Georgia. Both parents were kind and affectionate. His father, in particular, concerned himself actively with Theodore's development. He encouraged Theodore to build up his body by doing hard exercises and engaging in sports. He arranged for his son to be educated by excellent private tutors until it was time to enter college. And most important of all, he taught Theodore the difference between right and wrong and gave him an unusually strong sense of responsibility. When Theodore entered Harvard College in 1876, he was healthy in body and mind, except for a trace of snobbishness, which he later lost.

The Roosevelt family sat for this photo portrait in 1903. From left are Quentin, Theodore Roosevelt, Theodore, Jr., Archibald, Alice, Kermit, Edith Roosevelt, and Ethel. All the children except Alice are the children of his second marriage.

At Harvard, Roosevelt wrote a senior honors thesis and was elected to Phi Beta Kappa, the student honor society. He graduated 21st in a class of 158. He probably would have done even better, for his intelligence was high and his memory keen, but he spent much of his time in outside activities. He played tennis and boxed, read hundreds of books not related to his courses, and wrote the first two chapters of a quite good book, *The Naval War of 1812.* He also became so interested in politics and government that he decided not to become a professional naturalist as he had originally intended.

In 1880, a few months after graduation, Roosevelt married a charming young lady, Alice Hathaway Lee of Chestnut Hill, Massachusetts. After a short honeymoon he started to study law at Columbia University. He had little interest in legal details, however. In 1881, he gave up the study of law upon his election to the first of three terms in the New York State Assembly.

Roosevelt was only 23 years old when he took his seat in January, 1882. But his courageous support of good government soon earned him a state-wide reputation. He became the leader of a group of reform-minded Republicans and pushed through several bills strengthening the government of New York City. At the same time, he overcame a belief that government should not interfere in the economy and fought successfully for the regulation of tenement workshops.

Early in his third term, in 1884, Roosevelt's mother died. A few hours later his wife, who had given birth to a baby girl a short while before, also died. Though grief-stricken, Roosevelt carried on his duties until the end of the session. As he wrote to a close friend, "It was a grim and evil fate, but I have never believed it did any good to flinch or yield for any blow, nor does it lighten the blow to cease from working." That summer he retired temporarily from politics and went out to the Dakota Territory to raise cattle on his ranch on the Little Missouri River.

When Roosevelt first appeared in the West, veteran cowboys and hunters were amused by his thick glasses, eastern accent, and gentlemanly manners. But after he had knocked out a drunken stranger who threatened him with two pistols and had proved himself in a half dozen other incidents, he was accepted. Within a year he was regarded as one of the region's ablest young leaders. Besides running cattle, Roosevelt spent his time in the West writing a biography of Thomas Hart Benton, a Missouri senator of the pre-Civil War period. He also planned a four-volume history of the westward movement, later published under the title *The Winning of the West.*

PUBLIC SERVICE

Roosevelt returned from the West in the fall of 1886 to suffer defeat in a race for mayor of New York. That same year he married a childhood sweetheart, Edith Carow, and settled in a great rambling house on Sagamore Hill, overlooking Oyster Bay, Long Island. Four sons and a daughter were born to them.

But Roosevelt's energy was too great and his ambition too driving for him to be satisfied with life as a sportsman and writer. Besides, he felt that men of independent means were obligated to serve the public. So in 1889 he accepted an appointment to the United States Civil Service Commission. Roosevelt at once gave the commission new life, and for six years he enforced the laws honestly and fearlessly. When he resigned in 1895 to accept the presidency of the New York City Police Board, the civil service system had become an important part of American government.

As New York police commissioner, Roosevelt prowled the streets after midnight, overhauled the promotion system, and modernized the force. In 1897 he resigned from the Police Board to become assistant secretary of the Navy.

ROUGH RIDER AND GOVERNOR

Roosevelt's service in the Navy Department and in the war against Spain brought out his aggressive qualities. He believed at the time that power was necessary for a country to achieve greatness, and that war was a test of manliness. He also believed that civilized nations had a right to interfere in the affairs of less advanced nations in order to forward the march of civilization. He demanded that the United States build up its fleet, drive Spain from the Western Hemisphere, and acquire colonies of its own.

Soon after the Spanish-American War broke out in 1898, Roosevelt helped organize the First United States Volunteer Cavalry Regiment (the "Rough Riders"). He took command of the regiment in Cuba, and on July 1 he led an assault on a hill outside Santiago. For hours he braved withering gunfire from the heights as he rode up and down the line urging his men, who were on foot, to press the attack. His elbow was nicked, a soldier was killed at his feet, and he had several other narrow escapes. But he rallied his own and other troops, and the hill was captured.

As soon as Roosevelt returned to New York in the fall of 1898, Republican bosses nominated him for governor. They hoped that his war record and reputation as a reformer would cause the voters to overlook a series of recent scandals within the party. After being elected by a narrow margin, Roosevelt compelled the bosses to accept a number of reform measures. These included a tax on corporation franchises, regulation of sweatshops, a raise in schoolteachers' salaries, and a conservation program. This angered the businessmen who supported the bosses. So Republican leaders practically forced Roosevelt to accept the vice-presidential nomination in 1900, although he wanted a second term as governor. In the election McKinley and Roosevelt defeated the Democratic candidates, William Jennings Bryan and Adlai E. Stevenson.

Six months after their inauguration McKinley was dead and Roosevelt was the new president of the United States.

PRESIDENT

The main drive of Roosevelt's administration was toward a balance of economic interests. He believed that he should represent all the people—farmers, laborers, and white-collar workers as well as businessmen. Roosevelt called his program the Square Deal. He began to put it into effect five months after he took office by starting antitrust proceedings against the Northern Securities Company, a giant holding company. Holding companies

Roosevelt (center, with eyeglasses) is shown with his Rough Riders in Cuba in 1898 during the Spanish-American War.

Theodore Roosevelt.

Theodore Roosevelt

26th president, 1901–09 Republican

1858 Born on October 27 in New York, New York.

1880 Graduated from Harvard University. Married Alice Hathaway Lee on October 27.

1881–84 Served in New York state legislature.

1884 Wife died following birth of daughter, Alice. Mother died the same day. Dropped out of politics and became cattle rancher in Dakota Territory; also wrote history.

1886 Married Edith Kermit Carow on December 2. Four sons and a daughter would be born to the couple.

1887–89 Lived as sportsman and gentleman-scholar at Sagamore Hill, estate at Oyster Bay, New York. Continued career as historian. Most important work, *The Winning of the West*, was published in four volumes, 1889–96. He would write a total of some 40 books.

1889 Appointed to U.S. Civil Service Commission.

1895 Became police commissioner of New York City.

1897 Appointed assistant secretary of the Navy by President William McKinley.

1898 After outbreak of Spanish-American War, organized First U.S. Volunteer Cavalry (Rough Riders). As colonel, led charge up Kettle Hill in battle of San Juan. In November, elected governor of New York; as such, sponsored tax reform and fought spoils system.

1900 Elected vice president.

1901 On September 14, sworn in as 26th president after the assassination of President McKinley.

1912 Left GOP and ran for the presidency on his new Progressive ("Bull Moose") ticket. Shot during campaign, but recovered. Lost election to Democrat Woodrow Wilson.

1919 Died on January 6 at Sagamore Hill.

Highlights of Presidency

1903 Panama signed treaty for a canal under U.S. sovereignty. Department of Commerce and Labor was created.

1904 Won election to full term.

1906 Awarded Nobel Peace Prize for arbitrating end of Russo-Japanese War. Hepburn Act, authorizing Interstate Commerce Commission to regulate railroad rates, and the Pure Food and Drug Act were enacted.

1907 Financial panic and depression started. Supported William Howard Taft for the presidency.

A political cartoon of the early 1900s depicted President Theodore Roosevelt as a "trust-buster." Roosevelt's motto and philosophy was "Speak softly and carry a big stick."

controlled other companies and were thus able to reduce competition. Then in the fall of 1902, Roosevelt helped settle a long coal strike on terms favorable to the workers. This marked the first time that a president who took action in a strike had failed to side with management.

Despite his popular fame as a "trustbuster," Roosevelt continued to believe that bigness was good economically. He felt that large corporations should be regulated rather than destroyed. In 1903 he pushed through Congress a bill to form a Bureau of Corporations. That same year he gave his support to the Elkins Bill to prohibit railroad rebates. This was a practice in which railroads returned part of their payment to favored customers.

Foreign Policy

Roosevelt's foreign policy was guided by the belief that the United States must police the Western Hemisphere and should accept the responsibilities of world power. He felt that the United States was morally bound to uplift the people of the Philippines, which the United States had acquired from Spain. He worked conscientiously to improve the economy of the Filipinos and prepare them for self-government. In 1902 he persuaded Germany to arbitrate a dispute with Venezuela. In 1903 he acquired the Canal Zone after Panama broke away from Colombia. The circumstances left a feeling of ill will in Colombia.

In 1905, at the request of the government of Santo Domingo (now the Dominican Republic), Roosevelt took over control of customs collections in that misgoverned country. He did not want to do so. But he feared that European powers might take control for nonpayment of debts if the United States did not act. He then announced in a public letter that the United States had a right to intervene in the internal affairs of Latin American countries unable to keep order. This policy became known as the Roosevelt Corollary to the Monroe Doctrine.

Second Presidential Term

Roosevelt's flair for the dramatic combined with his solid achievements to assure him a term in his own right. In the election of 1904 he won a landslide victory over his conservative Democratic opponent, Judge Alton B. Parker of New York. The most productive years of his presidency followed. In a masterful display of leadership, Roosevelt forced the conservative Republicans into line by threatening to lower the tariff—the tax on imports. The conservatives then gave their support to the Hepburn Act (1906) to regulate railroads, a meat inspection measure (1906), the Pure Food and Drug Act (1906), and employers' liability legislation (1906 and 1908).

Meanwhile, Roosevelt and his chief forester, Gifford Pinchot, pushed conservation forward. Their program was based on the theory that (1) natural resources belong to all the people, (2) scientific forestry would provide a constant supply of timber, and (3) river valleys should be developed as entire units. Roosevelt and Pinchot were bitterly opposed by small lumber companies, electric power corporations, and states' righters. But progress was made. The Reclamation Act of 1902 provided for a large irrigation project in the Southwest. Many big lumber companies were won over to scientific forestry. More than 125,000,000 acres were added to the national forests, and the number of national parks doubled. Sixteen national monuments were created, and 51 wildlife refuges were established. On a less positive note, the city of San Francisco was partly destroyed by an earthquake and fire in 1906.

In foreign affairs Roosevelt's second term saw a retreat from his earlier imperialism. He tried mainly to protect the Philippines, support a balance of power in the Far East, and build up friendship with the Japanese. In 1905 he offered his good offices to end the Russo–Japanese War. His mediation proved successful and earned him the Nobel peace prize. On the other hand, he served notice that he still carried a "big stick" by sending the American fleet on a world cruise in 1907, which demonstrated America's naval strength. The U.S. Navy's first submarine, the *Holland*, was commissioned in 1900. Roosevelt became the first president to submerge in a submarine while in office.

As Roosevelt's term of office neared its end, Congress grew more and more resentful of his strong leadership and progressive policies. Again and again during his last two years Congress refused to do what he asked. Roosevelt's insight into the nation's problems con-

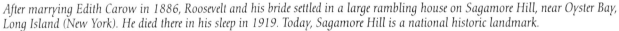

After marrying Edith Carow in 1886, Roosevelt and his bride settled in a large rambling house on Sagamore Hill, near Oyster Bay, Long Island (New York). He died there in his sleep in 1919. Today, Sagamore Hill is a national historic landmark.

DID YOU KNOW?

- *At 42, Theodore Roosevelt was the youngest president; Kennedy was the youngest elected president, at 43.*
- *The teddy bear is named for him.*
- *He lost the sight in one eye while boxing in the White House.*
- *Roosevelt had a photographic memory. He could read a page in the time it took anyone else to read a sentence.*
- *He was the first president to travel outside the United States—to Panama.*
- *Roosevelt craved attention. It was said that he wanted to be the bride at every wedding, the corpse at every funeral.*

tinued to deepen, however. On January 31, 1908, he sent Congress the most radical message written by a president to that time. It called, among other things, for better conditions for workers and for the arrest of businessmen who broke the law.

In spite of his troubles with Congress, Roosevelt's great energy and straightforward speeches appealed more than ever to the man in the street. He could have been renominated easily had he chosen. But he decided instead to support the candidacy of one of his dearest friends, Secretary of War William Howard Taft. Soon after Taft was inaugurated in 1909, Roosevelt left for Africa to hunt big game and collect specimens for the Smithsonian Institution.

The Bull Moose Party

While Roosevelt was in Africa, progressivism was gaining new force in the United States. But instead of encouraging its growth as Roosevelt had done, President Taft tried to hold it back. This put him on the side of the Republican conservatives who had opposed Roosevelt's policies.

In 1910 Roosevelt returned to the United States. Although irritated at Taft's policies, he at first tried to avoid hurting his old friend. But it was not in Roosevelt's nature to keep silent. In a series of speeches in the Midwest he set forth his own views, which he called the New Nationalism.

The New Nationalism was an extension of the progressive program he had urged in the last years of his presidency. It called for steeply graduated income and inheritance taxes and a long list of other social and political reforms. Finally, in 1912, Roosevelt yielded to the pleas of progressive midwestern Republicans and challenged Taft for the presidential nomination. But the Republican Convention failed to nominate Roosevelt in spite of his two-to-one victory over Taft in the primary elections. Roosevelt then organized the Progressive, or Bull Moose, Party. ("I am as strong as a bull moose," he had once said.) The new party was supported by most of the country's social workers, intellectuals, and progressive-minded citizens.

Roosevelt's leadership of the progressive movement stirred the social conscience of middle-class America. He was shot during the campaign but recovered. Though Woodrow Wilson, the Democratic candidate, won the three-cornered contest with about 42 percent of the popular vote, Roosevelt ran far ahead of Taft. In a sense, too, Roosevelt was vindicated in defeat. For by 1916 Wilson had written a great deal of Roosevelt's New Nationalism into law.

South American Exploration

After his defeat in 1912 Roosevelt wrote his autobiography. It is a colorful and vigorously written book and still the most informative memoir ever written by a former president. During this period, too, Roosevelt gave a memorable speech as president of the American Historical Association. In it he pleaded with professional historians to make history as interesting as literature.

Then, in 1913, Roosevelt decided to indulge his love of adventure once more by exploring an unknown South American river, the River of Doubt. It was a harrowing experience. He almost died of an injury suffered in a heroic effort to save two capsized boats. He was then stricken with malaria. Realizing that he was a burden, Roosevelt begged his companions, who included his son Kermit, to go on without him. But they insisted on bringing him out of the jungle.

World War I

Upon the outbreak of World War I in 1914, Roosevelt at first refused to take sides. But after a few months, he decided that the interests of the United States and the world would best be served by Germany's defeat. Early in 1915 he became a leader of the movement to prepare the United States for possible entry into the war. When the United States declared war against Germany in 1917, Roosevelt asked Wilson for permission to raise a volunteer division. But Wilson refused, and Roosevelt devoted himself to spurring the war effort at home. On January 6, 1919, 18 months after his youngest son, Quentin, was killed in an air battle over France, Roosevelt died in his sleep at Sagamore Hill. He is buried at Young's Memorial Cemetery in Oyster Bay, New York.

WILLIAM HOWARD TAFT

27th PRESIDENT OF THE UNITED STATES (1909–1913)

Born: *September 15, 1857, at Cincinnati, Ohio*
Occupation: *Lawyer, Public Official*
Party: *Republican*
Vice President: *James S. Sherman*
Wife: *Helen W. Herron*
Died: *March 8, 1930, in Washington, D.C.*

When William Howard Taft became president of the United States in 1909, great things were expected of him. The previous president, Theodore Roosevelt, one of the most popular in American history, had supported him enthusiastically, and Taft had promised to carry on Roosevelt's policies. Taft had already served the country for many years in a variety of important positions. In the 1908 election the people had chosen him over the Democratic candidate, William Jennings Bryan, by more than 1,000,000 popular votes. Yet Taft's administration was a disappointment to his supporters. He failed to win reelection in 1912 but later went on to a distinguished career as chief justice of the United States.

EARLY YEARS

Taft was born in Cincinnati, Ohio, on September 15, 1857. He came from an old and distinguished family, which traced its roots back to the 17th-century Puritan settlers of the Massachusetts Bay Colony. His father, Alphonso Taft, was a judge. Young William was intelligent and excelled at his studies. He graduated from Yale College in 1878, second in his class. He then returned to Cincinnati

and became a lawyer. A big, heavy man, he eventually weighed more than 300 pounds. He was friendly and warmhearted but rather lazy. His fine mind, however, soon made him a successful lawyer.

PUBLIC–SERVICE CAREER

Taft became interested in Republican politics in Ohio, and in 1881 he was appointed assistant prosecutor in Hamilton County. In 1887 he was named a judge on the Ohio superior court. In 1890, President Benjamin Harrison offered him the post of solicitor general of the United States, the second-ranking office in the Department of Justice. Taft accepted, but in 1892 he resigned this important office to become a federal circuit court judge.

Taft would have happily spent his entire life in this post. In 1899 he even turned down an offer of the presidency of Yale College. However, in 1900 he accepted President William McKinley's request that he become head of a special commission to oversee the government of the Philippine Islands. The Philippines had been acquired by the United States from Spain in 1898 after the Spanish-American War. In the Philippines, Taft demonstrated his ability as an administrator, and in 1901 he was appointed by McKinley as the first civilian governor of the islands.

Taft proved to be an excellent colonial governor. The Filipinos, objecting as much to American rule as to Spanish, were in rebellion against American troops when Taft arrived. Although he insisted that they lay down their arms, he developed a great affection for the people of the Philippines and carried out many important reforms. He saw to it that landless peasants were permitted to buy land at fair prices. He improved the school system, built many roads, and did everything possible to prepare the people for eventual independence. So interested was he in this

William Howard Taft

27th president, 1909-13   Republican

1857 Born on September 15 in Cincinnati, Ohio.

1878 Graduated from Yale University.

1880 Graduated from Cincinnati Law School and admitted to the Ohio bar.

1881 Became assistant prosecuting attorney of Hamilton county; served two years.

1886 Married Helen Herron on June 19. The Tafts would have three children.

1887 Appointed judge on the Ohio superior court. Elected to his own term the following year.

1890 Named U.S. solicitor-general.

1892 Chosen U.S. Circuit Court judge for the 6th district by President Benjamin Harrison.

1900 Named by President McKinley to head the commission charged with terminating U.S. military rule in Philippines.

1901 Became first civil governor of the Philippines.

1904 Appointed secretary of war by President Roosevelt.

1908 Won race for the presidency.

1913-21 Served as professor of law at Yale University. During World War I, was also joint chairman of the National War Labor Board.

1921 Appointed chief justice of the U.S. Supreme Court by President Warren Harding. Served until Feb. 3, 1930.

1930 Died on March 8 in Washington, D.C.

Highlights of Presidency

1909 Payne-Aldrich Act passed, lowering tariffs.

1911 Standard Oil Co. dissolved by Supreme Court under Sherman Antitiust Act. Administration also effected dissolution of tobacco trusts and proceeded with scores of other antitrust suits.

1912 New Mexico and Arizona admitted to the union, the last of the 48 contiguous states. President Taft won renomination by Republican Party but lost election to Democrat Woodrow Wilson. "Bull Moose" candidacy of Theodore Roosevelt split the Republican vote.

1913 The 16th Amendment to the U.S. Constitution, authorizing income taxes, was proclaimed on February 25. The 17th amendment, calling for direct popular election of U.S. senators, went into effect two months after Taft left office. Department of Commerce and Labor divided into separate departments.

Helen W. Herron Taft was an attractive and ambitious woman. She urged her reluctant husband to accept the nomination for the presidency in 1908.

work that he twice refused appointment to the United States Supreme Court—his highest ambition—because he felt that his work in the islands had not been completed.

In 1904, however, his friend Theodore Roosevelt, then president, appointed him secretary of war. This post enabled Taft to continue to supervise the Philippines. Heading the War Department also put him in charge of the building of the Panama Canal. He became one of Roosevelt's most trusted advisers, and soon he was being mentioned as a leading candidate for the office of president himself.

A RELUCTANT PRESIDENT

Taft did not want to be president. But his family, especially his wife, Helen Herron Taft, whom he had married in 1886, urged him to accept the nomination. When Roosevelt formally asked him to run, he reluctantly agreed.

This was a mistake. The hectic pressures of the White House made him an unhappy man. On the one hand, he spent too much time on the golf course. On the other, he complained that his work forced him to rush his meals and forego his afternoon nap. He hated to make speeches, and when he did, he was usually dull and long-winded. Too often he left important decisions to others. One critic called him "an amiable island completely surrounded by men who know exactly what they want." Taft had been an excellent administrator when working under someone else's direction. But he was not successful when faced with the final responsibility for establishing policy and directing the entire national government.

The Tariff

Taft's first move as president was to urge Congress to lower the tariff duties on foreign goods coming into the United States. Originally, high tariffs had seemed necessary to protect new American industries against European competition. But by 1900 American manufacturers were the most efficient in the world. High tariffs simply raised the cost of living for consumers and gave the manufacturers extra profits.

During the 1908 election campaign the Republican Party had promised to revise the tariff. This, everyone assumed, would mean lowering it. The new Payne-Aldrich tariff bill, however, made only very small changes in the law, and many reformers expected Taft to veto it. Taft was disappointed with the measure, but thought it at least better than the existing tariff. Therefore he signed it into law. Perhaps this was sensible. But Taft angered many citizens by actually praising the Payne-Aldrich Act, even calling it "the best tariff bill the Republican Party ever passed."

The Pinchot Controversy

Next Taft angered the liberals by seeming to reverse Roosevelt's conservation policies. Roosevelt was a great nature lover. He had been disturbed by the rapid destruction of the nation's forest and mineral resources by lumber and mining companies and had established many large national parks and reserves in the West. His chief forester, Gifford Pinchot, was a leading conservation expert. Taft also believed in conservation, and he kept Pinchot on as chief forester. But his secretary of the interior, Richard A. Ballinger, who was Pinchot's superior, soon got into an argument with the chief forester over a large tract of public land in Alaska. When Pinchot accused Ballinger of allowing this land to be gobbled up by a big coal-mining company, Taft ordered an investigation. The inquiry convinced Taft that Ballinger had done no wrong,

The opposition between Taft and Theodore Roosevelt for the Republican presidential nomination in 1912 is depicted in a political cartoon of the period.

so he ordered Pinchot to stop his attacks. Pinchot refused, and Taft then removed him from office. While he was probably justified in doing so, his action cost him much support among liberal Republicans.

Reforms

Taft did accomplish a number of major reforms. He was responsible for the creation of the Postal Savings System, which provided small depositors with a safe place for

President Taft weighed over 300 pounds when he posed for this photo in 1901. With him are his two sons, Charles (left) and Robert. He also had a daughter, Helen.

their savings. He strengthened the control of the Interstate Commerce Commission over the nation's railroads. He also continued and even expanded Roosevelt's "trust-busting" (antitrust) activities, which involved breaking up some of the large industrial monopolies that had grown up in recent years. But he came to rely increasingly on the conservative wing of the Republican Party and to criticize the reform, or progressive, wing. He believed the progressives were trying to ruin his administration and became so angry that he refused to invite them to White House dinners, receptions, and other social functions.

Income Tax. During Taft's term, the 16th Amendment to the Constitution was ratified in 1913. This made possible the adoption of the federal income tax, which is the mainstay of the modern federal revenue system. Before the income tax, the federal government had power to levy tariffs and excises, but it required that direct taxes be apportioned among the states according to population. Today, personal and corporate income taxes account for over half of the total federal revenue.

THE FEUD WITH ROOSEVELT

The reformers turned to Roosevelt for help. After his term had ended, the former president had gone off to Africa to hunt big game and collect specimens for a museum. In 1910 he returned to find himself in the middle of a bitter political fight. Roosevelt genuinely liked Taft and tried to

avoid opposing him. Yet all Roosevelt's progressive friends were insisting that Taft had sold out to the reactionaries. For a time Roosevelt tried to remain neutral. But this only angered Taft, who expected Roosevelt to back him up. Gradually they ceased to be friends. Mrs. Taft resented the fact that most people paid more attention to Roosevelt than to her husband. Finally, in 1912, Roosevelt moved to oppose Taft for the Republican presidential nomination.

Taft would actually have been happy to retire from the race. But he felt that he could not honorably step down under the circumstances. He remarked angrily that even a rat will fight when cornered. In the campaign for the nomination Roosevelt won the votes of most of the delegates from states where presidential primaries were held. However, a majority of the convention delegates were not chosen by the voters but by local politicians. Taft won most of their votes because of his power as head of the party. At the convention Taft was nominated on the first ballot.

Roosevelt felt that he had been cheated of the nomination. He therefore decided to form a new party and run for the presidency on his own. This Progressive, or Bull Moose, Party split the Republican vote, and the Democratic candidate, Woodrow Wilson, won the election. Taft ran a poor third, capturing only eight electoral votes.

LAW PROFESSOR AND CHIEF JUSTICE

When his term ended in 1913, Taft became a professor of constitutional law at Yale. During World War I he served as joint chairman of the National War Labor Board. After the war he was a leading Republican supporter of Woodrow Wilson's League of Nations. The failure of the Senate to accept American membership in the league greatly distressed him.

Then, in 1921, President Warren Harding named Taft chief justice of the United States. This was the post he had always wanted, and the last ten years of his life were probably the happiest. As a judge he was conservative. He opposed government control of business and objected particularly to laws giving special treatment to labor unions.

On the other hand, Taft succeeded in simplifying and making more efficient the procedures of the federal courts. Once again it was his skill as a manager, as distinct from ability to lead people, that came to the fore. He also persuaded Congress to construct the magnificent building that today houses the Supreme Court in Washington. Taft's administrative work while on the Supreme Court was probably his most important contribution in a lifetime devoted to public service.

Early in 1930 failing health forced Taft to retire. On March 8, 1930, he died in Washington, D.C., at the age of 72. He was buried in Arlington National Cemetery.

Taft was survived by his wife, two sons, and a daughter. His elder son, Robert Alphonso Taft, became a U.S. senator from Ohio and a leader of the Republican Party. His younger son, Charles Phelps Taft, was mayor of Cincinnati.

DID YOU KNOW?

- *Taft inaugurated the custom of the president throwing out the first ball to start the baseball season.*

- *Mrs. Taft was responsible for the planting of Japanese cherry trees in Washington.*

- *He appointed the first woman to a major federal post—Julia C. Lathrop—as director of the Children's Bureau.*

- *Taft, who weighed 332 pounds, got stuck in the White House tub the first time he used it; a larger one was ordered.*

- *The Tafts owned the last presidential cow and the first White House automobiles.*

28th PRESIDENT OF THE UNITED STATES (1913–1921)

Born: *December 28, 1856, at Staunton, Virginia*
Occupation: *Teacher, Public Official*
Party: *Democrat*
Vice President: *Thomas R.Marshall*
Wives: *Ellen Louise Axson; Edith Bolling Galt*
Died: *February 3, 1924, at Washington, D.C.*

Woodrow Wilson holds a secure place among the great presidents of the United States. Few if any presidents have been more successful in dealing with Congress. This ability enabled him to win passage of a number of laws that laid the foundations of modern American public policies. Wilson also led the United States in its first important participation in world affairs, during and after World War I. He was the man most responsible for the creation of the League of Nations, the parent organization of the United Nations. Historians and biographers have written hundreds of books about Wilson. Yet he is still largely unknown as a human being.

EARLY YEARS

Thomas Woodrow Wilson (he was called "Tommy" until his early twenties) was born in Staunton, Virginia, on December 28 or 29, 1856. He always gave December 28 as his birthday, but the Wilson family Bible indicates that he was born at 12:45 A.M. on December 29. His ancestry was Scottish and Scotch-Irish. Woodrow Wilson's mother, Janet Woodrow, was the daughter of a Presbyterian minister. Wilson's father, Joseph R. Wilson, was also a

Presbyterian minister. Although originally from the Midwest, he was a founder and leader of the southern branch of the Presbyterian Church in the United States. In 1857 the Wilsons moved to Augusta, Georgia. In 1870 they moved to Columbia, South Carolina, where Wilson's father became a professor in a Presbyterian theological seminary. Wilson's early memories were of Abraham Lincoln's election in 1861, the Civil War, and Reconstruction. Years later, he said he was glad that the North had won because its victory had meant the end of slavery.

Wilson had a remarkably normal boyhood, in spite of the war and political controversy raging around him. He had two older sisters, Annie and Marion, and a younger brother, Joseph, Jr. The family was close and made secure by a gentle mother and a learned father who valued religion and education above all things. Dr. Wilson was Tommy's teacher, constant companion, and friend. As Woodrow Wilson later said, he was "the best instructor, the most inspiring companion . . . that a youngster ever had."

There were no public schools in Augusta and Columbia during the Reconstruction period that followed the Civil War. Tommy went to private schools until he had learned enough English grammar, Latin, and Greek to qualify for admission, in 1873, to Davidson College in North Carolina. He withdrew from Davidson at the end of his freshman year. His father had moved to a large church in Wilmington, North Carolina. He could now afford to send his son to the older and better-known College of New Jersey, which later became Princeton University.

Wilson's years at Princeton were among the most important in his life. He was not an outstanding student in regular course work, graduating 38th in a class of 107. But he read widely on his own in history and literature.

(Thomas) Woodrow Wilson

28th president, 1913–21 Democrat

1856   Born on December 28 in Staunton, Virginia.

1879   Earned a B.A. from the College of New Jersey (now Princeton University).

1882   Admitted to the bar, but did not prosper as a lawyer. 1885. Married Ellen Louise Axson in Rome, Georgia on June 24. Three daughters would be born to the couple.

1886   Awarded a doctor's degree from Johns Hopkins University. His first book, *Congressional Government* (1885), analyzing the U.S. government, was his dissertation.

1890-1902   After teaching at Bryn Mawr College and Wesleyan University, served as a professor at Princeton University.

1902-10   Was president of Princeton University.

1911-13   Served as governor of New Jersey.

1912   Elected president.

1915   Married Edith Bolling Galt on December 18. (The first Mrs. Wilson died on Aug. 6, 1914.)

1919   Suffered a paralytic stroke in Washington, D.C.

1924   Died on February 3 in Washington, D.C.

Highlights of Presidency

1913   The Federal Reserve Bill became law.

1914   The Clayton Antitrust Bill and the Federal Trade Bill were enacted. In April, Wilson ordered the U.S. Navy to occupy Veracruz, Mexico, during a dispute with President Victoriano Huerta. In August, the president proclaimed neutrality as war broke out in Europe.

1915   More than 100 Americans were killed as a German submarine torpedoed the British liner *Lusitania* on May 7.

1916   Narrowly reelected.

1917   The United States purchased the Virgin Islands from Denmark. On April 6, Congress declared war on Germany.

1918   In January, outlined Fourteen Points as a basis for a peace settlement. On November 11, an armistice ending World War I was signed.

1920   For a second time, the U.S. Senate refused to ratify the 1919 Treaty of Versailles with Germany. Wilson was awarded the Nobel Peace Prize for 1919 for advocating the establishment of a League of Nations. The 19th amendment, giving woman the right to vote, was ratified. The 18th, or Prohibition amendment, had been proclaimed Jan. 29, 1919.

He was editor of the college newspaper, and he received excellent training in writing and public speaking. He also made many friends who stood by him to the end of his life. Most important of all, he established the basis for his future calling—politics and public service.

After graduation in 1879, he entered the University of Virginia to study law. Ill health forced him to withdraw in 1880, but he completed his studies at home. Then, in 1882, he moved to Atlanta, Georgia, the booming city of the new South, to begin his career. Wilson would have starved had he tried to live on his fees as a lawyer. Disappointed, he gave up his legal career forever and went to Johns Hopkins University in Baltimore to study political science and history. He made a brilliant record and received a Ph.D., or doctor of philosophy, degree in 1886. His doctoral dissertation (a requirement for the Ph.D. degree) was called *Congressional Government*. It is a study of the practical workings of Congress, and is still widely read.

TEACHER AND SCHOLAR

While in Atlanta, Wilson met Ellen Axson, daughter of the Presbyterian minister in Rome, Georgia. She was gentle, artistic, and widely read, and Wilson fell madly in love at first sight. They were engaged in 1883 and married in 1885. They made their home for the next three years in Bryn Mawr, Pennsylvania, where Wilson began his teaching career at the new Bryn Mawr College. Three daughters completed the close family circle—Margaret, born in 1886; Jessie, born in 1887; and Eleanor, born in 1889. It was a family bound together by religious faith, love, and fun. Wilson always had time to romp and play with his girls, or to read poetry and the Bible with his family in front of the fire at night.

Wilson served as president of Princeton University, his alma mater, from 1902 to 1910.

In 1888 Wilson moved to Wesleyan University in Connecticut. The following year he published *The State*, a textbook on modern governments. He acquired a growing reputation as a political scientist, and in 1890 Princeton asked him to become professor of jurisprudence, or constitutional law.

The next 12 years were extremely busy and happy years for Wilson. He quickly became the most popular lecturer on the campus, and hundreds of young men went out into the world under his influence. He furiously wrote articles and books to support his growing family and the numerous relatives who lived at the Wilson home. The best of these books was *Division and Reunion*, a history of the United States between the Andrew Jackson era and Reconstruction. The most well-known was a five-volume *History of the American People*. Wilson also dreamed of writing a great work on the philosophy of politics.

PRESIDENT OF PRINCETON

This dream was ended by Wilson's election as president of Princeton University in 1902. Princeton was an old college of excellent reputation, but it had failed to advance in the 1890s. Wilson first concentrated upon improving the work both of students and faculty. His greatest success was a new method of teaching undergraduates known as the preceptorial system, which he introduced in 1905. It brought teachers and students together in small groups to discuss lectures and reading.

Wilson next tried to abolish the undergraduate eating clubs. He wanted to organize students in colleges or quadrangles modeled after colleges at Oxford and Cambridge in England. There was a storm of protest, particularly from men who had graduated from Princeton, and Wilson had to give up the fight.

POLITICS

Wilson began to listen to friends who had been urging him to go into politics. One of his great admirers was George Harvey, editor of the magazine *Harper's Weekly*. A friend of Harvey's, former senator James Smith, Jr., was one of the "bosses" of the Democratic Party in New Jersey. Harvey persuaded Smith that Wilson would make a fine candidate for governor of New Jersey. Harvey had more trouble persuading Wilson to say that he would run. But Wilson finally agreed and was nominated. He conducted a brilliant campaign and won election in 1910 by a large majority.

Even more brilliant were Wilson's accomplishments with the New Jersey legislature during the early months of his administration. Over Smith's opposition he obtained passage of a number of reforms. These included a system of direct primary elections, in which the voters nominated party candidates; a public service commission with power over the charges and services of public utilities and railroads; and an insurance system to help injured workers.

First Lady Ellen Wilson serves tea to her three daughters during her husband's first term. Two of their daughters were married in the White House. Ellen died in 1914, and President Wilson married Edith Galt in 1915.

These successes made Wilson a national figure and a leading candidate for the Democratic presidential nomination in 1912. After a bitter struggle at the Democratic national convention in Baltimore, Wilson finally won the nomination on the 46th ballot.

Wilson's luck continued during the presidential campaign that followed. The United States was strongly Republican in 1912, and a popular Republican candidate would probably have been elected. But the Republicans renominated the very unpopular president William Howard Taft. Worse still for the Republicans, former president Theodore Roosevelt rebelled when his party refused to nominate him. He organized a third party, the Progressive, or Bull Moose, Party and thus split the Republican vote. Wilson called his program the New Freedom. He won a smashing victory in the Electoral College, though he won only 42 percent of the popular vote.

PRESIDENT

Wilson's first task after his election was to construct an administration. It was not easy, for the Democrats had been out of power since 1897. Wilson built his cabinet with the help of a soft-spoken Texan whom he had met in 1911 and liked immediately. He was Colonel Edward M. House, who later played an important role as Wilson's most trusted adviser and diplomatic agent. Wilson ap-

- *Wilson was the only president with a Ph.D. degree.*

- *In 1913, he held the first regular presidential press conference; afterwards he met the press twice a week.*

- *His second wife, Edith, was a great-granddaughter of Pocahontas, seven times removed.*

- *An avid golfer, Wilson used black golf balls when playing in the snow.*

- *Wilson is the only president buried in Washington, D.C.*

pointed the old Democratic leader William Jennings Bryan secretary of state in order to assure his support for domestic legislation. Josephus Daniels, a newspaper editor from North Carolina, was made secretary of the Navy in return for his support during the fight for the nomination. Most of the other cabinet members, as well as ambassadors and other high officials, were appointed for similar reasons. The difficulty of finding experienced men placed a heavy burden on Wilson. He often had to do the work of subordinates because he could not trust them to do it well. This was especially true in the field of foreign relations.

Wilson was sworn in as president on March 4, 1913. At once he showed what kind of president he planned to be. All his adult life he had written about the need for responsible party government and the necessity for strong leadership to make it work. He intended to be like an English prime minister, the leader of his party in legislation.

Breaking a custom of more than a century, Wilson appeared in person before Congress to demand fulfillment of the first Democratic campaign promise—reform of the tariff, the tax on imports. Then during the following weeks he worked closely with leaders in the House of Representatives who were writing a tariff bill. He gave the same leadership and put the same pressure on Democrats in Congress during all the planning and debate on important laws. He had great determination and power of persuasion.

Wilson pushed one bill after another through Congress. In the Underwood Simmons Tariff Act of 1913, he won considerable reductions in tariff rates and a modest income tax—the first under the 16th Amendment to the Constitution. Next he obtained reform of the nation's banking structure and creation of a new form of money—Federal Reserve notes in the Federal Reserve Act of 1913. During the following year Wilson won two measures for more effective control of business—the Federal Trade Commission Act and the Clayton Antitrust Act.

In 1916, while he was running for a second term as president, Wilson obtained passage of even more ambitious measures to promote social and economic welfare. Three of the most important were the Child Labor Act, which prohibited children under 14 from working in factories; the Federal Farm Loan Act, which provided loans to farmers on easy terms; and the Adamson Act, establishing the eight-hour day for interstate railroad workers. Wilson's great success in domestic reform was an important factor in his narrow victory over the Republican candidate, Charles Evans Hughes, in the election of 1916.

WORLD WAR I

Meanwhile, Wilson had been drawn deeply into foreign affairs. This was partly because he felt that he should take personal responsibility for American foreign policy. He learned valuable lessons in dealing with revolutions in Mexico and the Caribbean republics. Then came the outbreak of the World War in Europe in August 1914. At this same time Wilson was saddened by the death of his wife. He later met Mrs. Edith Bolling Galt, a beautiful and

The "Big Four" statesmen met in Paris after World War I. Seated, from left are: Vittorio Orlando of Italy, David Lloyd George of Great Britain, Georges Clemenceau of France, and Wilson.

Wilson's arrival in Paris at the end of World War I brought him a tremendous ovation from the French people for America's help against the Germans.

charming young widow, and they were married on December 18, 1915.

Both Wilson and the American people wanted very much to avoid being drawn into the war in Europe. But it was not easy to remain neutral. Great Britain blockaded the Central Powers of Germany and Austria–Hungary and prevented Americans from trading with them. Germany struck back by beginning a submarine campaign against Great Britain in 1915. Americans became much aroused when, on May 7, 1915, a German submarine sank the British liner *Lusitania*, killing over 1,000 passengers, including 124 Americans.

Wilson not only wanted to stay out of the war. He also wanted to end it by his own mediation. In December 1916, he called on the warring nations to state what they were fighting for and upon what terms they would end the war. Both sides, however, rejected Wilson's call for peace. The Germans began to sink all ships sailing in European waters, American as well as British and others. This led Wilson to break diplomatic relations with Germany on February 3, 1917. Finally, after it was clear that war could not be prevented, he asked Congress, on April 2, 1917, to declare war against the German Empire.

Wilson was an inspiring leader in war. He marshaled the nation's economic resources, raised an army of several million men, and maintained good relations with United States allies. Most important, he held out great moral objectives for peace. He first stated these in his war message to Congress and developed them most fully in his Fourteen Points speech of January 8, 1918. Wilson tried to make it clear that the American people were fighting to build a new world in which there would be peace and greater opportunity for all peoples.

After the armistice was signed on November 11, 1918, Wilson went to Paris to help write a just peace treaty. From January through June 1919, until the Versailles Treaty was signed with Germany, he worked harder than he had ever worked in his life, fighting for what he thought was right. One clause in the treaty provided for the establishment of a League of Nations. Wilson was sure that the league would help to heal the world's wounds and prevent future wars.

THE FIGHT FOR THE LEAGUE

Wilson returned to the United States on July 8, 1919. He presented the Versailles Treaty to the Senate for approval two days later. Most Democrats and some Republicans in the Senate—along with an apparent majority of thoughtful people—favored immediate approval of the treaty. But a group of Republican senators, led by Henry Cabot Lodge of Massachusetts, strongly objected to the promises that Wilson had made concerning American participation in the League. They would not agree to ratify the treaty unless certain changes were made regarding United States obligations to the League. Wilson said that this would cripple the League, and he refused to accept Lodge's demands. Wilson then went on a long speaking tour of the West to plead for public support for the treaty. But he broke down from overwork before the tour was completed. On October 2, 1919, he suffered a severe stroke and was very ill for a time. He recovered enough to run the government but never regained his old powers of leadership. The result was defeat of the treaty when the Senate voted on ratification.

After leaving the White House on March 4, 1921, Wilson retired to his home in Washington, broken in body but not in spirit. He never doubted that God would cause the people to understand and share his vision of a world united for peace and progress. He died on February 3, 1924, and was buried in Washington Cathedral.

WARREN G. HARDING

29th PRESIDENT OF THE UNITED STATES (1921–1923)

Born: *November 2, 1865, at Corsica, Ohio*
Occupation: *Editor-Publisher*
Party: *Republican*
Vice President: *Calvin Coolidge*
Wife: *Florence Kling DeWolfe*
Died: *August 2, 1923, at San Francisco, California*

money in it." He also worked as a printer's devil, or apprentice, and office boy on the Caledonia *Argus*, a local newspaper. There he learned how to set type and gained his first newspaper experience.

In 1879, at the age of 14, Harding entered Ohio Central College in Iberia. After graduating in 1882 he took a job as a schoolteacher. But he gave up teaching after one term, calling it the hardest job he had ever had. The following year the Hardings moved to Marion, Ohio. Harding studied law for a few months, but soon discovered that he did not like it. He also tried unsuccessfully to sell insurance.

NEWSPAPERMAN AND MARRIAGE

Finally, in 1884, Harding borrowed some money from his father and with two young friends bought the Marion *Star*. His partners soon dropped out, leaving him in control of the newspaper. The *Star* had no circulation and no reputation. To obtain money for his paper, the young editor talked the local merchants into advertising their goods.

At about this time Harding began courting Mrs. Florence Kling DeWolfe, a widow. In spite of her father's opposition, they were married in 1891. Florence Harding was far more industrious and ambitious than her husband. Under her influence the *Star* prospered, and Harding's career really began. One of his reporters later said of her: "Mrs. Harding blazed the way. She had faith in his future. She believed he had the makings in him of a great man. She urged him on and on."

POLITICS

As the *Star* prospered, Harding became one of Marion's leading citizens. He was a director of the county bank, a trustee of the local Baptist church, and a prominent member of many social organizations. Kind and good-natured, he was well liked in the small community.

I n the 1920 presidential election, Americans voted overwhelmingly for Warren G. Harding, who had promised to take the nation "back to normalcy" after the difficult times during and after World War I. As president, Harding saw his victory as a call to follow a conservative policy, both at home and abroad.

Friendly and handsome as a movie actor, Harding looked the image of a president. But less than three years after winning election, he was dead in office, his name tarnished by political scandals.

EARLY YEARS

Harding was born on November 2, 1865, in Corsica (now Blooming Grove), Ohio. He was the eldest of eight children. His father, George Tryon Harding, was a farmer and a doctor. His mother, Phoebe Dickerson Harding, was a "gentle, pious" woman who devoted herself to her children.

As a boy Warren helped his father on the farm. During summer vacations he worked in a sawmill making brooms and drove a team of horses for the Toledo and Ohio Central Railroad. His father later said of him, "Warren was always willing to work hard if there was any

In 1898, Harding won election as a Republican to the Ohio State Senate. In 1902 he was elected lieutenant governor of Ohio and served for two years. Harding left politics temporarily in 1906 and returned to Marion to devote himself to the *Star*. In 1910 he returned to politics to run for governor of Ohio. He was defeated, but in 1914 he was elected to the U.S. Senate.

Senator and Mrs. Harding particularly enjoyed the social life of Washington, D.C., and Harding thought the Senate "a very pleasant place." He showed the same good nature and personal modesty in Congress that he had in Marion, and he loyally supported the policies of the Republican leaders. He introduced no bills of national importance while in the Senate, and he attempted to cast his votes so as to avoid alienating any important group of his constituents. Harding did have an ability to bring opposing sides together and this caused the Republican party leadership to notice him. He sounded the call for unity after the Progressive Party split of 1912. And as a member of the important Senate Foreign Relations Committee, he gained additional national attention in opposing the League of Nations after World War I.

"He looks like a president." In the months before the 1920 Republican convention in Chicago, an Ohio admirer, Harry Daugherty, had been advancing Harding's candidacy for the presidential nomination. "He looks like a president," Daugherty later explained. Harding's other qualifications were so modest that few people took his candidacy seriously. But the stronger candidates at the convention, Leonard Wood and Frank O. Lowden, blocked each other from the nomination. As a result, a powerful group of senators and their allies met in a hotel room to select a compromise candidate. Because he could be controlled, Harding became their choice for the presidential nomination.

The Election of 1920. The Republican campaign slogan was "Back to normalcy with Harding." But it was

Before he entered politics, Warren Harding was a successful newspaper editor and publisher in Marion, Ohio.

not clear during the campaign just what this meant. It was especially difficult to determine from Harding's speeches whether he was for or against American entrance into the League of Nations which Wilson had so passionately endorsed. Harding was still trying to please everyone. The Democratic candidate, James A. Cox, campaigned vigorously for American participation in the League.

Florence Kling DeWolfe was a widow when she married Harding in 1891. She enjoyed entertaining and, with the president, opened the White House to the public.

Harding conducted a front-porch campaign, speaking to voters from the porch of his home. This put many people in mind of President William McKinley, who had done much the same thing 20 years before. After the hardships of World War I, a return to "normalcy" and the good times of McKinley appealed to many voters. Harding received 61 percent of the popular vote—126,143,000 to Cox's 9,130,000—and 404 electoral votes to Cox's 127. Calvin Coolidge was elected as Harding's vice president.

PRESIDENT

President and Mrs. Harding immediately won the goodwill of the country. They said they wanted to be thought of as "just folks." Harding opened the White House to the public and cheerfully greeted anyone who came to see him. He said that while he knew he could not be the best president the United States ever had, he wanted to be the best-loved.

Harding tried to form a cabinet made up of the "best minds" in the country. Some of his appointments, such

Warren G. Harding (signature)

Warren Gamaliel Harding

29th president, 1921–23   Republican

1865   Born on November 2 in Blooming Grove, Ohio.

1882   Graduated from Ohio Central College in Iberia.

1884   Bought the Marion *Star*, a small, struggling weekly, and devoted himself to it wholly for some 15 years. The *Star* eventually became one of the most successful small-town newspapers in the state.

1891   Married Florence Kling DeWolfe on July 8.

1898   Elected to the Ohio state Senate; reelected in 1900. Served as floor leader during second term.

1902   Elected lieutenant governor of Ohio.

1910   Ran unsuccessfully for governor.

1912   Delivered nominating address for President Taft at GOP convention. Political fortunes began to rise.

1914   Elected to U.S. Senate.

1920   Won Republican nomination for president and campaigned on "Return to Normalcy" slogan. Easily defeated James M. Cox in November election.

1923   Returning from a trip to Alaska, died in San Francisco on August 2.

Highlights of Presidency

1921   In May, Congress set up a national quota system for immigration. In June, the Budget and Accounting Act was signed into law; the Bureau of the Budget was created. On July 2, the president signed joint congressional resolution of peace with Germany, Austria, and Hungary. Treaties were signed in August. On November 12, the International Conference on Limitation of Armaments opened in Washington. It lasted until Feb. 6, 1922. Major powers agreed to limit naval construction.

1921-22   Ordered federal troops into West Virginia during coal strike of 1921. Sweeping federal injunction issued against Railway Shopmen's Strike of 1922.

1922   Fordney-McCumber Act, raising tariffs on manufactured goods to highest level to date, signed into law.

1923   In June, the president set out on transcontinental "Voyage of Understanding" to promote U.S. participation in the World Court. Took ill on his way back. For months, evidence of corruption in his administration had been coming to light. After his death, several high officials were linked to Teapot Dome and other scandals.

as Herbert Hoover as secretary of commerce, Andrew Mellon to the Treasury, and Charles Evans Hughes as secretary of state, were well made. (Hoover would win election himself as president in 1928.) But many others were not. Men like Secretary of the Interior Albert Fall and Attorney General Harry M. Daugherty later proved unworthy of the trust placed in them.

Administration. Harding interpreted his victory as a popular mandate to stay out of the League of Nations. He refused to cooperate with European nations in collective security plans. Instead, he called an international conference to reduce naval armaments and thus decrease the possibility of war. At the Washington Conference, which opened in 1921, Secretary of State Hughes recommended large cuts in the navies of the United States, Britain, and Japan. The resulting Five Power Naval Treaty of 1922 led an Englishman to remark: "Secretary Hughes sunk in 35 minutes more ships than all the admirals of the world have sunk in a cycle of centuries."

The more conservative Republicans in Congress were able to push through much of their program and to obtain the president's approval of their bills. They did away with remaining wartime government restrictions, cut taxes, and created a federal budget system. They reestablished the high protective tariff (a tax on imported goods) and for the first time in American history drastically restricted immigration. Under the Immigration Quota Act of 1921, the flood of immigrants was cut to no more than a trickle. During Harding's "normal" presidency, the Tomb of the Unknown soldier was dedicated in 1921 at Arlington National Cemetery, Virginia. Also, the Lincoln Memorial was dedicated in 1922 in Washington, D.C.

One of the positive gains of Harding's administration was not achieved while he lived. The President had appealed to the leaders of the iron and steel industry to eliminate the 12-hour day or 7-day week they were still

As president, Harding, shown here with baseball great Babe Ruth, sought to be a popular chief executive and return the country to "normalcy" after World War I.

Harding, the man who "looks like a president," is shown here flanked by Will Hayes (left) of the Republican National Committee and Calvin Coolidge, Harding's vice president. Coolidge became president when Harding died in office in 1923.

requiring of some employees. It was not until August 13, 1923, just 11 days after Harding's death, that the companies put into effect an 8-hour day.

Death. In June 1923, President Harding and his wife left Washington for a trip across the country. While returning from Alaska, Harding began to show signs of fatigue and illness. He was also worried about reports of a Senate investigation of men he had appointed to office. He remarked privately: "I have no trouble with my enemies. . . . But my friends, . . . they're the ones that keep me walking the floor nights!" Harding arrived in San Francisco apparently suffering from food poisoning. He developed pneumonia, complicated by a heart ailment, and died suddenly on August 2, 1923.

AFTERMATH

Harding was succeeded by Vice President Calvin Coolidge. At first the nation was plunged into grief over the president's death. Soon, however, scandals broke out that ruined his reputation.

The most spectacular of these was the Teapot Dome scandal, involving Secretary of the Interior Fall. Fall had accepted large bribes to lease to private oil companies some valuable oil deposits that belonged to the Navy—at Teapot Dome, Wyoming. He was fined $100,000 and sent to jail. Attorney General Daugherty was involved in another scandal. He was forced to resign and later was brought to trial but acquitted. Even so, the taint remained, and he had been a friend and confidant of Harding's. Other corruption came to light in the Veterans Bureau and the Office of the Alien Property Custodian. The president was never directly implicated in the disgrace. Nevertheless, his policy of leaving all responsibility to his cabinet members and advisors eventually destroyed his administration and its reputation. It is ironic that a man who wanted only to be well-liked should be remembered only by the scandals that came to light after his death.

Mrs. Harding died a year after her husband. She was buried at his side in Marion, Ohio, at Hillside Cemetery.

DID YOU KNOW?

- *Both of Harding's parents were doctors.*
- *One of his sisters was a Washington, D.C., policewoman.*
- *A newspaper publisher, he was the first businessman president.*
- *Harding was the first president to ride to his inauguration in an automobile.*
- *He was the first president to own a radio.*
- *While president, Harding played golf, poker twice a week, followed baseball and boxing, and sneaked off to burlesque shows.*

CALVIN COOLIDGE

30th PRESIDENT OF THE UNITED STATES (1923–1929)

Born: *July 4, 1872, at Plymouth Notch, Vermont*
Occupation: *Lawyer*
Party: *Republican*
Vice President: *Charles G. Dawes*
Wife: *Grace Anna Goodhue*
Died: *January 5, 1933, at Northampton, Massachusetts*

"SILENT CAL"

Young Calvin helped with the chores on the farm and went to the one-room village school. When he was 13, he entered Black River Academy at Ludlow, Vermont. In 1891 he was admitted to Amherst College in Massachusetts.

Coolidge was not a brilliant student at Amherst, but he studied hard and in 1895 he was graduated with honors. He did well as a debater and public speaker and was chosen as one of the speakers at his graduation. In private conversation, however, he was a man of few words. His nickname of "Silent Cal" was well earned. There is a story that is frequently told about him. A man once bet a friend that he could make Cal say at least *three* words in a conversation. When the man met Coolidge, he told him of the bet. All Coolidge said was, "You lose."

After graduation Coolidge decided to become a lawyer. He went to work in a law office in Northampton, Massachusetts, and studied for the bar examination. Although three years of study were required, he passed the examination after less than two years.

In 1898, at the age of 25, Coolidge opened his own law office in Northampton. He kept a careful account of his earnings and noted that in his first year of practice he earned $500.

Coolidge's upbringing made him place great emphasis on thrift. He never owned an automobile and, until he retired from the presidency, he never owned his own home. In later years he liked to remark that there were two ways to be self-respecting: "To spend less than you make, and to make more than you spend." Coolidge always spent less than he made.

EARLY POLITICAL CAREER

Coolidge had shown some interest in politics at college, and he soon began to take an active part in Northampton

For Americans, July 4 marks Independence Day and the birth of the United States. For John and Victoria Josephine Moor Coolidge of Plymouth Notch, Vermont, July 4, 1872, also marked the birth of a son. Their son, whom they named John Calvin Coolidge, was to become the 30th president of the United States. Later they had a daughter, Abigail.

EARLY LIFE

Calvin Coolidge's ancestors came to America from England in about 1630. The first Coolidge to live in Plymouth Notch was John Coolidge of Massachusetts, a soldier in the Revolutionary War, who settled there in the 1780's. The Coolidges were hardworking farmers and storekeepers. Some of Calvin's ancestors had been deacons in the community church and served in local political offices. Calvin's father had been elected to the Vermont legislature. The Coolidges' ideals of honesty, thrift, and hard work were passed down from generation to generation. And young Calvin Coolidge was brought up to believe in these ideals.

Calvin Coolidge (left), strikes a pose in 1895 while attending Amherst College. Coolidge (above), became Massachusetts Governor in 1918 and is shown with his wife and sons, Calvin (left), and John. She was the opposite of her quiet husband.

politics. He worked hard for the Republican Party, and in 1898 he was elected to his first office—city councilman.

In 1906 Coolidge was elected to the Massachusetts House of Representatives. He was a conservative in politics and did not trust reformers. But he did vote for two reform resolutions that later became amendments to the United States Constitution. One resolution called for the direct election of United States senators by the people (senators were then elected by the state legislatures). The other gave women the right to vote.

After two terms in the legislature, Coolidge returned to Northampton. In 1909 he was elected mayor. With his goal of thrifty government, Coolidge lowered taxes and reduced the city debt. At the same time he was able to raise the pay of many city employees.

While in Northampton, Coolidge met Grace Goodhue, a teacher at a school for the deaf. They were married in 1905 and had two sons. Mrs. Coolidge was gay and full of fun—just the opposite of her quiet, careful husband.

GOVERNOR OF MASSACHUSETTS

In 1911 Coolidge returned to the legislature as a state senator. His reelection to a second and third term in the Senate made him an important figure in state politics. In 1915 he was elected lieutenant governor, and three years later he became governor of Massachusetts.

The Boston Police Strike. In 1919 an event occurred that made Governor Coolidge a national figure. On September 9, 1919, most of the Boston police force went on strike for higher pay. For two days there was rioting and robbery in the city of Boston. Finally, in response to the mayor's call for help, Coolidge called out

the National Guard, and order was restored. In reply to a plea for sympathy for the striking policemen, Coolidge issued his famous statement: "There is no right to strike against the public safety by anybody, anywhere, any time." He became a national hero and a symbol of law and order.

DID YOU KNOW?

- *When governor of Massachusetts, Coolidge was once punched in the eye by the mayor of Boston.*

- *He was the only president sworn into office by his father, a justice of the peace and notary public.*

- *Grace Coolidge first saw her husband through a window; he was shaving while wearing long johns and a brown derby.*

- *Coolidge averaged nine hours of sleep a night and took afternoon naps of from two to four hours.*

Calvin Coolidge

30th president, 1923–29 Republican

1872 Born on July 4 in Plymouth Notch, Vermont.

1895 Graduated from Amherst College.

1897 Admitted to the Massachusetts bar.

1898 Elected city councilman of Northampton, Massachusetts.

1905 Married Grace Anna Goodhue on October 4. They would become the parents of two sons.

1906 Elected to the Massachusetts House of Representatives. Served two one-year terms.

1909 Elected mayor of Northampton. Reelected in 1910.

1911 Entered Massachusetts Senate. Won reelection twice. In third term, elected president of Senate.

1915 Ran successfully for lieutenant governor of Massachusetts. Served three years.

1918 Elected governor of Massachusetts. Gained prominence in 1919 by calling out the National Guard in the Boston police strike.

1920 Lost Republican presidential nomination to Warren G. Harding; selected as vice presidential candidate.

1923 On August 3, sworn in as 30th president after the death of President Harding.

1929 Published *The Autobiography of Calvin Coolidge*.

1933 Died on January 5 in Northampton.

Highlights of Presidency

1924 Pressed for investigations and prosecutions relating to scandals involving members of the Harding administration. Was elected president in his own right.

1925 U.S. Marines sent to Nicaragua after outbreak of civil war. In 1927, the president sent Henry Stimson to work out compromise, but Gen. Augusta César Sandino launched guerrilla war that lasted until withdrawal of U.S. troops in 1933.

1926 Vetoed the McNary-Haugen farm bill, which called for dumping of agricultural surpluses. Vetoed the relief measure again in 1928.

1927 Despite strong party support, announced on August 2: "I do not choose to run for president in 1928."

1928 Kellogg-Briand Pact, an agreement "to renounce war as an instrument of national policy," was signed in Paris by 15 nations on August 24.

In the 1920 Republican Party convention, Senator Warren G. Harding won the nomination as candidate for president. When one of the delegates suggested Coolidge's name for vice president, the cry of "We want Coolidge" rang out through the convention hall. Coolidge became the vice presidential candidate, and in the election of 1920 Harding and Coolidge won an overwhelming victory.

PRESIDENT

On the morning of August 3, 1923, Vice President Coolidge was in Plymouth, visiting his father, when the news of Harding's death reached him. Coolidge was now president of the United States. His father, a notary public, administered the oath of office to him.

Soon after Coolidge entered the White House, the scandals of Harding's administration came to public attention. The worst was the Teapot Dome oil scandal, which involved members of Harding's cabinet. Coolidge was never connected with the scandals, and his reputation helped to save the Republican Party from disgrace.

Coolidge was so popular that he had no trouble winning the election of 1924. His campaign slogan was "Keep Cool with Coolidge," and he received almost twice as many popular votes as his Democratic opponent, John W. Davis.

The Roaring 20s

Calvin Coolidge was president during one of the most colorful periods in American history. The 1920s are often called the Roaring 20s and the Jazz Age. It was the era of Prohibition. The Volstead Act, the 18th amendment to the Constitution, had made the sale of alcoholic beverages illegal. But many people ignored this highly unpopular law and purchased liquor from "bootleggers" or in "speakeasies." The most notorious of the bootleggers was a man who helped make the word "gangster" a part of the language—Al Capone.

But the 20s were more than an era of bootleg liquor and gangsters. The 19th amendment to the

President and Mrs. Coolidge are pictured on the way to his inauguration in 1925. Senator Charles Curtis is at right.

President Coolidge (above) opens the baseball season by throwing out the first ball. The president (right) celebrates a western-style Fourth of July at Rapid City, South Dakota. July 4 was also his birthday.

Constitution gave women throughout the United States the right to vote. Charles A. Lindbergh became the first man to fly nonstop and alone across the Atlantic Ocean. The first talking movie, *The Jazz Singer*, starring Al Jolson, was produced. It was a golden age of sports. Babe Ruth was hitting home runs, and Gene Tunney defeated Jack Dempsey for the heavyweight boxing championship of the world.

During the 1920s the population of the United States grew from less than 106,000,000 to almost 123,000,000. And for the first time in American history, more people lived in cities and towns than in rural areas. The country seemed prosperous, and everybody wanted to have a good time and not worry too much about tomorrow.

Coolidge's Popularity

Coolidge was popular because the people saw him as a symbol of the prosperous times. They also admired his old-fashioned virtues of thrift and common sense. As president he was conservative in his views on economics. He did not believe in government interference in private business. However, his support of a high protective tariff, or tax on goods imported into the United States, aided American business. With his respect for thrift, Coolidge worked to limit government spending, to reduce the national debt, and to lower taxes. But, though there was prosperity, not everybody shared in it. Many industrial workers were paid low wages, and farmers were hard hit by declining prices on their crops. A bill to raise the prices of farm products was vetoed by Coolidge.

Foreign Affairs

Coolidge took little interest in foreign affairs. He opposed the United States' joining the League of Nations. He did favor American membership in the World Court. But Congress' insistence on certain conditions before approv-

ing membership, and Coolidge's lack of real enthusiasm kept the United States out of the Court. The Kellogg-Briand Pact, an American and French plan to outlaw war, met with more success. It was signed by the United States and 14 other nations in 1928.

Coolidge showed more concern about Latin American matters. Revolutions in Nicaragua prompted him to send 5,000 marines to that country to protect American lives and business interests. When relations between Mexico and the United States became strained in a dispute over oil lands, the president appointed Dwight W. Morrow ambassador to Mexico. Morrow succeeded in improving relations between the two countries.

FINAL YEARS

Many people thought that Coolidge would run again for president. He surprised the nation when he said: "I do not choose to run for president in 1928." In the election of 1928, Herbert Hoover became president.

Some historians and economists have criticized Coolidge for a lack of forcefulness and political leadership. They say that his administration was partly responsible for the Great Depression that began in 1929, soon after President Hoover took office. However, during the 1920s, most Americans supported Coolidge's policies.

After Coolidge left the White House, he returned to Northampton, Massachusetts, where he spent the remaining years of his life. He wrote articles for a newspaper, giving his opinion on current events and politics, and he published his autobiography. On January 5, 1933, he died suddenly of a heart attack.

31st PRESIDENT OF THE UNITED STATES (1929–1933)

Born: August 10, 1874, at West Branch, Iowa
Occupation: Engineer
Party: Republican
Vice President: Charles Curtis
Wife: Lou Henry
Died: October 20, 1964, in New York, New York

Hoover wanted to be a mining engineer, and when he was 16, he took the entrance examinations for Leland Stanford, a new university in Palo Alto, California. He failed, except for the section on mathematics. Nevertheless, Hoover gathered his possessions—two suits, a bicycle, and $160—and went to Palo Alto anyway. After two months of studying, he took the tests again. This time he passed. In the fall of 1891 he entered Stanford as one of its first students.

Hoover worked his way through college. He clerked, delivered newspapers, ran a laundry, and managed special lectures and concerts. During summer months he worked on geological surveys in Arkansas and Nevada. Hoover soon showed his talent for business as financial manager of the Stanford football team. Once he arranged a game that sold over $30,000 worth of tickets.

ENGINEERING CAREER

After graduating in 1895, Hoover's first job was as a laborer in the goldfields of Nevada. In 1896 he went to San Francisco, where he was hired by a well-known firm of mining engineers. He started as an office boy, but in less than a year he was assistant to the superintendent of one of the company's mines. In 1897 a British company hired the 23-year-old Hoover to manage its gold mines in Australia. This was the start of a career that would take him around the world and make him a rich man.

Hoover spent two years in Australia. He returned home only long enough to marry Lou Henry on February 10, 1899. She had been a fellow student at Stanford. The next day they sailed for China, where Hoover had been appointed director of the Chinese bureau of mines. Soon after they arrived, the Boxer Rebellion—a revolt of Chinese against foreign domination—broke out. Hoover organized water and food supplies in the city of Tientsin. It was his first job in the kind of work that later made him famous.

The life of Herbert Hoover is an American success story. Orphaned at the age of nine, Hoover rose to become a successful mining engineer and a wealthy businessman. During World War I he headed a relief commission that provided food for millions of starving people in Europe. He became United States food administrator, then secretary of commerce in the 1920s, and in 1929 president of the United States.

EARLY YEARS

Hoover was born in West Branch, Iowa, on August 10, 1874. He was the second of three children of Jesse Hoover, a blacksmith, and Hulda Randall Minthorn Hoover. His parents were Quakers. In 1880, when Herbert was six, his father died of typhoid fever. Three years later his mother died of pneumonia, and Herbert went to live with an uncle, Allan Hoover, who had a farm near West Branch.

For a year he led a carefree life on his uncle's farm. Then he was sent to live with another uncle, Dr. Henry Minthorn, in Newberg, Oregon. There he attended a Quaker academy, helped with the chores, and worked at part-time and summer jobs.

During the next 15 years Hoover worked on engineering projects in Europe, India, South Africa, and Egypt. He also wrote *Principles of Mining* and, with his wife, translated a 16th-century Latin work, Agricola's *De Re Metallica* ("About Metals"). By 1914 he was known as the boy wonder of mining engineering. He was manager of a number of mining companies throughout the world and consultant to many others. Not yet 40 years old, he was already rich enough to retire.

PUBLIC SERVICE CAREER

Hoover was in London when World War I broke out in 1914. The American ambassador, Walter Hines Page, asked him to help with the thousands of Americans stranded in Europe by the outbreak of war. Hoover became head of the American Repatriation Committee, which helped the Americans borrow money to return home.

When the German Army invaded Belgium, Page again called on Hoover, who organized a group to send food to starving Belgians and Frenchmen in the war zones. This was the start of the Commission for Relief in Belgium, which fed 10,000,000 Belgians and Frenchmen during the war.

When the United States entered the war in 1917, President Woodrow Wilson appointed Hoover United States food administrator with the job of regulating and directing food production. It was especially important to supply more food to Allied and neutral countries. Hoover asked Americans to cooperate by saving food. His motto was "Food will win the war!" and "hooverize" came to mean "economize."

After the war ended in 1918, Eastern Europe was struck by a famine caused by crop failures. Hoover turned his food administration into a relief agency to send American surplus food to the starving people there. In 1918 and 1919 Hoover's agency provided food for 300,000,000 people.

POLITICAL CAREER

When his humanitarian task came to an end, Hoover planned to return to engineering. But by 1920 he was one of the most popular men in the U.S. Hoover clubs were formed to boost his nomination at the 1920 Republican convention. But Warren G. Harding won the nomination and the election. President Harding offered Hoover his choice of the posts of secretary of the interior or secretary of commerce. Hoover chose the commerce post. After Harding died in 1923, President Calvin Coolidge reappointed Hoover. For eight years he headed the Department of Commerce, which he reorganized and enlarged.

The Election of 1928

When Coolidge decided not to run again for president in 1928, Hoover's popularity made him the natural choice of the Republicans. His Democratic opponent was Governor Alfred E. Smith of New York. The campaign was a bitter one, centering on two issues. One was religion. The second was prohibition. Under a Constitutional amendment the federal government had banned the sale of liquor. Many voters opposed Smith be cause he was a Catholic, a big-city man, and against prohibition. Hoover campaigned on a platform of prosperity. The United States

Hoover (below, left) is shown during his early, spectacularly successful career as a young mining engineer in Australia. President Hoover in 1929 (below, right), delivers the Memorial Day speech at Arlington Cemetery in Washington, D.C.

Herbert Clark Hoover

31st president, 1929-33 Republican

1874 Born on August 10 in West Branch, Iowa.

1895 Graduated from Stanford University.

1897 Began his career as a mining engineer.

1899 Married Lou Henry on February 10. The couple would become the parents of two sons.

1912 Appointed a trustee of Stanford University.

1914-15 Directed the American Relief Committee, organized to aid Americans stranded in Europe as World War I began.

1915-19 Directed the Commission for Relief in Belgium.

1917-19 Served as U.S. food administrator.

1921-28 Was U.S. secretary of commerce.

1928 Defeated New York Gov. Alfred E. Smith in the presidential race.

1942 *The Problems of Lasting Peace*, written by Hoover with Hugh Gibson, was published.

1951-52 Published his memoirs in three volumes.

1955 On June 30, retired after serving as chairman of two Commissions on Organization of the Executive Branch of Government.

1959-61 *An American Epic*, a three-volume study of his experience in international relief work, appeared.

1964 Died on October 20 in New York, New York.

Highlights of Presidency

1929 After taking oath of office on March 4, the new president called Congress into special session in April. Two months later the Agricultural Marketing Act, designed to assist farmers suffering from low incomes during an era of prosperity, was enacted. The New York Stock Market crashed on October 29, beginning a severe economic depression that dominated the Hoover presidency.

1930 The London Naval Conference limited the number of small vessels, battleships, and cruisers various nations could construct. On February 3, the president named Charles Evans Hughes chief justice of the Supreme Court.

1932 On January 7, Secretary of State Henry L. Stimson announced the Stimson Doctrine, declaring that the United States would not recognize territorial conquest. Also in January, Congress established the Reconstruction Finance Corporation. In November, Hoover was defeated in bid for reelection by Franklin D. Roosevelt.

was rich and could grow even richer. Voters were promised "a chicken in every pot."

Hoover won a landslide victory, receiving 444 electoral votes to Smith's 87. The popular vote was 21,392,000 for Hoover and 15,016,000 for Smith. The orphan from Iowa had become president, the first from west of the Mississippi River.

PRESIDENT

But less than a year after Hoover took office, in October 1929, the stock market crashed, starting the United States toward the worst depression in its history.

Actually, the prosperity enjoyed by the United States during the 1920s had been misleading. Not everyone had shared in it. Farmers were hard hit because of falling prices on their crops. Stock prices were too high, and the stock market was weakened by the practice of buying stocks on credit.

The Smoot-Hawley tariff bill, passed by Congress in 1930, helped intensify the Depression. The bill was meant to help farmers meet European competition by raising tariffs (import taxes) on farm products. Hoover, who had promised during the campaign to help the farmers, signed the bill reluctantly, for it also raised tariffs on many manufactured goods. In retaliation, European countries raised their tariffs on American goods, thus reducing European purchase of American products.

The Depression

Hoover was faced with a task that made all others he had undertaken look small. The stock market crash had wiped out many investors. As businesses went bankrupt and banks failed, people lost their jobs and their savings. Many political leaders and businessmen thought that the Depression would not last long—that "Prosperity was just around the corner." Hoover was reluctant to interfere in the economy. Instead, he favored voluntary co-operation by business, and relief for the jobless and hungry through state and local agencies. He called businessmen to Washington to urge them to keep their factories going. Addressing the nation, he appealed to the people to have confidence.

But the Depression deepened, soon spreading to Europe. In 1931 Hoover introduced a one-year moratorium, or delay, on war debt payments owed to the United States by European nations. This helped them fight their own depressions and in turn helped the American economy.

In January 1932, at the president's urging, Congress established the Reconstruction Finance Corporation. This agency provided federal loans for banks and businesses and funds to the states for local relief. Huge public works projects were started to provide jobs for workers.

Foreign Affairs

Hoover's main concern in foreign affairs was for peace. The United States took part in the London Naval Conference in 1930, which was attended by the leading

Hoover's advice was sought by many during his long career, including President John F. Kennedy (left) in 1961.

nations of the world. The members of the conference hoped to prevent war by limiting the size and number of warships. When Japan invaded Manchuria in 1931, Hoover condemned the Japanese and refused to recognize their conquests in Manchuria. This policy of nonrecognition, named the Stimson Doctrine, after Secretary of State Henry L. Stimson, might better be called the Hoover Doctrine. Relations with Latin America were improved when Hoover removed United States Marines from Nicaragua, where they had been stationed since 1912.

The Election of 1932

As election time approached, Republicans did not expect victory. The Depression had become worse. Over 10,000,000 people were out of work, and almost everyone blamed Hoover for the hard times, often unfairly. Poor people lived in shanty towns, which they called Hoovervilles. Newspapers, used to keep out the cold, were nicknamed Hoover blankets. Hoover lost the election to the Democratic candidate, New York Governor Franklin D. Roosevelt, by a margin of more than 7,000,000 popular votes.

Hoover left the White House in 1933 and returned to Palo Alto, where he served as a trustee of Stanford University and founded the Hoover Library. Later he moved to New York City. He wrote lengthy memoirs and several books critical of President Roosevelt's New Deal. His two sons, Allan and Herbert, Jr., became mining engineers like their father. (Herbert, Jr., later served as undersecretary of state under President Eisenhower.)

LATER YEARS

During and after World War II, Hoover returned to humanitarian work, directing famine relief in Europe. In 1947 President Harry S. Truman appointed him to head a commission on reorganization of the executive branch of the government. A second Hoover Commission, as it was called, was established by President Eisenhower in 1953.

Hoover died in New York City on October 20, 1964, at the age of 90.

In a letter to a young admirer Hoover once summed up his personal philosophy: get the "constructive joy out of life"; be honest, sportsmanlike, and considerate of others; have "religious faith"; be "a man of education."

DID YOU KNOW?

SEAL OF THE PRESIDENT OF THE UNITED STATES

- *Hoover's great-grandfather anglicized the family name from the German Huber.*

- *He was the youngest member of Stanford University's first graduating class.*

- *During their first three years in the White House, the Hoovers dined alone only three times, each time on their wedding anniversary.*

- *He was the first president to donate his salary to charity.*

- *One of the most honored presidents, Hoover received 84 honorary degrees, 78 medals and awards, and the keys to dozens of cities.*

FRANKLIN D. ROOSEVELT

32nd PRESIDENT OF THE UNITED STATES (1933–1945)

Born: *January 30, 1882, at Hyde Park, New York*
Occupation: *Public Official, Lawyer*
Party: *Democrat*
Vice Presidents: *John N. Garner (1933–41); Henry A. Wallace (1941–45); Harry S. Truman (1945)*
Wife: *Anna Eleanor Roosevelt*
Died: *April 12, 1945, at Warm Springs, Georgia*

Franklin D. Roosevelt served longer than any other president of the United States. He held office from 1933 until his death in 1945 at the beginning of his fourth term. During his presidency he led the United States through two great crises—the Depression of the 1930s and World War II.

Roosevelt was a man of unusual charm and great optimism, which he was able to communicate to others. He had a broad smile and an easygoing way of nodding agreement to whatever proposals were made to him. But beneath his outward friendliness was an inner reserve and an iron will. He became one of the most beloved as well as one of the most hated of American presidents. His admirers emphasized the courage with which he met his illness—an attack of polio that left him permanently unable to walk—and the way in which, as president, he met the nation's problems. They praised him for insisting that the federal government must help the underprivileged and that the United States must share in the responsibility for preserving world peace. Roosevelt's opponents denounced him for increasing the role of the federal government in the economic life of the country and for the heavy spending of his administration. His opponents also criticized his wartime leadership. They claimed that he unnecessarily involved the United States in World War II and that he was fooled by the Communists.

Yet friend and foe alike agreed that Roosevelt made a vital impact upon his times, and that his policies exerted great influence on the future.

EARLY YEARS

Roosevelt was born on an estate overlooking the Hudson River at Hyde Park, New York, on January 30, 1882. He had a pleasant childhood. His father James Roosevelt, then in his middle 50s, was a well-to-do investor and vice president of a small railroad. His mother, Sara Delano Roosevelt, came from a wealthy family of New England origin. During his childhood Franklin was taught by a governess and was taken on frequent trips to Europe. Once his father took him to the White House to see President Grover Cleveland. Cleveland, saddened and worn by the burdens of office, said he hoped that young Franklin would never have the misfortune of becoming president.

At 14 Roosevelt entered Groton School in Massachusetts. From Groton he went to Harvard University. There he concerned himself more with social life and other activities than with his studies. He was especially proud of the fact that he was president (chief editor) of the Harvard *Crimson*, the student newspaper. He graduated in 1904 and went on to Columbia University Law School. Meanwhile, he had become engaged to his distant cousin, Anna Eleanor Roosevelt. At the wedding in 1905 Eleanor's uncle, President Theodore Roosevelt (who was Franklin's fifth cousin), gave her in marriage.

Roosevelt was an indifferent law student and did not bother to complete work for his degree after passing his bar examination. Nor was he much interested in his work with a prominent Wall Street law firm.

POLITICS

In 1910 the Democratic leaders in Dutchess County, New York, persuaded Roosevelt to run for the New York State Senate. The Senate contest seemed hopeless for a Democrat. Nevertheless Roosevelt conducted an energetic campaign, touring the Hudson River farming communities in a red Maxwell automobile. The Republicans were split that year, and he won his first election. Shortly before his 29th birthday he entered the New York Senate.

Roosevelt supported Woodrow Wilson for the presidential nomination, and when Wilson became president in 1913, Roosevelt was appointed assistant secretary of the Navy. He still seemed too handsome and too unpredictable to be taken very seriously. Some people said that his initials "F. D." stood for "feather duster." Yet Roosevelt was especially successful as an administrator during World War I. He was also achieving a reputation as a rising young progressive. In 1920, at the age of 38, he won the Democratic nomination for vice president, running with James M. Cox of Ohio. But the Democrats were buried in the landslide victory of Warren Harding.

ILLNESS

Biding his time, Roosevelt entered private business. Then, in the summer of 1921, while vacationing at Campobello Island in Canada, he was suddenly stricken with polio. Even after the worst had passed, he was still paralyzed from the waist down. Not yet 40, he seemed finished in politics. His mother wanted him to retire to Hyde Park. His wife, Eleanor, and his private secretary, Louis Howe, disagreed. They felt that his recovery would be aided if he kept his political interests. Eleanor, now the mother of five children (a sixth child had died in 1909), cast aside her acute shyness and learned to make appearances for her husband at political meetings. In spite of his illness, Roosevelt remained one of the dominant figures in the Democratic Party during the 1920s.

Above all, during these years Roosevelt turned his energies to recovering his health. He achieved the best results when be began swimming in the hot mineral waters at Warm Springs, a resort in Georgia. Roosevelt turned Warm Springs into a great national center for the treatment of polio. But he was still unable to walk without leg braces, a cane, and a strong arm upon which to lean.

Franklin Roosevelt had a sheltered childhood in Hyde Park, New York.

GOVERNOR

In 1928 Governor Alfred E. Smith of New York urged Roosevelt to run for governor of New York. Smith was then the Democratic candidate for president. Reluctantly, Roosevelt agreed; he had wanted to wait several years until he regained the use of his legs. Herbert Hoover defeated Smith for the presidency, but Roosevelt was elected governor by a narrow margin. His reelection in 1930 by a record majority made him the leading candidate for the Democratic presidential nomination in 1932.

During the 1932 election campaign the Depression overshadowed all other issues. In accepting the nomination, Roosevelt had promised the American people a "New Deal." A great majority of the voters were eager to try anything that might rescue them from their economic distress. They voted overwhelmingly for Roosevelt, who defeated Herbert Hoover by more than 7,000,000 votes.

Conditions became worse between Roosevelt's election on November 8, 1932, and his inauguration on March 4, 1933. (The 20th Amendment to the Constitution, changing the presidential inauguration date to January 20, did not go into effect until October 1933.) Thousands of banks failed as depositors, fearful of losing their savings, withdrew their money. A quarter of the nation's wage earners were unemployed, and many of the rest lived in misery. Families on relief sometimes received no more than 75 cents a week for food. Farmers were in an equally desperate plight because of low prices on basic crops.

PRESIDENT

Amid these grim conditions Roosevelt took his oath of office as president. He brought promise of immediate action to combat the Depression. "The only thing we have to fear is fear itself," he said in his inaugural speech. The words were not new, but the way Roosevelt said them gave people new hope. As a first step he closed all banks in the United States to prevent further collapse. Then he called Congress into special session to pass emergency banking legislation. Within a few days most banks were reopened, and people who had withdrawn their money redeposited it. (The Federal Deposit Insurance Corporation was established soon after. It insured bank deposits and protected people from losing their savings.)

Thus far Roosevelt had done little more than restore public confidence. But the American people were

Franklin Roosevelt's family posed with the family dog in 1920. Back row, left to right, are: Franklin Roosevelt, his mother Mrs. Sara Delano Roosevelt, and his wife Eleanor Roosevelt. Front row, left to right, are: Elliott, Franklin, Jr., John, Anna, and James.

so enthusiastic about him that Congress seemed his to command. During the first 100 days of his administration he presented to Congress a wide variety of legislation. This became the first New Deal program. These early measures contained one notable reform—the creation of the Tennessee Valley Authority (TVA). The TVA provided flood control, cheap electricity, and better use of the land for the entire poverty-stricken Tennessee River area.

Relief and Recovery

Most of the early New Deal measures were meant to bring immediate relief to the needy and recovery to the economy. A federal agency was set up to provide the states with funds to feed the hungry. Legislation was passed to aid farmers and homeowners in danger of losing their property because they could not keep up mortgage payments. The Civilian Conservation Corps (CCC) was organized, providing jobs for unemployed young men in forest conservation and road construction work. In December 1933, the 21st Amendment to the Constitution was ratified, ending the "noble experiment," Prohibition.

A series of recovery measures was enacted to raise farm and industrial prices, increase wages, and put people back to work. Many economists believed that low prices and wages (deflation) were at least partly responsible for the continuing Depression. At the president's urging, Congress took the United States off the gold standard and devaluated the dollar. This lowered its exchange value, allowing American products to be sold to better advantage abroad.

The AAA and NRA. At the heart of the recovery program of the early New Deal were the Agricultural Adjustment Administration (AAA) and the National Recovery Administration (NRA). Under the AAA, production of basic crops and livestock was limited in order to raise prices and thus increase farmers' incomes. Farmers were rewarded by benefit payments for reducing production.

The NRA was a more complicated plan. Created by the president under the terms of the National Industrial Recovery Act of 1933, it was meant to aid both business and labor. The NRA established codes of fair competition in major industries. Price cutting and various unfair business practices were prohibited in order to help manufacturers. In turn, businessmen were expected to pay at least minimum wages and to work their employees for no more than established maximum hours. Furthermore, under the terms of the Recovery Act, workers were given the right to bargain collectively; that is, to join unions of their choice, which would negotiate wages and working hours with the employers. These collective bargaining provisions were replaced in 1935 by the National Labor Relations Act (the Wagner Act). This law gave strong protection to unions and encouraged the growth of the labor movement.

None of Roosevelt's recovery measures worked quite satisfactorily, and the road to recovery was one of ups and downs. In 1935 the Supreme Court declared the NRA code system unconstitutional, and in 1936 they ruled against part of the AAA. Nevertheless, in 1935 and 1936 the economy was showing a marked improvement.

Other Measures. But although recovery seemed on the way, unemployment remained high. In the first winter of the New Deal, Roosevelt had tried a temporary work relief program for the unemployed—the Civil Works Administration (CWA). In 1935 he undertook a large-scale work program—the Works Progress Administration (WPA). Opponents of the New Deal criticized the government's heavy spending, which led to an increase in the national debt. And they denounced Roosevelt for interfering in the economy.

Three Reforms. In the summer of 1935 Roosevelt pushed through Congress three important reform measures. The Public Utility Holding Company Act placed restrictions on gas and electric utilities. The Revenue Act of 1935 placed heavier tax burdens on those in the upper income brackets. (Roosevelt's opponents called it the "soak the rich" tax.) Most important of the three was the Social Security Act. This provided for unemployment insurance, pensions for the aged, and aid to widows and orphans.

DID YOU KNOW?

- *Roosevelt was related by blood or marriage to 11 former presidents.*
- *A stamp collector, FDR received the first sheet of every new commemorative issue.*
- *In 1939, he became the first president to appear on television.*
- *He was the first president in office to visit an overseas war zone.*
- *During World War II, Mrs. Roosevelt visited Japanese-American internment camps to show her sympathy to the internees.*

President Roosevelt smiles for the camera in 1938, before delivering one of his "fireside chats" to the nation via radio.

Second Term

By 1936, Roosevelt had clearly become the champion of the underprivileged. He was reelected over the Republican candidate, Alfred M. Landon, by a margin so sweeping that he carried every state except Maine and Vermont.

The Supreme Court Crisis. Reelection by such a wide margin seemed to call for further reform. "I see one-third of a nation ill-housed, ill-clad, ill-nourished," Roosevelt declared in his second inaugural address. As a first step to aid the underprivileged, he wanted to end the Supreme Court's invalidation of New Deal measures. Roosevelt felt that these laws were constitutional but that the Supreme Court interpretation of them was sadly out of date. Therefore, in February 1937, he asked Congress to authorize him to appoint as many as six new justices to the Court.

A great controversy swept Congress and the country. Many people denounced the proposal as being the way a dictator would seek power. Roosevelt's plan failed, but the gradual retirement of the older justices brought more liberal ones to the Supreme Court. Even while the debate was going on, the Court had modified its decisions. Thereafter it approved of most government regulation of the nation's economy.

Toward Recovery. By 1937 the economy had reached almost the prosperity levels of the 1920s, although unemployment continued to be high. When Roosevelt cut New Deal spending in an effort to balance the federal budget, a sharp recession followed. He returned to heavy spending, and the trend toward recovery resumed. Large

Franklin Delano Roosevelt

32nd president, 1933–45   Democrat

1882   Born on January 30 in Hyde Park, New York.

1904   Earned B.A. degree from Harvard University.

1905   On March 17, married Anna Eleanor Roosevelt. A daughter and five sons would be born to the Roosevelts.

1907   Passed New York State Bar examination, withdrew from Columbia Law School, hired by Wall Street law firm.

1911–13   Was a New York state senator.

1913–20   Served as assistant secretary of the Navy.

1920   Ran unsuccessfully for vice president on Democratic ticket with James M. Cox.

1921   Stricken with polio while vacationing in Campobello, Maine.

1928   Elected to first of two terms as governor of New York.

1932   Elected president over incumbent Republican Herbert Hoover.

1945   Died on April 12 at Warm Springs, Georgia.

Highlights of Presidency

1933   During first 100 days as president, launched New Deal relief measures. Revived the banking industry; delivered the first of 28 "Fireside Chats." In December, the 21st Amendment, ending Prohibition, was ratified.

1934   Became the first president to visit Latin America.

1935   Social Security Act passed; Works Progress Administration (WPA) was established; Wagner Act, creating National Labor Relations Board (NLRB), was enacted.

1936   Reelected in a landslide over Alfred M. Landon. Also reelected in 1940 and 1944.

1937   President's plan to "reform" the Supreme Court was criticized and rejected.

1939   Hitler overran Poland, and war was declared in Europe.

1941   Congress enacted lend-lease, giving the president power to supply military equipment to U.S. allies. On December 7, Japanese launched surprise attack on Pearl Harbor. Congress declared war the next day.

1944   June 6, D-Day: Allied forces landed on the Normandy coast of France.

1945   Yalta Conference held in the Crimea in February. Roosevelt, Britain's Winston Churchill, and USSR's Joseph Stalin discussed the terms of peace and the postwar world.

sums were provided for the WPA and for a vast public works project—the Public Works Administration (PWA). Roosevelt also obtained from Congress the Fair Labor Standards Act of 1938. This set a national standard of minimum wages and maximum hours for workers and prohibited the shipping in interstate commerce (commerce between states) of goods made by child labor. It was the last important piece of New Deal reform legislation. Thereafter Roosevelt and the American people were concerned with events in Europe and Asia, where the aggressive policies of Hitler and Mussolini and the Japanese military leaders threatened to lead to war.

Life in the White House

Even under the great pressures of office Roosevelt found time to swim daily in the White House pool and to relax with his family and aides. The president's children and his many grandchildren often stayed at the White House, and during World War II, British Prime Minister Winston Churchill was a frequent guest.

Roosevelt enjoyed entertaining informally. When King George VI and Queen Elizabeth of Great Britain paid a state visit to the United States in 1939, the president took them to Hyde Park for a picnic of frankfurters and baked beans.

The Approach of World War II

In his first inaugural address, in 1933, Roosevelt had pledged the United States to a "good neighbor" policy. Roosevelt had carried out this pledge in Latin America. Indeed, he tried to follow a policy of goodwill throughout the world. As the threat of war became more ominous during the mid-1930s, both the president and the American public wished to remain neutral. But at the same time, Roosevelt did not want to see the aggressors triumph. When Japan invaded northern China in 1937, he declared in a speech that war, like a dangerous disease, must be quarantined.

While New York City held its first World's Fair in 1939, the country was divided about meddling in the affairs in Europe. War finally broke out in Europe when Hitler invaded Poland in September 1939. Roosevelt wished to help the democratic nations without involving the United States in war, but he did urge preparedness. Gradually, as the crisis deepened, he took greater risks of involvement. After the fall of France in 1940, Roosevelt, with the approval of Congress, rushed all possible weapons to Great Britain in order to help the British in the fight against Hitler. At this point, his strong feeling that the U.S. should enter the war led to his decision to run for a third term.

Third Term

In the election of 1940 Roosevelt ran against the Republican candidate, Wendell Willkie, who held similar views on aid to Great Britain. Isolationists, who wished the United States to keep out of European affairs, campaigned

British Prime Minister Winston Churchill, President Roosevelt, and Russian Premier Joseph Stalin met at the Yalta Conference in 1945. Roosevelt died shortly thereafter.

vigorously against Roosevelt. In spite of their opposition, he was elected to a third term.

Early in 1941, at the President's urging, Congress passed the Lend-Lease Act. This provided further aid to Great Britain and other nations fighting the Axis. Roosevelt was also trying to block Japanese advances into China and Southeast Asia. The Japanese felt they faced a choice of giving up their policy of expansion or fighting the United States. On December 7, 1941, Japanese planes attacked the American naval base at Pearl Harbor, Hawaii. The next day Congress declared war on Japan. On December 11, Germany and Italy declared war on the U.S. The nation had been swept into world war.

With the United States at war, Roosevelt temporarily set aside his plans for further New Deal reform. He now sought to increase American war production and to lead the country in a great alliance against the Axis powers. As commander in chief of the armed forces, he helped plan major offensives in Europe, leading to the Normandy invasion in 1944. At the same time, the Japanese were gradually pushed back in the Pacific.

Plans For the Future. From the beginning Roosevelt was concerned with planning a better postwar world. Even before the United States entered the war, he had declared that the American aims were the Four Freedoms: freedom of speech, freedom of worship, freedom from want, and freedom from fear.

As the war progressed, Roosevelt became increasingly interested in planning for the future self-government and economic development of colonial areas. He also hoped that an international organization could be created to prevent future wars. This organization was to be the United Nations. Roosevelt felt that the keeping of peace would depend to a considerable extent upon goodwill between the United States and the Soviet Union. He thus tried to establish friendly relations with Soviet premier Joseph Stalin at the Tehran Conference in 1943 and at the Yalta Conference in 1945.

Mrs. Roosevelt. All during her husband's political life, ever since he was stricken with polio, Eleanor Roosevelt worked tirelessly for a variety of social and political causes, until her own death in 1962. Among many other contributions, she served as a member of the U.S. delegation to the United Nations. She was a much-loved first lady.

Fourth Term

In 1944 Roosevelt was nominated for a fourth term, running against Thomas E. Dewey. Roosevelt appeared thin, worn, and tired, but late in the campaign he seemed to gain renewed energy. Again he was reelected. But his health, which had been declining since early in 1944, did not improve. After returning from the Yalta Conference, he went to Warm Springs to rest. There on April 12, 1945—less than a month before the war in Europe ended—he died of a cerebral hemorrhage. As the world mourned Roosevelt's death, Vice President Harry S. Truman took over as the new president.

At the time of his death Roosevelt had been working on a speech. In it he wrote: "We have learned in the agony of war that great power involves great responsibility. . . . The only limit to our realization of tomorrow will be our doubts of today. Let us move forward with strong and active faith."

33rd PRESIDENT OF THE UNITED STATES (1945–1953)

Born: *May 8, 1884, at Lamar, Missouri*
Occupation: *Farmer, Public Official*
Party: *Democrat*
Vice President: *Alben W. Barkley*
Wife: *Elizabeth Virginia Wallace*
Died: *December 26, 1972, at Kansas City, Missouri*

EARLY YEARS

Harry S. Truman was born in Lamar, Missouri, on May 8, 1884. He was the eldest of three children of Martha Ellen Young and John Anderson Truman. Because his parents could not decide which of his grandfathers to name him after, they gave young Harry the letter "S" instead of a middle name.

When Harry was six, the Trumans moved to Independence, Missouri. There he grew up, a bookish boy, so nearsighted that he had to wear thick glasses. After he finished high school, his father's financial difficulties prevented Harry from entering college. He held a number of jobs, eventually becoming a bank clerk. In 1906, at the age of 22, he went to work on the family farm, where he spent the next 11 years.

The entrance of the United States into World War I in 1917 gave Truman an opportunity to show his abilities. Soon after war was declared, he received his commission as a first lieutenant in the Missouri National Guard. In March 1918, he left for France with the 35th Division. Truman commanded a field artillery battery in several campaigns. Throughout the fighting he managed to maintain firm discipline among his unruly men yet retain their affection. He said afterwards: "I've always been sorry I did not get a university education in the regular way. But I got it in the Army the hard way—and it stuck."

After his discharge from the Army in 1919 with the rank of captain, Truman married his childhood sweetheart, Bess Wallace. Their only child, a daughter named Mary Margaret, was born in 1924. Soon after his marriage Truman entered into a partnership with one of his army friends and opened a men's clothing store in Kansas City. But in the postwar depression of 1921 the store

On April 12, 1945, President Franklin D. Roosevelt died suddenly of a cerebral hemorrhage. That same day Vice President Harry S. Truman was sworn in to succeed him.

Truman became president at a particularly critical time. World War II was coming to an end, and the Cold War with the Soviet Union was in its beginning stages. The new president was immediately called on to make a number of difficult and important decisions. A man of down-to-earth directness, he learned quickly and was willing to act vigorously. As a result, he was able to establish many of the basic foreign policies adopted by the United States following World War II. These included the Truman Doctrine to restrain Communist expansion and the Marshall Plan to aid war-devastated countries. Truman also is remembered for his resistance to the Soviet blockade of West Berlin and for his action in halting Communist aggression in South Korea.

Truman's domestic policy was known as the Fair Deal program. It emphasized the need for greater employment opportunities and for increased civil rights for members of minority groups.

failed. Truman lost his life savings and owed $20,000 in debts. He refused to go into bankruptcy, however, and instead scraped for 15 years to pay off the money he owed.

POLITICS

Truman's friends urged him to enter politics. Like his father, he was a Democrat with strong views. In 1922, Truman won election as one of three judges of the Jackson County Court. His friends called him Judge Truman, but his duties were administrative rather than judicial. Since he felt that his new responsibilities called for a knowledge of law, he studied at night for two years at the Kansas City School of Law. In 1926 he was elected presiding judge, an office he held until 1935.

During these years Truman was allied with the notorious political machine of Kansas City boss Thomas J. Pendergast. In spite of this, Truman maintained his reputation as a man of strict honesty and unusual efficiency. Pendergast complained frequently that Truman was "the contrariest cuss in Missouri" but respected him as a popular vote getter. In 1934 he backed Truman for election to the United States Senate.

During his first term in the Senate, Truman seldom spoke and was handicapped by his tie with Pendergast. With difficulty he won reelection in 1940. In his second term as a senator, however, he became famous.

The Truman Committee. Truman felt that Missouri was not getting its fair share of defense contracts. He also

Harry S. Truman (right) appears at the age of four with his younger brother, Vivian, in 1888. The "S" didn't stand for anything.

was disturbed by reports of inefficiency and corruption in the defense program. He proposed that the Senate investigate the national defense program. A committee was formed, with Truman as chairman. It was called the Senate War Investigating Committee, but was better known as the Truman Committee. The Truman Committee became a financial watchdog for President Franklin D. Roosevelt's administration during World War II. By uncovering corruption and waste, the committee saved the government hundreds of millions of dollars—perhaps as much as $15,000,000,000. And by its efficiency it caused government officials and defense contractors to be more careful.

VICE PRESIDENT AND PRESIDENT

The success of the committee and his support of Roosevelt's policies led Truman's political supporters to back him for the Democratic nomination for vice president in the election of 1944. President Roosevelt was running for a fourth term, and he and Truman were elected easily.

During his 12 weeks as vice president Truman saw little of Roosevelt. He received no special briefings on the major issues facing the administration, such as the deteriorating relations with Soviet Russia and the development of the atomic bomb. Roosevelt's health was failing, but he optimistically expected to regain it. Thus Truman was far from prepared for the responsibilities that suddenly fell on him when Roosevelt died. The day after his inauguration he remarked to reporters: "Boys, if you ever pray, pray for me now. . . . Yesterday . . . I felt like the moon, the stars, and all the planets had fallen on me."

Truman's first task was to bring World War II to a triumphant conclusion. On May 8, 1945, just a few weeks after he took office, the unconditional surrender of the German forces ended the war in Europe. There remained the task of forcing the surrender of Japan and of meeting the increasing difficulties with the Soviet Union. The Soviets, in violation of the agreements reached with President Roosevelt and British Prime Minister Winston Churchill at the Yalta Conference, were gradually taking over political control of the countries of Eastern Europe.

The Atomic Bomb

In July 1945, President Truman went to Potsdam, Germany, to meet with Churchill and Soviet premier Joseph Stalin. While there, Truman received word of the first successful test of the atomic bomb. Truman could arrive at no useful agreements with Stalin at Potsdam. However, the president did issue a warning to Japan that unless it surrendered, it faced complete devastation. When the Japanese ignored the ultimatum, Truman ordered the atomic bomb dropped on Japan. The target was the city of Hiroshima. In spite of the frightful damage done by the bomb on August 6, Japan did not surrender until a second bomb was dropped on Nagasaki on August 9. On September 2, 1945, aboard the battleship *Missouri*, the

Japanese signed the surrender documents. "Let there be no mistake about it," Truman said later. "I regarded the bomb as a military weapon and never had any doubt that it should be used."

Problems at Home

With the long war finally at an end, millions of Americans in the armed forces and in defense plants were eager to return to peaceful pursuits. The armed forces were demobilized (disbanded) at top speed, and wartime economic controls were rapidly abandoned. In September 1945, President Truman sent to Congress a message containing his recommendations for domestic legislation. Among other things, the president asked for expanded social security, an increase in the minimum wage, a permanent Fair Employment Practices Act, a bill to provide full employment, and public housing and slum clearance. Additional recommendations called for federal aid to education and for health insurance, medical care, and federal control of atomic energy.

But the mood of the United States during the next two years favored more conservative policies, and Congress enacted only two of Truman's recommendations. In 1946 it passed the Atomic Energy Act, which created the Atomic Energy Commission to exercise control over research and development of atomic energy. Congress also passed a limited version of the president's full employment program. This was the Maximum Employment Act. Among other things, this act established the Council of Economic Advisers to assist the president and issue a yearly report on economic conditions.

Meanwhile, the United States was suffering the pains of the hurried change to a peacetime economy. A scarcity

General Charles de Gaulle of France met with President Truman in 1945 after the surrender of the Germans in World War II.

Harry S. Truman

33rd president, 1945–53 Democrat

1884 Born on May 8 in Lamar, Missouri.

1901 Graduated from high school.

1906-17 Worked on family farm in Grandview, Missouri.

1917-18 Served with the American Expeditionary Force.

1919 On June 28, married Elizabeth (Bess) Wallace. A daughter, (Mary) Margaret would be born in 1924.

1922 Failed to succeed in clothing business. Elected judge of the Jackson county court. Lost reelection in 1924.

1923-25 Studied at the Kansas City Law School.

1926-34 Was presiding judge of the Jackson county court.

1934 Won first of two terms to the U.S. Senate.

1941-44 Served as chairman of a special Senate committee on defense.

1944 Running with F. D. Roosevelt, elected vice president.

1945 On April 12, sworn in as president following the sudden death of President Roosevelt.

1953 Began retirement during which he traveled widely, wrote memoirs, and remained politically active.

1972 Died in Kansas City on December 26.

Highlights of Presidency

1945 On May 7, Germany surrendered ending World War II in Europe. On June 26, the UN Charter was signed. From July 17 to August 2, Truman attended the Potsdam Conference. After atomic bombs were dropped on Hiroshima and Nagasaki, Japan surrendered in September.

1946 Ordered the seizure of nation's railroads in face of a strike threat.

1947 On March 12, outlined the Truman Doctrine—U.S. aid to Greece, Turkey, and other nations "threatened by armed minorities and outside pressure." In June, the Marshall Plan (economic and technical assistance for Europe) was announced, and Congress overrode presidential veto of Taft Hartley labor bill.

1948 In a "political upset," won full term.

1949 In January, granted recognition to new state of Israel. The North Atlantic Treaty Organization was set up.

1950 U.S. forces entered combat in Korea.

1951 Relieved Gen. Douglas MacArthur of his command in the Far East.

of goods, rising prices, and workers' strikes for higher wages led to inflation. Truman had enjoyed general sympathy and popularity when he became president. But now he became the butt of jokes. Voters, tired of wartime and postwar shortages, swept Republicans into control of both houses of Congress in 1946. The new Congress followed a conservative course in economic legislation. In 1947, over Truman's veto, it passed the Taft–Hartley Act, which placed certain restrictions on labor unions.

The Election of 1948

In 1948, Truman prepared to run for election for a term as president in his own right. His Republican opponent was Governor Thomas E. Dewey of New York. In addition, the president was faced with a split in his own party. A small group of radical Democrats nominated former vice president Henry A. Wallace as the Progressive Party candidate. Southern Democrats, who were angered at the strong civil rights plank in the regular Democratic platform, formed the Dixiecrat, or States' Rights, Party, with Governor (later Senator) J. Strom Thurmond of South Carolina as their candidate for president.

In spite of predictions of his defeat by every poll-taker in the United States, Truman planned a vigorous campaign. He told his vice-presidential running mate, Senator Alben W. Barkley of Kentucky, "I'm going to fight hard. I'm going to give them hell." Truman campaigned across the nation, denouncing what he called the "do-nothing" Congress. He appealed for voter support for his program of welfare and civil rights legislation, aid to farmers, and repeal of the Taft–Hartley Act. To practically everyone's surprise but his own, Truman defeated Dewey by over 2,000,000 popular votes and by an electoral vote of 304 to 189. The Progressive and Dixiecrat parties received relatively few votes. The Democrats also regained control of both houses of Congress.

Domestic Affairs

With renewed vigor Truman urged upon Congress his domestic program, which he was now calling the Fair Deal. But Congress was dominated by a conservative alliance of Southern Democrats and Republicans, and the president was able to obtain little beyond the strengthening of such earlier measures as social security, public housing, and the minimum wage.

In 1951, the 22nd Amendment to the Constitution was ratified, which limited the president to two four-year terms.

By the end of 1949, reverses in the Cold War had made Communism the nation's major domestic issue. Shortly after the USSR announced that it had tested its first atomic bomb came a stunning series of Communist espionage cases. In 1950 Republican Senator Joseph R. McCarthy made repeated charges of Communist infiltration of the State Department and other key government agencies. It is now thought that most of the investigations that followed bordered on hysteria and should have been stopped.

Foreign Affairs

In his foreign policy President Truman was more successful in winning the backing of Congress. His achievements in foreign affairs were so notable that a group of 75 historians, in a poll taken in 1962, ranked him among the near-great presidents.

Throughout his presidency Truman hoped that the United States could help maintain peace through international cooperation. On June 26, 1945, at San Francisco he witnessed the signing of the charter establishing the United Nations. He hailed it as a "declaration of great faith by the nations of the earth—faith that war is not inevitable, faith that peace can be maintained." In this same spirit Truman proposed international control of atomic energy to harness it for peaceful uses. But the Soviet Union refused to accept the American plan submitted to the United Nations in 1946. Instead, Soviet leaders worked at top speed to develop their own bomb.

The Truman Doctrine. Gradually, Truman realized that more vigorous measures had to be taken if the spread of Communism was to be stopped. In 1947 he became especially alarmed by Soviet pressure on Turkey and by Soviet aid to Communist guerrillas in Greece. He requested funds from Congress to assist the armed forces of these countries. He also set forth the policy that came to be called the Truman Doctrine: "to support free peoples, who are resisting attempted subjugation. . . ." It allowed the

Truman relaxes from the cares of office on a vacation in Key West, Florida, in 1951. He is reading about Abraham Lincoln.

After leaving the presidency, Truman was able to spend time with his family. Here, in 1960, are the former president; daughter Mary Margaret Daniel, holding the Trumans' grandson, William; son-in-law Clifton Daniel, holding their grandson, Clifton; and Bess Truman.

United States to send aid to nations who are "threatened by armed minorities and outside pressure."

The Marshall Plan. The need for help to war-torn Europe led to Truman's proposal, in 1947, of what came to be known as the Marshall Plan, after Secretary of State George C. Marshall. Under the Marshall Plan, large amounts of U.S. aid were sent to the nations of Western Europe, which brought about their rapid economic recovery. Truman also called for aid, under his Point Four program, to developing nations of Africa and Asia.

The Berlin Airlift. In 1948, Soviet forces blockaded the western sectors of Berlin, the former capital of Germany, which had been under the control of the four Allied powers since the end of World War II. Truman did not want to risk war by sending land convoys through the Soviet lines. Instead, he ordered West Berlin supplied by air, which forced the Soviets to lift the blockade in 1949.

NATO. To meet any further Soviet military threats to Western Europe, in 1949 Truman helped shape a new alliance called the North Atlantic Treaty Organization (NATO). It was originally signed by representatives from 12 nations, although later others were included. The signing of the North Atlantic Treaty in Washington, D.C., in April paved the way for the first peacetime alliance participated in by the United States. The key article states: "The Parties agree that an armed attack against one or more of them . . . shall be considered an attack against them all."

China. Truman was severely criticized for not having sent massive military aid to President Chiang Kai-shek's Nationalist government before the mainland of China fell to Communist forces in 1949. However, Truman's advisers, chiefly George C. Marshall, had decided that nothing the United States could do would save the Nationalists, who withdrew to Taiwan.

The Korean War. When Communist North Korea invaded South Korea in 1950, Truman called for armed assistance to the South Koreans under a United Nations command headed by the United States. Technically, the Korean War was what Truman called a "police action by the United Nations." After Communist Chinese forces entered the war in great numbers, Truman refused to allow the United Nations commander, U.S. General Douglas MacArthur, to bomb bases within China for fear that it might lead to all-out war. When MacArthur sought through Republican leaders in Congress to reverse Truman's policy, the president relieved MacArthur of his command. An armistice in Korea was not obtained until July, 1953, after Truman had left the presidency.

FINAL YEARS

After leaving office in January, 1953, Truman returned to his home in Independence, Missouri. He traveled widely, published his memoirs in a two-volume set in 1955-1956, and enjoyed the status of an elder statesman. He died on December 26, 1972, and was buried in Independence.

DID YOU — SEAL OF THE PRESIDENT OF THE UNITED STATES — KNOW?

- *The middle initial "S" in Truman's name is not an abbreviation and has no significance.*
- *At 60, he was the oldest vice president to succeed to the presidency.*
- *In recognition of Truman's contribution to medical insurance, President Johnson presented the first two Medicare cards to Mr. and Mrs. Truman.*
- *It was Truman who popularized the phrase, "If you can't stand the heat stay out of the kitchen."*
- *A Confederate sympathizer, Truman's mother refused to sleep in Lincoln's bed during a White House visit.*

DWIGHT D. EISENHOWER

34th PRESIDENT OF THE UNITED STATES (1953–1961)

Born: October 14, 1890, at Denison, Texas
Occupation: Soldier
Party: Republican
Vice President: Richard M. Nixon
Wife: Mary Geneva Doud
Died: March 28, 1969, at Washington, D.C.

Before winning election to the presidency in 1952, Dwight D. Eisenhower had spent most of his adult life as an army officer, rising to the highest military rank, general of the army. Both as a general and as president, Eisenhower aroused an enormous affection in the people of the United States and indeed in people throughout the world. This was because in a time of national danger, of changing values and uncertainty, he possessed the virtues that most Americans feel represent the United States at its best. He was brave, kind, steadfast, idealistic, friendly, and so completely honest that even his political opponents never questioned his integrity.

EARLY YEARS

Eisenhower was born on October 14, 1890, in Denison, Texas, the third son of David and Ida Stover Eisenhower. His ancestors on his father's side had emigrated from Germany to Pennsylvania in 1732. The family name meant "iron axe" or "iron hitter." The boy was christened David Dwight Eisenhower. Later his names were accidentally reversed to Dwight David. This was agreeable to him, since he was called Dwight by his family.

Eisenhower was two years old when the family moved to Abilene, Kansas. Although his father never made more than $1,500 a year, he managed to save enough to buy a small house and a ten-acre farm. The five Eisenhower boys worked the farm and raised almost all the food for the family. They had virtually no money, but they ate well. The boys went to the local school, where Dwight was nicknamed "Ike."

West Point. After he graduated from high school, Eisenhower went to work in a creamery, partly to enable one of his older brothers to attend college. When Dwight realized that the only chance of getting his own college education was to try for a free one, he took the competitive examinations for both the U.S. Naval Academy at Annapolis and the U.S. Military Academy at West Point. He placed first for Annapolis and second for West Point. He wanted to go to the Naval Academy, but he discovered that at 20 he was too old. At the Military Academy the age limit was 21.

Eisenhower entered West Point in 1911. His academic record was average. He stood 61st in a class of 164, but he was very popular. Eisenhower was a big, powerful young man with a friendly grin. He was a star halfback on the football team until he hurt his knee. The knee bothered him the rest of his life.

MARRIAGE AND EARLY MILITARY CAREER

Upon graduation in 1915, Eisenhower was commissioned a second lieutenant in the 19th Infantry and ordered to Fort Sam Houston in San Antonio, Texas. There he met Mary (Mamie) Geneva Doud of Denver, Colorado, and fell in love with her. They were married in Denver in 1916, on the day that Eisenhower was promoted to first lieutenant.

Dwight David Eisenhower

34th president, 1953–61 Republican

1890 Born on October 14 in Denison, Texas.

1915 Graduated from the U.S. Military Academy.

1916 Married Mary (Mamie) Geneva Doud on July 1. The couple would have two sons; one died in childhood.

1918 Took command of a tank training center in Gettysburg, Pennsylvania.

1929-33 Served under the assistant secretary of war.

1935-39 Was a senior assistant to Gen. Douglas MacArthur in the Philippines.

1942 With United States fighting in World War II, became commander of the European Theater of Operations.

1943 Appointed supreme commander of the Allied Expeditionary Force.

1944 Directed the landing of allied forces in Normandy.

1945 Succeeded George Marshall as Army chief of staff.

1948 Installed as president of Columbia University.

1950 Became supreme commander of the forces of the North Atlantic Treaty Organization.

1952 Retired from the Army; elected president.

1955 Suffered a heart attack.

1961 Restored to the rank of general of the Army.

1965 The second and final volume of his memoirs was published.

1969 Died on March 28 in Washington, D.C.

Highlights of Presidency

1953 The Department of Health, Education, and Welfare was established. The Korean War ended. Eisenhower nominated Earl Warren as chief justice of the Supreme Court.

1956 After Egypt nationalized the Suez Canal, the president refused to join Britain, France, and Israel in an invasion of Egypt. Denounced the USSR for crushing Hungarian uprising. Reelected to a second term.

1957 Signed the Eisenhower Doctrine, promising that the United States would resist Communist aggression in the Middle East. Sent federal troops to Little Rock, Arkansas, to ensure the integration of Central High School.

1959 The National Aeronautics and Space Administration was formed.

1960 After Soviets downed a U.S. reconnaissance flight, summit conference with Premier Nikita Khrushchev collapsed.

World War I. Eisenhower was promoted to captain in 1917 and then served as an instructor at several Army training camps. With the United States involved in World War I, he sought active service in France. But he was too good at training troops, and in 1918 he was assigned to command the Tank Training Center at Camp Colt, Pennsylvania. He was quickly promoted to major (temporary), and by the war's end, in November 1918, he held the temporary rank of lieutenant colonel.

Peacetime Years. The peacetime years were routine for Eisenhower. He went back to his regular rank of captain and served at Camp Meade, Maryland, and in the Panama Canal Zone. In 1924 he was promoted to major again. In 1926 he studied at the Command and General Staff School at Fort Leavenworth, Kansas, from which he graduated first in his class.

During the next few years Eisenhower served on the Battle Monuments Commission in France. He also attended the War College in Washington, D.C. He served under the assistant secretary of war from 1929 to 1933, when he was appointed to the staff of General Douglas MacArthur, who was then chief of staff of the Army. When MacArthur undertook the task of building a Philippine army in 1935, he asked Eisenhower to go along as his assistant. In the Philippines, Eisenhower had a major role in planning the defense of the islands. In 1936 he was promoted to lieutenant colonel.

WORLD WAR II

Eisenhower remained in the Philippines for four years. When World War II broke out in Europe in 1939, he was anxious to get home, for he foresaw that the United States

Newly promoted Lieutenant Eisenhower married Mamie Doud of Denver in July 1916.

must eventually become involved. He returned to the United States in December 1939, and was assigned to the 15th Infantry as regimental executive officer. In 1941 he was promoted to colonel and made chief of staff of the U.S. Third Army. Later that year he was promoted to brigadier general.

Pearl Harbor. On December 7, 1941, Japanese planes attacked U.S. bases at Pearl Harbor, Hawaii, bringing the United States into World War II. Eisenhower was promoted to major general in March 1942, and in April he was appointed to the position of chief of operations under Army Chief of Staff General George C. Marshall.

In May 1942, Marshall sent Eisenhower to England. That June, Eisenhower was chosen to command all U.S. forces in Europe. He was promoted to lieutenant general.

North Africa. When the Allied invasion of North Africa was agreed on, Eisenhower was given command of all British and U.S. forces. On November 8, 1942, the troops were successfully landed in Algeria and Morocco. However, the German Army in Africa reacted sharply, beginning six months of bitter fighting. Eisenhower had never commanded even a division in the field, and he had to learn the techniques of command while fighting. The Americans suffered an almost disastrous defeat at Kasserine Pass in Tunisia, before Eisenhower got hold of the situation and his raw American troops settled down. In February 1943, he was promoted to full general. The British and U.S. forces, assisted by the Free French, defeated the Germans and their Italian allies in North Africa, taking more than 250,000 prisoners.

Italy and Supreme Commander. Allied forces under Eisenhower's overall command had occupied the Italian island of Sicily by the summer of 1943. In September 1943, they landed at Salerno, on the mainland of Italy. In the winter of 1943, President Roosevelt, British Prime Minister Winston Churchill, and Soviet leader Joseph Stalin met at Teheran, in Iran, and agreed on plans for the invasion of France the following year. At the Cairo Conference, which followed, it was decided that Eisenhower was to be appointed supreme commander of the Allied expeditionary force. In January 1944, Eisenhower arrived in England to take command. D–Day, the date for the Allied invasion of Normandy in western France, was set for June 5, 1944.

As supreme commander of Allied forces in Europe during World War II, General Eisenhower (above) addressed the troops just before the 1944 D-Day landing in Normandy. The First Family (right) celebrates Christmas in the White House in 1960. President and Mamie Eisenhower are at center. At the far left are son John and his wife, Barbara Jean, with their children (from left), Barbara Anne, David, Mary Jean, and Susan.

DID YOU KNOW?

- *Eisenhower was the last president born in the 19th century.*

- *He was the only president to serve in both world wars.*

- *A pacifist, Eisenhower's mother wept at the fact that her son was going to West Point.*

- *In their married life the Eisenhowers moved 28 times before their retirement to Gettysburg, Pennsylvania.*

- *A skilled chef, he was famous for his vegetable soup, steaks, and cornmeal pancakes.*

- *He was the first president licensed to pilot a plane.*

D-Day. On Saturday, June 3, the weather was bad. The invasion was postponed one day. Monday morning, June 5, at 4:00 A.M., forecasters said weather conditions might clear enough by Tuesday, June 6, to make the landings possible. Otherwise they must be put off for about three weeks. Eisenhower asked his generals for their opinions. Some were for going on, some for postponement. He got a final weather check; then he said the historic words: "O.K. We'll go ahead!"

By early September 1944, Paris was liberated and the Germans were driven back to the borders of Germany. But the Allied armies had outrun their supplies and had to stop. This gave the Germans time to recover.

Battle of the Bulge. On December 16, 1944, the Germans launched their last great offensive, which became known as the Battle of the Bulge. German armored divisions almost succeeded in breaking through the thin, stretched-out Allied lines. In this dangerous position Eisenhower never lost his calm optimism. He made the necessary decisions to meet and counter the German attack. Then he took to his jeep and rolled over the snowy roads of France and Belgium to encourage the hard-pressed front-line troops.

Victory. When the Germans were stopped at the Bulge, Eisenhower, now holding the rank of general of the Army, proceeded with his plan for the conquest of Germany. His British and U.S. generals sharply disagreed

about these plans. By tact, persuasion, and finally the assertion of authority, Eisenhower got them to work as a team. The British themselves said that no one but "Ike" could have kept such temperamental characters as British General Bernard Montgomery and U.S. General George Patton working in harmony. Their armies swept through Germany from the west while the Soviet Army attacked from the east.

On May 7, 1945, the German High Command signed an unconditional surrender at Eisenhower's headquarters in a schoolhouse in Rheims, France.

POSTWAR YEARS

Eisenhower returned home to great demonstrations of affection and enthusiasm by the American people. In November 1945, he succeeded General Marshall as Army chief of staff.

Eisenhower retired from active military service in 1948. He published an account of his wartime experiences, *Crusade in Europe,* and in 1949 accepted the post of president of Columbia University.

Eisenhower returned to active duty in 1950, at the height of the Cold War with the Soviet Union. President Harry S. Truman appointed him supreme commander of the forces of the recently formed North Atlantic Treaty Organization (NATO), a defensive military alliance made up of the United States, Canada, and a number of European nations.

As early as 1947 both the Democratic and Republican parties had sought to make Eisenhower their presidential candidate. In the tradition of American military leaders, Eisenhower had never taken part in partisan politics. He firmly refused offers from both parties. However, by 1952, he had come to feel in tune with the principles of the Republican Party. He resigned his NATO command that year to campaign for the Republican presidential nomination.

PRESIDENT

Eisenhower easily won the Republican nomination on the first ballot. In the 1952 election, he defeated the Democratic candidate, Adlai E. Stevenson, by 442 to 89 electoral votes. Eisenhower's vice president was Richard M. Nixon, who was later to win election to the presidency himself.

First Term. As president, Eisenhower tried to lead the United States in a program of cooperation with all free nations and strong opposition to Communism. In this he relied heavily on the advice of his secretary of state, John Foster Dulles. Eisenhower was not completely successful, but he did have some notable achievements. The first of these was bringing an end to the fighting in the Korean War in 1953. The truce that was concluded in July ended the war without a victory. His Atoms for Peace program assisted other nations in developing atomic energy for peaceful uses. The Southeast Asia Treaty Organization (SEATO) was set up in 1954 to prevent Communist aggression in Southeast Asia. (SEATO was phased out in 1977.)

The president's integrity was seen during the 1956 Suez crisis, when he criticized three U.S. allies—Britain, France, and Israel—for their attack on Egypt after it had nationalized the Suez Canal.

Illness and Reelection. In 1955, Eisenhower suffered a severe heart attack. But after a few months he was again able to resume his full activities. Twice more he was stricken with serious illnesses, once by an intestinal attack that required a major operation and later by a slight stroke.

Despite his illnesses, Eisenhower decided to run for reelection in 1956. Again his opponent was Adlai E. Stevenson. Eisenhower received 457 electoral votes to Stevenson's 73. His popular vote of nearly 35,590,000 was the largest ever received by a U.S. president up to that time.

Second Term. During his second term, President Eisenhower was even more heavily involved in foreign affairs. To help protect the nations of the Middle East from Communist aggression, Eisenhower in 1957 offered to send them military aid if they requested it. This proposal became known as the Eisenhower Doctrine. In 1958, under the terms of the doctrine, Eisenhower sent U.S. Marines to Lebanon to prevent a Communist takeover of its government.

He also ordered ships of the U.S. Seventh Fleet to Taiwan to prevent a possible invasion, by the Communist

Eisenhower's boyhood home in Abilene, Kansas, is part of the Eisenhower Center, which includes the presidential library and the grave sites of the president and his wife.

Chinese, of the islands of Quemoy and Matsu, which were held by the Nationalist Chinese. Closer to home was the problem of Cuba. The seizure by Cuba of U.S. property and the establishment of a Communist government on the island prompted Eisenhower to break relations with Cuba in 1961. The U-2 incident, in which a U.S. spy plane, the U-2, was shot down over the Soviet Union, was an embarrassment to the administration.

In 1954 the U.S. Supreme Court declared that the segregation of white and African–American children in public schools was unconstitutional. Eisenhower had hoped for peaceful integration, but he did not hesitate to send U.S. military units to a Little Rock, Arkansas, high school in 1957, in order to enforce the law.

Two massive, self-financed federal public-works projects were pushed through by Eisenhower. Construction for the St. Lawrence Seaway, which linked the Great Lakes with the Atlantic Ocean, was finished in 1959. The Interstate Highway System, begun in 1944, was greatly expanded in 1956 to 41,000 miles

Alaska and Hawaii were admitted to the Union in 1959 as the 49th and 50th states, respectively.

RETIREMENT

Eisenhower supported Richard M. Nixon, his vice president, for the Republican nomination in 1960. Nixon lost to John F. Kennedy in a very close election. After leaving the White House in 1961, Eisenhower retired with Mamie to the farm he had purchased at Gettysburg, Pennsylvania. One of the first acts of the new president, John F. Kennedy, was to restore Eisenhower to his rank of general of the Army. Eisenhower wrote several books, including *Mandate for Change* (1963) and *Waging Peace* (1965). He died on March 28, 1969, in Washington, D.C., and was buried in Abilene, Kansas.

Eisenhower (left) met with Soviet leader Nikita Khrushchev during the latter's visit to the U.S. in 1959, at the height of the Cold War.

JOHN F. KENNEDY

35th PRESIDENT OF THE UNITED STATES (1961–1963)

Born: *May 29, 1917, at Brookline, Massachusetts*
Occupation: *Author, Public Official*
Party: *Democrat*
Vice President: *Lyndon B. Johnson*
Wife: *Jacqueline Bouvier*
Died: *November 22, 1963, at Dallas, Texas*

John F. Kennedy, whose ancestors came from Ireland, was the first Roman Catholic to become president of the United States. At 43 he was also the youngest man ever elected to the highest office of his country, although he was not the youngest to serve in it. Theodore Roosevelt was not quite 43 when the assassination of President McKinley elevated him to the presidency.

Communist control of Cuba and the discovery of Soviet nuclear missiles in that country almost brought the United States to the brink of war during President Kennedy's second year in office. His support of black demands for equality in civil rights shook the Democratic Party's long-standing grip on the South and tested his political leadership. Racial integration, economics, and other issues stirred fierce antagonisms throughout the United States. Yet for millions of his countrymen John F. Kennedy held great charm and even greater hopes, and his assassination in 1963 brought many to tears.

EARLY LIFE

The United States under President Woodrow Wilson had just entered World War I when John Fitzgerald Francis

Kennedy was born on May 29, 1917, in Brookline, Massachusetts. Brookline was the suburb of Boston where his grandfathers, Patrick J. Kennedy and John F. ("Honey Fitz") Fitzgerald, had been elected to many public offices. John F. Fitzgerald had been mayor of Boston and had served in Congress. Joseph P. Kennedy, father of the future president, was at 25 the youngest bank president in the country. He was to build one of the great private fortunes of his time. He and Rose Fitzgerald Kennedy raised a family of nine children. John was the second born.

Joseph Kennedy was a politician, too, though not the candidate type. In the 1930s he became deeply committed to the policies of President Franklin D. Roosevelt, whom he served in three important posts, including that of ambassador to Great Britain.

When the first Kennedy child, Joseph, Jr., was born, father Joe was reported to have said, "He'll be the first Kennedy to become president of the United States."

Young Joe, likable, outgoing, and aggressive, developed all the characteristics of a successful politician. But he was killed while piloting a bomber in World War II, and the Kennedy mantle passed to John.

Thus young John Kennedy inherited a background of politics, wealth, and determination. The family circle was close and warm. The boys learned competition first in sports. They played hard to win, a family trait in sports and politics all their lives. Jack, as he came to be known, was often overshadowed by his older, sturdier brother.

Although father Joe could provide all the money his children needed, he insisted they learn that work and study had its values and rewards. If Jack's school reports were not always what they should have been—and sometimes they were not—his father would encourage him to try harder. When the reports improved, the boy was left in no doubt about his parents' pleasure.

Once, when Jack was a child, he asked for a raise in his allowance of 40 cents a week. His father told him to write a letter to justify a raise. Jack drafted a petition. It was studded with bad spelling and errors of grammar, but the youngster's intellectual resourcefulness was evident:

A Plea for a Raise by Jack Kennedy Dedicated to my father, Mr. J. P. Kennedy. Chapter I.

My recent allowance is 40¢. This I used for aeroplanes and other playthings for childhood but now I am a scout and I put away my childish things. Before I would spend 20¢ of my 40¢ allowance and in five minutes I would have empty pockets and nothing to gain and 20¢ to lose. When I am a scout I have to buy canteens, haversacks, blankets, search licgs [lights], poncho things that will last for years and I can always use it while I can't use chocolate marshmallow sunday ice cream and so I put my plea for a raise of thirty cetns [cents] for me to buy schut [such] things and pay my own way around.

Finis,
John Fitzgerald Francis Kennedy

There is no document to prove the results, but it is likely that Jack got his raise.

Young Kennedy attended private schools in Brookline and New York City; and then in 1931 he entered Choate School, in Wallingford, Connecticut, to prepare for college. He chose Princeton University. His father was a Harvard man, and brother Joe was at Harvard. Father Joe kidded the young man about fleeing his older brother's shadow. Jack simply said that he wanted to be with his Choate friends, who were going to Princeton. First, though, Jack's father insisted that he spend the summer at the London School of Economics, where he could learn how people in other environments thought. Jack went to London in 1935, but in a short time jaundice, a liver ailment, forced him to return home. He entered Princeton as planned the following fall, but a second attack of jaundice forced him to leave school. He spent months recuperating and the following year reentered college. This time it was Harvard.

Young Manhood

Harvard professors found Jack Kennedy "a pleasant, bright, easygoing student." Although his marks were seldom higher than C in his first two years, he worked on the college newspaper and went out for swimming, football, sailing, and other sports. One day in a junior varsity football scrimmage he had trouble getting off the ground after a pile-up. His back had been hurt. Not until years later did he realize how difficult and painful that injury was to be.

Travels in Europe. Political movements at home and abroad apparently did not concern young Kennedy. But a visit to Europe in the summer of 1937 increased his interest. He decided that most Americans were completely uninformed about affairs abroad. In Spain the relationship between church and state was much too close, he wrote. He was to take a strong position on this issue in his campaign for the presidency 23 years later. Kennedy thought his travels gave him greater incentive to study. But the improvement in his grades at Harvard did not become striking until his senior year. Another trip, this time to Eastern Europe in 1939, sharpened his intellectual interests noticeably. In 1940 he graduated from Harvard *cum laude* (with honor). World War II had begun in Europe, with young Kennedy almost an on-the-spot witness. His senior thesis reflected his observations so well that he turned it into a successful book, *Why England Slept*. It was his explanation of the dawdling by democratic nations in the face of Hitler's threats of war.

THE WAR YEARS

Lieutenant John F. Kennedy was a hero in the South Pacific in 1943.

Out of college, Kennedy groped for his future. He thought about attending Yale Law School, went to business school at Stanford University for six months instead, then toured South America. In 1941 he tried to enlist in the Army but was rejected because of his old back injury. After five months of exercise to strengthen his back, he tried the Navy and passed the fitness test. He found his assignments, mostly paperwork, dull. When the Japanese attacked Pearl Harbor on December 7, 1941, he applied for sea duty. But more than a year passed before he shipped out for the South Pacific. There Lieutenant John F. Kennedy became the central figure in one of the dramatic episodes of the war.

PT-109. In the dark hours before dawn on August 2, 1943, Kennedy, in command of the torpedo boat PT-109, was on patrol near the Solomon Islands. Suddenly the Japanese destroyer *Amagiri* ploughed through the blackness and knifed Kennedy's boat in half. Two of the 12-man crew disappeared and a third was badly burned by the gasoline flames that sprang up on the water. Others were injured, and some of the men could not swim. Kennedy himself was thrown to the deck, and his back was reinjured. Nevertheless, he gathered his men on the bobbing bow, all that remained of his boat. As the hours passed and it seemed as if the bow would sink, Skipper Kennedy made a decision. He ordered all hands to make for an island about three miles away. Those who could were to swim. The others were to hang onto a plank,

DID YOU KNOW?

- *In 1938, at age 21, Kennedy received a $1 million trust fund from his father.*

- *His favorite writer was Ernest Hemingway.*

- *Kennedy was the only president to win a Pulitzer Prize—for his biography* Profiles in Courage.

- *He was the first president who had served in the U.S. Navy.*

- *He was the only president to appoint his brother to a cabinet post.*

once part of the gun mount, and push. Kennedy grabbed the burned crew member, McMahon, clenched his teeth on the straps of the man's life vest, and swam for the island. They all made it, about five hours later.

The next problem was how to summon help without arousing the enemy. Kennedy swam to other islands, got caught in a current on the return trip, and passed out. His life vest saved him. Kennedy and Ensign Ross repeated these swimming explorations and eventually found two natives in a canoe. Scratching a message on a coconut, Kennedy handed it to the natives and pointed to Rendova, a United States Navy base 38 miles away. The message was delivered, and the men were rescued after five days on the island. For his courage and leadership Kennedy won the Navy and Marine Corps medal. He refused a chance to quit active duty. But malaria and then his old back injury eventually forced him into a hospital in the summer of 1944. After a disk operation and recuperation he retired from the Navy.

POLITICAL CAREER

In 1945 the Hearst newspapers hired Kennedy to cover the United Nations preliminary conference in San Francisco. There he first saw the Russian diplomats in action. He was pessimistic. He covered the British elections that year, then decided he had had enough of journalism. He did not know whether he would like politics, but decided to try it. In 1946 he ran for Congress as a Democrat, in a Boston district. Though he did not live there, Kennedy, by hard campaigning, defeated a large field of rivals. He was reelected twice. Then he tried for election to the United States Senate against Republican Henry

Cabot Lodge, who was supposed to be unbeatable in Massachusetts. It was a big Republican year in 1952, in Massachusetts and elsewhere, but Jack Kennedy beat Lodge by 70,000 votes.

On September 12, 1953, Kennedy and Jacqueline Bouvier were married at Newport, Rhode Island. They had three children—Caroline; John, Jr., whom his father called John-John; and Patrick Bouvier, who lived but a few days.

IN CONGRESS

Kennedy's legislative record—six years in the House of Representatives, eight in the Senate—defied easy labeling. His strong liberal streak led him, for instance, to oppose the loyalty oath that students had to take to get a loan. His support of workmen's demands for higher minimum-wage laws and other welfare benefits also stamped him as a liberal. But when some of his liberal friends resisted union reform legislation, Kennedy disagreed. He did not join the anti-union reformers, but took a moderate position. Only a master of the art of politics could, in those days, insist on any union reforms at all and still command the strong support of most union leaders, as Kennedy did.

McCarthyism. Kennedy displeased the liberals by failing to take a strong position against McCarthyism. He was in the hospital when the Senate voted on December 2, 1954, to censure (reprimand) its Wisconsin Republican member, Joseph R. McCarthy. McCarthy's methods of investigating Communism had led to one of the great controversies of the decade. Liberals felt that McCarthy had violated rules of fair play and had unjustly damaged reputations. They criticized Kennedy for evading the issue. Later Kennedy accepted all or most of the liberal position on McCarthy. He said that he would have voted for McCarthy's censure if he had not been in the hospital. However, he had a hard time convincing the liberals of his sincerity.

THE PRESIDENCY

Kennedy missed being nominated for vice president by a few votes in 1956. But he gained an introduction to millions of Americans who watched the Chicago Democratic convention on television. When he decided to run for president in 1960, his name was widely known. Many thought that his religion and his youthful appearance would handicap him. Kennedy faced the religion issue frankly. He declared his firm belief in the separation of church and state. His wealth enabled him to assemble a staff and to get around the country in a private plane. He drew many doubting Democratic politicians to his side by winning delegate contests in every state primary he entered. On winning his party's nomination, Kennedy amazed nearly everybody by choosing Lyndon B. Johnson, who had opposed him for the nomination, to run for vice president. Again he used his unusual political skills to convince doubting friends that this was the practical course.

John F. Kennedy is sworn in as president by Chief Justice Earl Warren in 1961. He was the youngest president elected in his own right.

Kennedy's four television debates with the Republican candidate, Richard M. Nixon, were a highlight of the 1960 campaign. In the opinion of one television network president, they were "the most significant innovation in presidential campaigns since popular elections began." The debates probably were important in Kennedy's close victory—303 electoral votes to 219 for Nixon. The popular vote was breathtakingly close; Kennedy received only 18,574 more votes than Nixon—a fraction of one percent of the total vote.

Kennedy's Administration

Kennedy's big problems as president were the Cold War with Communism, the resistance of Southerners in his own party to the demands of blacks for full civil rights equality, and unemployment.

Berlin. The Communists had chosen to make Berlin the chief battleground of the Cold War. As if to test Kennedy's courage, they intensified their pressures on West Berlin. That city, under the protection of the Western Allies, was entirely surrounded by Communist territory. Kennedy's response was to alert the nation and to strengthen its military position. Soon the Soviet threat subsided in Berlin. But the Communists were busy elsewhere—the Republic of the Congo (now Zaire), Laos, Viet Nam, and Cuba.

Cuba. In Cuba, Fidel Castro had turned a people's revolt into a Communist revolution. Anti-Castro Cubans in the United States organized. With United States aid they launched an invasion of their country in April 1961. The invasion, which took place at the Bay of Pigs, failed. President Kennedy, without revealing the errors of planning and operation, accepted responsibility for the results.

John Fitzgerald Kennedy

35th president, 1961–63   Democrat

1917 Born on May 29 in Brookline, Massachusetts.

1935 Studied at the London School of Economics.

1940 Graduated from Harvard University.

1941 Commissioned an ensign in the U.S. Navy.

1944 Received the Navy and Marine Corps Medal for his conduct while commander of a PT boat that was sunk by the Japanese in the Solomon Islands in 1943.

1945 Worked as a newspaper correspondent.

1947–53 Represented Massachusetts' 11th district in the U.S. House of Representatives.

1952 Elected to the U.S. Senate, defeating the Republican incumbent, Henry Cabot Lodge, by more than 70,000 votes.

1953 Married Jacqueline Bouvier on September 12 in Newport, Rhode Island. A daughter and a son would be born to the Kennedys. A second son died two days after birth in August 1963.

1956 Defeated in an open contest for the Democratic vice-presidential nomination.

1957 Won a Pulitzer Prize for *Profiles in Courage.*

1958 Reelected to the U.S. Senate.

1960 Defeated Richard M. Nixon for the presidency.

1963 Assassinated on November 22 in Dallas, Texas.

Highlights of Presidency

1961 Established the Peace Corps. In April, a force of anti-Castro Cubans, trained by the Central Intelligence Agency, staged an unsuccessful attempt to establish a beachhead at the Bay of Pigs, Cuba. In August, East Germany constructed a wall separating East and West Berlin.

1962 On February 20, Lt. Col. John H. Glenn, Jr., became the first American to orbit the earth. After U.S. aerial reconnaissance revealed that Soviet offensive missiles were being installed in Cuba, the United States established a naval "quarantine" around Cuba in October. The Soviets then withdrew their missiles.

1963 On August 5, the United States, Britain, and the USSR signed a nuclear test-ban agreement, prohibiting atmospheric testing of nuclear weapons. On August 28, more than 200,000 persons staged a march in Washington, dramatizing the demands of blacks for equal rights. South Vietnam President Ngo Dinh Diem was overthrown on November 1.

President and Mrs. Kennedy vacation with their children, John, Jr., and Caroline, at Hyannis Port, Massachusetts, in the summer of 1963.

Kennedy brothers Robert, Edward, and John pose at the White House in 1962. Robert playfully bends his knees to emphasize that he is the shortest of the three. Oldest brother Joseph died in WW II.

The Cuban issue became far more serious in the fall of 1962. Photographs and other sources of information revealed Soviet missiles and soldiers in Cuba. The president insisted on their withdrawal. He surrounded the island with ships and mobilized land and air strength in Florida and elsewhere on the continent. Then he addressed the nation in grave terms. The crisis passed when Soviet Premier Nikita Khrushchev agreed to withdraw the missiles and soldiers. Whether the Soviet leader fully kept his promise was still an issue in the United States at the time of Kennedy's death over a year later. However, relations between the United States and the Soviet Union improved steadily after the missile crisis, on the surface at least. A hopeful sign was the agreement to suspend nuclear testing in the atmosphere.

Civil Rights. Black demonstrations and white resistance in the South caused Kennedy to declare a "moral crisis" at home. He called for legislation supporting equal rights for blacks. Federal marshals backed by national guardsmen forced the University of Mississippi to accept the registration of James Meredith, a black. This led to anti-Kennedyism in the South, directed not only at the president but also at his brother Robert, the attorney general.

Other Issues. The delaying tactics of Congress, more than actual rejections, marred President Kennedy's record of legislative achievements. His hopes for new civil rights laws and a tax cut to help provide more jobs were unfulfilled at the time of his death. The Alliance for Progress, the president's plan for a partnership in prosperity between the United States and Latin America, also had borne little fruit. However, Congress did pass the Trade Expansion Act, which enabled the president to lower tariffs (taxes on imports) to compete with nations of the European Common Market. One of Kennedy's most popular achievements was the Peace Corps, a volunteer organization which carried education and skills to underdeveloped countries.

A TRAGIC END

Throughout his presidency, Kennedy wore a back brace and suffered more than the public knew. Yet he loved life and politics. The image of vigor and his humor were real. He wrote *Profiles in Courage* in 1956, which won a Pulitzer Prize, and *Strategy of Peace* in 1960. He conveyed his thoughts in clear, forceful language and had a deep sense of history and an appreciation of scholarship. Kennedy appointed a cultural affairs adviser to his staff and, with Mrs. Kennedy, invited famous figures in the arts and entertainment to the White House.

But the hope that millions saw in the young president was wiped out on November 22, 1963, when he was assassinated in Dallas, Texas. Lee Harvey Oswald, who was arrested for the crime, was shot to death himself two days later. With great dignity, First Lady Jacqueline Kennedy led the nation in mourning during the Washington funeral. She remained much admired until her death from cancer in 1994.

LYNDON BAINES JOHNSON

36th PRESIDENT OF THE UNITED STATES (1963–1969)

Born: August 27, 1908, near Johnson City, Texas
Occupation: Teacher, Public Official
Party: Democrat
Vice President: Hubert H. Humphrey
Wife: Claudia Alta Taylor
Died: January 22, 1973, near Johnson City, Texas

Ninety-nine minutes after the assassination of President John F. Kennedy in Dallas, Texas, on November 22, 1963, Vice President Lyndon Baines Johnson took the oath of office as president of the United States. He was flown immediately to Washington, D.C. At the Washington airport he spoke briefly over television to the stunned nation, saying: "This is a sad time for all people. We have suffered a loss that cannot be weighed. For me it is a deep personal tragedy. I know the world shares the sorrow that Mrs. Kennedy and her family bear. I will do my best. That is all I can do. I ask for your help, and God's."

President Johnson had the most thorough training for his new office of any man who had succeeded to the presidency from the vice presidency. All his adult life had been spent in public service, and he had built a notable record of accomplishment.

EARLY YEARS

Lyndon Johnson was born on August 27, 1908, on a farm near Johnson City, Texas. He was the eldest of five children born to Samuel Ealy Johnson, Jr., and Rebekah Baines Johnson. The early years of his life were spent on the farm and in the neighboring town of Johnson City. The town had been named for Lyndon's paternal grandfather, Sam Ealy Johnson, Sr., and his brother (Lyndon's great-uncle), Tom Johnson. The brothers had settled in the area before the Civil War to raise cattle, which they then drove over the trails to Kansas.

Young Lyndon was brought up neither in poverty nor in luxury. The Johnson family was not terribly poor, but it certainly was not rich. There was always enough simple food on the table, decent clothes, and at least one pair of shoes for each member of the family. Lyndon had a pony to ride to school—but ponies were commonplace in that area. There were few extras, however, and money was never plentiful. Lyndon earned his own spending money by delivering newspapers and shining shoes. He went to school in Johnson City. His grades were generally good, and his mother was determined that he should receive an adequate education.

When young Johnson graduated from high school, however, he resisted the idea of going to college. With several of his friends he decided to go to California to make his own way in life. He soon found that this was not easy, although he worked at any job he could get. He washed dishes, waited on tables, ran an elevator, and did farm work whenever he could find it. Finally, homesick, he worked and hitchhiked his way back to Texas. There he obtained a job doing hard manual work with a road construction crew.

After a few months of this work he began to listen more carefully to what his father and mother constantly advised him about the value of education. At last he told them that he was going to try to learn to work with his head instead of his hands. He borrowed $75 for his tuition and entered Southwest Texas State Teachers College

Lyndon Baines Johnson

36th president, 1963–69 Democrat

1908 Born on August 27 near Johnson City, Texas.

1930 After graduating from Southwest Texas State Teachers College in San Marcos, Texas, taught school in Houston.

1931 Became secretary to U.S. Rep. Richard M. Kleberg.

1934 Married Claudia Alta ("Lady Bird") Taylor on November 17. The Johnsons would become the parents of two daughters.

1935-37 Headed the National Youth Administration in Texas.

1937-49 Served in the U.S. House of Representatives.

1941 Defeated in a special election for the U.S. Senate.

1942 After President Roosevelt ordered all congressmen on active military duty to return to Washington, concluded a brief tour of duty with the U.S. Navy.

1948 Elected to the U.S. Senate. Won reelection in 1954.

1955 In January, elected Senate majority leader. In July, suffered a major heart attack.

1960 Lost the Democratic presidential nomination to John F. Kennedy. Elected vice president.

1963 Sworn in as 36th president following the assassination of President Kennedy.

1971 The president's memoirs, *The Vantage Point: Perspectives of the Presidency, 1963-1969,* were published.

1973 Died on January 22 near Johnson City, Texas.

Highlights of Presidency

1964 Signed an $11.5 billion tax-reduction bill and a major civil-rights bill. Proclaimed a war on poverty. Elected to a full presidential term.

1965 On February 7, ordered the bombing of targets in North Vietnam and began escalating U.S. troop strength in Indochina. In April, ordered U.S. troops into the Dominican Republic to end a rebellion. Signed legislation setting up Medicare and the Department of Housing and Urban Development.

1966 The Department of Transportation was formed.

1967 Nominated Thurgood Marshall, a black, as an associate justice of the Supreme Court. Met with Soviet Premier Aleksei Kosygin in Glassboro, New Jersey.

1968 Withdrew from the 1968 presidential race and ordered a reduction in the bombing of North Vietnam.

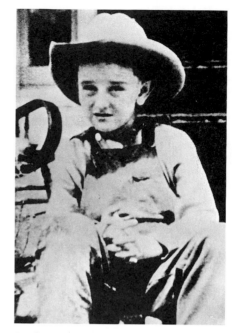

Lyndon Baines Johnson grew up on a ranch near Johnson City, Texas, which was named after his grandfather and great uncle.

in San Marcos, Texas. He majored in history. To help pay his expenses, Johnson worked as a janitor. Later he obtained a better paying job as a secretary in the college president's office.

Johnson led the college debating team, edited the college newspaper, and was a member of the literary society. In 1930 he was graduated with a bachelor of science degree.

POLITICS

After his graduation from college Johnson became a teacher in the public school system of Houston, Texas. This was not for long, however. Political activity was a tradition in the families of both his parents, and Lyndon Johnson was fascinated by politics. In 1931 he left the teaching job to become secretary to a newly elected congressman, Richard M. Kleberg, a family friend.

In Washington, Johnson benefited from the friendship of Representative Sam Rayburn. Johnson's father had served with Rayburn in the Texas House of Representatives. Now Rayburn was rising to a position of great power in Washington. He was responsible for Johnson's appointment in 1935 as Texas state director for the National Youth Administration.

In 1937 Johnson resigned the NYA post to become a candidate for Congress. Campaigning on a firm pledge of support for President Franklin D. Roosevelt and his New Deal, he received almost twice as many votes as his nearest opponent. He was reelected for five successive terms.

President Roosevelt showed a personal interest in the young Texan from the time he entered Congress. Johnson was immediately named to the powerful Naval

Affairs Committee. This was an assignment of unusual importance for a freshman member of the House of Representatives. In 1941 Johnson ran for the United States Senate in a special election, but he was defeated.

World War II. On December 8, 1941, the United States declared war on Japan. Johnson, a member of the Naval Reserve, asked to be called up for active duty. He was the first member of the House of Representatives to go into uniform. He served a little over seven months before President Roosevelt ordered all members of Congress in military service to return to their duties in Washington. During most of his service Johnson, holding the rank of lieutenant commander, was assigned to the Pacific Theater of Operations. He was awarded the Silver Star medal.

SENATOR

In 1948 Johnson again ran for the United States Senate and won. He was assigned to the Armed Services Committee. In 1950, when the Korean War broke out, Johnson helped establish the Preparedness Investigating Subcommittee. He became its chairman and conducted a series of investigations of defense costs and efficiency. These investigations brought him national attention. They also earned him the respect of senior members of the Senate, something very important to a young senator.

Johnson quickly advanced to a position of leadership in the Senate. In 1953 he was elected minority floor leader. He was the youngest man ever named floor leader by either major political party. Texas voters reelected him to the Senate in 1954. The Democrats had gained control

As a working vice president, Johnson traveled to West Berlin in 1961 on one of many errands for Kennedy.

of the Senate, so Johnson became majority floor leader. His duties were to schedule legislation and to help pass measures favored by the Democrats.

VICE PRESIDENT

Johnson's great success as Senate majority leader led to his being widely mentioned as a possible Democratic presidential candidate. He was Texas' "favorite son" candidate at the party's national convention in 1956. It was not until 1960, however, that he made a serious bid for the nomination. He received 409 votes on the first and only ballot at the Los Angeles convention. But the nomination went to Senator John F. Kennedy of Massachusetts. Johnson was then nominated for vice president, having been personally chosen by Kennedy as his running mate. The Kennedy-Johnson ticket was elected by the closest popular vote margin of any presidential election in the 20th century.

Always an active man, Johnson became known as a working vice president. He traveled throughout the country on speech making tours to present the viewpoint of the Kennedy administration on issues of the day. He also journeyed to many foreign countries as an emissary of the United States Government. When he was in Washington, he regularly attended meetings of the National Security Council, cabinet sessions, and meetings of the President with congressional leaders. Johnson served as chairman of the National Aeronautics and Space Council. He was also chairman of the President's Committee on Equal Employment Opportunity and of the Peace Corps Advisory Council.

President Franklin Roosevelt took a liking to young Congressman Johnson in 1937.

PRESIDENT

The assassination of President Kennedy aroused fears and doubts among the shocked people of the United States and throughout the world. Johnson's first efforts were devoted to calming these fears. In an address before a joint session of Congress, five days after assuming the presidency, he called for passage of President Kennedy's legislative program. He immediately took up problems of national security and foreign policy. In his first week in office the new president conferred with leaders of most of the great nations who were in Washington for President Kennedy's funeral. He planned military policy with the Joint Chiefs of Staff. He created a presidential commission, headed by Chief Justice Earl Warren, to investigate the assassination.

In his first State of the Union message on January 8, 1964, President Johnson presented a broad program of legislation to Congress. Most of his major proposals were enacted during the long session of Congress that followed. Among them were a substantial reduction in taxes, a far-reaching civil rights bill, and an antipoverty program called the War on Poverty.

The Election of 1964. In 1964 Johnson ran for a full term as president. His vice-presidential running mate was Senator Hubert H. Humphrey of Minnesota. The Republican candidates were Senator Barry Goldwater of Arizona for president and Representative William E. Miller of New York for vice president.

Johnson received 61 percent of the popular votes cast—43,121,085 votes to 27,145,161 for Goldwater—and 486 electoral votes to Goldwater's 52. It was the most one-sided presidential election since 1936.

The Great Society. Acting on what President Johnson called the "Great Society" program, Congress passed much legislation in 1965. Federal aid to education, funds for the depressed Appalachia region, creation of a new Department of Housing and Urban Development, hospitalization insurance for the elderly (Medicare), and changes in the immigration laws were some of the

Following President Kennedy's assassination on November 22, 1963, Johnson (above) was sworn in as president on a plane in Dallas, Texas. Mrs. Johnson is at left, Mrs. Kennedy at right. Before a large audience, President Johnson (right) signs the historic Civil Rights Bill on July 2, 1964.

measures pushed through. The Voting Rights Act of 1965 was designed to protect the voting rights of African Americans.

In 1966, at the president's urging, another new cabinet-level department was created—the Department of Transportation. Legislation passed by Congress in 1967 included a 13 percent increase in Social Security benefits and a federal air-pollution control bill. In 1968 a civil rights bill with strong open-housing provisions was passed by Congress. However, racial tension still increased, flaring into violence in many urban areas between 1965 and 1968.

Foreign Affairs. In foreign affairs, events in Panama, the Dominican Republic, the Middle East, and Vietnam caused the administration particular concern. In Panama, dissatisfaction with the existing Panama Canal treaty led to rioting in 1964 and the temporary breaking of diplomatic relations with the United States. Relations with Panama were improved by President Johnson's agreement to undertake a new treaty. Reports of Communist influence in a rebel movement in the Dominican Republic prompted the President to send troops to that country in 1965. The troops were withdrawn after a peaceful election the following year. In the Middle East the situation remained tense following the Arab-Israeli war of June 1967.

President Johnson's most controversial decision was to increase the number of American troops in South Vietnam and to bomb sites in North Vietnam. In 1968,

President and Mrs. Johnson with Lynda Bird (left) and Luci Baines (left, rear). Both daughters were married while Johnson was president.

U.S. troops in Southeast Asia numbered 500,000, up from 16,000 at the time of Kennedy's death. The Vietnam War became the most critical foreign and domestic issue facing President Johnson in 1967 and 1968, as protests against the war mounted.

JOHNSON'S FAMILY

Johnson was married in 1934 to Claudia Alta Taylor of Marshall, Texas. When Mrs. Johnson was a baby, she was nicknamed Lady Bird, and she has been so known ever since. Their two daughters, Lynda Bird and Luci Baines, were both married while their father was president. Lynda married Charles S. Robb, who went on to become governor and later U.S. senator of Virginia, as a conservative democrat.

FINAL YEARS

In March 1968, in an address to the nation, Johnson announced that he would not seek renomination as president. He cited the growing division within the country over the war. In the same speech he also said he would stop the bombing in most of North Vietnam and seek to negotiate an end to the war. He supported his vice president, Hubert H. Humphrey, as the Democratic candidate. After Republican Richard M. Nixon's win and inauguration on January 20, 1969, Lyndon Johnson retired to his ranch in Johnson City, Texas. Frequently the victim of ill health, he suffered from a heart ailment and died suddenly on January 22, 1973, at the age of 64. He is buried in Johnson City. Mrs. Johnson returned to Texas where she became active in promoting numerous environmental and social causes.

DID YOU KNOW?

- *Johnson and his wife were married with a $2.50 wedding ring bought at Sears.*

- *He was the only president to take the oath of office from a female official, Judge Sarah T. Hughes.*

- *He rejected his official portrait painting, saying it was "the ugliest thing I ever saw."*

- *The Johnsons entertained more than 200,000 guests during their five years in the White House.*

- *He was the first incumbent president to meet with a pope.*

RICHARD M. NIXON

37th PRESIDENT OF THE UNITED STATES (1969–1974)

Born: *January 9, 1913, at Yorba Linda, California*
Occupation: *Lawyer, Public Official*
Party: *Republican*
Vice Presidents: *Spiro T. Agnew (1969–73); Gerald R. Ford (1973–74)*
Wife: *Thelma Catherine Ryan*
Died: *April 22, 1994, at New York, New York*

Humphrey and Senator Edmund S. Muskie of Maine, the Democratic candidates, and former governor George C. Wallace of Alabama and retired general Curtis LeMay, of the American Independent Party.

EARLY LIFE

Nixon was born January 9, 1913, in a house built by his father in Yorba Linda, California, a small farming community near Los Angeles. His parents ran a small lemon farm. Today, the lemon trees are gone and the grounds are owned by the Richard M. Nixon Elementary School. But the white frame house is still there.

Young Nixon's parents were poor. His father, Francis Anthony Nixon, was of Irish ancestry. He was a native of Ohio who came west in 1906. In 1922, when Nixon was nine, the farm failed and the family moved to Whittier, California. There Francis Nixon operated a combination general store and gas station. The Nixon boys—there were five altogether—did chores, helped out in the store, and pumped gas. Nixon's mother, Hannah Milhous Nixon, was born in Indiana. The Nixons were serious and hard-working Quakers.

Although the Nixons endured several years of hard times, Nixon was able to attend local public schools and, at 17, to enter Whittier College, a small Quaker school.

EARLY CAREER

At Whittier, Nixon quickly developed a taste for politics. He excelled in debating and won a Southern California college speaking contest. He also won his first election, becoming president of the student body. He was a good student and graduated second in his class. His greatest disappointment was that he never played first string on the football team. In 1934 Nixon received a scholarship to Duke University Law School in North Carolina, from which he graduated third in his class.

Richard M. Nixon's rise to the presidency was one of the most astonishing political comebacks of modern times. Few men have run for the highest office in the United States and lost—as Nixon lost in 1960—and then won election on a second attempt. And few men have been written off as finished in political life more often than he. Some people believed that his public career had come to an end when he narrowly lost the presidential election to John F. Kennedy in 1960. Two years later, he ran for the governorship of California and again was defeated. Afterward, Nixon himself announced that his days in politics were over.

But by the middle of 1966 a combination of events—including the weaknesses of his own party and a sharp decline in the popularity of Lyndon Johnson's administration—had pushed Nixon to the forefront again. He won a series of impressive victories in the presidential primaries in early 1968, and then won the Republican presidential nomination on the first ballot at the Republican National Convention in Miami Beach, Florida. In the election, Nixon and his vice-presidential running mate, Governor Spiro T. Agnew of Maryland, defeated Vice President Hubert H.

The Nixon family moved to Whittier, California, in 1922. Richard (left) is shown here at age 14 with a friend in 1927.

Nixon returned to Whittier to practice law. There he met Thelma Catherine Patricia Ryan, who was then teaching shorthand and typing at the local high school. They were married in 1940 and later had two daughters, Patricia ("Tricia") and Julie. Julie married David Eisenhower, grandson of former president Dwight D. Eisenhower. Tricia married Edward Cox.

Nixon practiced law in Whittier for several years. In 1942 he entered the Navy. Commissioned a lieutenant, he served for four years and was discharged with the rank of lieutenant commander. As a Quaker, Nixon could have avoided military service, but he said later that "the thought never occurred to me."

POLITICAL CAREER

In 1946 Nixon won election to the House of Representatives. Reelected to Congress in 1948, he served on the Education and Labor Committee and the House Un-American Activities Committee. In 1948, the House Un-American Activities Committee began its investigation of a State Department official named Alger Hiss, who was accused of passing secret documents to a Soviet spy ring. Nixon played a major role in the Hiss case. In his book, *Six Crises*, Nixon later wrote: "The Hiss case brought me national fame. I received considerable credit for spearheading the investigation which led to Hiss's conviction [for perjury]. . . . But it also left a residue of hatred and hostility toward me—not only among the Communists but also among substantial segments of the press and the intellectual community. . . ."

Nixon's name appeared frequently in the headlines, and in 1950 he ran for the United States Senate from California. Some observers believed it was one of the roughest, most bitter campaigns in political history. During the campaign, Nixon, continuing his crusade against Communism in the United States, accused his opponent, Helen Gahagan Douglas, of ignoring the threat of internal subversion. He defeated Mrs. Douglas by nearly 700,000 votes. Nixon's prominent role in the investigation of domestic Communism tended to obscure his positions on other important issues. Generally he showed himself as a moderately cautious conservative on domestic issues and an internationalist on foreign affairs.

By 1952 Nixon had become a national figure. His work in the House of Representatives and Senate had attracted the attention not only of the voters, but also of Dwight D. Eisenhower. When Eisenhower was nominated for the presidency that year, he asked the Republican convention to make Nixon his running mate. Nixon was accused of having illegally accepted $18,235 in campaign contributions from wealthy Californians. Amid demands from his opponents that he leave the race, Nixon delivered an emotional speech—the so-called Checkers speech, named for his dog—defending himself. Eisenhower kept him on the ticket.

When Nixon was elected in the Republican landslide of 1952, he was the second youngest vice president in American history. Only John C. Breckenridge, who became James Buchanan's vice president at the age of 35 in 1856, was younger.

Vice President Nixon (at right) negotiates with Soviet Premier Nikita Khrushchev at a meeting in Moscow in 1959. Later on this trip the two had their famous "kitchen debate."

During his years as vice president, Nixon visited 56 countries and five continents as the personal representative of President Eisenhower. On a tour of Latin America at a time when feeling against the United States was running high, Nixon's car was stoned in Caracas, Venezuela. In 1959 he visited Moscow. At the kitchen display of an American exhibition he engaged in the famous "kitchen debate" with the Soviet premier, Nikita Khrushchev, debating the merits of the free enterprise system.

THE ELECTIONS OF 1960 AND 1968

Nixon was the overwhelming choice of his party for the presidency in 1960 and was nominated with Eisenhower's blessing. The contest between Nixon and Kennedy was one of the closest in American history. Campaigning at top speed for nine weeks, Nixon drove himself, his staff, and his wife, who went with him every step of the way, to the edge of exhaustion. He lost the election by only 118,574 popular votes—two tenths of one percent.

Following his defeat, Nixon returned to California to practice law. He ran for governor of the state in 1962 and lost by a wide margin. Most people thought his political career was finished. Nixon himself told reporters that he was leaving the political arena.

Moving to New York to practice law, he kept a close eye on the course of Republican politics. Barry Goldwater's shattering defeat in the 1964 presidential election and Nixon's successful efforts for Republican candidates for Congress in 1966 raised Nixon once again to the top of his party. After long, careful consideration he decided in 1967 to become an active candidate for the presidency. By the time he arrived at the 1968 Republican Convention, he had accumulated so much strength that his nomination was a foregone conclusion. In the election he defeated Vice President Hubert Humphrey in a very close contest.

NIXON'S ADMINISTRATION

Probably the most difficult problem facing the president as he took office in 1969 was the still unresolved war in Vietnam. As the Paris peace talks continued with no obvious success, President Nixon announced a program of phased withdrawal of American forces from Vietnam and a policy of "Vietnamization" of the conflict. The president's plan was criticized by some, but it seemed to be approved of generally by what the Administration termed the "silent majority" of Americans. However, the sudden military operation by American and South Vietnamese troops against Communist supply bases in Cambodia in 1970 received harsh criticism.

The president's proposal for the Safeguard antiballistic missile system (ABM) also provoked great controversy before it was approved by the Senate in 1969 in a close vote. Congress also passed the president's tax reform bill in 1969. More favorably received was the change in the selective service system to provide for a draft lottery. Congress established the United States Postal Service in 1970 as an independent government agency. Also in 1970

Richard Milhous Nixon

37th president, 1969–74 Republican

1913 Born on January 9 in Yorba Linda, California.

1934 Graduated from Whittier College.

1937 Received a law degree from Duke University.

1940 Married Thelma Catherine ("Pat") Ryan on June 21. Two daughters would be born to the Nixons.

1942-45 Served in the U.S. Navy.

1947-51 Served as U.S. congressman.

1948 Participated in the House Committee of Un-American Activities investigation of Algier Hiss.

1950 Won election to the U.S. Senate.

1952 Elected as Dwight D. Eisenhower's running mate on the Republican presidential ticket.

1955 Performed various presidential duties as President Eisenhower recuperated from a heart attack.

1956 The Eisenhower-Nixon ticket was reelected.

1960 Lost close presidential race to John F. Kennedy.

1962 His first book, *Six Crises*, was published. Lost California's gubernatorial contest.

1968 Elected president.

1994 Died on April 22 in New York City.

Highlights of Presidency

1969 On July 20, Neil A. Armstrong became the first man to walk on the moon.

1970 On April 30, announced that U.S. combat troops were being sent into Cambodia to destroy enemy sanctuaries.

1972 Visited China in February. Meeting in Moscow with Soviet General Secretary Leonid Brezhnev in May, signed agreements limiting antiballistic missile (ABM) systems and offensive missile launchers. In June, five men were arrested for breaking into the headquarters of the Democratic National Committee. The subsequent investigation of the "Watergate affair" led to the downfall of the Nixon presidency. Overwhelmingly reelected.

1973 The Vietnam cease-fire agreement was signed in January. On October 10, Spiro T. Agnew resigned as vice president and pleaded no contest to one count of income tax evasion. The president named Gerald R. Ford as his successor.

1974 Toured Middle East in June. Resigned as president, effective at noon on August 9.

President Nixon dines with Chou En-Lai, premier of the People's Republic of China, in Shanghai in 1972. Nixon's visit opened the way for U.S. Chinese trade, cultural, and scientific exchanges.

President Nixon began the Strategic Arms Limitation Talks (SALT) with the Soviet Union.

President Nixon suffered a rebuff when the Senate twice refused to confirm his nominations to a vacant seat on the Supreme Court. Critics of the Administration also accused it of following a "Southern strategy" by allowing a slowdown in the rate of desegregation of schools in the South. A number of other serious problems confronted the president. The Middle East remained potentially explosive. At home, inflation was causing concern, as was continued student unrest, particularly after the deaths of several college students during campus demonstrations.

During 1969, the most widely followed event was the Apollo 11 space flight in July, which carried American astronauts to man's first landing on the moon.

Some Events of 1971–1972

The war in Vietnam and Cambodia continued and spilled over into Laos in 1971. The reduction of American troops continued, however, in spite of a large-scale North Vietnamese offensive in the South in the spring of 1972. Earlier the President had announced a peace offer he had made to the Communist representatives in Paris. It called for new presidential elections in South Vietnam to include participation by the Communists; a cease-fire followed by withdrawal of all American forces; and the freeing of American prisoners of war. The plan was denounced by the North Vietnamese and by some critics of the Administration.

Other aspects of the war heightened its controversy. One was the 1971 trial of Army lieutenant William Calley, who was convicted of murder in the death of Vietnamese civilians at the village of Mylai. Another was the issue of the so-called Pentagon Papers. These secret government documents relating to the war were made public by a former government employee opposed to the war.

The president's legislative program did not gain much ground in 1971. More successful was the effort to lower the voting age to 18, accomplished by the 26th Amendment to the Constitution. An equal rights for women amendment passed Congress in 1972 and was sent to the states for ratification. Controversy arose over the question of busing children to school to achieve racial integration.

Abroad, the Middle East remained tense, but the cease-fire along the Suez Canal held. But the most dramatic event in foreign affairs was President Nixon's visit to Communist China in 1972. This was followed by a trip to the Soviet Union, during which the president signed an arms limitation agreement with the Russians. President Nixon also ordered the resumption of the bombing of North Vietnam and the mining of Haiphong Harbor in response to the North's invasion of the South. This provoked renewed criticism of the war. In 1972 the last American ground combat units left Vietnam. By the end of 1972 hopes for a settlement rose as a result of intensified negotiations between the United States and North Vietnam.

In June 1972, an incident took place that was to have the most serious consequences for the president and some of his closest advisers. Five men were caught raiding the Democratic National Committee headquarters in the Watergate building in Washington, D. C.

In the 1972 election President Nixon and Vice President Agnew were opposed by the Democrats Senator George S. McGovern of South Dakota and R. Sargent Shriver, the former director of the Peace Corps. Nixon and Agnew were reelected by a wide margin.

DID YOU KNOW?

- *Nixon's mother wanted him to become a Quaker missionary.*
- *He parted his hair to the right to hide a large scar resulting from a childhood accident.*
- *By coincidence Nixon was in Dallas on the day Kennedy was assassinated.*
- *With his trip to China in 1972, Nixon became the first president to visit a nation not recognized by the United States.*

Nixon's daughter Julie married Eisenhower's grandson, David. From left are: Edward and Tricia Nixon Cox, Mrs. Pat Nixon, Nixon, Mrs. Mamie Eisenhower, Julie Nixon Eisenhower and David Eisenhower.

Nixon leaving for San Clemente, California after his resignation on August 9, 1974. He is the only president to have resigned. One month later he was pardoned by his successor, President Ford.

Second Term

Early in 1973 the peace negotiations in Paris culminated in a cease-fire in Vietnam. The agreement called for a halt in the fighting and the release of all prisoners of war. Henry Kissinger, the president's adviser, helped negotiate the agreement. He was later appointed secretary of state to succeed William P. Rogers, who resigned.

The outbreak of war in the Middle East in October 1973, between Israel on the one hand and Egypt and Syria on the other, threatened the new détente, or easing of relations, between the United States and the Soviet Union. The United States had supported Israel, and the Soviet Union had aided the Arab countries. Still the two superpowers were able to work out an acceptable United Nations cease-fire. An oil embargo by the oil-producing Arab countries threatened the United States and other countries with an energy crisis.

Intensive negotiations by Secretary Kissinger brought about a pullback of Arab and Israeli forces and an end to the oil embargo. In June 1974, President Nixon made a five-nation trip to the Middle East to cement the agreement, and in July had a summit meeting with officials in the Soviet Union.

Resignation. From the moment President Nixon had been sworn in there were signs of political trouble ahead. The men arrested for the Watergate break-in had gone on trial in Washington, D.C., before Judge John Sirica. A month later a special Senate committee was formed to investigate 1972 presidential campaign irregularities and Watergate. Some of President Nixon's top aides resigned, and charges were made that the president himself might be involved. A special prosecutor, Archibald Cox, was named by Attorney General Elliot L. Richardson. The president asserted that he had no knowledge of any attempt to cover up Watergate. He refused to turn over White House tape recordings.

In a further dispute over the tapes, the president dismissed the special prosecutor. Richardson promptly resigned in protest at the dismissal. Under great pressure, which included calls for his impeachment or resignation, the president agreed to turn over the tapes. A new prosecutor, Leon Jaworski, was appointed. The House of Representatives began an impeachment inquiry.

The Nixon administration was further jolted by a federal grand jury investigation of Vice President Agnew. It ended with Agnew's resignation and his no-contest plea to a tax-evasion charge. President Nixon nominated Michigan Congressman Gerald R. Ford for the vice presidency. Ford was confirmed by Congress and sworn in as vice president.

In 1974 the special prosecutor asked for more tapes. Nixon again refused, claiming executive privilege. The Supreme Court ruled unanimously that the president must surrender the tapes. At last he did so.

After months of hearings, the Judiciary Committee of the House of Representatives voted three articles of impeachment. In accordance with the Supreme Court decision President Nixon released more tapes. He acknowledged that the tapes did not agree with statements he had made previously. The tapes showed that president Nixon had ordered a halt to aspects of the FBI investigation only six days after the break-in. With the release of this information, impeachment and a Senate trial were certain.

On August 8, Richard Nixon announced that he would resign from the presidency, effective the following day, even though he admitted no criminal wrongdoing. Gerald R. Ford was immediately sworn in as the new president and, on September 8, granted Nixon "a full, free, and absolute pardon" for all offenses he might have committed against the United States. In the last 20 years of his life, Nixon earned a reputation as an "elder statesman" an expert on international affairs.

GERALD R. FORD

38th PRESIDENT OF THE UNITED STATES (1974–1977)

Born: July 14, 1913, at Omaha, Nebraska
Occupation: Lawyer, Public Official
Party: Republican
Vice President: Nelson A. Rockefeller
Wife: Elizabeth Bloomer Warren

Gerald R. Ford became president of the United States under unique circumstances. As vice president, he succeeded to the presidency on the resignation of Richard M. Nixon in 1974, during the Watergate scandal. It was the first time in U.S. history that a vice president had assumed the presidency because of the resignation of the chief executive.

Ford was also the first person to become president without having been elected president or vice president. He had been appointed vice president by President Nixon in 1973 to replace Vice President Spiro T. Agnew, who had been forced to resign his office.

Ford came to the vice presidency and the presidency after a long career in the U.S. Congress. He had served in the House of Representatives for 25 years, the last nine of them as Republican minority leader.

EARLY YEARS

Ford was born on July 14, 1913, in Omaha, Nebraska, the only child of Leslie Lynch King and Dorothy Gardner King. He was originally named Leslie Lynch King, Jr., after his father. His parents were divorced when he was two

years old, and his mother moved with him to Grand Rapids, Michigan. There she married Gerald Rudolph Ford, who adopted the boy and gave him his own name.

Young Ford saw his natural father only a few times in later years. He learned that he had remarried and raised a family, which included Ford's half brother and two half sisters.

Jerry, as the boy was called, attended local grade schools and South High School in Grand Rapids. A husky, athletic youth, with a keen sense of competition, he was a star football player on his high school team. He also became an Eagle Scout.

EARLY CAREER

Ford entered the University of Michigan in 1931. He concentrated on pre-law studies and was elected to Michigauma, the senior honor society. He also played center on Michigan's undefeated national football championship teams of 1932 and 1933. After graduation in 1935, he turned down offers to play professional football and accepted a job as assistant football coach and freshman boxing coach at Yale University. He attended the Yale Law School, receiving his law degree in 1941. After passing the bar examination, he returned to Grand Rapids, where he opened a law office with a college friend.

Ford's law practice was interrupted by the entry, in 1941, of the United States into World War II. He enlisted in the U.S. Navy as an ensign and served nearly four years on active duty, 18 months of them aboard an aircraft carrier in the Pacific. He earned ten battle stars and was released to inactive duty in 1946 with the rank of lieutenant commander.

POLITICS AND MARRIAGE

Ford resumed his law practice in Grand Rapids and became active in local Republican politics. Michigan Senator Arthur Vandenberg, who also came from Grand Rapids,

At the age of two, Gerald Ford (left) had blond bangs and a dog named Spot. Ford (below) played center on the University of Michigan's national championship football teams of 1932 and 1933.

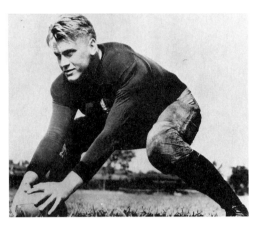

encouraged him to run for Congress. Ford won election to the House of Representatives from Michigan's Fifth Congressional District in 1948. He was reelected twelve times, until he resigned from the House in 1973 to become vice president.

Elizabeth Ford. On October 15, 1948, during the election campaign, Ford had secretly married Elizabeth (Betty) Bloomer Warren. Her previous marriage, to William C. Warren, had ended in divorce in 1947. Born in Chicago, Betty Ford had studied dance with Martha Graham, had been a model in New York, and had worked as a fashion coordinator for a Grand Rapids department store.

After their marriage the couple moved to Washington, D.C. They eventually moved into a house in nearby Alexandria, Virginia, where they lived until Ford entered the White House. The couple had four children Michael, John, Steven, and Susan.

CONGRESSIONAL CAREER

In Congress, Ford was a conservative in money matters and a vigorous supporter of a strong national defense policy. He was highly respected for his political skill. Assigned in 1949 to the House Committee on Public Works, he declared that he intended to guarantee taxpayers "100 cents of value out of every dollar their government spends."

Gerald R. Ford

Gerald Rudolph Ford

38th president, 1974-77 Republican

1913 Born on July 14 in Omaha, Nebraska.

1935 Graduated from the University of Michigan, where he starred on the football team.

1941 After graduating from Yale Law School, returned to Grand Rapids to practice law. While at Yale, served as assistant football coach and boxing coach.

1942-46 During 47 months in the U.S. Navy, was awarded ten battle stars for service in the South Pacific.

1948 Elected to the U.S. House of Representatives from Michigan's fifth district. Won reelection 12 times. Married Elizabeth Bloomer on October 15. Three sons and a daughter were born to the couple.

1963 Elected chairman of the House GOP Conference. Named by President Johnson to serve on the Warren Commission, the official investigation into the assassination of President Kennedy.

1965 Successfully challenged Charles A. Halleck for the post of House minority leader.

1973 Under the terms of the 25th Amendment, took the oath as vice president on December 6.

1974 Following the resignation of President Nixon, inaugurated as the 38th chief executive on August 9.

1980 An attempt by Ronald Reagan to persuade the former president to join him as the vice-presidential candidate on the GOP ticket failed.

Highlights of Presidency

1974 Nominated Nelson A. Rockefeller as vice president. Granted Richard M. Nixon an "absolute" pardon for all federal crimes he may have "committed or taken part in" while president. In Vladivostok, USSR, joined Soviet General Secretary Brezhnev in signing a tentative agreement listing the number of offensive strategic nuclear weapons and delivery vehicles through 1985.

1975 In April, South Vietnam surrendered to the Communists, ending the war in Southeast Asia. U.S. evacuation airlift from the nation was completed. In May, U.S. forces rescued 39 crewmen of the U.S. merchant ship *Mayagüez*, seized by Cambodia.

1976 Led the nation in marking its 200th birthday. Defeated by Jimmy Carter in his bid to win a full term.

In 1951 he was appointed to the House Committee on Appropriations, often called the watchdog of government spending, and from 1953 he also served on that committee's subcommittee on defense. He was increasingly regarded as a hardworking legislator. In his 25 years in the House, in fact, Ford had an attendance record of more than 90 percent. He was not, however, the author of any major legislation during that period, preferring instead to round up support for proposals he favored.

Favorite Son Candidate. In 1959, Ford's colleagues already were considering him as a possible leader of the House Republicans. In 1960, Michigan Republicans endorsed him as their favorite son candidate for the Republican vice-presidential nomination. However, the eventual presidential nominee, Richard M. Nixon, chose Henry Cabot Lodge, Jr., as his running mate instead.

In 1963, Ford was elected by his fellow Republicans to the chairmanship of the Republican House caucus. As the third-ranking member of his party's congressional leadership, Ford fought hard for his positions. But he tried to avoid making enemies of his opponents. He was well liked by both moderate and conservative Republicans and by the Democratic opposition as well.

House Minority Leader. In 1964, Ford decided to seek the post of Republican minority leader. At the time, Republicans were becoming increasingly concerned over

DID YOU KNOW?

- *Both Ford and his wife, Betty, had been models before their marriage.*
- *Running for Congress in 1948, Ford campaigned on his wedding day.*
- *He was the first president to release to the public a full report of his medical checkup.*
- *Ford was the only president whose two assassination attempts against him were made by women.*

Ford (right) spent 25 years in the House of Representatives. He is shown here in 1965, as Republican minority leader, with Speaker of the House John McCormack.

what they felt was weak leadership in Congress. Ford became the champion of those anxious for fresh leadership, and when the issue came to a vote, he was swept into the leadership post.

As House minority leader, Ford became a national Republican leader and a spokesman for the party's conservative wing. Following the election of Richard Nixon to the presidency in 1968, Ford supported the administration's policies in Congress.

VICE PRESIDENT

In 1973 it became known that Vice President Spiro Agnew was under investigation for possible violations of the criminal law. Agnew resigned on October 10, 1973. Two days later President Nixon nominated Ford to succeed Agnew under a provision of the 25th Amendment to the Constitution. The amendment, ratified in 1967, states that when there is a vacancy in the vice presidency, the president is to nominate a vice president, who takes office on confirmation by a majority vote of Congress. Ford thus became the first appointed vice president.

As vice president, he traveled throughout the country addressing Republican gatherings, seeking support for President Nixon, who was under the cloud of the Watergate scandal. Ford was at home with his family when, on August 8, 1974, Nixon, faced with almost certain impeachment, announced his resignation.

PRESIDENT

On August 9, 1974, the day Nixon's resignation went into effect, Ford was sworn in as president. In his address on the occasion he declared, ". . . our long national night-

As Betty Ford looks on, Vice President Ford is sworn in as president on August 9, 1974. Ford succeeded President Richard M. Nixon, who resigned after the Watergate scandal.

mare is over. Our Constitution works. Our great republic is a government of laws and not of men. Here, the people rule."

Ford's succession to the presidency was received with general approval. His reputation for integrity and his openness appealed to most Americans.

A Pardon and Conditional Amnesty. Ford chose Nelson A. Rockefeller, a liberal Republican and four-term governor of New York, as his vice president. Then, in his second major act as president, Ford announced that he was pardoning former President Nixon. Ford cited "compassion" and a desire to end controversy as his reasons. The pardon was applauded by some people but criticized by others.

The Ford family strikes a casual pose in front of the White House. From left are: son Michael, his wife Gayle, President and Mrs. Ford, son John, daughter Susan, and son Steven.

Ford then proclaimed a conditional amnesty for Vietnam War resisters. Under its terms those who had resisted service in the war were to be pardoned in return for civilian service not to exceed two years. The program had limited success, since many war resisters chose not to take part in it. Critics of the program insisted that Ford should have offered unconditional amnesty. President Jimmy Carter pardoned most draft evaders, who numbered some 10,000, in January 1977.

The Economy. Ford inherited a troubled economy. Inflation, recession, and unemployment had all become worse in the final months of the Nixon administration. Ford attacked the problem with a tax cut and a reduction in federal spending. But although the inflation rate dropped considerably, unemployment remained high. Critics of the president said that he was not doing enough to reduce unemployment, and they called for legislation to create jobs. Such a measure, a public-works bill, was passed by Congress in 1976. Ford vetoed it on the grounds that it would be inflationary, but his veto was overridden. Ford vetoed many bills passed by Congress. This was partly for reasons of economy and partly because of his own ideas of government. Ford believed that the federal government and its bureaucracy had become too big and too complex. Many federal programs, he felt, should be cut back or abandoned entirely.

Foreign Affairs. The fall of the governments of South Vietnam and Cambodia to Communist forces in 1975 was a blow to the administration. Cambodian Communists seized an American merchant ship, *Mayagüez*, in 1975. This incident attracted worldwide attention. The president ordered U.S. Marines to recover the ship and its remaining crew, which they did successfully. Later the same year, Ford attended a summit conference of world leaders held in Helsinki, Finland.

The Election of 1976. Ford edged out former California governor Ronald Reagan for the Republican presidential nomination in 1976. He was defeated in the election, however, by the Democratic candidate, James Earl (Jimmy) Carter of Georgia.

Although disappointed at not having won a full term as president in his own right, Ford was gracious in defeat. After retiring from the presidency, he served on the board of directors of several corporations. His autobiography, *A Time to Heal*, was published in 1979. With the status of elder statesman, Ford was called on for advice on several occasions in the 1980s, during the presidency of Ronald Reagan.

39th PRESIDENT OF THE UNITED STATES (1977–1981)

Born: *October 1, 1924, at Plains, Georgia*
Occupation: *Farmer, Public Official*
Party: *Democrat*
Vice President: *Walter F. Mondale*
Wife: *Rosalynn Smith*

When we think of Abraham Lincoln, we see him as a poor boy of the frontier, studying by candlelight, working in a country store, splitting logs, striving to make something of himself. We may wonder at his ability to travel from a log cabin to the White House. His story has helped form the American dream—that a person coming from a modest background can attain spectacular success.

James Earl (Jimmy) Carter, Jr., achieved that dream. His roots were in the southwestern part of Georgia, where members of his family had struggled to make a living for 150 years. He was the first Carter to finish high school. From such beginnings he went on to become president of the United States.

EARLY YEARS

Carter was born in the little town of Plains, Georgia (population about 650), on October 1, 1924. He was the first child of James Earl Carter and Lillian Gordy Carter. Later two daughters, Gloria and Ruth, and another son, William, were born to the Carters. The elder Carter was the manager of a grocery store. In time he was able to ac-

quire some farmland of his own in Archery, just outside Plains.

When Jimmy was not going to school, he was working on the farm. He sold peanuts as a sideline and saved the money he earned. Of his childhood, Carter later said: "In general, the early years of my life on the farm were full and enjoyable, isolated but not lonely. We always had enough to eat . . . but no money to waste."

NAVAL OFFICER AND BUSINESSMAN

Jimmy graduated from high school with very high marks. From his first days at school, he had wanted to attend the United States Naval Academy at Annapolis. An uncle whom he idolized had been in the Navy. At the same time, it meant a chance for an education, for there was little money in the family to pay for college.

Carter received an appointment to the Naval Academy in 1942. But first he spent a year at the Georgia Institute of Technology in Atlanta, taking courses that would help him to pass the entrance examinations to Annapolis. He entered the Academy in 1943. There he adapted to the strict discipline, did well in his studies, ran track and cross country, and played on the lightweight football team. He graduated in 1946 in the upper ten percent of his class. Soon after, he married Rosalynn Smith, whose family lived near Plains. He had met her in his last year at the Naval Academy. The Carters had four children: John, James Earl 3rd (Chip), Jeffrey, and Amy.

Carter spent seven years in the Navy, attaining the rank of lieutenant (senior grade). During part of that time he worked with Admiral Hyman G. Rickover in the nuclear submarine program. Carter's ambition then was to become an admiral. But when his father died in 1953, Carter felt that it was necessary to return to the family farm.

But he was not content to be just a peanut farmer. He bought a peanut sheller and began to supply large

Born in the small town of Plains, Georgia, Jimmy Carter plays the part of a barefoot boy in a school play.

peanut processors. Then he expanded his operation into peanut warehousing. Eventually, with some hard work, the Carters became relatively prosperous.

STATE SENATOR AND GOVERNOR

Carter's interest in politics can be traced at least in part to his father, who had served a year in the Georgia state legislature. In 1962, Carter ran for the state Senate. He lost by a few votes. But when violations of voting rules were discovered, he challenged the results and was declared the winner.

In 1966, Carter first declared himself a candidate for the U.S. House of Representatives but then decided to try for the Democratic nomination for governor of Georgia. He lost in the primary election, but he made a good showing. Carter devoted himself to his business and to civic affairs until 1970. Then he tried again for the governorship. He defeated a former governor of the state in the primary and won the election easily.

Perhaps Carter's most important contribution as governor was in increasing efficiency in the state government. Hating waste, he reduced the number of state agencies from 300 to 22. He appointed a considerable number of African Americans to state jobs. He also ordered that a portrait of Martin Luther King, Jr., be placed alongside portraits of other famous Georgians in the state capitol building. It was the first portrait of an African American to hang in the capitol, a gesture Carter felt was long overdue.

CAMPAIGN FOR THE PRESIDENCY

Carter announced his candidacy for the presidency late in 1974. He campaigned tirelessly, sought the support of Democratic leaders, and built an efficient political staff. His soft southern drawl and wide smile became familiar

---

Jimmy Carter (signature)

James Earl ("Jimmy") Carter, Jr.

39th president, 1977–81 Democrat

1924 Born on October 1 in Plains, Georgia.

1935 Baptized into the First Baptist Church of Plains.

1946 Graduated from the U.S. Naval Academy. Married Rosalynn Smith on July 7. The couple would become the parents of three sons and a daughter.

1946–53 Served in the U.S. Navy. Duty included work under Hyman Rickover.

1953 Following the death of his father, resigned from the Navy and returned to Plains to run the family farm.

1963–67 Served two terms in the Georgia Senate.

1966 Ran third in Georgia's Democratic primary for the gubernatorial nomination.

1971–75 Served as governor of Georgia.

1975 Published his first book, *Why Not the Best?*

1976 Defeated Gerald R. Ford for the presidency.

1982 Named a distinguished professor at Emory University. His memoirs, *Keeping Faith: Memoirs of a President*, were published.

1986 Carter Center established at Emory University.

Highlights of Presidency

1977 In September, signed treaties providing for U.S. operation of the Panama Canal to the end of 1999 and for the permanent neutralization of the canal.

1978 With Israeli Prime Minister Menahem Begin and Egypt's President Anwar el-Sadat, signed the "Framework of Peace in the Middle East" and the "Framework for the Conclusion of a Peace Treaty Between Egypt and Israel," following 11 days of U.S.-sponsored talks at Camp David. In December, China and the U.S. agreed to establish diplomatic relations.

1979 Signed a bill creating the U.S. Department of Education; Department of Energy was established in 1977. Reached Strategic Arms Limitation Agreement with Soviet President Brezhnev. Protesting U.S. support of the Shah, radical Iranian students seized a group of American diplomats and embassy officials in Teheran in November. The "hostage crisis" clouded the remaining months of the Carter presidency.

1980 After defeating Sen. Edward M. Kennedy for the Democratic presidential nomination, lost election to Ronald Reagan by a wide margin.

across the country. By the time of the Democratic National Convention in New York in the summer of 1976, he had already won enough delegates to assure his nomination. The only question that remained was whom he would pick as the vice–presidential candidate. He chose Walter F. Mondale, a liberal senator from Minnesota. In the election, Carter defeated the Republican candidate, President Gerald R. Ford. Carter received 297 electoral votes to Ford's 240.

THE WHITE HOUSE YEARS

The new president adopted a casual style. Carter chose to walk instead of ride down Pennsylvania Avenue after his inauguration. He also requested that the presidential theme, "Hail to the Chief," not be played every time he entered a public place. Many people welcomed this simplicity. But others were critical of Carter's style, which sometimes seemed less than forceful. They wondered how he would deal with the country's problems.

Domestic Issues. At home, Carter's administration faced major problems in the areas of energy supply and the economy. Soon after taking office, Carter asked Congress to create a new Department of Energy. He proposed legislation to reduce oil consumption, increase U.S. oil production, and encourage the use of other energy sources. Congress approved the new department and, after much debate, some of the legislation.

Inflation soon became the leading economic problem. In 1978, Carter called for voluntary limits on wage and price increases. The limits had little effect. Later, controls were imposed on credit. The government hoped that by discouraging borrowing, it would lessen the rate of inflation.

DID YOU KNOW?

- *Carter was the first president born in a hospital.*
- *His nickname as a boy was Hot, short for Hot Shot.*
- *He was the first president to graduate from the U.S. Naval Academy.*
- *Carter was the first president sworn in using his nickname, Jimmy.*
- *He was the first president to send his mother on a diplomatic mission.*
- *When he conducted the first presidential phone-in, over nine million people tried to call him.*

However, a new gasoline shortage and continuing economic problems brought Carter's popularity at home to an all-time low by July, 1979. In a televised speech, Carter said that the United States was facing a "crisis of confidence." He promised to provide strong leadership, and he outlined a new energy program.

Carter and his vice president, Walter Mondale, shown here with Mrs. Mondale, (below, left) ran a relaxed, but unsuccessful campaign in 1984. The First Family (below, right) at the White House are Rosalynn and President Carter and their youngest child, Amy.

Iranian Muslim extremists seized the U.S. Embassy in Tehran in 1979 (above), holding Americans hostage for over 14 months. Carter's attempts to free them were unsuccessful. President and Mrs. Reagan (below) attended the opening of the Jimmy Carter Library with Mr. and Mrs. Carter in 1986.

Carter's Foreign Policy. In foreign policy, Carter often stressed moral principles. His goals, he said, were peace, arms control, economic cooperation, and the advancement of human rights. His efforts toward peace in the Middle East were widely acclaimed. In the fall of 1978, the leaders of Egypt and Israel met with him at Camp David, Maryland, and agreed on basic principles for a peace treaty. A treaty was signed in 1979. But negotiations on details of the peace made slow progress.

Carter concluded new treaties with Panama, giving the country control of the Panama Canal by the year 2000. These treaties were controversial, but they were ratified by the U.S. Senate in 1978. Diplomatic relations with the People's Republic of China were established in 1979. In June 1979, Carter signed a new strategic arms limitation treaty with the Soviet Union. But this treaty met with strong opposition in Congress.

The Iran Crisis and Afghanistan. At the end of 1979 two issues arose that severely tested Carter's leadership. In November, Iranian militants seized the U.S. Embassy in Tehran and held the Americans there hostage. In December, the Soviet Union sent troops into Afghanistan to put down a rebellion against that country's Communist government.

To free the hostages, the United States attempted to negotiate with Iranian leaders. Carter also halted trade with Iran. He appealed to the United Nations and the World Court. When these measures were not successful, Carter ordered military action to try to free the hostages, but the rescue mission failed.

As a result of the Soviet action in Afghanistan, Carter asked Congress to delay consideration of the new arms treaty. He limited trade with the Soviet Union and called for a boycott of the 1980 Summer Olympic Games, which were held in Moscow.

Support for the President was strong at the start of these crises. But as 1980 wore on, there seemed to be little progress toward solving them. At the same time, economic problems continued—especially high interest rates and double-digit inflation.

The 1980 Election. In the election of 1980, Carter faced Ronald W. Reagan, a Republican and a former governor of California. Representative John B. Anderson of Illinois was also in the race, as an independent. Reagan won the election by a wide margin, with 489 electoral votes to Carter's 49. Meanwhile, Carter continued his efforts to obtain the release of the hostages. On January 20, 1981, the day he left office and Reagan was sworn in, they were set free.

After returning to Plains, Carter published his memoirs in 1982 and did other writing. In 1986, the Carter Center at Emory University in Atlanta, Georgia, was set up. The Carters continued to work for such causes as Habitat for Humanity, which provides housing for the poor. The former president also served as an observer of various national elections and as a mediator of international disputes.

40th PRESIDENT OF THE UNITED STATES (1981–1989)

Born: February 6, 1911, at Tampico, Illinois
Occupation: Actor, Public Official
Party: Republican
Vice President: George Bush
Wives: Jane Wyman; Nancy Davis

His mother, Nelle Wilson Reagan, was of English and Scottish ancestry. Neither parent had more than an elementary school education. Ronald had one brother, Neil, who was two years older. Neil picked up the nickname Moon, and Ronald was called Dutch.

Reagan's father often moved the family around the state in search of a better-paying job. But life in the small towns of Illinois was pleasant. "My existence turned into one of those rare Huck Finn–Tom Sawyer idylls," Reagan recalled in his autobiography, *Where's the Rest of Me?* "Those were the days when I learned the riches of rags."

Dixon, a small town to which the family moved when he was nine, was the place where Reagan got most of his schooling. He was not an outstanding student. But his interests in drama, sports, and politics began early. His mother gave dramatic readings before clubs and in prisons and hospitals, and he was first exposed to acting before he started school. He began to play football—one of the great loves of his life—before he was ten years old, in neighborhood games arranged on the spur of the moment.

"There was no field; no lines, no goal. Simply grass, the ball, and a mob of excited youngsters," he later wrote. "Those were the happiest times of my life." Reagan graduated from that kind of football to action as a guard and end on the Dixon High School team. He also participated in basketball and track, acted in school plays, and was president of the student body. During most of his high school and college summers, he worked as a lifeguard at a summer resort near Dixon.

After his high school graduation in 1928, Reagan enrolled at Eureka College, a small college in Eureka, Illinois. He majored in economics; joined the college football, track, and swimming teams; and acted in school plays. He washed dishes at his fraternity house and saved money from summer jobs to help pay his expenses. His grades

The life of Ronald Wilson Reagan is a story of unlikely successes. Reagan was born of poor parents in a small town in Illinois. He graduated from college during the Depression of the 1930s. Yet he became a successful actor in motion pictures and on television. When his entertainment career began to decline, he began a new career—in politics. In 1966 he ran for governor of California as a Republican. He won, despite the fact that most California voters were Democrats.

In 1968 and again in 1976, Reagan sought the Republican nomination for president. He lost both times. After that, many people thought that Reagan's age—then 65—would prevent his party from nominating him. But he worked hard for the nomination in 1980. And he demonstrated to the voters' satisfaction that he could stand up to the stress of a job that is perhaps the most difficult in the world.

EARLY YEARS

The 40th president of the United States was born in Tampico, Illinois, on February 6, 1911. His father, John Edward Reagan, was an Irish-American shoe salesman.

Ronald Reagan (near right) had a happy childhood with his parents and older brother, Neil. In the movie Knute Rockne, All American *(far right), Reagan drew on his love of football to play star halfback George Gipp. The future president appeared in more than 50 motion pictures.*

were not exceptional. But he earned acceptable marks through "quick studies" before tests. He also served for one year as president of the student body.

As a freshman, Reagan took part in a student strike that resulted in the resignation of the college president, who had proposed cutting back the curriculum and the teaching staff because of a shortage of funds. Reagan made the main speech at a rally that won support for the strike from nearly all the students. He later said that he learned then what it was like to succeed with an audience. His skill with audiences was to be a major factor in his successes in later life.

ACTING CAREER

Reagan earned a B.A. degree from Eureka in 1932, at a time when the Depression had left many people without jobs. He spent one last summer as a lifeguard. Then he set out to obtain a job as a radio announcer. He won a tryout for a job announcing football games at WOC in Davenport, Iowa, not far from Dixon. His tryout consisted of making up a play-by-play broadcast

for an imaginary football game. He did well enough, and he was signed on. That job led to work at WOC's larger affiliate, WHO in Des Moines. By the time he was 25, he was one of the top sports broadcasters in the Middle West.

In 1937, Reagan traveled with the Chicago Cubs to their spring training camp near Los Angeles, California. While there, he managed to obtain a screen test from Warner Brothers, and he was offered an acting contract. He quickly accepted. Reagan's movie career spanned more than 20 years and over 50 movies. His most successful roles were in *Knute Rockne, All American* in 1940 and in *King's Row* in 1941. In *Knute Rockne*, Reagan played star halfback George Gipp, who died imploring his coach to have his teammates "win one for the Gipper."

In 1942, during World War II, Reagan entered the Army as a second lieutenant. He was disqualified for combat duty because of poor eyesight, and he spent the next four years making military training films. He then returned to acting. Until this time, Reagan had been a Democrat and had supported liberal causes. But after his

DID YOU KNOW?

- As a college freshman, Reagan led a successful student strike against curriculum cutbacks.

- He was the first president to have headed a labor union.

- He was the first president to have been divorced.

- As a result of his many television appearances while president, he was known as the Great Communicator.

- He was the oldest president.

Army experiences, he became more conservative. He served as president of the Screen Actor's Guild from 1947 to 1952. In the 1950s and 1960s, he appeared on television as the host of "General Electric Theater" and "Death Valley Days." Reagan had married Jane Wyman, an actress, in 1940. They had a daughter and an adopted son. The marriage ended in divorce in 1948. In 1952, Reagan married another actress, Nancy Davis. They had two children.

GOVERNOR OF CALIFORNIA

Reagan's entry into politics was helped by a speech he gave in 1964. It appeared on television and brought him to the attention of powerful Republicans. They urged him to run for governor of California.

In the 1966 election, Reagan faced Edmund G. (Pat) Brown, who had been a popular Democratic governor for eight years. Reagan was critical of state government spending and welfare payments that he believed were too high. He won the election by nearly 1,000,000 votes. Four years later, Reagan easily won reelection. He served as governor until 1975.

THE ROAD TO THE PRESIDENCY

Reagan first sought the Republican presidential nomination in 1968 but lost to Richard M. Nixon. In 1976, Reagan narrowly lost the nomination to President Gerald R. Ford.

The 1980 Campaign. Most Republicans considered Reagan to be too old for the office of presidency, and many considered him as no more than a former movie actor with simplistic views. However, he immediately began his campaign for the 1980 nomination. In the primary contests, he called on his skills as a speaker to win support. His views seemed to reflect growing conservatism in the country, and he won the nomination easily. His nearest opponent, George Bush, was chosen as his vice–presidential running mate.

In the election campaign, Reagan favored reducing total government spending while increasing the amount spent on defense. He also supported large tax cuts and state or local control of programs such as welfare. Reagan called this policy "getting the government off our backs." And he felt that the United States should take firmer stands against Communism.

In the election, Reagan overwhelmingly defeated the Democratic candidate, President Jimmy Carter, running for reelection. Reagan won 489 electoral votes to Carter's 49.

First Term. Reagan's presidency began dramatically in 1981. Minutes after he was sworn in, Iran released the 52 Americans who had been held hostage for more than 14 months. The release had been negotiated by the Carter administration. Then, on March 30, Reagan was shot in Washington, D.C., by John W. Hinckley, Jr. Reagan quickly recovered.

Domestic Issues. During his first term, Reagan launched a "revitalization" program that called for heavy budget cuts, tax cuts, and less regulations. This was based on "supply–side economics" and was designed to speed growth. Congress passed Reagan's requests for cuts in taxes and in some government programs. He also won increased funds for defense. By 1982, however, the country was in an economic recession. The economy improved in 1983. But the increased defense spending and tax cut had

As governor of California, Reagan signs a bill into law as members of the state legislature look on.

Ronald Wilson Reagan

40th president, 1981–89 Republican

1911 Born on February 6 in Tampico, Illinois.

1932 After graduating from Eureka College, worked as a sports announcer for radio stations in Davenport and Des Moines, Iowa.

1937 Made film debut in *Love Is on the Air.* Appeared in more than 50 movies during a 27-year career as an actor.

1940 Married Jane Wyman on January 25. The couple would become the parents of a daughter and an adopted son, and he divorced in 1948.

1942–45 Served in the U.S. Army Air Forces.

1947–52; 1959 Was president of the Screen Actors Guild.

1952 Married actress Nancy Davis on March 4. The couple would have a daughter and a son.

1952-62 Served as a spokesperson for General Electric.

1962 Officially joined the Republican Party, after being a liberal Democrat for years.

1967–75 Was governor of California.

1976 Failed to capture the GOP presidential nomination from the incumbent Gerald Ford.

1980 Elected president in a landslide win over Jimmy Carter and third party candidate John Anderson.

Highlights of Presidency

1981 On January 20, inaugurated as the 40th president. Moments later, 52 Americans, who had been held hostage in Iran since November 1979, were released. In July, nominated Sandra Day O'Connor as an associate justice of the U.S. Supreme Court.

1983 With U.S. forces participating in a multinational peacekeeping force in Lebanon, 241 U.S. servicemen are killed in terrorist attack in October. That same month, U.S.troops invade the Caribbean island of Grenada in an "effort to restore order and democracy."

1984 Reelected in a landslide.

1985 In November, met with Soviet General Secretary Mikhail Gorbachev in Geneva.

1986 American warplanes bombed "terrorist-related targets" in Libya, in April. Second summit meeting with Gorbachev in Iceland. The Iran-Contra affair becomes public.

1987 Stock market collapse in October raises doubts about Reagan's economic program. Arms-control agreement signed with USSR in December.

1988 Goodwill visit to Russia in spring. Supports Bush in presidential election.

led to a record budget deficit. Democrats attacked Reagan for cutting social welfare programs and called for reduced defense spending and a tax increase in order to lower the deficit.

Reagan's appointment in 1981 of Sandra Day O'Connor as the first woman justice of the U.S. Supreme Court was a popular one. But the administration's support for prayer in the public schools and its opposition to abortion aroused much controversy.

Foreign Affairs. In 1983, Reagan sent U.S. Marines to Lebanon as part of a peacekeeping force. The Marines were recalled after 241 were killed in a terrorist attack in 1984. Reagan also sent U.S. troops to Grenada in 1983, to prevent what the administration saw as a Cuban attempt to take over the Caribbean island nation. The president denounced the left-wing Sandinista government of Nicaragua as a threat to peace in Central America, and he repeatedly sought military aid for the anti-Sandinista guerrillas, or contras.

SECOND TERM

The 1984 Election. At the Republican National Convention in Dallas, Reagan and Vice President Bush were renominated without opposition. Their Democratic opponent was former vice president Walter F. Mondale. Congresswoman Geraldine A. Ferraro of New York was named as his running mate, the first time in history a woman ran for the vice presidency. Reagan won a sweeping victory. He received 525 electoral votes to 13 for Mondale, and he carried 49 states.

Domestic Issues. Reagan underwent successful surgery for cancer in 1985. His call for extensive changes in the federal income tax laws helped bring about passage of the Tax Reform Act of 1986. Congress also passed

Reagan hosted a gathering of former presidents at the White House in October 1981. From the left are Richard Nixon, President Reagan, Gerald Ford, and Jimmy Carter.

The Reagan family gathers to celebrate the president's 1984 reelection. From the left are daughters Patti and Maureen and their husbands; son Ron and his wife; Nancy and Ronald Reagan; and the president's brother, Neil Reagan. Eldest son Michael is absent.

a major immigration bill that year. Reagan made two Supreme Court appointments in 1986—Associate Justice William Rehnquist as U.S. Chief Justice and Antonin Scalia as an associate justice. Nominees Robert Bork and Douglas Ginsburg failed to win a Supreme Court seat in 1987. A third nominee, Anthony Kennedy, won approval.

A stock market crash in 1987 raised questions about the nation's economic health. A new bill to balance the federal budget became law in 1987, but the huge deficit continued to trouble the government.

Congress passed several important pieces of legislation in 1988. It approved a new cabinet post, the Department of Veterans Affairs. Federal welfare laws were reformed, and Medicare was expanded to cover "catastrophic" illness. A trade bill was agreed to that also offered some protection to workers facing layoffs. A free-trade pact with Canada was approved, and an anti-drug bill was passed.

Foreign Affairs. Reagan ordered the bombing of military targets in Libya in 1986 in retaliation for its role in international terrorism. His policy of reflagging (flying the U.S. flag on) Kuwaiti oil tankers and providing them with a U.S. naval escort in the Persian Gulf led to clashes with Iran in 1987. The president's greatest diplomatic achievement was the 1987 treaty with the Soviet Union banning intermediate-range nuclear forces (INF), approved by the Senate in 1988.

The Iran-Contra affair proved embarrassing to the administration, even though the president was not directly involved. Congressional hearings in 1987 revealed that presidential aides had secretly sold arms to Iran in an effort to free U.S. citizens being held hostage in the Middle East. The aides had then illegally diverted some of the arms money to contra guerrillas in Nicaragua.

In November 1985, Reagan met with Soviet leader Mikhail Gorbachev in Geneva for a summit conference. A second summit in Iceland in October 1986, did not go as well. Reagan continued to press for his costly Strategic Defense Initiative, nicknamed "Star Wars," and many felt his persistence showed that he was out of touch. At the age of 75, Reagan was perhaps too old to carry out these delicate negotiations. However, in December 1987, an arms-control agreement was signed in Washington, D.C., that eliminated short and intermediate-range missiles in Europe. Reagan visited Moscow in 1988, where he met with Soviet dissidents.

Retirement. With his two terms of office completed, Reagan left the White House in January 1989. He was succeeded by George Bush, the winner of the 1988 presidential election. When Reagan retired, his ratings were the highest of any president since World War II. Yet during his presidency the national debt went from approximately $900 billion to more than $2 trillion. The United States therefore went from being the world's leading creditor (in 1983) to the world's leading debtor (by 1986). More than $400 billion was owed abroad when his second term as president came to an end.

But these economic woes notwithstanding, Reagan's leadership style overcame most doubts. His optimism about U.S. strength touched a responsive public chord. The country's mood had been pessimistic after the Vietnam War, Nixon's resignation, and the Iranian hostage crisis. Reagan preached defense and pursued policies in foreign affairs that he claimed were instrumental in ending the Cold War.

In 1994, it was revealed that President Reagan was suffering from Alzheimer's disease. The disclosure heightened public awareness and concern about the illness, which afflicts some 4 million Americans.

GEORGE BUSH

41st PRESIDENT OF THE UNITED STATES (1989–1993)

Born: June 12, 1924, at Milton, Massachusetts
Occupation: Businessman, Public Official
Party: Republican
Vice President: J. Danforth Quayle
Wife: Barbara Pierce

Few presidents in recent years have entered the White House with as much broad experience in government as George Bush. He served as a member of Congress and as U.S. representative to the United Nations. He was one of the first officials to represent the United States in the People's Republic of China. He is a former director of the Central Intelligence Agency (CIA). And he was vice president under President Ronald Reagan for eight years, before winning the presidency himself in 1988. Bush was the first sitting vice president to be elected president since Martin Van Buren won office in 1836.

EARLY YEARS

George Herbert Walker Bush was born in Milton, Massachusetts, on June 12, 1924. His parents were Prescott Sheldon Bush and Dorothy Walker Bush. His father was a Wall Street investment banker and later served as a U.S. senator from Connecticut. Four other children, three sons and a daughter, were born to the Bushes. George was named after his maternal grandfather, George Herbert Walker, who established the Walker Cup trophy for American and British amateur golfers.

When George was still an infant, the Bush family moved to Greenwich, Connecticut. There he was raised amid wealth. Three maids tended to the needs of the family. A chauffeur drove young George to the Greenwich Country Day School. The Bushes spent the summers at their vacation home in Kennebunkport, Maine, where George loved to go boating and fishing for mackerel in the waters of the Atlantic Ocean. Bush still maintains a summer home in Kennebunkport.

Bush attended an exclusive prep school, Phillips Academy, in Andover, Massachusetts. He was captain of the basketball and soccer teams, played on the baseball team, and was elected president of his senior class. During his senior year, on December 7, 1941, the Japanese attacked Pearl Harbor, Hawaii, drawing the United States into World War II. Bush was impatient to graduate in 1942 so that he could volunteer for the Navy air service.

WAR SERVICE, MARRIAGE, AND COLLEGE

On his 18th birthday, Bush enlisted in the Navy as a seaman second class. Following flight training, he was commissioned as an ensign in 1943 and became a torpedo bomber pilot. At age 19, he was the youngest pilot then serving in the U.S. Navy. During 1943 and 1944, he took part in 58 combat missions in the Pacific. His worst wartime experience occurred in 1944, when his plane was hit by Japanese anti-aircraft fire over Chichi Jima, one of the Bonin Islands. His two crewmen were killed. Bush parachuted to the water. He lay helpless in a rubber raft until he was rescued by a U.S. submarine.

In 1945, while still in uniform, Bush married Barbara Pierce, the daughter of a magazine publisher. The Bushes had five children who lived to maturity, George W., John (known as Jeb), Neil, Marvin, and Dorothy. Another daughter, Robin, died in 1953.

Bush (above) was the youngest U.S. Navy pilot at the time he entered World War II. He later graduated from Yale University, where he played on the baseball team (right).

Corporation. From 1953 to 1966, Bush was the head of the Zapata Off Shore Company, which was a supplier of the drilling equipment used to explore for oil beneath the ocean floor.

Meanwhile, Bush had settled his family in Houston, Texas, and had become active in Republican Party politics. In 1964 he ran for the U.S. Senate, but was defeated. Setting his sights a little lower, Bush won election to the U.S. House of Representatives in 1966. He was the first Republican to represent Houston in Congress. He was re-elected in 1968. In 1970, Bush again ran for the Senate and again was defeated.

APPOINTIVE OFFICES

United Nations Representative. In 1971, President Richard M. Nixon appointed Bush U.S. Permanent Representative to the United Nations. It was a crucial time for the world organization. The United States had agreed to allow the admission of the People's Republic of China to the United Nations for the first time since 1949, when the Communists took over the mainland of China. Bush argued forcefully for a so-called "two-China" policy. Under this compromise, a special seat would have been created for the Republic of China (Taiwan), which had held the China seat since the founding of the United Nations in 1945. But the United Nations rejected the two-China plan and expelled the Taiwan government in favor of the People's Republic.

When the war ended in 1945, Bush was discharged from the Navy with the rank of lieutenant, junior grade. He had won the Distinguished Flying Cross and three Air Medals.

Bush resumed his education at Yale University, where he majored in economics. Still interested in sports, he played first base on the Yale baseball team. In 1948, during a home game against Princeton University, Bush got a chance to meet one of his baseball heroes, Babe Ruth. In one of his last public appearances before his death that year, Babe Ruth presented Bush, then the team captain, with the manuscript of his autobiography, which he was donating to Yale.

OIL AND POLITICS IN TEXAS

On his graduation from Yale in 1948, Bush was offered a job in his father's investment banking firm. But Bush preferred to make it on his own. With his wife and young son, he headed for Texas. His first job was painting oil rigs. But soon he was selling oil drilling equipment. In 1950 he and a partner formed a company that bought land in hopes of finding oil or natural gas. Three years later, Bush merged the company with the operations of other oil speculators, founding the Zapata Petroleum

DID YOU KNOW?

- *With Bush the first president born in June, presidents now have been born in all 12 months.*

- *When he received his commission in 1943, he became, at 19, the youngest pilot then in the Navy.*

- *Bush was the first president to have been chairman of his political party.*

- *His inauguration cost $25 million, by far the most expensive in U.S. history.*

- *Bush, distantly related to Benedict Arnold and Marilyn Monroe, is also related to Presidents Pierce, Lincoln, Theodore Roosevelt, and Ford, and to Winston Churchill.*

George Bush

41st president, 1989–93 Republican

1924   Born on June 12 in Milton, Massachusetts.

1942   Enlists in U.S. Navy as seaman second class.

1943-45   Becomes youngest pilot in Navy and serves to end of war. Married Barbara Pierce on January 6. They would become parents of four sons and one daughter.

1948   Graduates from Yale University. Moves to Texas.

1964   Defeated, as Republican, in run for U.S. Senate.

1966   Runs successfully for Congress, the first Republican from Houston to do so.

1968   Reelected to House.

1970   Defeated again in run for Senate.

1971   Appointed U.S. Permanent Representative to the United Nations by President Nixon.

1973   Named chairman of the Republican National Committee.

1974   Appointed chief of the U.S. Liaison Office to the People's Republic of China by President Ford.

1976   Appointed director of the Central Intelligence Agency by President Ford.

1980   Ran successfully as Ronald Reagan's vice president.

1984   Reelected as Ronald Reagan's vice president.

1988   Ran successfully for president with J. Danforth Quayle as running mate.

Highlights of Presidency

1989   Savings and loan bail-out plan passed. Exxon Valdez leaves history's largest oil spill in Alaska. Federal minimum hourly wage increased. Authorized the use of U.S. troops to oust Panama's General Noriega.

1990   Named David H. Souter as Supreme Court Justice. Iraq invades Kuwait in August. Communist governments of Eastern Europe fall. German unification completed.

1991   In January, U.S. troops lead U.N. forces to quick victory over Hussein, pushing the Iraqis out of Kuwait. Soviet hard-liners attempt coup against Gorbachev which fails. African-American Clarence Thomas confirmed to Supreme Court after controversial hearings. USSR collapses and new Russian Commonwealth formed.

1992   Wins Republican Party nomination for second term in August. Suffers defeat at the hands of Democratic nominee Bill Clinton in November 3 general election.

Party Chairman. In 1973, Bush was named chairman of the Republican National Committee. At this time, President Nixon and the Republican Party were under the cloud of the Watergate scandal. For a long time, Bush defended Nixon, because he believed the president when he said that he had taken no part in attempts to cover up illegal activities by some members of his administration. But when the White House tape recordings were made public and exposed Nixon's involvement, Bush, acting for the Republican Party, asked Nixon to resign. Nixon did so on August 9, 1974.

Envoy to China and CIA Director. The new president, Gerald R. Ford, appointed Bush to what was then the top diplomatic post in the People's Republic of China, chief of the U.S. Liaison Office, in 1974. He remained in China until he was called home at Ford's request to become director of the Central Intelligence Agency (CIA). Bush served in that post from late January 1976 until the beginning of Jimmy Carter's administration in January 1977.

VICE PRESIDENT

Bush lost the Republican presidential nomination to Ronald Reagan in 1980 but was named as his vice-presidential running mate. The Reagan–Bush ticket won easily in 1980. They were reelected overwhelmingly in 1984.

Two Presidential Emergencies. On March 30, 1981, President Reagan was shot in an assassination attempt. While Reagan was recovering, Vice President Bush met regularly with the cabinet, White House officials, and congressional leaders. On July 13, 1985, the powers of the presidency were transferred temporarily to Bush while Reagan underwent cancer surgery.

The Iran-Contra Affair. In 1986 it became known that presidential aides had secretly sold arms to Iran in exchange for the release of American hostages in the Middle East. Some of the arms profits were used, illegally, to help contra guerrillas in their war against the government of Nicaragua. Bush's role in the arms sale to Iran was unclear.

Bush served two terms as vice president in the administration of President Ronald Reagan, from 1981 to 1989.

The Bush family gathers at their summer home in Kennebunkport, Maine. The president and Mrs. Bush (in dark sweater) are seated to right of center. The eldest son, George W., is at far right, with his wife and daughter. Seated at left front are sons Neil and Marvin (in white sneakers), with their wives and children. Son John, known as Jeb, is at rear left (in dark shirt). Daughter Dorothy is to John's left, with her husband and children.

The Presidential Campaign. With Reagan forced to retire after two terms, Bush again sought the Republican presidential nomination in 1988. At the Republican convention in New Orleans, Louisiana, he won the nomination without opposition. Bush surprised many people by selecting 41-year-old Senator John Danforth Quayle of Indiana as his vice-presidential running mate. Bush and Quayle went on to defeat the Democratic candidates for president and vice president, Governor Michael Dukakis of Massachusetts and Senator Lloyd Bentsen, Jr., of Texas. The Bush–Quayle ticket won 54 percent of the popular vote and received 426 electoral votes to 111 for the Democrats.

PRESIDENT

After being sworn in as the nation's 41st president, Bush began putting his own conservative stamp on the office.

Domestic Affairs

In February 1989, Bush proposed a major plan to bail out the nation's troubled savings and loan associations. Although Congress passed a $159 billion ten-year plan to rescue the industry, the scope of the problem grew. In November 1989, Bush signed into law a bill raising the federal minimum hourly wage to $4.25 in 1991, after first vetoing a higher raise.

Although during his first year as president Bush had received high ratings in the polls, the dilemma of the enormous budget deficit was becoming a problem he could no longer ignore. In his campaign he had promised no new taxes, but the increasing costs of the savings and loan bailout plan, a sluggish GNP, and rising inflation

forced him to change his mind. Budget debates dragged on all during 1990, and a when a budget was finally enacted by Congress in late October, almost no one was happy with it. His popularity fell in the polls by over 20 points.

Bush's campaign promise to become "the education president" was also met with criticism. Early in 1991 he unveiled his "America 2000" education program which featured broad national standards for students in five core subjects, a new voluntary nationwide examination system, and incentives for local school systems to allow parents greater opportunity to choose schools for their children.

Like his predecessor, Bush took a strong anti-abortion stance. His call for a constitutional amendment to prohibit flag burning was rejected. Worried about America's dependence on oil imports, his "national energy strategy" depended heavily on expanding domestic supplies of oil and increasing the use of nuclear power. There was little attention paid to conservation and alternate energy sources.

Following the resignation of U.S. Supreme Court Justice William J. Brennan in 1990, Bush named Judge David H. Souter of New Hampshire to the post. In 1991 he appointed Clarence Thomas, a 43-year-old African-American federal judge, to the court to succeed the retiring Thurgood Marshall. Thomas was confirmed after much controversy. Bush agreed to a compromise civil rights bill in 1991, after he had vetoed a measure in 1990 that he said would have led to quotas in hiring.

Foreign Affairs

If Bush was hampered by what some saw as indecisive leadership on domestic issues, global events transpired to

President and Mrs. Bush and congressional leaders visited U.S. troops involved in Operation Desert Shield in Saudi Arabia on Thanksgiving 1990.

give him a leadership role. Late in 1989, Bush authorized the use of U.S. troops to oust Panama's General Manuel Noriega. The deposed dictator was brought to the United States and went on trial on drug charges in Miami in September 1991.

On a more positive note, in July of 1990, a harmonious North Atlantic Treaty Organization (NATO) summit cleared the way for further agreements between even more nations. In late 1990 Bush attended the 35-nation Conference on Security and Cooperation in Europe (CSCE) in Paris. A number of foreign-policy successes were scored, including a European conventional arms agreement.

One by one, nearly all of the Communist governments of Eastern Europe fell and were replaced by Western-style democracies. The reunification of Germany in the fall of 1990 was certainly welcomed by all. It looked as if the Cold War was really winding down as Bush met several times with Soviet leader Mikhail Gorbachev and in 1991 signed the Strategic Arms Reduction Treaty (START) with the Soviet leader. He later announced that the United States would do away with all land and sea tactical nuclear weapons.

Invasion of Kuwait. After Iraq invaded Kuwait in August 1990, Bush led a global effort to counter the aggression. When Iraq's President Saddam Hussein ignored a deadline of mid-January 1991, imposed by the United Nations for evacuating Kuwait, a U.N. coalition headed by U.S. forces attacked and overwhelmed the Iraqis in a ground war that was over in a few days. Total U.S. armed forces numbered over 400,000 and were joined by British, French, Egyptian, and Syrian units, along with small contingents from other nations. Other countries sent monetary aid, and Gorbachev supported the U.N. decision.

Although the military success did much for Bush's image, questions were raised about the wisdom and legality of authorizing war against Iraq. The subject of presidential war-making powers again was debated. Many felt the U.S. was defending its own oil supply, not the worried neighbors of Iraq in Saudi Arabia or the oppressed Kuwaitis.

Following the end of the fighting, the administration organized a Middle East peace conference, which convened in Madrid, Spain, in late October 1991. With Russia immersed in problems of its own, the countries of the Middle East were coming to rely more heavily on the U.S.

Collapse of USSR. In August 1991, Communist hard-liners attempted a coup by forcing out Soviet President Mikhail Gorbachev. Largely because of the efforts of Russian Republic President Boris Yeltsin, the coup fell apart. In the aftermath, the Soviet Communist Party was dissolved. By the end of the year, Gorbachev had resigned, and the USSR no longer existed. The U.S. and the rest of the world recognized the independence of the former Soviet republics.

The 1992 Election

In his bid for reelection in 1992, Bush won renomination easily. Arkansas Governor Bill Clinton emerged as the Democratic nominee. Despite President Bush's record-high popularity ratings following the 1991 Iraqi war, voters elected Clinton to the presidency. An economic downturn and effective campaigning by the Democrats contributed to Bush's defeat.

After leaving the White House, the Bushes divided their time between a new home in Texas and their summer home in Maine. The former president remained active politically. In November 1994, the Bushes' eldest son, George W., was elected governor of Texas.

WILLIAM CLINTON

42nd PRESIDENT OF THE UNITED STATES (1993–)

Born: August 19, 1946, in Hope, Arkansas
Occupation: Lawyer, Public Official
Party: Democrat
Vice President: Albert Gore, Jr.
Wife: Hillary Rodham

In January 1993, William (Bill) Clinton, at age 46, became the youngest person to assume the presidency of the United States since John F. Kennedy took the oath office in 1961 at age 43. Despite his youth, Clinton entered the White House with considerable experience in executive government. At the time of his election victory in November 1992, he already had served for nearly 12 years as governor of Arkansas, his native state. There, too, Clinton had been distinguished for his youth as well as his accomplishments. With his rise to the presidency, he became the first of the generation born after World War II, the so-called "baby boomers," to achieve the nation's highest office.

EARLY YEARS

Clinton was born William Jefferson Blythe IV in Hope, Arkansas, on August 19, 1946. Three months before his birth, his father, William Jefferson Blythe III, had been killed in an automobile accident. At the age of two he was sent to live with his grandparents, who also resided in Hope, while his mother, Virginia Blythe, studied nursing in New Orleans. When he was four, his mother married

Roger Clinton, a car salesman, and they moved together as a family to Hot Springs, Arkansas. The boy later took his stepfather's last name.

Young Bill attended school in Little Rock. He was an honors student, played the saxophone, and was popular with his classmates. But life at home was not always pleasant. The elder Clinton was an alcoholic, and when he had too much to drink he often beat Bill's mother. One day, when Bill was about 14, he stood up to his stepfather, warning him never to strike his mother again. Although his stepfather kept drinking, he never again raised a hand to his family. As Bill grew older, he came to understand his stepfather's problem and so was able to forgive him before his death. Bill's mother, who had a successful career as a nurse, lived to see her son become president.

YOUTHFUL AMBITION AND EDUCATION

Clinton thought of becoming a doctor or a reporter or even a musician. But after a fateful meeting with President John F. Kennedy while still in high school, he made up his mind to enter politics. The meeting came about in 1963, when he was a delegate to the American Legion Boys' Nation, a youth program in which students learn about the roles of government leaders. Clinton was part of a group that was invited to the White House to meet the president. Kennedy, who only months later was to be assassinated, shook hands with the eager young Clinton and made a lasting impression on him.

After graduating from Hot Springs High School in 1964, Clinton enrolled at Georgetown University in Washington, D.C. In his spare time he worked in the office of U.S. Senator J. William Fulbright of Arkansas. Upon graduation from Georgetown in 1968 with a degree in international affairs, Clinton won a two-year Rhodes scholarship at Oxford University in England. He returned to the United States in 1970 to study law at Yale University. In 1972 he took time off from his studies to work for the presidential campaign of Democratic candidate George McGovern, who was defeated by Richard M. Nixon. The following year, Clinton received his law degree.

EARLY CAREER AND MARRIAGE

Clinton served briefly as a staff lawyer for the U.S. House of Representatives Judiciary Committee before joining the faculty of the University of Arkansas Law School in 1973. The following year he tried, unsuccessfully, to launch his own political career, running for Congress against a popular four-term Republican. Although Clinton lost, he received more votes than any other Democratic candidate in the district in 25 years. One reason Clinton did so well was that many voters had turned against Republicans because of the Watergate scandal.

In 1975, Clinton married Hillary Rodham, whom he had met at the Yale Law School. Mrs. Clinton established her own very successful law practice in Little Rock. The Clintons have one child, a daughter named Chelsea.

As a teenager in Hot Springs, Arkansas, Bill Clinton took up the saxophone—a lifelong hobby. He also excelled in school and was popular with his classmates.

William (Bill) Clinton

42nd President, 1993–   Democrat

1946 Born William Jefferson Blythe IV on August 19 in Hope, Arkansas.

1968 Graduates from Georgetown University with a bachelor's degree in international affairs.

1968–70 Attends University College, Oxford University (England) as a Rhodes Scholar.

1973 Graduates from Yale University Law School with a J. D. degree.

1973–76 Serves as professor of law at the University of Arkansas at Fayetteville, while pursuing a limited law practice.

1974 Is defeated in a race for the U.S. House of Representatives from the Third Congressional District of Arkansas.

1975 Marries Hillary Rodham on October 11. A daughter, Chelsea Victoria, would be born to the couple in 1980.

1977–79 Serves as attorney general of Arkansas.

1979–81 Serves first term as governor of Arkansas.

1980 Loses bid for a second term as governor.

1981–82 Practices law at the firm of Wright, Lindsey & Jennings in Little Rock, Arkansas.

1983–92 Serves again as governor of Arkansas.

1992 Accepts the Democratic Party nomination for president in July; names Senator Albert Gore, Jr., as his vice-presidential running mate. Defeats Republican incumbent George Bush in the general election on November 3.

Highlights of Presidency

1993 Inaugurated as 42nd President. Names Ruth Bader Ginsburg as an associate justice of the U.S. Supreme Court. In a White House ceremony, representatives of Israel and the Palestine Liberation Organization (PLO) sign a declaration of principles for interim Palestinian self-rule. Congress approves legislation implementing the Clinton-supported North American Free Trade Agreement (NAFTA), linking Canada, Mexico, and the United States.

1994 With U.S. backing, Jean-Bertrand Aristide, Haiti's democratically elected president who was overthrown in a 1991 coup, is restored to office. Congress fails to enact legislation reforming the health-care system, a Clinton priority. In midterm elections, the Republican Party gains control of both houses of Congress for first time since 1954.

Clinton's second try for political office was more effective, winning him election as attorney general of Arkansas in 1976. He also ran the state campaign for Democratic presidential candidate Jimmy Carter. As state attorney general for the next two years, Clinton aggressively defended the rights of consumers. He worked to curb the high cost of electricity and other public utilities and enforced the state's laws on the environment.

GOVERNOR OF ARKANSAS

Victory and Defeat

Clinton won election as governor of Arkansas in 1978. Then 32, he was at the time the nation's youngest governor. His political rise had been so swift and sure that Democratic Party leaders were already talking about his presidential prospects in the years ahead. He was chosen to deliver an important speech at the Democratic National Convention in New York City in 1980. He also served for a time as chairman of the National Conference of Democratic Governors.

But the people of Arkansas began to resent seeing their new young governor distracted from the problems at home. They were also unhappy with tax increases that Clinton imposed on gasoline and automobile licenses, revenue that he had wanted to pay for improving the state's highway system. These and other issues led to his defeat for reelection in 1980 at the hands of Frank White, a banker with no political experience. At the age of 34, Clinton had the dubious distinction of being the youngest ex-governor in U.S. history. Stunned by his defeat, he joined a law firm in Little Rock and tried to sort out what had gone wrong.

Political Comeback

Two years later, Clinton ran again for governor. This time he promised Arkansas voters that he would talk less and listen more to their needs. Partly because the voters blamed Governor White for a steep increase in electricity costs during his term, Clinton was able to win back many of his former supporters, and he defeated White easily. He went on to win reelection in 1984, 1986, and 1990. (The term for governor was extended from two to four years, beginning in 1986.)

The centerpiece of Governor Clinton's policy agenda was to improve the state's educational system. In 1983 he won passage of a major educational reform package, which required teachers to pass a test demonstrating their qualifications. It was the first time any state had required its teachers to take such an examination, and many teachers resented it. But he also offered a pay raise to those who qualified. To lower their high dropout rate, students were required to remain in school until at least age 17. To pay for these reforms, the new law increased the sales tax. Over the next several years, the quality of education began to improve.

In other matters, Clinton helped create new manufacturing jobs in Arkansas, though sometimes at the ex-

- *Clinton is the first U.S. president born after World War II. He was also the first Arkansan to win a major party nomination for the office.*

- *In high school, Clinton played saxophone in a jazz trio. The three musicians wore dark glasses on stage, and they called themselves "Three Blind Mice."*

- *Clinton is known as a card shark with near-photographic memory. His favorite game is hearts.*

- *An attorney of national reputation, Hillary Clinton has sat on the boards of directors of several major corporations and charities.*

pense of the environment. He also upgraded health care for pregnant women and infants, and improved race relations between blacks and whites in the state.

ROAD TO THE PRESIDENCY

Clinton was expected to run for president in 1988, but at the last minute he changed his mind. His explanation was that he thought the ordeal of the campaign would be too hard on his daughter, Chelsea, who was then just seven years old. Governor Michael Dukakis of Massachusetts, the Democratic presidential candidate that year, chose Clinton to deliver his nominating address at the party's convention in Atlanta, Georgia. But Clinton, who was usually an interesting speaker, failed to capture the attention of the delegates or the vast television audience. The election proved a disaster for the Democrats, with Dukakis losing heavily to the Republican nominee, Vice President George Bush.

Candidate

In October 1991, Clinton announced his candidacy for the 1992 Democratic presidential nomination. Because President Bush was so popular following the U.S.-led victory in the 1991 Persian Gulf War, many leading Democrats chose not to challenge his reelection bid. Besides Clinton, the major Democratic candidates included former Governor Jerry Brown of California, former

On Jan. 20, 1993, William Jefferson Clinton was sworn in as the 42nd president by Chief Justice William H. Rehnquist. Hillary Rodham Clinton held the Bible during her husband's swearing in. Their daughter Chelsea was at her father's side.

Senator Paul Tsongas of Massachusetts, Senator Bob Kerrey of Nebraska, and Senator Tom Harkin of Iowa.

Platform

Among other issues, Clinton supported lower taxes for working people, tougher requirements for receiving welfare, and more money for education. He proposed an innovative program to enable more young people to attend college, favored some form of national health insurance, and supported a woman's right to choose an abortion. The heart of Clinton's program was a detailed economic plan designed to create jobs, reform the health care system, and improve education and worker training. It called for an investment of $200 billion over four years to upgrade the nation's transportation and communications system and to train young people for the highly technical jobs of tomorrow.

Nomination and Election

With the best campaign organization in the field, Clinton jumped to an early lead in the race for the Democratic nomination. But he was soon dogged by questions about his character. Among other things, he was criticized for avoiding military service during the Vietnam War and seeming to try to cover it up. Despite intense media coverage of such matters, Clinton continued to draw support, so that by the end of the primary campaign, he had won enough delegates to assure his swift nomination at the Democratic National Convention in New York City in July 1992.

Still, many Democrats and Republicans throughout the country expressed disappointment with their presidential choices. Tapping into that discontent was H. Ross Perot, a billionaire Texas businessman who put together an independent grass-roots campaign for president, which drew considerable support.

For his vice-presidential running mate, Clinton chose Senator Albert (Al) Gore, Jr., of Tennessee. In selecting Gore, Clinton ignored the usual practice of forming a balanced ticket: both were young (Gore was 44 at the time) political moderates from neighboring states. The combination proved effective, however. Emphasizing the need for economic reform, Clinton and Gore defeated Bush and his vice president, Dan Quayle. It was only the second time in 28 years that the Democrats had won the presidency. And with Democratic majorities in both houses of Congress, a period of sweeping domestic policy reform seemed in the offing.

THE PRESIDENCY

Much of Bill Clinton's first year as president was devoted to domestic issues, including the economy and health-care reform, as well as winning congressional approval of a major trade agreement with Canada and Mexico. A series of crises—including continued hostilities in the former Yugoslavia, economic difficulties in Russia, North Korea's nuclear program, and the restoration of democracy in Haiti—drew Clinton's attention in 1994. A peace agreement between Israel and Jordan and a peace initiative regarding Northern Ireland, as well as major crime legislation, were highlights of Clinton's second year in the White House. The character issue, including some financial dealings while he was governor of Arkansas, continued to cause him difficulty, however.

In November 1994, he watched his Democratic Party lose control of both houses of Congress. The GOP now was offering its own Contract with America. The federal budget deficit, affirmative-action programs, and diplomatic recognition for Vietnam were topics of presidential concern in 1995. By midyear, President Clinton's eyes already seemed to be turning toward 1996 and a bid for a second term.

	Parties	Popular Vote	Electoral Vote
1789 George Washington			69
John Adams			34
John Jay			9
R. H. Harrison			6
John Rutledge			6
John Hancock			4
George Clinton			3
Samuel Huntington			2
John Milton			2
James Armstrong			1
Benjamin Lincoln			1
Edward Telfair			1
(Not voted)			12
1792 George Washington	Federalist		132
John Adams	Federalist		77
George Clinton	Dem.-Rep.		50
Thomas Jefferson			4
Aaron Burr			1
1796 John Adams	Federalist		71
Thomas Jefferson	Dem.-Rep.		68
Thomas Pinckney	Federalist		59
Aaron Burr	Anti-Federalist		30
Samuel Adams	Dem.-Rep.		15
Oliver Ellsworth	Federalist		11
George Clinton	Dem.-Rep.		7
John Jay	Ind.-Fed.		5
James Iredell	Federalist		3
George Washington	Federalist		2
John Henry	Independent		2
S. Johnston	Ind.-Fed.		2
C. C. Pinckney	Ind.-Fed.		1
1800 Thomas Jefferson	Dem.-Rep.		73
Aaron Burr	Dem.-Rep.		73
John Adams	Federalist		65
C. C. Pinckney	Federalist		64
John Jay	Federalist		1
1804 Thomas Jefferson	Dem.-Rep.		162
C.C. Pinckney	Federalist		14
1808 James Madison	Dem.-Rep.		122
C. C. Pinckney	Federalist		47
George Clinton	Ind.-Rep.		6
(Not voted)			1
1812 James Madison	Dem.-Rep.		128
DeWitt Clinton	Fusion		89
(Not voted)			1

	Parties	Popular Vote	Electoral Vote
1816 James Monroe	Dem.-Rep.		183
Rufus King	Federalist		34
(Not voted)			4
1820 James Monroe	Dem.-Rep.		231
John Q. Adams	Ind.-Rep.		1
(Not voted)			3
1824 John Q. Adams	No distinct	108,740	84
Andrew Jackson	party	153,544	99
Henry Clay	designations	47,136	37
W. H. Crawford		46,618	41
1828 Andrew Jackson	Democratic	647,286	178
John Q. Adams	Nat.-Rep.	508,064	83
1832 Andrew Jackson	Democratic	687,502	219
Henry Clay	Nat. Rep.	530,189	49
William Wirt	Anti-Masonic	—	7
John Floyd	Nullifiers	—	11
(Not voted)			2
1836 Martin Van Buren	Democratic	765,483	170
William H. Harrison	Whig		73
Hugh L. White	Whig	739,795	26
Daniel Webster	Whig		14
W. P. Mangum	Anti-Jackson		11
1840 William H. Harrison	Whig	1,274,624	234
Martin Van Buren	Democratic	1,127,781	60
1844 James K. Polk	Democratic	1,338,464	170
Henry Clay	Whig	1,300,097	105
James G. Birney	Liberty	62,300	—
1848 Zachary Taylor	Whig	1,360,967	163
Lewis Cass	Democratic	1,222,342	127
Martin Van Buren	Free Soil	291,263	—
1852 Franklin Pierce	Democratic	1,601,117	254
Winfield Scott	Whig	1,385,453	42
John P. Hale	Free Soil	155,825	—
1856 James Buchanan	Democratic	1,832,955	174
John C. Fremont	Republican	1,339,932	114
Millard Fillmore	American	871,731	8
1860 Abraham Lincoln	Republican	1,865,593	180
J. C. Breckinridge	Democratic (S)	848,356	72
Stephen A. Douglas	Democratic	1,382,713	12
John Bell	Con. Union	592,906	39
1864 Abraham Lincoln	Republican	2,206,938	212
George B. McClellan	Democratic	1,803,787	21
(Not voted)		—	81

		Parties	Popular Vote	Electoral Vote
1868	Ulysses S. Grant	Republican	3,013,421	214
	Horatio Seymour	Democratic	2,706,829	80
	(Not voted)		—	23
1872	Ulysses S. Grant	Republican	3,596,745	286
	Horace Greeley	Democratic	2,843,446	
	Charles O'Connor	Straight Dem.	29,489	—
	Thomas A. Hendricks	Ind.-Dem.	—	42
	B. Gratz Brown	Democratic	—	18
	Charles J. Jenkins	Democratic	—	2
	David Davis	Democratic	—	1
	(Not voted)		—	17
1876	Rutherford B. Hayes	Republican	4,036,572	185
	Samuel J. Tilden	Democratic	4,284,020	184
	Peter Cooper	Greenback	81,737	—
1880	James A. Garfield	Republican	4,453,295	214
	Winfield S. Hancock	Democratic	4,414,082	155
	James B. Weaver	Green.-Labor	308,578	—
	Neal Dow	Prohibition	10,305	—
1884	Grover Cleveland	Democratic	4,879,507	219
	James G. Blaine	Republican	4,850,293	182
	Benjamin F. Butler	Green.-Labor	175,370	—
	John P. St. John	Prohibition	150,369	—
1888	Benjamin Harrison	Republican	5,447,129	233
	Grover Cleveland	Democratic	5,537,857	168
	Clinton B. Fisk	Prohibition	249,506	—
	Anson J. Streeter	Union Labor	146,935	—
1892	Grover Cleveland	Democratic	5,555,426	277
	Benjamin Harrison	Republican	5,182,690	145
	James B. Weaver	People's	1,029,846	22
	John Bidwell	Prohibition	264,133	—
	Simon Wing	Soc. Labor	21,164	—
1896	William McKinley	Republican	7,102,246	271
	William J. Bryan	Democratic	6,492,559	176
	John M. Palmer	Nat. Dem.	133,148	—
	Joshua Levering	Prohibition	132,007	—
	Charles H. Matchett	Soc. Labor	36,274	—
	Charles E. Bentley	Nationalist	13,969	—
1900	William McKinley	Republican	7,218,491	292
	William J. Bryan	Democratic	6,356,734	155
	John C. Wooley	Prohibition	208,914	—
	Eugene V. Debs	Socialist	87,814	—
	Wharton Barker	People's	50,373	—
	Jos. F. Malloney	Soc. Labor	39,739	—
1904	Theodore Roosevelt	Republican	7,628,461	336
	Alton B. Parker	Democratic	5,084,223	140
	Eugene V. Debs	Socialist	402,283	—
	Silas C. Swallow	Prohibition	258,536	—
	Thomas E. Watson	People's	117,183	—
	Charles H. Corregan	Soc. Labor	31,249	—
1908	William H. Taft	Republican	7,675,320	321
	William J. Bryan	Democratic	6,412,294	162
	Eugene V. Debs	Socialist	420,793	—
	Eugene W Chafin	Prohibition	253,840	—
	Thomas L. Hisgen	Independence	82,872	—
	Thomas E. Watson	People's	29,100	—
	August Gillhaus	Soc. Labor	14,021	—
1912	Woodrow Wilson	Democratic	6,296,547	435
	Theodore Roosevelt	Progressive	4,118,571	88
	William H. Taft	Republican	3,486,720	8
	Eugene V. Debs	Socialist	900,672	—
	Eugene W. Chafin	Prohibition	206,275	—
	Arthur E. Reimer	Soc. Labor	28,750	—
1916	Woodrow Wilson	Democratic	9,127,695	277
	Charles E. Hughes	Republican	8,533,507	254
	A. L. Benson	Socialist	585,113	—
	J. Frank Hanly	Prohibition	220,506	—
	Arthur E. Reimer	Soc. Labor	13,403	—
1920	Warren G. Harding	Republican	16,143,407	404
	James M. Cox	Democratic	9,130,328	127
	Eugene V. Debs	Socialist	919,799	—
	P. P. Christensen	Farmer-Labor	265,411	—
	Aaron S. Watkins	Prohibition	189,408	—
	James E. Ferguson	American	48,000	—
	W. W. Cox	Soc. Labor	31,715	—
1924	Calvin Coolidge	Republican	15,718,211	382
	John W. Davis	Democratic	8,385,283	136
	Robert M. LaFollette	Progressive	4,831,289	13
	Herman P. Faris	Prohibition	57,520	—
	Frank T. Johns	Soc. Labor	36,428	—
	William Z. Foster	Workers	36,386	—
	Gilbert O. Nations	American	25,967	—
1928	Herbert C. Hoover	Republican	21,391,993	444
	Alfred E. Smith	Democratic	15,016,169	87
	Norman Thomas	Socialist	267,835	—
	Verne L. Reynolds	Soc. Labor	21,603	—
	William Z. Foster	Workers	21,181	—
	William F. Varney	Prohibition	20,106	—
1932	Franklin D. Roosevelt	Democratic	22,809,638	472
	Herbert C. Hoover	Republican	15,758,901	59
	Norman Thomas	Socialist	881,951	—
	William Z. Foster	Communist	102,785	—
	William D. Upshaw	Prohibition	81,869	—
	Verne L. Reynolds	Soc. Labor	33,276	—
	William H. Harvey	Liberty	53,425	

Parties		Popular Vote	Electoral Vote
1936 Franklin D. Roosevelt	Democratic	27,752,869	523
Alfred M. Landon	Republican	16,674,665	8
William Lemke	Union	882,479	—
Norman Thomas	Socialist	187,720	—
Earl Browder	Communist	80,159	—
D. Leigh Colvin	Prohibition	37,847	—
John W. Aiken	Soc. Labor	12,777	—
1940 Franklin D. Roosevelt	Democratic	27,307,819	449
Wendell L. Willkie	Republican	22,321,018	82
Norman Thomas	Socialist	99,557	—
Roger Q. Babson	Prohibition	57,812	—
Earl Browder	Communist	46,251	—
John W. Aiken	Soc. Labor	14,892	—
1944 Franklin D. Roosevelt	Democratic	25,606,585	432
Thomas E. Dewey	Republican	22,014,745	99
Norman Thomas	Socialist	80,518	—
Claude A. Watson	Prohibition	74,758	—
Edward A. Teichert	Soc. Labor	45,336	—
1948 Harry S. Truman	Democratic	24,179,345	303
Thomas E. Dewey	Republican	21,991,291	189
Strom Thurmond	States' Rights	1,176,125	39
Henry Wallace	Progressive	1,157,326	—
Norman Thomas	Socialist	139,572	—
Claude A. Watson	Prohibition	103,900	—
Edward A. Teichert	Soc. Labor	29,241	—
Farrell Dobbs	Soc. Workers	13,614	—
1952 Dwight D. Eisenhower	Republican	33,936,234	442
Adlai E. Stevenson	Democratic	27,314,992	89
Vincent Hallinan	Progressive	140,023	—
Stuart Hamblen	Prohibition	72,949	—
Eric Hass	Soc. Labor	30,267	—
Darlington Hoopes	Socialist	20,203	—
Douglas A. MacArthur	Constitution	17,205	—
Farrell Dobbs	Soc. Workers	10,312	—
1956 Dwight D. Eisenhower	Republican	35,590,472	457
Adlai E. Stevenson	Democratic	26,022,752	73
T. Coleman Andrews	States' Rights	111,178	—
Eric Hass	Soc. Labor	44,450	—
Enoch A. Holtwick	Prohibition	41,937	—
1960 John F. Kennedy	Democratic	34,226,731	303
Richard M. Nixon	Republican	34,108,157	219
Eric Hass	Soc. Labor	47,522	—
Rutherford L. Decker	Prohibition	46,203	—
Orval E. Faubus	Nat. S. Rights	44,977	—
Farrell Dobbs	Soc. Workers	40,165	—
Charles L. Sullivan	Constitution	18,162	—
1964 Lyndon B. Johnson	Democratic	43,129,566	486
Barry M. Goldwater	Republican	27,178,188	52
Eric Hass	Soc. Labor	45,219	—
Clifton DeBerry	Soc. Workers	32,720	—
E. Harold Munn	Prohibition	23,267	—
1968 Richard M. Nixon	Republican	31,785,480	301
Hubert H. Humphrey	Democratic	31,275,166	191
George C. Wallace	Amer. Ind.	9,906,473	46
Henning A. Blomen	Soc. Labor	52,588	—
Dick Gregory		47,133	—
Fred Halstead	Soc. Workers	41,388	—
Eldridge Cleaver	Peace-Freedom	36,563	—
Eugene J. McCarthy		25,552	—
E. Harold Munn	Prohibition	15,123	—
1972 Richard M. Nixon	Republican	41,170,000	520
George McGovern	Democratic	29,170,000	17
John Schmitz	American	1,099,482	—
Benjamin Spock	People's	78,756	—
1976 Jimmy Carter	Democratic	40,831,000	297
Gerald Ford	Republican	39,148,000	240
Eugene McCarthy	Independent	756,691	—
Roger MacBride	Libertarian	173,011	—
1980 Ronald Reagan	Republican	43,904,000	489
Jimmy Carter	Democratic	35,484,000	49
John Anderson	Independent	5,720,060	—
Ed Clark	Libertarian	921,299	—
1984 Ronald Reagan	Republican	54,455,000	525
Walter Mondale	Democratic	37,577,000	13
David Bergland	Libertarian	228,314	—
Lyndon H. LaRouche	Independent	78,807	—
1988 George Bush	Republican	48,881,278	426
Michael Dukakis	Democratic	41,805,374	111
Ron Paul	Libertarian	431,616	—
Lenora Fulani	New Alliance	217,200	—
David Duke	Populist	46,910	—
Eugene McCarthy	Consumer	30,903	—
1992 Bill Clinton	Democrat	44,909,889	370
George Bush	Republican	39,104,545	168
H. Ross Perot	Independent	19,742,267	—
Andre Marrou	Libertarian	291,628	—
James "Bo" Gritz	Populist/ America First	107,002	—
Lenora Fulani	New Alliance	73,708	—

(Several other candidates received less than 50,000 votes.)

The Vice Presidents

1. JOHN ADAMS (1735–1826). Federalist. Served under George Washington, 1789-97; home state: MA; profession: lawyer.

2. THOMAS JEFFERSON (1743–1826). Democratic-Republican. Served under John Adams, 1797-1801; home state: VA; profession: lawyer, planter, public official.

3. AARON BURR (1756–1836). Democratic-Republican. Served under Thomas Jefferson, 1801-05; home state: NY; profession: public official.

4. GEORGE CLINTON (1739–1812). Democratic-Republican. Served under Thomas Jefferson, 1805-09, James Madison, 1809-12; home state: NY; profession: public official.

5. ELBRIDGE GERRY (1744–1814). Democratic-Republican. Served under James Madison, 1813-14; home state: MA; profession: public official.

6. DANIEL D. TOMPKINS (1774–1825). Democratic-Republican. Served under James Monroe, 1817-25; home state: NY; profession: lawyer and public official.

7. JOHN C. CALHOUN (1782–1850). Served as Democratic-Republican under John Quincy Adams, 1825-29; as Democrat under Andrew Jackson, 1829-32; home state: SC; profession: lawyer and public official.

8. MARTIN VAN BUREN (1782–1862). Democrat. Served under Andrew Jackson, 1833-37; home state: NY; profession: lawyer and public official.

9. RICHARD M. JOHNSON (1780–1850). Democrat. Served under Martin Van Buren, 1837-41; home state: KY; profession: public official.

10. JOHN TYLER (1790–1862). Whig. Served under William H. Harr son, March 4-April 4, 1841; home state: VA; profession: lawyer and public official.

11. GEORGE M. DALLAS (1792–1864). Democrat. Served under James K. Polk, 1845-49; home state: PA; profession: public official and diplomat.

12. MILLARD FILLMORE (1800–1874). Whig. Served under Zachary Taylor, 1849-50; home state: NY; profession: teacher, lawyer, public official.

13. WILLIAM R. D. KING (1786–1853). Democrat. Served under Franklin Pierce, March 4-April 18, 1853; home state: AL; profession: lawyer, public official, diplomat.

14. JOHN C. BRECKINRIDGE (1821–75). Democrat. Served under James Buchanan, 1857-61; home state: KY; profession: lawyer and public official.

15. HANNIBAL HAMLIN (1809–1891). Republican. Served under Abraham Lincoln, 1861-65; home state: ME; profession: lawyer and public official.

16. ANDREW JOHNSON (1808–1875). National Union (Republican). Served under Abraham Lincoln, March 4-April 15, 1865; home state: TN; profession: tailor and public official.

17. SCHUYLER COLFAX (1823–1885). Republican. Served under Ulysses S. Grant, 1869-73; home state: IN; profession: newspaperman and public official.

18. HENRY WILSON (1812–1875). Republican. Served under Ulysses S. Grant, 1873-75; home state: MA; profession: factory owner and public official.

19. WILLIAM A. WHEELER (1819–1887). Republican. Served under Rutherford B. Hayes, 1877-81; home state: NY; profession: businessman and public official.

20. CHESTER A. ARTHUR (1829–1886). Republican. Served under James A. Garfield, March 4-Sept. 20, 1881; home state: NY; profession: lawyer.

21. THOMAS A. HENDRICKS (1819–1885). Democrat. Served under Grover Cleveland, March 4-Nov. 25, 1885; home state: IN; profession: lawyer and public official.

22. LEVI P. MORTON (1824–1920). Republican. Served under Benjamin Harrison, 1889-93; home state: NY; profession: banker and public official.

23. ADLAI E. STEVENSON (1835–1914). Democrat. Served under Grover Cleveland, 1893-97; home state: IL; profession: public official.

24. GARRET A. HOBART (1844–1899). Republican. Served under William McKinley, 1897-99; home state: NJ; profession: lawyer and public official.

25. THEODORE ROOSEVELT (1858–1919). Republican. Served under William McKinley, March 4-Sept. 14, 1901; home state: NY; profession: historian and public official.

26. CHARLES W. FAIRBANKS (1852–1918). Republican. Served under Theodore Roosevelt, 1905-09; home state: IN; profession: financier and public official.

27. JAMES S. SHERMAN (1855–1912). Republican. Served under Wiliam Howard Taft, 1909-12; home state: NY; profession: public official.

28. THOMAS R. MARSHALL (1854–1925). Democrat. Served under Woodrow Wilson, 1913-21; home state: IN; profession: lawyer and public official.

29. CALVIN COOLIDGE (1872–1933). Republican. Served under Warren G. Harding, 1921-23; home state: MA; profession: lawyer and public official.

30. CHARLES G. DAWES (1865–1951). Republican. Served under Calvin Coolidge, 1925-29; home state: IL; profession: financier and diplomat.

31. CHARLES CURTIS (1860–1936). Republican. Served under Herbert Hoover, 1929-33; home state: KS; profession: lawyer and public official.

32. JOHN N. GARNER (1868–1967). Democrat. Served under Franklin D. Roosevelt, 1933-41; home state: TX; profession: public official.

33. HENRY A. WALLACE (1888–1965). Democrat. Served under Franklin D. Roosevelt, 1941-45; home state: IA; profession: editor and agribusinessman.

34. HARRY S. TRUMAN (1884–1972). Democrat. Served under Franklin D. Roosevelt, Jan. 20-April 12, 1945; home state: MO; profession: public official.

35. ALBEN W. BARKLEY (1877–1956). Democrat. Served under Harry S. Truman, 1949-53; home state: KY; profession: public official.

36. RICHARD M. NIXON (1913–1994). Republican. Served under Dwight D. Eisenhower, 1953-61; home state: CA; profession: public official.

37. LYNDON B. JOHNSON (1908–1973). Democrat. Served under John F. Kennedy, Jan. 20, 1961-Nov. 22, 1963; home state: TX; profession: public official.

38. HUBERT H. HUMPHREY (1911–1978). Democrat. Served under Lyndon B. Johnson, 1965-69; home state: MN; profession: public official.

39. SPIRO T. AGNEW (1918–   ). Republican. Served under Richard M. Nixon, Jan. 20, 1969-Oct. 10, 1973; home state: MD; profession: public official.

40. GERALD R. FORD (1913–   ). Republican. Served under Richard M. Nixon, Dec. 6, 1973-Aug. 9, 1974; home state: MI; profession: public official.

41. NELSON A. ROCKEFELLER (1908–1979). Republican. Served under Gerald R. Ford, Dec. 19, 1974-Jan. 20, 1977; home state: NY; profession: public official.

42. WALTER F. MONDALE (1928–   ). Democrat. Served under Jimmy Carter, 1977-81; home state: MN; profession: public official.

43. GEORGE BUSH (1924–   ). Republican. Served under Ronald Reagan, 1981-89; home state: TX; profession: oilman and public official.

44. J. DANFORTH QUAYLE (1947–   ). Republican. Served under George Bush, 1989-93; home state: IN; profession: lawyer and public official.

45. ALBERT A. GORE, JR. (1948–   ). Democrat. Served under Bill Clinton, 1993–   ; home state: TN; profession: public official.